WALTER HINES PAGE

The
FRED W. MORRISON
Series in Southern Studies

BUST OF WALTER HINES PAGE,
executed by Jo Davidson,
presented in 1965 to the Walter Hines Page Library,
Randolph-Macon College

(by permission of Randolph-Macon College, Ashland, Virginia)

WALTER HINES PAGE

The
Southerner as American
1855–1918

by

JOHN MILTON COOPER, JR.

The University of North Carolina Press
Chapel Hill

Library of Congress Cataloging in Publication Data

Cooper, John Milton.
  Walter Hines Page: the Southerner as American, 1855–
1918.

  (The Fred W. Morrison series in Southern studies)
  Bibliography: p.
  Includes index.
  1. Page, Walter Hines, 1855–1918. 2. Ambassadors—
United States—Biography. 3. Journalists—United States
—Biography. 4. Reconstruction. I. Series.
e664.P15C66   973.8'092'4 [B]   77-4390
ISBN 0-8078-1298-6   12-1-77

FOR MY MOTHER

CONTENTS

ILLUSTRATIONS

ACKNOWLEDGMENTS

For me as a biographer, Walter Hines Page has proved unfailingly good company during nearly eight years of research and writing. He likewise introduced and brought me into contact with many people who proved equally good company and rendered my work much easier and more enjoyable than it would otherwise have been. Institutions, too, aided me by providing released time and financial support that facilitated my tasks. A fellowship from the National Endowment for the Humanities allowed me to pursue research full time during 1969–70. A grant from the Wisconsin Alumni Research Foundation, through the University of Wisconsin Graduate School, permitted me to spend a semester in 1972 entirely on research. Another grant from the Spencer Foundation, through the University of Wisconsin School of Education, enabled me to spend the summer of 1973 in uninterrupted work on Page. Final revisions and editing were done while I was spending a thoroughly enjoyable and highly profitable semester at the Institute for Research in the Humanities, University of Wisconsin. Grants from Wellesley College, the American Philosophical Society, the University of Wisconsin Graduate School, and the Spencer Foundation also enabled me to do extended traveling and photocopying in this country and Britain. The Department of History of the University of Wisconsin supplied both a stimulating environment for research and writing and an excellent secretarial staff, particularly Cecile Henneman, Helen Hull, Ruth Koontz, and Margaret Moore. To these people and institutions, I wish to extend my heartiest thanks.

Librarians and archivists played invaluable parts in my research, too. The Houghton Library at Harvard University, which houses the Page papers, provided a second home for me during many months of work. Special thanks must go to Carolyn Jakeman and Marte Shaw for innumerable kindnesses and courtesies. The staffs of the Wellesley College Library, especially Marion

Kanaly, and the State Historical Society of Wisconsin repeatedly demonstrated resourcefulness and indefatigability in finding and obtaining materials for me. The staff of the Walter Hines Page Library of Randolph-Macon College, particularly Flavia Reed Owen and Cecil A. Reid, Jr., likewise furnished great help in unearthing and providing materials. Many other libraries in Britain and the United States similarly aided my research, as did the National Archives and the Public Record Office.

More than most biographers and historians, I owe a profound debt to private individuals who retain the papers of members of their families. My greatest debt of this kind or of any kind in my research is to Martha and Robert Rusnak of Elmhurst, Illinois, who hold the papers of her grandfather, Burton J. Hendrick. On their own initiative, the Rusnaks informed me of the existence of these papers, which were almost indispensable to the biography, and then allowed me to copy whatever I wished. As if that were not enough, they fed and entertained me and became my good friends. This acknowledgment of my warmest thanks is small recompense for the Rusnaks' contribution to this biography.

In the same vein, I wish to thank Lady Elizabeth Mary Arthur of London and Mr. Richard Bassett of Milton, Massachusetts. Lady Arthur generously lent me the private papers of her father, Sir Cecil Spring Rice, which were then in her possession, and she introduced me to other people who facilitated my research in England. She and her husband, the late Sir Raynor Arthur, also went far out of their way many times to do nice things for my whole family. They added much more than they know to the pleasure of our stay in England. Mr. Bassett allowed me to examine and copy from the papers of his father, John Spencer Bassett, and he and Mrs. Bassett extended me their warm hospitality.

Many people have been helpful in furnishing information about Page through correspondence and interviews. These include Lady Elizabeth Arthur, Richard Bassett, Jonathan Daniels, Margaret Digby, John H. Finley, Sir Ralph Hawtrey, Mrs. Richard Lovering, Broadus Mitchell, the late Raymond Moley, the late Thad S. Page, and Lady Percy of Newcastle. Fellow scholars who have likewise come to my aid on many occasions with advice and leads on sources and interpretations include Robert Bannister, Sally Cross, Carl Degler, David Herbert Donald, Robert H. Elias, Martin Gilbert, Noel Griesy, Cameron Hazelhurst, the late Richard Hofstadter, Robert A. Hohner, Sterling Kernek, Arthur S. Link, Peter Lyon, George W. Pierson, Keith Robbins, Blair Rouse, Morton P. Sosna, Zara S. Steiner, A. J. P. Taylor, George B. Tindall, Franklin Trenaby Walker, Samuel F. Wells, Jr., and Sherrill Brown Wells. Three medical friends, Dr. Edward Larkin, Dr. David Greenblatt, and Dr. William Craig, offered opinions on matters regarding Page's health and cause of death. I wish to thank all of these people for supplying information and perspectives that I could not otherwise have gotten.

Six historians and writers have aided me still more by reading parts or all of the manuscript of this biography, giving the kinds of suggestions and criticisms that are deserved by better efforts. Jonathan Daniels drew upon his intimate acquaintance with North Carolina and his father, Josephus Daniels, in reading chapter 3. Ellen B. Ballou brought to bear both her familiarity with the history of Houghton Mifflin Company and the *Atlantic* and her sharp critical skills in evaluating chapter 5, greatly to my profit. One of my Wisconsin colleagues, Daniel T. Rodgers, shared with me his great knowledge of late-nineteenth-century American history and the magazines of the period in going over chapters 4 through 6. Two other distinguished colleagues, Paul K. Conkin and Paul W. Glad, took many hours away from busy schedules to read the entire manuscript and give me the benefit of their clear thinking, wide learning, and devotion to good writing. The leading historian of the Wilson era, Arthur S. Link of Princeton University, extended his generosity far beyond the bounds of friendship not only by sharing advice and information in the research but even more by reading the whole manuscript with his unparalleled scholarship and judgment. To these people I wish to render my thanks and express my hope that this book goes some of the way toward meeting their standards.

To The University of North Carolina Press, especially its director, Matthew N. Hodgson, I owe not only the normal debts for promptness, efficiency, and sympathy but also a special debt for a service that harks back to an earlier, more gracious era of American book publishing. On Matt Hodgson's initiative, the press enlisted the services of its director emeritus, Lambert Davis, who has contributed more than anyone else to giving the book its present shape. A prince of editors, Mr. Davis has brought to the manuscript his incomparable skills and his extensive acquaintance with many of the same fields that Walter Hines Page traversed. Beyond that, Mr. Davis has given a care and devotion reminiscent of the contributions to far better writers than me of such men as Maxwell Perkins. I can only offer Mr. Davis my deepest thanks and the hope that this book comes somewhere not too far from justifying his part in it.

As any reader of acknowledgments knows, the most self-conscious part comes last, when an author speaks of his family's contribution. In this case I can leave most things unsaid because my wife knows well what has gone into this book and how much she has given to it. Our children have been born within the span of the work. We have all lived with it in our own ways. The dedication bespeaks both my gratitude to my mother and the fitness that in different forms and for a different generation this was her story.

INTRODUCTION

The Southerner as American

As the election of 1976 showed, the South has finally trod the road to reunion. Jimmy Carter's election gained added significance by coming one hundred years after the end of Reconstruction. It has taken a century since the nation was supposedly restored from the Civil War for the South to be brought fully back into the American mainstream. Obviously, sectional reconciliation has been a long and difficult job, and the work has had to be done with few prophets or heroic leaders and in the face of enormous frustrations. For many southerners the greatest frustration of all has been the conviction that alienation between their section and the rest of the country has been wrong and unnecessary. One of the first southerners after Reconstruction to argue that sectional hostility was needless and one of the most important advocates of national reunion during his lifetime was the North Carolina–born editor, publisher, and reformer, Walter Hines Page. Ironically, he has been better remembered as the United States ambassador to Great Britain during World War I than as the proponent of the views that helped shape his life and most influenced his times.

Page was an early exponent of the viewpoint that was encapsulated in the title of a collection of essays published in 1960— *The Southerner as American.* The authors of those essays believed, stated the editor, Charles G. Sellers, Jr., "that the traditional emphasis on the South's differentness and on the conflict between Southernism and Americanism is wrong historically." In support of that thesis and its corollary that mistaken notions of separateness warped southern thinking, Sellers quoted several pungent observations made by Page around the turn of the century. Further, Sellers maintained, Page's own life and career symbolized the way that southerners during the last century found themselves torn between the unpalatable alternatives of clinging to nostalgic myths about themselves and bowing to the realities of an urban, industrial North. "Page's personal dilemma," Sellers concluded, "was the dilemma of the modern South."

That phrase, "the Southerner as American," and the evocation of Page as a figure caught in the classic dilemma of the post-Reconstruction South suggest both his historical significance and the great theme that he illuminated. Born in 1855, Page came of age at the end of Reconstruction, and he spent all but the last five years of his adult life in the front lines of the struggle to restore the South to full participation in national life. Starting as a newspaperman in the South and continuing as an editor of national magazines in New York and Boston until 1913, he wrote and reflected constantly on the meanings of the twin identities of southerner and American. At the same time, he was advocating and—as a philanthropist, social reformer, and amateur politician—promoting reconciliation between those identities. His ambassadorship to Britain, which occupied the last five years of his life, until his death in 1918, came as a political reward for aiding the presidential candidacy of his friend Woodrow Wilson, whom Arthur S. Link has called "the American as Southerner." An uncanny combination of circumstances and personal traits made Page, moreover, one of the most richly revealing figures of his time, especially regarding the manifold ramifications of the problem of reunion between North and South. Walter Hines Page shed a light that reached a long way down the road that finally ended with Jimmy Carter in 1976.

The time, place, and family into which Page was born engaged him from the beginning with being at once a southerner and an American. For the rest of his life he could remember how, as a child of eight, he had watched coffins bearing the remains of Confederate soldiers being returned to the village in North Carolina where his family lived. At the end of the war, the conflict itself briefly intruded when a Union army occupied the Page home and encamped on the grounds. Not long afterward, as a boy of thirteen at a nearby military school, he first encountered the thralldom in which the Lost Cause had come to grip so much of the white South. Those youthful experiences with the Civil War and its romantic legends raised problems of divided loyalties, because of where Walter Page was born and who he was.

His birth and upbringing in rolling Piedmont country a few miles west of Raleigh made him a North Carolinian, or "Tar Heel." In the antebellum South, North Carolina had occupied an uncomfortable spot. There, as elsewhere in the Upper South, plantation agriculture and large-scale slaveholding had not flourished nearly to the extent it had in the Deep South. Tar Heels had also suffered from poverty and backwardness since colonial days, and they had long smarted under the contempt of aristocratic Virginians and South Carolinians. The differences between the two parts of the South and between North Carolina and its neighbors had become most readily apparent in 1861, when the states of the Upper South had seceded only after the firing on Fort Sumter and President Lincoln's call for armed suppression of the Confederacy. North Carolina had left the Union last of all, after Virginia's secession had ruled out any other course. Being a Tar Heel tended to inject at least a few reservations into Page's southern identity.

Deeper reservations sprang from his family background. Since Walter's grandfather's time, the Pages had been staunch Whigs, originally admirers of Henry Clay and his nationalism and, like most members of their party in North Carolina, opponents of sectional extremism and secession. Walter Page later insisted that his father had been a "Union man." That did not mean that the elder Page had sided with the North during the Civil War or joined the Republicans during Reconstruction. But his father had been a less-than-ardent Confederate and had not fought under the Stars and Bars. Coming from such a family, Page could hardly have avoided predispositions toward questioning the Lost Cause and rejecting distinctive southernism and northern-defined Americanism as mutually exclusive categories.

Another, more intimate aspect of his family background added further dimensions to his embodiment of dual loyalties. Beginning in his childhood, Page found himself caught in a celebrated but seldom-analyzed American family conflict. On one side, a warm, sympathetic, cultivated mother who had almost exclusive charge of the early upbringing of Walter, the oldest child, fostered his somewhat romantic inclinations toward intellectual and literary callings. On the other side, a hard-bitten businessman father, who played a larger role in his son's life after 1865, insisted upon practical work and active involvement in the world. It was significant in itself that such a family conflict, which has usually been thought peculiar to later periods and to more sophisticated urban precincts, could arise in a rude southern community during the Civil War era. The conflict created divisions within Page between intellect and action, with certain inescapable sex-role connotations, that lasted throughout his life and shaped his attitudes and actions.

Those divisions and Page's responses to them naturally affected his performance in his twin roles as southerner and American. The young man met his opposing parental influences by trying to satisfy them both, thereby fashioning a personal model for sectional reconciliation. When he began to address the problem after 1876, Page tended to depict the South as an extension of his own romantic, literary side and the North as an extension of his practical, commercial side. But he did not draw simple analogues. The North also represented culture for Page, and the South's shortcomings in that area troubled him profoundly. Likewise, his father's practical, worldly outlook ran counter not only to the sentimentality of the Lost Cause but also to its heroism and military glory, which exerted a powerful attraction over Page.

Beneath those complications in his outlook toward the South and the national scene lay a further twist in his internal divisions. Unlike others who have found themselves torn between intellect and action, Page was pulled, not in two directions, but three. The first direction was toward intellectual and literary aspirations. The second was a desire to exert social, cultural, and political influence. The third was a drive to make money. That three-way division partially reflected another facet of Page's family background—their strong Methodist faith. His parents' wishes and his own initial inclination toward the Methodist ministry provided him with a fruitful way to satisfy literary and public leanings, with an exemption from the business influence. But when Page forsook his ministerial vocation in college, the family conflict exploded in his face, while his subsequent skepticism about religious orthodoxy supplied another reservation to his southern identity. Seeking an alternative career to the ministry that might satisfy all three of his inclinations ultimately led Page into journalism and the other public activities that made him such an important spokesman and promoter of national reunion.

The origins of his involvement in public affairs gave his viewpoint toward the South a special slant. Page's own youthful interests had run almost entirely toward literature and religion, and he turned to journalism after a flirtation with an academic career. In 1876, Page joined the illustrious first group of Fellows of the newly opened Johns Hopkins University, but he abandoned higher education after two years, both because he could not stomach the narrowly positivistic approach prevalent at the Johns Hopkins and because teaching did not satisfy his worldly longings. Yet those early inclinations left their mark. Page's original concern in advocating reform in the South was cultural. His first known published writing, a series of letters to a Raleigh newspaper in 1877, urged the adaptation of northern and German scientific methods to southern colleges and universities. Likewise, his preferred avenue for improvement in the South was, from the beginning, through education. Page taught at the University of North Carolina and at a high school in Louisville, Kentucky, in 1878 and 1879, and in 1881, in one of his earliest magazine articles, he asserted that above everything else the South needed "popular and practical education."

The cultural origins and educational thrust of Page's reform ideas marked him off from other contemporary spokesmen for southern uplift and sectional reconciliation. He differed particularly from his sometime acquaintance, the renowned "New South" advocate Henry Grady, in not embracing industrial capitalism and northern investment with nearly the same uncritical ardor. Thanks in part to his father's influence, Page called for greater commercial and industrial development, but he hedged his espousal of those means to improvement in several ways. In his first important newspaper writing, a series of reports from different parts of the South for leading northern papers in 1881, he argued that the sole path to genuine progress lay through "the way of agricultural improvement." In those reports, Page also dismissed "large railroad projects and mammoth manufacturing establishments" as improper for the South. At the outset of his journalistic career, Page was formulating his basic viewpoint toward improvement in his native section.

The young North Carolinian expanded his role as a southern reform spokesman in 1883 when, after a stint on the staff of the *New York World*, he started his own weekly newspaper in Raleigh, the *State Chronicle*. In the *State Chronicle* Page revealed more of the differences between himself and other New South advocates. He disclosed a trinity of reform approaches in which education ranked first, agricultural improvement came next, and industrial development came last. Similarly, although the paper ran special industrial editions and bragged about "ADVERTISING NORTH CAROLINA AT HOME AND ABROAD," Page still rejected large-scale manufacturing and denied the necessity for outside investment. Along the same line, he refused to expound on the cheapness and docility of southern labor. In fact, Page's thinking about southern labor ran in the opposite direction. His major crusade as editor of the *State Chronicle* and as founder of a civic improvement organization was the establishment of an agricultural and mechanical college that would provide training in the latest technology for farming and manufacturing. Finally and most important, Page developed his distinctive viewpoint toward the competing claims of southern and American loyalties.

Whereas other New South advocates mixed their wooing of northern capital with profusions of nostalgia for the Old South and the Lost Cause, the *State Chronicle* editor tried to forget the past and set his face toward the future. Actually, Page had to suppress a seething resentment toward the worshipers of departed glories who dominated the post-Reconstruction South. He later spewed forth his resentment in a blast of sarcasm in which he dubbed the old guard "mummies" who stifled new ideas and made North Carolina "the laughingstock among the States." But Page did not issue that blast until after he had stepped down from the *State Chronicle* and gone to New York. As long as he remained in Raleigh, he preached and practiced a gospel of cheerful, patient uplift to be achieved mainly through individual and small-group efforts by native southern whites. He likewise went out of his way to avoid controversy, especially in those three most sensitive areas—religion, race, and southern identity.

Despite the amiable facade, Page began to enunciate the positions toward the major issues of sectional reconciliation that would continue to characterize his thinking. Inasmuch as religion was a personal and local problem for him, he succeeded largely in steering clear of it. Only after he left North Carolina did he divulge his scorn for preachers and their followers as retrograde social and political influences in the South. Race was another area into which Page did not care to stray too far, but that was as much out of conviction as from prudence. Even before he started the *State Chronicle*, Page had displayed a sympathetic attitude toward black people and argued that hard work, patience, and avoidance of agitation would improve their lot almost as much as that of whites. As editor of the *State Chronicle*, he capitalized the word "Negro," then an unusual practice in the South and most other parts of the country, and he deplored excessive attention to racial issues, which he strove to avoid. Page's racial attitudes were of a piece with his larger outlook on the South.

He had begun to develop his southern outlook as soon as he had resolved to enter journalism, drawing together his personal inclinations, family background, and North Carolina origins. Two points formed the basis of his position. One was a condemnation of antebellum plantations, slavery, and aristocratic pretensions for having perverted an earlier democratic society that had been at once more authentically southern and more like the rest of the United States. In his 1881 newspaper reports Page had condemned "the narcotic influences of slavery" and the "aristocratic shackles" that still bound so many whites. When he had first decided upon a journalistic career, Page had immediately read a biography of Thomas Jefferson, and in the *State Chronicle* he recommended an immersion in Jefferson's writings as the best means of maintaining correct political and social bearings. Page's expression of those views in the 1880s was significant because during the first half of the twentieth century they came to dominate white southern liberal and moderate thinking. He had formulated both what C. Vann Woodward has termed the "hill-country point of view," which found its most influential expression in W. J. Cash's *The Mind of the South,* and the belief in a preslavery democratic, Jeffersonian South that was purveyed in the works of such leading historians as William E. Dodd.

The other basic point in Page's southern outlook was a corollary of the first. Since the South had its own democratic past to draw upon, it did not need to change its basic character in order to reenter the national mainstream. This was the point on which Page encountered the most misunderstanding and aroused the greatest hostility. Especially after he loosed his blast at the "mummies" and subsequent criticisms of southern backwardness, fellow southerners charged him with disloyalty and seeking to ape Yankee ways. Page insisted repeatedly that the South must be highly selective in transplanting alien customs and institutions. For example, in 1881, in his first national magazine article, he had cautioned against "pressing blindly forward" and called for "the proper fusion of the old and the new." With those arguments and with his invocation of Jefferson as a talisman of legitimacy, Page was erecting the defenses that succeeding generations of southern liberals would use against allegations of disloyalty.

Page seldom needed such defenses while he edited the *State Chronicle.* His few brushes with controversy occurred when he refused to refer to political candidates by their Confederate military ranks and lamented their preoccupation with outworn issues. Those were not serious slips. Yet in February 1885, less than two years after starting his paper, Page resigned the editorship, departed for New York, and later fired back barrages of criticism. Although pent-up frustration played a part in his withdrawal, he was knowingly defying his own counsel of patient, local uplift. At first he maintained in his series of critical letters to the *State Chronicle* that he planned to return, but he privately admitted that he was casting his lot with New York journalism. Another reason for his move lay in the *State Chronicle*'s small earnings, although the paper continued to publish and pay for itself for another seven years.

However, Page's strongest motive for departing sprang from the third side of his ambitions—his literary and intellectual aspirations. Public influence in his home state and modest business success did not compensate for low cultural standards. Page hankered for not just the money but also the glamor and excitement of the metropolitan arena. In that way, too, he was acting out another aspect of his roles of southerner and American. By leaving the South at the age of thirty and spending the rest of his life in the United States in northern cities, Page made himself part of another chapter in sectional reconciliation—the story of the southern expatriate.

Leaving the South did not end Page's engagement with his native section, but it did alter the context in which he approached his twin identities. In 1887, after spending two years at newspaper jobs in New York, he joined the *Forum*, a nonfiction magazine, and four years later he became its editor. Page's assumption of command of the *Forum* in 1891 opened a highly successful and influential twenty-two-year career as a magazine editor. He boosted the *Forum*'s circulation by anticipating the trend toward lower-priced quality periodicals, and he pioneered in investigative reporting and discussion of public affairs. Then, after losing a fight for control of the *Forum*, he moved to Boston to work for Houghton, Mifflin & Company, the publishing house that owned *The Atlantic Monthly*. In 1896, Page assumed direction of the *Atlantic*, and in 1898 he became the first southerner and only the second non–New Englander, after William Dean Howells, to occupy the magazine's exalted editorial chair.

Page brought new departures to the *Atlantic*, especially when he used the magazine as his own editorial platform to promote American imperialism in 1898 and 1899. He also encouraged fledgling southern writers, and through the Houghton, Mifflin connection he moved into book publishing, which became his second most important career. Yet it is ironic that the *Atlantic* editorship was the most noteworthy post that Page held in the United States. Boston and the *Atlantic* really represented a detour in Page's magazine career. Although Page was an innovator with the *Atlantic*, he showed less resourcefulness and imagination there than he had earlier or did again later, and he had less public impact during those years than he did before or after. Fittingly, he resigned the *Atlantic* editorship after only a year.

In 1899, Page returned to New York for a brief fling at a venture with the irrepressible S. S. McClure before teaming up with Frank N. Doubleday to found the publishing house Doubleday, Page & Company. The firm not only blossomed swiftly into a major book publisher, which afforded Page another outlet for southern authors, but it also gave him the opportunity in 1900 to start his own magazine, *World's Work*. The magazine was a nonfiction monthly illustrated entirely with photographs—another journalistic departure. It stressed public affairs, and each issue opened with Page's own extended editorial commentary. Both successful commercially and influential socially and politically, *World's Work* established a national platform for Page and developed the main features of twentieth-century newsmagazines.

Success in the North as a magazine editor and book publisher provided the former Tar Heel with a new base from which to attempt to influence southern affairs. Almost at once after leaving Raleigh, Page resumed his earlier function of interpreting North and South to each other, and gradually, as he gained eminence and expanded his activities, he began to act as a kind of intersectional ambassador. Page perceived his new mission through a more sharply defined version of his previously formulated viewpoint. In 1885, in his first magazine article after going to New York, Page asserted that no separate "Southern problem" existed. Rather, the South's troubles were variations of general American conditions, worsened and complicated by economic and cultural backwardness, racial tensions, and misguided notions left over from the Lost Cause.

That was a remarkable viewpoint for anyone, especially a southerner, to advance so soon after Reconstruction. That perspective, unlike Page's other views of the South, would not gain currency for another seventy or eighty years, until the appearance of such works as *The Southerner as American*. Even today, despite the 1976 election, to maintain that the South is basically like the rest of the country remains controversial. Yet though that proposition meets resistance from some of the South's leading interpreters, most notably C. Vann Woodward, opponents of the viewpoint have had to concede it a measure of validity. Page's insistence upon the essential unity of southern and American experience staked his strongest claim to the rank of prophet.

From 1885 to 1913, he hammered away at his messages of basic similarity between North and South and hopefulness about solving his native section's problems. Besides in his own magazine articles and editorials, two books, and scores of speeches, Page propagated his views by offering means for others who shared them to speak out. During the 1890s, he found an ideological brother across the color line in Booker T. Washington. Page ran so many stories by and about Washington and others like him that *World's Work* published more material about black people than any other national magazine. Page also encouraged Washington to write his autobiography, *Up from Slavery*, which became one of the Doubleday, Page firm's first best-sellers. The former North Carolinian retained a sometimes credulous optimism about the willingness of southern whites to treat blacks humanely if left alone, but he largely avoided the paternalism of such other leading white moderates of the time as Robert C. Ogden and Edgar Gardner Murphy. Like Washington, Page sincerely believed that hard work and material progress would achieve a just society for blacks and whites alike.

Insistence upon the underlying similarity of the South to the rest of the United States cut both ways. Nearly all of Page's stands on national issues stemmed from his southern views. Such a ready transference of southern-based attitudes to the national scene introduced strengths and weaknesses into his thinking. On the positive side, Page's rural origins and early advocacy of agricultural improvement led him to perceive and try to bridge the widening gap between city and country in the United States.

Although Page moderated his hostility toward big business after 1900, he never reconciled himself to urban and industrial dominance. In 1908, he declared that America was "and always will be mainly an agricultural country." Page's fondest cause on the national scene was the effort to redress the balance between rural and urban America. His first official post came in connection with that effort, when President Theodore Roosevelt appointed him in 1908 to the Commission on Country Life.

Page also suffered from the way that he applied his southern views to the nation as a whole. For example, his rejection of the populists and of William Jennings Bryan and his Democratic followers sprang from distaste for agrarian rabblerousers in his native section. As a result, Page never adequately appreciated the reform impulse that arose from those quarters, and his magazine supported measures aimed at curbing the powers of big business and political machines, but often with reticence and skepticism. Conversely, Page's unexamined Democratic fealty stood in the way of his sympathizing as much as he should have with the leader to whom he came closest in views and temperament— Theodore Roosevelt. Page's congruence with Roosevelt, which extended to their foreign-policy views as well, contained a certain irony, since the editor had been a Jeffersonian while the president was an outspoken neo-Hamiltonian. Page labored under a confusion of political identity that later led him to try to invest William Howard Taft and Woodrow Wilson with traits they did not possess.

In addition to writing and talking about southern uplift and national reunion, the former Tar Heel sought to promote those ends through philanthropy and politics. Starting in 1901, Page plunged into the efforts of a coalition of southern white reformers and northern philanthropists to upgrade and expand all levels of education in the South. The coalition operated through two select organizations whose membership largely overlapped—the Southern Education Board, which was founded by Ogden and Murphy and primarily aided local initiatives, and the General Education Board, which dispensed huge contributions from John D. Rockefeller. As a leading southern expatriate, Page played an important part as a link between the two elements in the coalition. The Southern and General boards in turn formed the core of an interlocking directorate of other agencies concerned with aiding black and rural education. Moreover, thanks to Page's personal intervention, these groups became involved in public-health work in the South, particularly the spectacular Rockefeller-funded drive to eradicate hookworm. In all, these philanthropic efforts enabled Page to give practical meaning to his intersectional ambassadorship.

Politics remained an inescapable concern for him, despite his reluctance to become directly involved. Page continued to believe that southern and American politics needed to be disenthralled from outworn issues and that old allegiances ought to be dissolved. During Roosevelt's second term, the *World's Work* editor made his first foray into president-making by publicizing Taft's candidacy and by managing overtures from Taft to the South during and after the 1908 election. Those moves went awry in the general disintegration of the Taft administration, but Page soon found a more attractive alternative. At the beginning of 1911, he became one of the handful of original backers of Woodrow Wilson's presidential candidacy. Page had known and admired Wilson, a fellow southern expatriate, since 1882, and he aided his old acquaintance's drive for the White House through organization, fund raising, and especially publicity. In return, Page nearly received a place in Wilson's cabinet as secretary of agriculture or secretary of the interior. Either post would have made a fitting capstone to his pursuit of being a southerner and an American.

As matters turned out, the chances of politics supplied an unexpected last chapter to Page's life. In 1913 Wilson appointed him ambassador to the Court of St. James's. The ambassadorship to Great Britain meant a change for Page, who had previously taken just two widely separated summer trips abroad and had never seen the inside of an American embassy. Page nevertheless warmed to his new tasks, and during his first year in London, before the outbreak of World War I, he promoted Anglo-American concert as his latest cause. With the coming of the world war in

August 1914 his work became more critical, in the face of the British blockade and German submarine warfare. Page began sympathizing with the Allies soon after the outbreak of the war, and after the sinking of the *Lusitania* in May 1915 he tirelessly urged intervention on the Allied side. The entry of the United States into the war in 1917 seemed to vindicate his stand. Finally, a sudden breakdown in his health at the middle of 1918 and his death shortly after the Armistice appeared to cast Page as a heroic martyr to the Allied victory.

The wartime ambassadorship brought great posthumous fame. Following the publication in 1922 of the best-selling *Life and Letters of Walter Hines Page*, his services were commemorated with memorials on both sides of the Atlantic. That reputation cracked in the later disillusionment with the world war and with the disclosure of how little influence he had actually had with Wilson. Page was neither a hero nor a villain of American intervention. He was simply the southerner as American on the international scene. There, as at home, his ready extrapolation of southern-based views entailed strengths and weaknesses. Anglo-American concert became for him an analogue to sectional reconciliation, and during his first, peacetime year in London, he was able to pursue that end with his usual stress on speaking, publicity, and informal organization. During the war, his manifest sympathy for Britain helped reduce friction and at certain junctures, such as the disclosure of the Zimmermann telegram, his presence may have made a difference in the course of events. But Page suffered even more from the weaknesses of his approach. Envisioning the United States and Britain as equivalent to the North and South heightened his diplomatic naiveté and led him to misconceive many of his dealings with the British. Similarly, Page's confused political bearings helped create a gulf of misunderstanding between himself and Wilson.

His failings as ambassador did not detract much from his historical significance. Page's main contributions lay in his domestic career, and those contributions derived added importance from their variety. Partly because of the circumstances of where and when he lived but more because of his incredible versatility,

Page involved himself and rendered observations in important ways in at least twelve fields—southern affairs, race relations, politics, diplomacy, philanthropy, education, public health, agriculture, business, literature, book publishing, and journalism. Such versatility, combined with buoyant optimism and persistent faith in technology, made him resemble no southerner or American so much as Thomas Jefferson. Unlike Jefferson, however, Page did not derive his versatility solely from superabundant gifts and curiosity. Page was a man of too many parts. His versatility was the upshot of the three-way internal conflict that he never successfully resolved. Yet that conflict also led him into the fields where his best talents lay—journalism, publishing, philanthropy, and certain kinds of amateur politics and peacetime diplomacy. Page's inner divisions brought him personal success and, through his versatility, greater historical significance.

In one other, final way the pull of his three sets of aspirations enhanced Page's place in his time and after. His unrequited literary yearnings complemented his versatility to make him one of the most illuminating figures in the United States during the last century and a half. Throughout his life, Page remained a literary man who ached to do significant writing. He took time away from his many involvements in the 1900s to write a novel, and during the world war he made repeated attempts to record the momentous events that he was witnessing. Page's literary aspirations influenced his political and social views in some surprising areas, particularly war and rural uplift. Those aspirations likewise impelled him to leave the sort of intimate, self-revelatory record that rarely enlightens a career in the thick of affairs. Van Wyck Brooks once observed that it is easier to do a first-rate biography of a second- or third-rate writer than of a first-rate businessman, soldier, or politician. Writers by calling, Brooks explained, examine themselves and leave records, whereas men of action do not. Thanks to his internal conflict, Page offers an exception that proves Brooks's rule.

An individual character in history has sometimes been compared to a tracer bullet fired in the night. Walter Hines Page always liked images such as that, and this one suits him. It is hard to imagine a better aimed or more brightly illuminating tracer than he was through the years from Reconstruction to World War I. Because his trajectory sped straight down the road traveled by the southerner as American, his life showed much about where the nation has come from to reach the place where it stands today.

PART I

Southern Beginnings

1855–1885

———

BIRTHPLACE OF WALTER HINES PAGE,
Cary, North Carolina

*(by permission of the Division of Archives and History,
Raleigh, North Carolina)*

CHAPTER I

Civil War Youth

The locomotive whistle brought the two boys running. The station was too small to be a regular stop, and the whistle signaled a special event, perhaps the arrival of a visitor to the settlement. Instead, the boys found only a large wooden box, which the train crew placed in the shade of the fence adjoining the station building. A man who had come by asked the boys to stay with the box for a few minutes, explaining that it was a coffin containing the body of a young man of the village who had fallen in battle. The two boys, one black, the other white, stayed even after the man returned. They waited until the soldier's parents drove up in a lint-covered wagon to take his coffin away. The father, a farmer, had been hauling his crop to the cotton gin when he learned of his dead son's return home.

Similar scenes occurred regularly in the autumn of 1863. The coffin contained the remains of a Confederate soldier being returned to a village in North Carolina. The boys who watched the scene were among countless children, particularly in the South, who would retain memories of the Civil War. The vigil by the coffin made the war real to the two boys. Before then, they had heard talk about the war, but they had suspected that it was just a story fabricated mainly for their benefit. The arrival of the coffin changed that. Over forty years later, Walter Hines Page, who had been the white boy, wrote, "We found out the truth that day, and for this reason it is among my clearest early recollections."

Repeated revelations of that truth followed. More coffins arrived at the station, which stood close by young Walter Page's home. Women gathered to sew stockings and make bandages. Church bells rang out for victories in the field and tolled for funerals. Finally, at the end of the war, fighting armies burst upon the scene. One morning the same two boys saw a troop of grey-coated Confederate cavalrymen galloping by, fleeing from blue-jacketed pursuers. Then, as the boys peeked from a second-floor window, the main host of a Union army marched down the road in front of the Page house. A tense hour or two ensued after a band of irregular troops, or "bummers," broke into the house and ransacked the interior. Presently, a Union officer informed Walter's mother that he required the house for his headquarters. The officer and his staff occupied the first floor, while the family lived upstairs; troopers pitched their tents and built cooking fires under the oak trees in the yard. The whole experience proved exciting for Walter Page, who was then nine years old. Except for some mutterings when word came of President Lincoln's murder, few hard feelings marred the interlude. After about three weeks, the soldiers departed, and the boy and his playmates went back to their usual summer pastimes.[1]

The North Carolina village where Walter Hines Page was born on 15 August 1855 had no name. The tiny settlement stood in rolling country still largely forested with stands of tall, straight pines, in Wake County, about eight miles west of the state capital Raleigh, a town of four thousand. Popularly called "Page's" and designated by the railroad as "Page's Station," the settlement centered on the Page house, which his parents had bought the year before Walter's birth. The two-story frame building served both as the family's home and, at various times, as a store and hotel. Except for the little train station and some outbuildings, the house stood alone on a slight rise. Down the road was a Methodist church where Walter Page was christened as a baby. The boy's father, Allison Francis—known as "Frank"—Page erected several sawmills in the neighborhood to cut the pines into lumber and to make turpentine. During and after the war the village grew into a town, and in 1871 it was incorporated, at Frank Page's request, as Cary, North Carolina.

Boyhood in that North Carolina village savored of a sylvan

idyll. Wat, as his family called him, wandered barefoot in the woods, fished in the streams, hunted with his own rifle, and swam in a nearby millpond. Trips to Raleigh afforded glimpses of town life, with big houses, wide streets, stores, blacksmiths' and carpenters' shops, taverns, and the Greek-revival-style stone capitol building. The railroad displayed smoke-belching, whistle-screeching marvels of speed and power practically in front of the boy's doorstep. For a while not even school disrupted his young existence. Wat did not enter a classroom before he was ten but received private tutoring from his mother. She taught him his lessons in the Page house or often, when the weather was fine, under the trees in the backyard and by the pond.

A distinctively southern feature of Wat's early upbringing was slavery. In 1860 Frank Page owned four Negro slaves—two men, a woman, and a boy named Tance, who was about seven years older than Wat. Tance became his young master's closest friend, constant companion, and sometime tutor and protector. But Wat did not grow up on one of the fabled plantations of the Old South. Owning only four slaves did not make his father a planter, and Wake County was hardly plantation country. Although Frank Page listed his occupation in 1860 as "farmer," he did not engage primarily in agriculture. Six feet five inches tall, with a rangy build, craggy features, coarse dark hair, bristly beard, and warm brown eyes, Frank Page conveyed an impression of homely strength. He had displayed a restless money-making urge from an early age, having left home by the time he turned twenty to engage in sawmilling and turpentine distilling in the pine forests of the eastern Piedmont region of North Carolina. Agriculture held few charms for him, not even the booming cotton cultivation that attracted so many southern whites. "I can make more money out of a pine log than a bale of cotton," Frank Page supposedly avowed. During the six years between Wat's birth and the outbreak of the war, he ran a store but concentrated most of his attention on sawmilling. During the war he turned over his lumber to the Confederate government.

As Frank Page's enterprises prospered, he enlarged his house, adding a whole new structure onto the front of the simple dwelling in which Wat had been born. The new edifice became one of the finest houses in the neighborhood, with freshly painted white clapboards, a big brick chimney, and a wide veranda. The prevailing smells came from the pines and a small peach orchard, from the railroad's wood smoke, from the sawmill's sawdust, and from the pungent odor of turpentine. The scent of magnolia neither literally nor figuratively pervaded the Page place, and the house's one-story veranda was not the columned portico of the plantation legend.

Wat's boyhood resembled those of Mark Twain's characters, especially Tom Sawyer. Wat, too, often reveled in anarchic freedom, and the woods and the railroad evidently excited his young mind the way the river and steamboats aroused Tom Sawyer's imagination. The slave boy Tance seems to have played much the same role for Wat that Nigger Jim played for Tom Sawyer—playmate, foil, instructor, instigator. Like Tom Sawyer, Wat Page spun rich romantic fantasies, becoming a reader of Sir Walter Scott's novels at an early age and conjuring up knightly trappings for the Union and Confederate soldiers. Wat also shared Tom Sawyer's most renowned trait—guile in escaping work. He usually got Tance to do his gardening chores while he lounged in the shade reading a book. In common with Tom Sawyer, too, Wat had a woman-dominated childhood. Although Frank Page later took a strong hand in the boy's upbringing, during Wat's early years his father was away much of the time on extended business trips. The major responsibility for raising the boy fell to his mother, Catherine Frances Raboteau—or "Kate"—Page. She was the strongest influence in Wat's early childhood.

In December 1876, when he was twenty-one, Walter Page described memories of his earliest years in a letter to his mother. "Do you know," he wrote, "that I have dim recollections of a mother who was hardly more than a girl? Indeed I do. Not that you are *old* now; no, not that—you'll never grow old, in one sense, to me. But then, it seems to me, you had less to do, less to wear your life out with. You were a young mother and I a little boy. . . . However we may seem to others, you are a young mother yet to *me*, and I am yet to you only the same little boy." The letter conveyed an accurate impression of the early relationship between mother and son.[2]

Circumstances made Kate Page about as close to Wat as a mother could be. She and Frank Page had been married for six years when the boy was born. Two children born previously had both died shortly after birth. During the first few years of his life, Wat often looked as if he might not survive. He was sickly and required constant care. Wat did not share his mother with siblings until his brother Robert arrived when he was four. The Page family eventually expanded to include seven other children, four boys and three girls, the youngest being born nearly twenty years after Wat. Those circumstances carved a special place for Wat in Kate Page's affections and almost certainly made him her favorite. Twenty-two at the time of Wat's birth, she was an attractively slender young woman, with blue eyes, blond hair, and a fair complexion. The boy likewise grew into an appealing youngster with deep brown eyes, thick and curly brown hair, and lively curiosity.

Closeness to his mother did much to shape his character. Not only did she teach him to read and write, but she filled him with genuine love of learning and feeling for culture. Before her marriage to Frank Page at the age of sixteen, Kate Raboteau had received a better education than many women of her time. Not from a pretentious background, she was the second child and eldest daughter of John Raboteau, a saddlemaker in the market town of Fayetteville, North Carolina. Yet Kate attended a girls' academy in Raleigh and a female seminary in Louisburg, North Carolina, where she acquired some knowledge of French and algebra. More remarkable than her education was her devotion to reading, which she kept up after marriage and the arrival of her children. She read while knitting and usually carried a book on her household rounds. Through her care and gentle tutelage Kate Page provided her son with an introduction to learning that added to the idyllic quality of his boyhood. She often took Wat for walks in the woods, where they picked wildflowers and learned the names of plants and trees. Or they went fishing at the stream, where she read aloud from novels of Scott or Charles Dickens.

Nor did Kate fail to have an apt, appreciative student. From the time he learned to read, Wat devoured books, and he, too, was seldom without one. Schoolwork came easily to him from the outset. When a neighbor opened an academy for boys two miles down the road in 1865, Wat began his formal education. Despite a prankish streak, he became the star pupil. A fellow student later remembered him as "wonderfully precocious. When still a boy he wrote remarkably well and also spoke well." After going to college, Wat admitted to his mother in half-mocking self-reproach, "Ever since I can remember, I have always been called smart, and many a foolish teacher and friend (I suppose they intended to be) has [sic] praised my *great abilities* to the skies. Is it unnatural that under such circumstances I should think myself extraordinarily brilliant?"[3]

The boy's intellectual and imaginative inclinations received further support from his paternal grandfather, Anderson Page. A short, stocky, taciturn man of sixty-five at the time of Wat's birth, Grandfather Page supplied the element in Wat's boyhood that came closest to the plantation South. He lived about ten miles away at a home called "Oaky Mount," but known to the family simply as the "Old Place." The house was a large, plain dwelling set atop a hill in a grove of oaks. A big gate led into the grounds. The twenty slaves whom Anderson Page owned in 1860 entitled him to be classed as a planter, and he ranked as one of the more substantial people of the area. His cotton gin had fallen into disuse, however, and even with twenty slaves, his personal property was valued at only $24,300, as compared with the $10,000 value set on his son's personal property, with just four slaves. Whatever its shortcomings as a plantation, the Old Place excited Wat's fancy, especially the cotton gin, the slave cabins, and the family cemetery. Best of all, the house harbored a small library and an attic with old family papers and a musket and blue jacket, which the boy was convinced had come from the American Revolution. Wat developed a special attachment to the Old Place, returning for long stays during his school and college years and later.

Anderson Page, too, had a strong interest in education. In 1839 he had opened a girls' school at his home, and later one of Wat's uncles maintained a boys' school in a house on the grounds.

ALLISON FRANCIS PAGE,
father of Walter Hines Page

(by permission of the Houghton Library, Harvard University)

CATHERINE FRANCES RABOTEAU PAGE,
mother of Walter Hines Page

(by permission of the Houghton Library, Harvard University)

Most of Frank Page's seven brothers had pursued studies in academies and colleges. One was a Methodist minister and two of the family's four daughters married Methodist ministers. One of those ministers was Hines Whittaker, for whom Wat received his middle name. Another Page uncle became a lawyer and Whig party politician, and reputedly the most accomplished of them was a bachelor physician who lived at the Old Place.[4]

Whatever the influence of his father's family, the boost that his mother gave Wat's nascent intellectual bent had the most lasting consequences. Two people who knew Page well later singled out Kate Page's influence as the most important force in molding her son. Page's first biographer recorded that his brother Robert, who was closest to him in age, "always thought that Walter's taste and to a great extent, his character, were the product of the first five years of his life." Robert Page believed that the early intimacy with his mother not only fostered literary tastes and a dreamy temperament in his older brother but "also had a softening effect upon his nature. As he grew up he developed all the boy's fondness for sports and games, yet there was a general feeling in the crowd that he was of finer texture than the rest." Augustus White Long, who worked on Walter Page's newspaper and lived in his house in Raleigh during the early 1880s, expanded on the same point: "Walter was the oldest living child and the only one with literary tastes and ambitions, which he inherited from his mother. His father was of the pioneer breed, bold, aggressive, dominant. Walter leaned to the feminine type rather than the masculine: he was feminine in the gentleness of his manner, his sensitiveness to impressions, and the generosity of his enthusiasms; but there was nothing in the least effeminate about him."[5]

The year 1865, when he was ten, formed a dividing point in Wat Page's childhood. No longer a little boy, he started school and ventured out more into the world. At the same time, both because he was older and because Frank Page's business enterprises now centered closer to home, his father began to exert greater influence. As a result, the boy found himself thrust into a psychological conflict that was to be fought many times in fact and fiction in modern America. It was the story of the bright, sensitive boy who, under his mother's influence and protection, dreamed of becoming an artist or intellectual; from the surrounding society, however, he met scorn, and he encountered opposition from a domineering, worldly father.

Some values of the larger society hit thirteen-year-old Wat Page hard when he entered Bingham School in the fall of 1868. Located at Mebane, about forty miles west of the Page home, Bingham enjoyed wide renown as one of the oldest and best boys' boarding schools in North Carolina and the whole South. It was also a military school, permeated with customs and attitudes borrowed from the Confederate officer corps. The boys not only wore grey uniforms, carried rifles, and drilled in close formation, but they also caught a certain martial spirit from their elders. Among the students a status hierarchy held sway, based primarily upon their fathers' military ranks. The son of a former Confederate general was cock of the walk, while sons of colonels also commanded great prestige. Because not all the boys had formerly military fathers, ambiguities clouded the standings of sons of governors, judges, and legislators. Religion also entered into the juvenile social gradations. Clergymen's sons counted for something, and in the absence of other distinguishing marks, the church affiliation of a boy's family fixed his standing. Episcopalians took the top spot, followed by Presbyterians, while Methodists and Baptists contended for the bottom rung of the ladder.

By his peers' criteria, Wat Page was a loser. Twenty-three years later he recalled in a speech, "How greatly I suffered in my own childhood at our foremost school. . . . The boys rated one another according to the military prominence of their fathers, and my father was so unthoughtful as not to be even a colonel." Worse, his father was a Methodist and had not served the Confederacy in any official capacity, military or civilian. Wat evidently endured a few rough times because of his family background. According to the account of his school days in his largely autobiographical novel, *The Southerner*, he got into a swinging, scratching fight with a boy who twitted him about his father's lack of a war record. But Wat did not suffer greatly. He did well at Bingham and became popular with his schoolmates. Thanks to his quick, retentive mind, studies caused him no more difficulty than before, as he continued his voracious reading and began algebra and the rudiments of Greek. Nor did the military side of Bingham bother Wat. A classmate who had been his company officer later remembered, "There was no foolishness about him. He went at it [drill] with the determination to master every detail of the manual at arms." Wat followed orders "like a real soldier."[6]

But schoolboy successes and pleasures did not erase an unpleasant realization. In his novel, Page also wrote about his father, "If it had become known among the boys that he had been a 'Union man'—I used to shudder at the suspicion in which I should be held." As a man in his sixties, Page recalled a conversation between his father and a local judge at the outbreak of the Civil War. The two men had taken out a piece of paper and drawn up a balance sheet of the war-making potential of the North and South. Their estimates had included the two sections' populations of military age, numbers of ships, manufacturing output, skilled labor forces, stocks of rifles and guns, aggregate wealth, and productive capacities. The totals had revealed a two-to-one superiority for the North. "Judge," Frank Page had concluded about secession, "this is the most foolhardy enterprise that man ever undertook." Both the reasoning and the remark were characteristic of his father. Frank Page had not been a secessionist and, to his son's later pain, he did not join the fight.[7]

Although Frank Page left little account of his opinions, the motives that impelled him toward antisecessionism and coolness toward the Confederacy most likely sprang from personal and family views, as well as the place of North Carolina in the antebellum South. Little disposed this hardheaded businessman to become a secessionist or ardent Confederate. He did not grow cotton or tobacco, the two great cash crops of the plantation system. He apparently regarded slavery as an available labor system, not a hallowed institution. Such attitudes came easily to a member of the Page family of North Carolina. These North Carolina Pages were farmers, who had migrated from England to Virginia sometime in the mid-seventeenth century. The first rec-

ord of them in America was of Samuel Page, who was born in
Lunenburg County, in south central Virginia, in 1672. The family
lived in that area for over a century until Lewis Page, Frank's
grandfather and Wat's great-grandfather, moved across the bor-
der into Granville County, North Carolina, where his son Anderson was born in 1790. Anderson Page, in turn, moved further
down into North Carolina to Wake County, where Frank Page
was born in 1824. Lewis Page supposedly held as many as fifty
bondsmen at one time, but Anderson Page's ownership of twenty
slaves and small-scale cultivation of cotton represented the family's nearest recent approach to the planter class.[8]

Politics also helped dispose Frank Page toward antisecession-
ist views. He and his father and brothers were staunch Whigs
before the Civil War. In North Carolina, as in most of the South,
Whigs were less inclined toward secession than Democrats. Walter later remembered his grandfather as an admirer of Henry
Clay and an adherent to an old-fashioned nationalism that antedated the sectional controversy of the 1840s and 1850s. Partly
because of Whig leanings, opposition to secession and halfhearted
devotion to the Confederacy were common in North Carolina.

Also behind North Carolinians' attitudes lay a long-standing
alienation from the rest of the South. Except in a few eastern
counties, large-scale plantation agriculture had never taken hold.
Landholding and slaveholding remained smaller in scale than in
most of the South, while much of the state was poor and backward. From early on, economic and social disadvantages had
made North Carolina an object of ridicule from outsiders, especially Virginians and South Carolinians. In turn, "Tar Heels," as
white North Carolinians called themselves, grew defensive and self-
critical, and issues in state politics perennially revolved around
how to pull the state out of its slough of torpor and inferiority.
This "Tar Heel" perspective toward the South had an impact on
Walter Page not only when he was an adolescent, but also when
he grew up to become a well-known editor and commentator.
From the late 1870s, he criticized much in southern life from a
standpoint resembling the outlook of North Carolinians of his
father's generation. He blamed most of the ills of the South on

the legacy of slavery and sentimentality toward the Lost Cause. As cures for the section's failings, Walter Page preached what Frank Page practiced—thrift, industry, and an unsentimental attitude toward the past.

But the boy did not have to accept the views of his father and his class and locality. He might have rejected everything that Frank Page stood for. He was closer to his mother, and some members of her family were ardent Confederates. To a boy entering the potentially rebellious period of adolescence, identifying himself with the Lost Cause might have seemed appealing. At one point Wat apparently did feel some attraction to the swashbuckling officers in grey and their nostalgic legend. The boy at the military school in *The Southerner* found himself stirred when he attended ceremonies unveiling a bust of General Stonewall Jackson. In his bunk that night he remembered "that my father had once spoken of the Confederacy as 'a foolish enterprise,' and I fell asleep wondering if he had been mistaken." Later, Page eagerly supported the two wars that the United States fought during his adult lifetime. Qualms about his father's part in the Civil War may have gone deeper than he realized.[9]

Nevertheless, Wat remained a dutiful son who admired his father and sought his approval. Though the bookish son plainly differed from the hard-driving businessman father, people only had to look at Wat to know that he was Frank Page's boy. His hair was softer, curlier, and a lighter shade of brown, but he unmistakably resembled his father. By the time he reached his teens, Wat had begun to acquire the big, bulbous nose, high forehead, and overall homeliness that marked most of the male Pages. His eyes were his most striking feature. They were large and a lively dark brown, like his father's. Only in one respect did he look more like his mother. From her he appears to have inherited unusually heavy eyelids, which, seemingly half-closed, often made Page as an adult look sleepy. In early photographs of him, the eyelids framed his large dark eyes in a way that gave the young man a dreamy appearance. What made Wat look most like Frank Page was his build. He shot up in height to well over six feet, and in his growth he acquired the same lanky, loose-jointed physique.

That rangy appearance was evidently another common characteristic of the men in the family. When Walter later described his oldest son to Frank Page as a stocky, heavyset child, he concluded, "There is nothing Pagey about him."[10]

The resemblance between father and son was more than physical. Whether from heredity or paternal example, Wat's temperament paralleled Frank Page's in several respects. The boy may have disliked chores around the home place, but he was hardly lazy. From an early age, Wat displayed his father's nervous energy and addiction to work. Little remains to indicate how Frank Page regarded his oldest boy. Because they were so different, the father evidently lacked understanding toward his son. That did not mean, however, that he disliked the boy or tried to force him to follow his own ways. Frank Page seems to have viewed Wat with affectionate, though distant, tolerance. "There's my book-worm," he once remarked, pointing his son out to a visitor in the house. Josephus Daniels, who later knew both father and son, wrote that Frank Page "never quite understood his son Walter though he admired his brilliancy. He didn't think Walter knew a thing about a dollar."[11]

Harmony between father and son stemmed in part from the family's staunch Methodism. Both Kate and Frank Page were strict, enthusiastic members of the church. Kate Page practiced a gentler and more intellectual faith, while her husband's religion was narrower and sterner. Frank Page disliked tobacco, although he did tolerate it; but he fired any black or white employee whom he heard swearing. Of all the vices, he most vehemently abhorred liquor and prohibition became his pet cause. He named the town that had grown up around his Wake County home after Samuel A. Cary, a former Union general and temperance crusader from Ohio, who had lectured in the town in the late 1860s. When the town was incorporated in 1871, Frank Page insisted that the charter include an ordinance forbidding the sale of liquor. He stood his ground even though he knew that the "dry" clause might keep profitable tobacco factories from being built in Cary.

Methodists formed the second-largest denomination in membership, behind the Baptists, in Wake County and North Carolina.

Generally they occupied the same low social status as they did at Bingham School. In the eyes of the best people, Methodism suffered from both the social standing of its adherents and the revivalistic character of its worship. Methodist revivalism played a big part in Wat Page's boyhood. Circuit-riding preachers conducted services at the little church down the road from his home. Outdoor revival meetings also took place in the area, featuring vociferous conversions of sinners—young and old—frenzied preaching, and singing of spirituals. But the greatest impact of the Page family's Methodist faith on Wat lay in pointing toward a future career. Frank Page and the community at large esteemed the ministry, and Kate and Frank Page could hardly help envisioning a clerical career as soon as the boy began to show bookish leanings. The desire to see their son a Methodist minister united both parents, father almost as much as mother, in their approval of his fondness for books.

Wat seems to have responded to his family's interest in a clerical career. He became a devout young Methodist evidently inclined toward the ministry as a vocation. After two years at Bingham, he returned for a year at a new, coeducational academy that Frank Page had helped to found in the town. In the fall of 1871, when he was sixteen, he left home again, to enter Trinity College, the only Methodist institution of higher education in North Carolina. An impoverished, struggling school, Trinity had attained collegiate rank just before the war and in 1871 did not present an inspiring appearance. The campus consisted of a clearing in the woods at the village of Old Trinity, some fifty miles west of the Page home. Two or three crude brick buildings housed classrooms, the chapel, and the literary societies, and students boarded out at homes in the area. Instead of embarking on the four-year program that led to the bachelor's degree, Wat found himself placed for a year in the preparatory course. That experience filled him with contempt for Trinity's academic standards. "You know that I would not [give] a horse-apple for Trinity's first distinction in any way," he announced to his mother the following year. "And I have good reason to believe that *your* opinion isn't a high one—am I not guessing correctly?"[12]

Clashes with the college's president, Braxton Craven, evidently deepened the youth's unhappiness. A stocky, rugged man with thick black hair and dark eyes, "Brack" Craven ran Trinity like a paternal autocrat. He set the curriculum, taught many of the classes, supplied one of the libraries, and nursed students when they got sick, while his superabundant energies also allowed him to serve as a local patriarch and cultural arbiter. Traditions around the college later depicted the gargantuan president and the lanky, curly-haired student as two strong wills in collision, supposedly over student organizations. Wat Page belonged to the literary society that Craven did not favor, and he helped found the first Greek letter fraternity, over the president's objections. Although those stories have an apocryphal ring, the young man did feel totally dissatisfied. Soon after he began his freshman year in the regular college course in the fall of 1872, he warned his parents that he could not possibly get high marks because he believed that other students cheated and the professors played favorites. A good grade would give "grounds for suspicion, of being a professor's pet, a boot-lick, or a scoundrel [with] no sense of honor."

The youth's complaints really stemmed from insufficient intellectual challenge. His grades, nearly all 99s and 100s, betrayed little trace of his discontent. Craven scrawled on the bottom of his first-term report card, "Be sure to send him back." Some of the deficiencies in the instruction Walter made up for by continued reading on his own and discussions with acquaintances until a chance event presented him with an opportunity to escape Trinity. In October 1872 a prominent Methodist divine came to preach in the chapel. He was the president of Randolph-Macon College in Ashland, Virginia, Dr. James E. Duncan, whom Page called "the best orator I ever heard." The Virginian appeared at Trinity on an errand that was not solely spiritual. He was conducting a raiding party for students—a common practice among presidents of struggling denominational colleges in those days. Duncan's autumn expedition to Trinity fulfilled at least part of his mundane purpose. Page and two other leading students from the college transferred to Randolph-Macon at midyear. When he took the train north to Virginia in January 1873, Page left his native state for the first time. The journey had an appropriate symbolism, for he was moving beyond the horizons of North Carolina Methodism. When Page went to Randolph-Macon, he did not think that he was leaving home intellectually or spiritually. Yet the signs pointed north. At seventeen he had outgrown the highest education offered by his church in his native state. He might wander further still, beyond the intellectual borders of Methodism and the South.[13]

Walter Page probably felt a twinge of apprehension as he climbed down from the train in Ashland in January 1873. Located on a flat expanse of land sixteen miles north of Richmond, Ashland was not a large or impressive town. Most of the buildings were frame structures, many in need of paint and repairs. Open fields stretched out behind the single street. Because Ashland had been founded as a summer resort before the Civil War, a hotel stood close by the railroad station. About fifty yards beyond the hotel was the college, which at first glimpse must have reminded Wat of Trinity. Randolph-Macon, too, had a wooded campus with a few simple buildings, which contained a chapel, classrooms, and literary societies. The only immediately discernible differences were a few small cottages that served as dormitories for some of the students. Set in a drab winter landscape, the town and the college may not have looked entirely inviting to an uncertain seventeen-year-old further away from home than he had ever ventured before.

Walter's collegiate career at Randolph-Macon did not get off to a promising start. A few days after arriving he developed a case of measles that kept him confined to bed for eleven days. After recovering, he joined another transfer student from Trinity in a rooming house across the railroad tracks—"Unhappy week or two!"—and then switched to a more acceptable residence. Those unfortunate first impressions quickly wore off. Even the measles were not all bad, because they provided an occasion for religious reflections and devotions, which Walter remembered as "better than I have experienced in an emotional way, before or since." President Duncan's preaching in the chapel added to both religious fervor and enjoyment of life at Randolph-Macon. Class-work came easily, as usual, and brought further success. At the end of the school year, after only a semester's attendance, he received certificates of distinction in mathematics, Greek, and English and was chosen Orator, the freshman speaker at the commencement exercises in June 1873. He was, he told his mother, "getting on finely now, so don't be troubled about me, in any way."

Randolph-Macon gave Walter more than academic success and a religious environment. Slight as differences between the two colleges initially appeared, Randolph-Macon possessed advantages over Trinity in satisfying the young North Carolinian's intellectual appetite. Whether because of twenty years' longer establishment, gentler surroundings, or the contrast between "Brack" Craven and James Duncan, the Virginia college had a less rigid, more open spirit. The institution's name seemed odd for a denominational college, inasmuch as both John Randolph and Nathaniel Macon had been Christian rationalists. The name attested regard for the southern agrarian and states' rights traditions associated with those men; no tolerance of religious skepticism was implied. Yet the college did not require attendance at daily chapel or Sunday church services; only one member of the faculty belonged to the Methodist church; and many students freely read books that expressed skepticism about orthodox Christianity. Those conditions reflected President Duncan's philosophy. The college operated, the catalog announced, "not according to any mere system of arbitrary regulations." Nor did the institution practice "mere enforcement of outward formal obedience to restrictive regulations," which fostered "a hollow morality" and blind obedience to rules. Instead, Randolph-Macon followed a "plan of making moral *improvement*—not mere *restraint*—a part of the education of the student." This was a remarkably tolerant philosophy for a college anywhere in the United States in the 1870s, particularly a denominational college in the South.[14]

As much as the general spirit of Randolph-Macon, the presence of one faculty member furthered Walter Page's development. He was Thomas Randolph Price, the professor of Greek and English. Thirty-four in 1873, Price still looked like the Confederate cavalry officer he had recently been. He had an erect bearing, alert gaze, and passionate manner that added to the romantic aura supplied by tales of his wartime service. A native Virginian, Price had studied before the war at the University of Virginia with the South's greatest classicist, Basil L. Gildersleeve, and later in Europe, principally in Germany. After recrossing the ocean in disguise to fight for the Confederacy, he had mounted a daring exploit in running the Union blockade at Wilmington, North Carolina. His dashing reputation made Price an attractive model to young men. He also believed in the practical value of his teaching. As the Randolph-Macon catalog stated, training in English would help "to solve the much-mooted question of practical education," by giving students skill "in the use of their mother tongue. . . . It ought no longer to be seen that young men, at the end of their studies, should often be unable to write a letter decently, or to express with ease, or even correctness, the knowledge that they have won." According to one student, the professor quipped, not completely in jest, that "he did not believe a man would ever go to heaven who did not use good English."[15]

Price proved a godsend to Walter. He furnished an important example in the young man's life, suggesting an alternative to a career in the pulpit as a way of reconciling literary tastes with useful work. Price's views on the practical value of English prefigured Page's subsequent justifications of his journalistic career and his ideas about teaching writing in universities. But the impact of Price's example still lay ahead. At the outset, the professor simply discovered an able, sympathetic pupil. In a college with fewer than two hundred students, Price would have had trouble not noticing Walter's ability. English was initially the better of his two subjects with Price. The professor gave him a mark of "high distinction" in second-year English, calling him "a young scholar of extraordinary promise." Again in his second year at Randolph-Macon, Walter earned distinctions in all his subjects, including Greek, Latin, mathematics, and logic, in addition to English.[16]

Fellow students also made Randolph-Macon congenial. During his first semester, Walter seems to have stayed close to the other two transferees, but in his second year he branched out somewhat in his friendships. Though attracting mainly sons of pious Methodist families, Randolph-Macon drew better students from a broader area. During his second year Walter became a close friend of two sons of Methodist ministers, one from North Carolina and the other from Georgia. His fellow Tar Heel was Wilbur F. Tillett, a later transferee from Trinity. Tall, smooth-faced, serious, Tillett subsequently entered the Methodist ministry and became a professor and dean of theology at Vanderbilt University. The Georgian was John Banks Wardlaw, a curly-haired youth a year older than Walter. The three were, as Tillett recalled, "dearest and best friends." Constant companions during the school years from 1873 to 1875, they became known as "the Triumvirate," a trio of college luminaries who captured the most sought-after prizes at the 1875 commencement—Tillett in mathematics and literature, Wardlaw in oratory, and Page in Greek.

These two friends appealed to different sides of Walter's maturing mind and personality. Wilbur Tillett remembered himself as being slower, less imaginative, and more conventional than his fellow North Carolinian. Years later he reminded Page of "the helpful and healthful intellectual, moral and religious influence which you exerted upon me at a time when I needed just such a liberal and enlarging influence." Walter spent part of the summer vacation of 1875 at the Tillett home in Oxford, North Carolina, where he made a strong impression. Long afterward Wilbur's younger brother could remember their older sister's admonishing him to "be a smart, good, clean man like Walter Page."[17]

With "Jack" Wardlaw, influences seem to have run in the opposite direction. He came from a more sophisticated background than Walter and he had evidently gone further in many of his reflections and speculations. He was also the companion to whom the younger man felt the stronger bond. "I count our spiritual alliance a steadfast one," Wardlaw declared in 1876, "and, indeed, one of the best manifestations of Providence's interest in my destiny." For his part, Walter seems to have hero-worshiped his friend, following him as a mentor in the pursuits of the mind and spirit. Wardlaw, he later explained, "is my constant companion in these things. He's a talented boy who pushes his way among men and has the outside go ahead manliness of masculine beings ten-fold stronger than I; and in this soul-life we are brothers. We felt together the uprising within us of these strong incomprehensible things simultaneously, several years ago, in our first coming to know each other." Walter called their friendship a "soul-union."[18]

The two friends were together just two years. Wardlaw transferred to Princeton in the fall of 1875, but he corresponded regularly with Walter, who visited him at Princeton once or twice before his graduation in 1877. From the first, they had common interests in literature, especially in such newly famed English poets and critics as Alfred Tennyson and Matthew Arnold. Later they also shared a growing ambivalence toward their families' desires for them to enter the ministry. After finishing Princeton, Wardlaw became a newspaperman and contributor to magazines. His example seems to have influenced Page toward a journalistic career. Tragedy clouded Wardlaw's life following college. His wife was killed in an accident a year after their marriage in 1879. Wardlaw himself contracted tuberculosis around 1877, suffering from the disease until his death in 1881, at the age of twenty-seven. Page visited him twice during his frequently bedridden last years, and he eulogized his friend just after his death as one of the South's finest products, "of that youth, fresh as spring, yet sprung from the strength of centuries."[19]

These companions helped to make Walter's second and third years at Randolph-Macon a triumph. The tall, gawky young Tar Heel seems to have enjoyed a campus reputation, even among "the Triumvirate," as most likely to succeed. Walter did especially well in oratorical contests. His voice, now turned warm and deep, and his plain, forceful delivery helped him defeat exponents of the more common, florid southern style of speaking. Other students tended to look up to Walter Page as a model of studiousness and clean moral character, although his "cussing" pained Tillett. Walter concentrated most of his studies on literature, progressing in the classics to the Latin poets and Homer and devoting himself in English to Shakespeare and Chaucer. Additional mathematics, French, and a year of natural science, but no history, economics, or government, which Randolph-Macon did not offer, rounded out his studies. Religion and literature remained the students' central concerns, both in class and out. Price often conducted smoke-filled evening sessions of readings and talk at his house, where the subjects ranged from ancient writers to modern poets, particularly Tennyson. Smoking evidently represented the prevalent student vice. Walter and Jack Wardlaw both became devotees of cheap tobacco and corncob pipes.

Intellectual development and student success hardly formed the Page family's main reasons for sending Walter to college. His mother hoped and his father evidently expected that their studious, devout son would enter the Methodist ministry. During his first year and a half at Randolph-Macon Walter seems to have shared their desire, and the anticipated climax to his youthful religious fervor came in April 1874, when he wrote home, "I have settled upon the determination to become a minister. . . . Of course I know that you and Papa would be pleased to see me become a faithful minister; but I have never had either of you to say what you think of *my* becoming one." Walter also discussed his ministerial vocation with Wilbur Tillett, suggesting that they both take out "preaching certificates," which would allow them to begin conducting Sunday services in country churches. Tillett demurred because he wanted to be surer of his own faith.[20]

Instead of forming the expected capstone to his college career, the announcement marked the prelude to a storm that broke over Page's eighteen-year-old head. Two months later, in June 1874, he received a letter from his father that "took me somewhat by surprise, I must acknowledge," he replied to his mother. Did she know anything about the letter? "I shall be much pleased with the nice office he spoke of; but I have something I'd like to say about his plan. I cannot write, however. So we shall talk the matter over, the office, stopping college, the University etc." What Frank Page had in mind is not known. Neither his letter to Walter nor anything else has survived to elucidate his plans for his son. The "office" may have been a political position. The "University" was most likely the University of North Carolina, which was then trying to reopen after closing down during Reconstruction. Frank Page may have secured a minor political sinecure in Raleigh, with which Walter might pay his own way for the rest of his education at the nearby state university.[21]

Two circumstances gave rise to his father's plans. One was financial hardship. Frank Page's lumbering business had collapsed with the Confederate defeat, and in the hard times following the war he had tried other enterprises, including turning part of the family home into a hotel. Early in the 1870s he opened a cotton-spinning factory, but that venture failed in the nationwide depression that began in 1873. But more than lack of money prompted Frank Page to try to end his son's studies at Randolph-Macon. The other circumstance behind his action was Walter's evident renunciation of his ministerial calling. Page never said exactly when or why he lost interest in the ministry. In *The Southerner* he depicted the central character as frustrated by a taboo on subjecting Christianity to critical scientific scrutiny. But religious skepticism was not Page's reason for renouncing the ministry almost immediately after announcing his call, at the age of eighteen. Tillett remembered that he simply "gave up entirely any and all ideas that looked toward making the Christian ministry his life-calling." In fact, at almost the same time that he avowed his ministerial intentions, he was becoming attracted to a secular career. Sometime during 1873 or 1874 he wrote a notation in his college catalog. Next to the title "Professor of Greek and English," which was printed under Price's name, he penciled "Walter H. Page."[22]

A harrowing summer followed his father's announcement. Long afterward, one of Walter's cousins remembered his arguing repeatedly with Frank Page about his becoming a minister. The youth reportedly declared, banging his fist on the table, "I'm damned if I'll become a Methodist preacher." The elder Page, according to a family friend, was so disappointed that he vowed never to educate another of his sons. About the quarrel Walter himself later noted in his college catalog for the 1874–75 school year, "This session, owing to the struggle I had with Father about going to college, I was 5 wks. behind the beginning of the session. I was very economical. My tuition I left unpaid, without pa's knowledge, as a Divinity Student." His subterfuge derived from the practice that Randolph-Macon followed, in common with other Methodist schools, of waiving tuition for students preparing for the ministry.[23]

Echoes of the conflict sounded through Page's remaining two years at Randolph-Macon and beyond. At commencement in June 1875, an inspiring sermon by President Duncan prompted him to tell his mother, "I thought this evening of the anxiety that being able to return to college caused me last fall, and of Pa's inability to bear my expense; and calmly I concluded that the lessons I have learned today are worth thribbly [sic] it all." In that same letter in June 1875, Page also revealed that the dispute over his staying in college involved more than money. "Life— what is it to be for me?" he pondered. "Failure or success? Easy enough it is to talk about doing great things but great talkers oftentimes greatly fail. Have I principles and the strength that make *men*?" College success struck him as meaningless compared with trying to "live a pure, active life. Can I never get up the strength required for that?" He could not escape self-reproach. "The same old question evermore comes up: 'How are you going to stand whatever may come?' 'What are you going to do, preach or dig?' Oh! The thing frets me eternally. Let's let it go, for the present at any rate."[24]

At bottom, the conflict between father and son involved Frank Page's and other people's beliefs that some kinds of work were fit for men and others were not. Doubts about his own manliness infested Walter's mind. He later contrasted his character with Jack Wardlaw's "outside go ahead manliness of masculine beings ten-fold stronger than I." Although some of his doubts sprang from guilt over inability to support himself, Walter's feelings of inadequacy went deeper. The final question posed in his letter—"What are you going to do, preach or dig?"—did not refer to the ministry; he never again mentioned a clerical calling in any letters to his parents. The question betrayed his acceptance of the belief that the only truly masculine calling was a life of action, not talk.

Walter Page admired action and scorned talk for the rest of his life. In *The Southerner*, the novel he wrote when he was in his fifties, the central character declares, "I suspect, in fact, that the builders of things are the happiest of mortals, and always have been—the builders of things, whether of states and laws or of 'works' and mills or of colleges; for these are the men who satisfy their own longings, who find life good, and to whom we look for guidance." In 1881, in his first signed magazine article, he contrasted crotchety southern gentlemen, "who talk so much," with vigorous mercantile types, who had "a sort of business air, . . . a fresher tone of voice, a more energetic step." As a magazine editor, he deplored narrow, scholarly writing, especially literary criticism, as "talk-ee, talkee, talkee." Of the three books Page wrote in his lifetime, the only one to bear his name was a collection of speeches entitled *The Rebuilding of Old Commonwealths*. It was dedicated "to the *honoured memory of my father* whose work was the work that built up the commonwealth."[25]

The family fracas over Walter's returning to college plunged the young man into the broader psychological conflict over "manly" and "unmanly" vocations. On one side, he had intellectual inclinations, which ran almost exclusively toward literature. Oddly for a white boy growing up in the South, especially during Reconstruction, he seems to have taken no interest in politics. Except for religious books, Walter's reading consisted mostly of poetry, novels, and literary criticism. He was interested in contemporary British and American authors, and he became particularly drawn to the young southern poet who had died shortly after the war, Henry Timrod. Probably starting in college, he also wrote his own poetry. On the other side, thrust into opposition, stood his father's insistence upon useful work and paying his own way. Frank Page remained true to his word about never educating another son. None of the other boys went to college, except Frank Jr., who was twenty years younger than Walter and briefly attended the University of North Carolina. Besides Walter, only his sister Emma received a bachelor's degree or did post-graduate study. Despite their differences, Frank Page's eldest son plainly took to heart his conviction that only active, profitable occupations were manly vocations.

These two sides established the opposite poles of Walter Page's internal conflict. One was a literary ambition that waxed and waned throughout his life. Page's interest in poetry faded within a few years after college, but into the early 1900s he continued to draft short stories and fictional sketches. In 1905, when he was nearly fifty years old and a busy, successful editor and publisher, he began writing what eventually became his only novel, *The Southerner*. To the end of his life he kept hatching plans for articles and books. The other pole was Frank Page's influence, which lent an inescapably commercial slant to all notions about acceptable occupations. The surest way to gain his father's approval was to make money. The few surviving letters to his father show that he repeatedly assured Frank Page that he was paying his debts, supporting himself, and turning a profit. Even as he dreamed of literary triumphs, he displayed keen interest in money-making ventures, including not only books and magazines but also stocks, inventions, and real estate.

In the end, those opposing poles of influence—toward literature and toward business—spread too far apart for Page to resolve his internal conflict for long. He sought political, social, and cultural influence as a secular substitute for a clerical career. In one way, his search for an alternative calling proved a boon. Page directed himself toward fields that mediated between the high culture of art, literature, and speculative thought and the workaday world of business, politics, and domestic life. His best talents lay in such fields—education, journalism, publishing, philanthropy, and social service. Unfortunately, the polar influences within him never let him remain completely at peace on those happy, fruitful middle grounds. The quarrel that erupted in the Page family during the summer of 1874 opened a conflict that lasted for over forty years and carved the basic outlines of the rest of Walter's life.

Wondering what to do with his life troubled the young man less than it might have during his last two years at Randolph-Macon. Price's example made teaching seem a fine alternative to the ministry, and Walter's few surviving letters indicate that he absorbed himself in his studies even more than before. Yet in June 1875 he also confessed, "Everything to my mind is in confusion. As for plans for anything, I have none, nor can I make any." His main reason for uncertainty was ironic. Not only did Walter win the prize for being the best student in Greek at the 1875 commencement, but he also received his bachelor's degree, after less than three years at Randolph-Macon. Early graduation raised the problem of going to work, until Professor Price came to Walter's rescue with the offer of a teaching assistantship in his Greek course. The job paid a small stipend, not enough to live on, but it did allow him to do further study in a postgraduate program.[26]

Working for Price turned out to be inspiring and demanding. Walter insisted to his mother that what he was gaining "in scholarship and in ideas is richly worth all my work." Price had the young man to tea at his house once or twice a week, "and he takes such occasions to criticise, sharply too, me and my work and to talk about every thing that I wish. His way of managing will force me into thoroughness." Walter found Randolph-Macon less pleasant than earlier. Of his two closest friends, Wilbur Tillett was still around, but Jack Wardlaw had left for Princeton. A pall had fallen over the whole college owing to the bad health of the president; Duncan could no longer preach in the chapel, nor could he make recruitment trips. The Randolph-Macon student body had shrunk in the fall of 1875, Walter observed, because of "Dr. D's inability to travel around last summer."[27]

Some of his worst perturbations during his final year at Randolph-Macon and in the months following stemmed from his being at least intermittently in love. A year or so later he supposedly told Tillett that he was "in love with three women all at once, all charming, otherwise quite different." Of these three loves, only one, whom he reportedly called "a scholar, almost a blue-stocking," can be identified with much certainty. This must have been Sarah Jasper, his mother's first cousin, who spent the summer of 1876 at the Page home. Although Sarah was eight years older than Walter, devotion to literature immediately formed a common bond between them. She introduced him to Timrod's poetry, while he shared his taste for Wordsworth. That summer formed an idyllic interlude for Walter. Frank Page was often away on business and after the younger children had gone to bed Kate Page, Sarah, and Walter would sit on the front porch and talk into the night about books and people, especially the great men of the past. Kate Page confided to Sarah that ever since Walter's recovery from his early childhood illnesses she had looked upon him as "a chosen vessel of the Lord" for great works. "I used to tell her," Sarah recalled, "she reminded me of Napoleon and his 'star.' "[28]

Walter's romance with his cousin flourished only briefly. At the end of the summer Sarah went to teach in Arkansas and he left to pursue graduate study in Baltimore. They did not see each other again for almost two years, and although Walter often wrote to Sarah, almost all his surviving letters were cool and lightly platonic. He and Sarah tried afterward to pretend that they had been no more than "brother-cousin" and "cousin-sister." Yet at one time they meant more to each other. Over forty-five years later, after Page's death, when Sarah Jasper was a widow in her seventies, she confessed that his letters had "formed the best and brightest part of my existence." Walter once testified directly about his feelings about Sarah. In a letter written in the fall of 1876, he affirmed, "How very sweet it is to love you with me in my work too. Had you ever thought of that? And your love giveth me ever a good hope—in all things where you say hope." The letter also suggested that religion drove Sarah and Walter apart. He went on to declare, "Hope, yes; but Faith: Help me my own Sarah, and maybe I can grow to it." The letter concluded with five stanzas of rhymed lines about the value of love and its ability to rekindle religious conviction.[29]

The young man's short-lived love for his cousin added a further emotional wrench to overstepping the intellectual horizons of the Page family, the Methodist church, and the South.

Walter's sharpest personal pain usually arose from his attitude toward churches and Christianity. That fact later made Page exaggerate the malignant power of clerical influences in both his own life and southern society. Preachers and their ignorance and superstition became handy scapegoats, along with the devotees of the Lost Cause, for many troubles. What part Sarah Jasper had in developing that cast of mind is impossible to say. Walter's longer-running frictions with his family and others over the ministry and religious beliefs almost certainly played a larger role. But this early love must have helped form the pictures that Walter Page carried in his head of southern women as handmaidens of the preachers and the Confederates and thus as retrograde influences on their homeland.

The biggest step in Walter's journey away from home came after his final year at Randolph-Macon. In January 1876 he mentioned to his mother "a hazy, half seen vision of a plan that is rather a pet of mine." Although Walter never disclosed what the scheme was, he probably wanted to study in Germany. Then an exciting new possibility arose. The Johns Hopkins University in Baltimore, Maryland, was to begin offering instruction in the fall of 1876. The Johns Hopkins was the first university in the United States to be devoted primarily to graduate work. The new university's dynamic president, Daniel Coit Gilman, had spent two years conducting a search for faculty on both sides of the Atlantic. Gilman's earliest and one of his most eminent catches came in classical philology, when he hired Basil Gildersleeve away from the University of Virginia. Gildersleeve's appointment established a connection that benefited twenty-year-old Walter Page. The great classicist's protégé was Price, who took Gildersleeve's place at Virginia in the fall of 1876. Price, in turn, urged Walter to apply for a fellowship at the Johns Hopkins, and he recommended the young man glowingly to Gildersleeve and Gilman.[30]

Walter had some trouble gaining the fellowship. Largely because no other financial support for genuine graduate study existed in America, the Johns Hopkins attracted a greater number and a higher caliber of applicants than anyone had anticipated. In philology, Gildersleeve informed Walter that one candidate

I submitted "two elaborate essays—one in Latin—on the traces parody in Latin comic poets; another has been pursuing Sanskrit studies for several years." Such work lay beyond Walter's competence. Professor Gildersleeve regretted that his application essay could hardly be considered "such proof of philological attainments as the Board expects." Walter immediately wrote to President Gilman to withdraw his application, but the list of fellowship winners, with his name among them, had already been published. Gildersleeve valued Price's recommendation so highly that he asked Walter to submit an additional essay to justify his admission. Over the summer of 1876 he put together work that showed, in Gildersleeve's estimation, "sufficient progress to justify the confirmation of the appointment." It was a signal honor for a southerner who had just turned twenty-one and who had received his entire education in the denominational colleges of his native region.[31]

This time there could be no question that Walter Page was mentally and spiritually leaving home. When he crossed the Potomac River in the fall of 1876, he ventured to the edge of the South. Maryland might have had slavery before the Civil War, but the state had not joined the Confederacy. In 1876 Baltimore had a population of about three hundred thousand, more than five times as large as Richmond, which was the biggest town Walter had yet seen. Baltimore was also a bustling seaport with a cosmopolitan air and polyglot citizenry to be found nowhere else in the South except in faraway New Orleans. The Johns Hopkins occupied from its inception a position of leadership in American education, boasting a distinguished faculty and a spirit of scholarly enterprise and critical thought unmatched anywhere in the United States, much less south of the Potomac. No matter how much he protested to the contrary, Walter Page was leaving behind most of the values of his youth.

CHAPTER 2

The Search for Vocation

Walter Page's journey in the fall of 1876 filled him with both excitement and misgiving. Before going to Baltimore, he traveled as far north as Philadelphia, where he visited the Centennial Exposition commemorating the hundredth anniversary of the Declaration of Independence. Besides getting his first impressions of a large city, the young man jostled with a quarter of a million visitors when he went to the exposition to view the marvels of industrial America and works of art from all over the world. The homemade exhibits included the new Pullman sleeping car for railroads, a gigantic engine that powered hundreds of machines, a complete watch factory, and, for a time, Alexander Graham Bell's novel device, the telephone. To a young southerner on his first trip away from his homeland, the experience was breathtaking. After Philadelphia and the exposition, Walter wrote to Sarah Jasper, "Baltimore with all the noise of its trading season, seems quiet indeed to me now."

At first, Baltimore also brought loneliness and uncertainty. Cold and rainy weather, the Johns Hopkins's drab quarters—Gilman had decided to concentrate on "men not buildings"—and unfamiliarity with other students all had a depressing effect. "I am 'feeling around,'" Walter recounted to Sarah, "as the North Carolina phrase goes, and being 'felt around,' living the while a sort of miserable dog-life of it." The first meeting with Gilman dispelled loneliness and restored excitement. Early in October 1876, the group of twenty-one Fellows gathered in a small, bare auditorium to be addressed by a trim, compact man with flowing moustaches. With his normal exuberance, the president announced that the university would be "a temple of learning and upon its altar we shall light the sacred flame," and he enjoined each Fellow "to light his own torch at the altar flame and to maintain it burning as brightly as possible so long as he shall live."

One member of the audience noticed that a thin, pale-faced young man sitting next to him hung on Gilman's words. When the president finished speaking, the intent listener exclaimed in a southern accent, "Isn't he splendid!" As the meeting broke up and most of the Fellows began chatting in small groups, Walter Page sat by himself on top of a table, dangling his long legs over the side. Presently, another Fellow perched beside him and struck up a conversation. He was William W. Jacques from Massachusetts, a student in physics. The pair got on well at once and decided to room together. He and Page soon found a situation conducive to study in the home of two aged spinsters. They bought some large, comfortable chairs and a broad table and settled in for the rest of the school year.[1]

Page could hardly have helped responding excitedly to the Johns Hopkins, for the new university pulsated with intellectual adventure. A fitting symbolism linked its opening in 1876 with the Philadelphia Exposition. America's first institution of graduate education was expected to usher in a new era of intellectual sovereignty. Before Page and the other Fellows arrived, the Johns Hopkins's first convocation, on 12 September 1876, had sounded the note of cultural nationalism. The renowned English biologist and writer, Thomas Henry Huxley, who was then on a lecture tour of the United States, had challenged Americans to strengthen the "intellectual clearness of the individual citizen" and make their universities "the fortresses of the higher life of the nation."[2] In selecting faculty and students, Gilman sought to match the luster of European universities. The faculty sparkled with eminence, despite numbering only eight members. Basil Gildersleeve held undisputed premiership among classical scholars in the United States. Equally renowned was James Joseph Sylvester, who was considered the greatest British mathematician of his time. Almost as distinguished were the British and German-trained American professors of biology, Latin, chemistry, and physics.

As impressive as the faculty at the Johns Hopkins was the band of twenty-one Fellows, who formed the core of the student body. They were over double the number originally authorized and included men with far more advanced qualifications than Gilman and the trustees had anticipated. That first group of Fellows at the Johns Hopkins was, as has often been noted, probably the most remarkable band of students ever to gather in one place in America. In many ways the Fellows were more than students, since Gilman expected them to lend a hand in establishing the institution. Some were asked to lecture, even in their first years, and all were consulted about buying books for the library. Scientists such as Page's roommate Jacques traveled to other universities to inspect laboratories, with a view to purchasing equipment and setting up facilities at the Johns Hopkins. The more advanced men had chosen the Johns Hopkins fellowships over positions in colleges where they would have had to teach students on levels far below their own attainments. They belonged to a wave of academic specialists who were waiting for American higher education to catch up with them. Less highly trained Fellows also had excellent preparation and a fervent academic vocation, and most were in their middle or late twenties. Page and Jacques were the youngest, both having just turned twenty-one in August 1876.

In such company, it was no wonder that Walter Page felt ill at ease. "My chief difficulty is my lack of advancement," he informed Sarah in October 1876. Beyond this, Page began to doubt his academic calling. Germanic-inspired examples of scholarly dedication appalled him. Some of the Fellows, he told Sarah, "read Homer to catalogue grammatical peculiarities; they see nothing in Sappho but forms of grammar!" At the end of November he instructed her to call him "a Greek drudge. . . . There is little encouragement in it, I confess; and I am sure that I have mistaken my work, or would mistake it, if I considered Greek-teaching my life work." Sticking with his studies did, however, have certain advantages. "There's no other place of half the advertising power for a young scholar as the place I hold." He believed further that "a home-feeling in Greek literature" was essential to any "claims to high literary culture." Page apparently never planned to make studying and teaching the classics his profession. At the end of November 1876, he also told Sarah that he planned, in studying classical literature, "to break my way into it and then leave it, as a main work." Aversion to minute scholarship formed his biggest obstacle. "In dead earnest, I have a strong mind to throw up all my scholarly plans," he confessed to Sarah in the same letter, "and go to work, go among men, I mean—go into politics, for example. Active work is worth tenfold more than book speculation."[3]

Basil Gildersleeve epitomized nearly everything about the Johns Hopkins that Page liked and disliked. Eminence, awesome command of his subject, and physical appearance—a massive build, protruding beard, and forceful manner—made the professor a truly impressive figure. Like his former student Price, Gildersleeve was a Confederate veteran. He still limped from a leg wound and he had a fund of war stories, which he delighted in telling. Also like Price, Gildersleeve contained within himself a radical split between artistic love of literature and commitment to rigorous, scientific study of language. Years later he remarked, "I have never forgotten that my original purpose in life was to be a man of letters."[4]

Gildersleeve rarely showed students his artistic or lighter sides. He was a professor and seminar leader directing scholars in philological investigation. The lanky, curly-haired North Carolinian was the youngest member of a seminar of five Fellows who met weekly with Gildersleeve. Although the professor allowed some latitude in choosing subjects, he did not permit the seminar to stray from the path of philological method. Students orally presented introductions to classical authors or interpretations of assigned texts. The professor offered criticism. The exercises stressed close analysis of words, grammar, and syntax, especially origins and changing usage. A severe, demanding atmosphere pervaded the seminar. Page evidently fitted in well. Another Fellow, who later became a distinguished classicist, recalled that

Page read aloud well, in a soft southern accent. Less extensive preparation than the others did not prevent him from participating in the seminar, and Gildersleeve expressed satisfaction with his work.[5]

However, Page did not live with his nose constantly in classical texts. He enjoyed rooming with Jacques, a lively person with whom he engaged in intimate late evening talks. Other Fellows often stopped by, to sit by the fire, smoke, and talk about all manner of topics. Page "lost all of his shyness," Jacques remembered years afterward, and he displayed "the happy faculty of drawing out the best there was in those with whom he came in contact." The young man also ventured out into broader circles, attending lectures in mathematics, visiting Jacques's physics laboratory, and attending beer hall get-togethers with other Fellows. He and Jacques likewise plunged into the whirl of polite Baltimore society, and Page developed a taste for opera.[6]

The youthful North Carolinian was venturing into areas of thought and culture that extended far beyond anything in his earlier experience. His first year at the Johns Hopkins, Page told his mother, "has opened up my eyes more than any year before has ever done." He began to relax his sectional prejudices. In October 1876, Page attributed one reclusive Fellow's peculiarities to his being "a native of Connecticut; and Connecticut, I suppose, is capable of producing any unholy phenomenon." Rooming with Jacques, whom he affectionately called "damned Yankee," lessened his suspicion of northerners. By February 1877, he was describing "my Boston friend" as "a *rare* thing, viz. a *complete* Christian Yankee gentleman."[7]

The reference to Christianity betrayed Page's agitation about orthodox religion. Born four years before the publication of Charles Darwin's *Origin of the Species*, the young North Carolinian had grown up at the outset of perhaps the fiercest religious controversy since the Reformation. On both sides of the Atlantic disputes had arisen, particularly within the Protestant denominations, over whether the Englishman's evolutionary theories could be reconciled with the biblical account of Creation. American colleges and universities became hotbeds of argument among faculty and students alike over the validity of Darwinian explanations and their compatibility with Christianity. According to Page's account in *The Southerner*, he first encountered the tension between science and religion at Randolph-Macon. Wilbur Tillett later recalled that "during the last year that he was at R. M. College, under the influence of such writers as Matthew Arnold, Huxley and others, he began drifting away not only from the ministry but from the *evangelical* type of faith characterizing his earlier years."[8]

Page knew from the start that going to the Johns Hopkins would aggravate the already-sore subject of his religious beliefs. The university proclaimed its dedication to critical, scientific inquiry in all areas, and Huxley's appearance at the September 1876 convocation dramatized the potential for conflict with the forces of orthodoxy. The biologist's fame rested not only on his scientific research but also on his public skepticism toward traditional Christianity and articulate championship of Darwin's theories. Huxley's stress on the "interpretation of nature" in his Johns Hopkins address, together with the absence of a prayer at the convocation ceremony, raised what Page called "a very great outcry against the godlessness of Johns Hopkins." He found the charges groundless because, he told Sarah in October, "there are here no religious influences pro or con." Yet Page feared the consequences of the Huxley incident. "For whatever be the peculiar religious views that I may have, what is objectionable to my friends will be attributed to my connection with the university."[9]

The controversy between science and religion preoccupied Page during his first year at the university. On the back of his Greek notes he scribbled several fragmentary essays on the conflict between the two realms. In one entitled "the Scientific Method applied to Religion/Christianity," he maintained that science was not destroying religion. "Religion is *fact* not theory," he wrote, and "facts in religion" could be investigated in the same manner as "facts in physiology." Moreover, science deserved praise for "tearing away some of the cumbersome gear of religious thought. . . . How much time of how many working people will be saved, for better work." Those essays represented a last attempt to maintain his faith against skepticism. But it was evidently a losing fight, as Page engaged in discussions with his fellow students in his rooms and in the beer halls of Baltimore. In June 1877, at the end of his first year at the Johns Hopkins, he admitted to Sarah that the "men who lead me in thought and whom I honor are at least what I should formerly have called infidels."[10]

Page's first year at the Johns Hopkins marked the climax of his youthful religious involvement. Thereafter, churches and doctrines rarely held much interest for him and he attended services only sporadically. The only religious matter that continued to concern him was a growing conviction that preachers often exercised a retrograde social influence. But Page's later attitudes were anticlerical rather than anti-Christian. These fragmentary essays revealed that he responded to the controversy between science and religion in the same way that he met the conflict between his parental influences, not by taking sides but by trying to reconcile the opposing parties. His proposed settlement disclosed a lasting habit of mind. Stress on "facts" and relish for saving time for "better work" later became Page's main response to all kinds of controversies—to shun them for the sake of practical activity. Notions of salvation through action were common in America, and the young Tar Heel had a compelling personal example of an activist approach in the life of his father.

During the summer of 1877 Page went to Germany with his roommate Jacques. They sailed as soon as classes ended, and by the beginning of July they were settled into a comfortable rooming house in Berlin. While Jacques visited laboratories, Page read Greek and went to the Berlin Museum, which contained the world's finest collection of classical antiquities. The two young Americans also attended concerts and the opera and drank in beer gardens. Page later journeyed by himself to Copenhagen, Dresden, and Darmstadt before returning to Baltimore at the end of the summer. The trip contained all the fun and adventure of a first voyage abroad. Page insisted to his mother that "this living a little in the old world is so educating" that he would never "regret what I had feared Papa would think of my rashness."[11]

Equally important, Page's European summer provided his first chance to try his hand at journalism. He sent a series of descriptive letters to a North Carolina newspaper, the *Raleigh Observer*. Nine contributions, his first published work, eventually appeared over the signature "WHP." His descriptions dwelled mainly on obvious contrasts between America, particularly North Carolina, and Germany, with special stress on Germany's efficiency, order, cleanliness, and the absence of political freedom. In his last letter to the *Observer*, in September 1877, Page stated that Germany had a "lesson" to teach North Carolina. "It is the lesson of scholarship," he declared, "the lesson of education, the lesson of culture." The lesson had two principal messages. The first was work; "in this thing of higher culture mere preaching is no good." Second, Tar Heels must "domesticate" German methods to their society. "For it is not a method of indigenous growth in democratic soil—this method of scientific exactness." Yet if North Carolina properly followed Teutonic examples, the feat could work miracles. "German accuracy wedded to such endurance as we show in many directions of labor might beget giants amongst us."[12]

This first foray into journalism foreshadowed Page's more mature work in style and ideas. Though still on the flowery side, his *Observer* letters contained some of the forceful, colloquial writing that already characterized his private correspondence. Lighter touches of human interest often relieved their overall seriousness. Concern for education and advocacy of borrowing from other societies prefigured basic arguments that Page later reiterated constantly in advocating southern reform. The dismissal of "mere preaching" about education reflected both his stress on practical work and his contempt for talk.

The letters from Europe hinted at the frame of mind in which Page returned to the Johns Hopkins in September 1877. His second year at the university went wrong from the beginning. For some reason, Page did not room with Jacques again. He lived alone, and though he claimed to "make all my arrangements fit my work," he complained to his mother after only a few days, "it's a dreary sort of existence." He tried to pursue his studies, but, as he admitted to Sarah early in the academic year, his heart was not in the work. He did not wish "to find out any new grammatical fact, nor prepare myself to teach Greek." Having to "read for grammar's sake" and compile "dry statistics from dry Greek" grew wearisome. "In strict truth I ought not to hold the place I do here. I am not working in the line that it requires and ought to require." At the end of February 1878 he fell ill and went home to North Carolina.[13]

That was the end of Walter Page's career at the Johns Hopkins. He never returned to the university as a student. "A disorder of the liver," he explained to Gildersleeve in May, "keeps me continually incapable of application." Declining the professor's suggestion that he finish a dissertation, Page protested that "my lack of preparation weighed heavily on me always, and the confining private work I did in consequence is what is now telling on my health." The plea of ill health was an excuse. Page hardly remained bedridden during the first three months after leaving the Johns Hopkins. He spent most of the time at his grandfather's house, the Old Place, where he read intensively in Shakespeare and Chaucer. During those three months he probably wrote his first magazine article and may have written some poems and short stories. In May 1878, on almost the same day that he pleaded ill health to Gildersleeve, Page accepted an appointment to teach English in the summer school at the University of North Carolina, and in June he went to Chapel Hill to begin a vigorous six weeks of lecturing.[14]

Like ill health, insufficient preparation was an excuse. Page's trouble at the Johns Hopkins lay not in lack of ability but in lack of desire to keep up with the other Fellows. Even during his first year he had had a hard time not being distracted from philological research. During the second year, he admitted, "I manage to steal much time to read generally in fine literature." Nor was his main problem that of not wanting to make teaching Greek his career. Although Page may have been contemplating journalism, he had not yet renounced university teaching as a career. He greeted his summer appointment at North Carolina as a chance to put "myself earnestly & prominently into the greatest educational movement, as I take it, of the age for us—the scientific study of English." He confessed that he felt "considerable elation at thus being able to strike a good blow, if a weak one, just where I think a blow will most help in shaping the uncouth metal of our state."[15]

Page's basic difficulty at the Johns Hopkins lay in the subject and method of his studies. His reading preferences showed that his deepest interest was English literature. If he could have pursued graduate study in English, Page might have stuck it out. Unfortunately, the only available route to teaching English literature, which was then in its infancy as a college course, lay through the classics. Rigorous emphasis on "scientific" research in philology also bothered the young North Carolinian. In November 1877 he commented in another letter to the *Observer*, "In these days when science, physical and philosophic, is absorbing the whole force of mind and youthful studiousness among us, who is to take care of our literature and our literary culture?"[16]

Page indicated where his interests lay when he published his first magazine article in March 1878. The eight-page, unsigned review essay entitled "Henry Timrod" appeared in *The South-Atlantic*, a literary review published in Wilmington, North Carolina. "Timrod was no great genius," Page asserted. He was "not Titanic, nor is his work likely to be remembered forever." Yet Timrod did strike Page as having one claim to greatness. His Civil War poems correctly answered the question, "What is there in our history, in our society, in our life, that is poetically graspable? One thing surely, if none other—our war; our war not so much in the battlefield sense, nor in the political sense, but socially." Despite his limitations, Timrod had captured the essence of the war for the South, "a passionate giving up to an all-enveloping cause." Whatever northern poets might achieve, Page asserted, "for real poetry, we must look to the Southern side; and of all the songs the war inspired, there are none comparable to Timrod's."[17]

To a young North Carolinian anxious to play a part in the literature and culture of his native region, the Johns Hopkins now seemed to offer little. Page was not alone in disliking the university's dominant intellectual atmosphere. Charles D. Morris, the university's Latin professor, clung to older ideals of classical education as a broad, humanistic influence. Sidney Lanier, the southern poet who then lived in Baltimore and later lectured at the Johns Hopkins, argued for studying literature solely as art. Lanier wanted to combat, as he told Gilman, "that very lamentable narrowness of range which seems peculiarly incident to the absorbed specialist in modern physical science and linguistics." Page's decision to depart evidently left few regrets. He remained friendly with Gildersleeve, Gilman, and others whom he had met at the university, and he later participated in the Johns Hopkins Alumni Association. The Johns Hopkins did instill in Page a lasting sense of excitement about the expansion and application of knowledge. In 1900 he recalled wistfully to Gilman "men like me who coming out of a poor Southern community, might never have got a wide view of the great world and of the great things in it in proper coordination but for the help that the university gave us." Otherwise, he felt well quit of the place.[18]

For nearly two years after leaving the Johns Hopkins, Page went through one of the most frustrating periods in his life. At first he must have felt happy at being freed from the grind of classical philology. He especially enjoyed teaching English literature at Chapel Hill during the summer of 1878. His students were "normalites," young men and women taking a crash course before they went out to teach in the public schools. Many were at least as old as their twenty-three-year-old instructor, and they seem to have delighted in his youthful fervor. One student was Edwin Alderman, who remembered Page's exhorting "with fierce eagerness and a kind of defiant intellectual confidence" about the value of reading the classics. Alderman appreciated Page's flouting "the oratorical pomposities" then prevalent on most public platforms. The lanky, intense young teacher wore a rough tweed suit rather than a frock coat, and he put his hands in his pockets instead of grasping his lapels. Except when he "bawled out" his listeners in bursts of enthusiasm, he spoke in a conversational manner and made few gestures. Another observer, Augustus

White Long, then a teenager about to enroll at the university, recalled how visiting one of Page's classes incited him to read Shakespeare on his own. "Page opened windows in my mind."[19]

Much of the young teacher's fervor derived from a sense of mission. Writing to the *Observer* from Baltimore in November 1877, Page had maintained, "If the Southern people are to attain any enviable eminence in culture it is likely to be in literature rather than in science. Our climate and our blood point that way." His problem was how to participate personally in the hoped-for cultural renaissance. The question threw him back into the thorny path of vocational choice. Page's immediate concern was what to do after the end of the summer session at Chapel Hill. He had hopes of joining the faculty of the university, but a position never materialized. Then and later he thought that suspicions of religious unorthodoxy had prevented his appointment. In fact, Page's inability to secure a position probably sprang from the university's lack of money. Reopened only in 1875, the University of North Carolina was no larger and it stood on no better financial footing than a college such as Randolph-Macon. In the autumn of 1878, Kemp P. Battle, the president of the university, bragged to Page about having nearly two hundred students. Unfortunately, not all of them paid tuition, and "until hard times pass our resources will be limited."[20]

A professorship at Chapel Hill was not Page's only possibility in North Carolina. During the summer of 1878, he declined an offer to head a boys' school at Hillsboro, about twenty miles from the Page home. Some of the young man's reasons for turning down the post can be inferred from a letter written to him in July 1878 by George T. Winston, the professor of Latin at Chapel Hill. Winston did not blame his friend for kicking at "the traces of the N.C. pedagogue. . . . Your ideas of happiness and your thirst for something more elevated and purely literary, on which to expend your energies, are strongly at variance with the work required by the man that takes charge of the Hillsboro School." Put another way, Page's problem was whether his newly cultivated thoughts and tastes had outgrown his native state.[21]

The young man had not yet become totally disaffected. His

restiveness toward his native state did not apply to the whole South. In 1881 he noted in a magazine article, "Very few Southerners go away from the newer towns or larger cities." Page himself went to one of the larger cities on the edge of the South in the fall of 1878. At the end of August two telegrams arrived, offering Page a "professorship" of English at the Boys' High School in Louisville, Kentucky, at a salary of fifteen hundred dollars. Price had recommended him for the job, and Page accepted apparently because of the salary and a welcome change of scene. Louisville, a city of 120,000, was mounting a local economic and cultural revival. The city's greatest single force was Henry Watterson, the owner and proprietor of the *Courier-Journal*, who vociferously championed the "New South" doctrines of sectional reconciliation and industrialization below the Mason-Dixon line. At the Boys' High School Page taught English courses that ran from grammar through Shakespeare and Chaucer. Once again he performed well in the classroom. His work, he told his mother in December, "seems to bear very excellent results."

But success as a teacher no longer satisfied him. "Some day or other I shall quit teaching," Page also told his mother, "—some day when I have grown enough in my studies to do some higher scholarly work." Page busied himself trying to get started on a literary career. He registered with a literary agency in New York, which was to try to sell some poems and to advertise him as "a student of Literature, especially of Poetry" who had been a "contributor, chiefly on educational and poetic subjects, to several Southern papers." Over the Christmas holidays, Page traveled to Georgia to visit Jack Wardlaw, whose health had taken a turn for the worse. Wardlaw evidently discussed his journalistic work and plans to write a social history of the South. His friend's example again seems to have inspired Page. Shortly after the visit, the young teacher embarked on a venture that represented both his first stab at professional journalism and an attempt to strike a blow for southern culture.[22]

The venture was *The Age*, a newly founded weekly magazine. *The Age* called itself "A Representative Southern Paper. An independent Democratic weekly review of Politics, Literature and Art." The magazine strove "to represent and give expression to the more intelligent thought and opinion of the democratic party" and to demonstrate the capacity of the South and West "to do their own thinking in national affairs, and to pass their own judgments on the World's literature." The journal's founder was William Thompson Price, a buoyant thirty-three-year-old bachelor who had served in the Confederate cavalry and studied in Germany. Price was a friend of Henry Watterson and he continued working as a reporter and drama critic for the *Courier-Journal* after he founded *The Age*. Price's model for *The Age* was E. L. Godkin's journal, *The Nation*, which combined political commentary from an independent Republican standpoint with essays on cultural topics and book reviews. In its political columns *The Age* urged the Democratic party to use clean, respectable methods.[23]

Page made his first appearance in *The Age* a little over a month after its founding, with a review of Bayard Taylor's verse play, "Prince Deukalion." The youthful critic applauded the poet's "great virility." According to Page, Taylor had grasped the truth that "poetry is not mere dainties." Later, Page published more essays and reviews in *The Age*. All the material in *The Age* was unsigned, but a marked copy of one issue, which Page apparently saved, indicates that he wrote an editorial about a possible Democratic presidential nominee. Style and subject suggest that Page may also have written an editorial entitled "Southern Journalism." The editorial observed that a new breed of "practical men" were taking southern newspapers "in hand," making them professional enterprises and getting rid of "accidental [Confederate] colonels and useless brigadiers." Their efforts showed awareness "that journalism is as much a profession as pleading cases or healing diseases, with as hard work in it as in the trade of blacksmithing or bootmaking." These new journalists and other enterprising southerners should gain the respect of "the honest-minded in the North. . . . Let the politicians and the marplots and the intermeddlers know that they have opinions of their own."[24]

More important than writing for *The Age*, Page borrowed a

thousand dollars to become half-owner of the magazine in April 1879. He had become, he exulted to his father, "free from anybody's domineering," and he felt sure that he had laid the "foundation of a life-time's independence." He seemed particularly anxious to convince Frank Page that he had acted wisely. Referring to *The Nation*, he pointed out that a comparable journal in New York "that is Republican in politics and infidel in religion" had made a million dollars in the past fourteen years. Southerners, Democrats, and "Christian people will support a similar publication if it be Democratic, & religious in its tone, if it suit their views." It would have been "a weak thing for a man of my chance and working habits to miss this for the lack of $1000." Page insisted that "in the end I shall gain enough money to live comfortably."[25]

The Age did not last long. The publication came to an end in June 1879, less than three months after the young North Carolinian bought in. When the school year was over Walter Page once more returned home. He was not only jobless because he had not sought another year at Boys' High School, but he was also in debt. Page seldom talked about *The Age* in later years, but the experience helped to shape his future. *The Age* gave him a taste for magazines, which later proved to be his journalistic forte. "I am going to write," he vowed to one of his cousins in the summer or fall of 1879, "—I am going to edit a magazine." The bitter financial lesson in no way diminished his determination to be his own boss. He also vowed to his cousin, with a determined look in his eye, "And I am going to own the magazine that I edit." Nor did Page lose his soft spot for enthusiastic characters with big ideas, like Price, or, for that matter, like himself. "A man who won't bet on himself isn't worth a damn," he quipped twenty years later, as he prepared to try yet another publishing venture that might give him independence. Living in Louisville also exposed Page to Watterson's "New South" views. His likely authorship of the editorial "Southern Journalism" showed that Page had begun to develop New South views of his own, which he soon articulated further. Still, the failure of *The Age* must have deepened his pessimism about the cultural possibilities and opportunities for himself in the South.[26]

Page returned to North Carolina in the summer of 1879 filled with frustration and self-doubt. Bold words from the preceding year may have come back to haunt him. The previous December he had written, "And all the while, dear Mama, I am trying to grow to be a man—every inch a man; and to [work?] so that nobody need keep charitable [. . .] for my sake." In March he had asserted, "There is a living for me in my pen, once I get started." His problem remained where to find that living and how to get started, and he spent the rest of 1879 trying to solve those problems. In the end, Page left North Carolina again, but, he reminded his mother, "did I not wait 8 months at home trying to get a place as teacher, or as anything else? I could not have chosen differently. You must know how I tried month after month to get even any business place in Raleigh—all the way up to a professorship in the University."[27]

His father's activities could not help adding to the young man's disquiet. After the failure of his cotton mill in 1873, Frank Page had returned to his vocation of lumbering and had begun to explore opportunities in the pine forests a hundred miles to the south of Cary. When Walter returned from Louisville in the summer of 1879, his father was getting ready to sell the house in which the family had lived for twenty-five years and in which his eight children had been born. They were moving to Aberdeen, in Moore County, North Carolina, where Walter's brothers and one of his sisters would eventually join their father in exploiting new lumbering opportunities. Frank Page was embarking on the path that would lead him over the next twenty years to build a substantial set of family businesses, which would include not only sawmills but also a railroad, a bank, and extensive agricultural, real-estate, and stock holdings. At the age of fifty-four Frank Page was once more demonstrating his unsentimental, enterprising approach to life. His example was not lost on his unemployed, literary eldest son.

Walter Page's adversities had some compensations. During these months he was able to devote himself to reading, writing, and thinking. He turned out a number of fragmentary poems and short stories. He also began to read history and to take an interest in public affairs, in pursuit of his now-settled determination to enter journalism. On long walks in the woods with Cary Page, another "cousin-sister," he described his "dreams and aspirations" of becoming an editor and owning his own magazine. "You are the only one I can talk to about this," Cary remembered his telling her. "My family wouldn't understand what I was talking about. They'd think me a visionary—think I was crazy." Page sent job inquiries to newspapers in North Carolina, Baltimore, and Louisville and to a literary magazine in Atlanta. He likewise placed a classified advertisement in some magazines stating, "A journalist of experience desires an editorial position on a first-class journal."[28]

Page's newfound interest in public affairs came as a natural outgrowth of his literary vocation. In December 1878 he had written to the *Raleigh Observer* from Louisville that North Carolina and the whole South must strive toward "keeping our life and our civilization in companionship with the leading life and the leading civilization of the times." He also wrote fragmentary essays on the need for a cultured public to foster literature in the South. Page perceived all the requirements for a great "literary outburst" at hand, "a heroic age behind—The balancing benefits of Reverence & of Conservatism in Religious and Political Thought —an unparalleled field for caricature and humour." If only his neighbors would devote "the hours & the brains that are wasted around your courthouse" to truly cultivated pursuits, "the result would attract the attention of the whole world."[29]

These origins of Page's concern over public issues later had important effects on both his career and his political and social views. He was a loyal, self-conscious southerner who desired material advancement in order to support the highest forms of art and learning. He did not view making money as an end in itself. Page did subsequently allow involvement in journalism, public service, politics, and diplomacy to overshadow his original bent toward literature. He gave up writing poetry after this period in his life, and although he kept on puttering at fiction, his main energies went elsewhere. Yet Page never completely lost his literary vocation. To the end of his life he yearned to write great literature and that yearning continued to influence his behavior and decisions. Similarly, no matter how enamored of wealth and power he sometimes later grew, he clung to cultural standards as the ultimate tests of human achievement. These viewpoints grew out of his initial concern with expanding the cultural horizons of his homeland so that he could find a suitable career.

After he returned from Louisville in the summer of 1879, Page's personal life grew more complicated. He had fallen in love again. This time the young woman was Willia Alice Wilson, whom Page had known for several years. Alice, as she was called, was twenty-one years old in 1879 and a native of Michigan. Orphaned at an early age, Alice Wilson had come to North Carolina after the Civil War with an older half sister and her family, who settled near the Pages. She first met Walter during the year before he entered Trinity, when they both attended the local academy. After returning to Michigan for several years, Alice had come back to North Carolina in 1877. During the summer of 1878 she had gone to Chapel Hill as a "normalite." She renewed her acquaintance with Page when she sat in his class, but a romance between the two evidently did not develop until after his return from Louisville. Alice Wilson was a short, slender young woman with lively dark eyes and brown hair. Used to acting and thinking independently, she was well read and had been an excellent student. Alice shared most of Page's interests, although she did not hesitate to utter strong opinions or disagree with him.

Fortunately, the two agreed about religion. Page's earliest surviving letter to Alice, from January 1880, was a confession of his own unorthodoxy. He reminded her of their conversation around Christmastime "about the dogmatic interpretation of scripture." That, he explained, "was the one absorbing subject of my life's thought for a good many years, and it caused me much groveling darkness of mind, rending my very life asunder at times. And through it all, I was utterly alone." His religious views weighed heavily at that moment because he was thinking that he might "go away from my old people & join the Unitarians. I have been often tempted to do it. Why not? All that I

ALICE WILSON, 1879,
just before her marriage to Walter Hines Page

(by permission of Randolph-Macon College, Ashland, Virginia)

WALTER HINES PAGE, *1878*,
probably taken in Louisville

(by permission of the Houghton Library, Harvard University)

should regret would be the necessity of being expatriated. But I have half a mind to suffer expatriation for a season."[30]

Page was serious—at least for the moment—about entering the Unitarian ministry. In January 1880 he also wrote to Edward Everett Hale, the country's most famous Unitarian clergyman, expressing both his interest and his qualms. Becoming a Unitarian minister would, he explained, subject him to the pain of leaving the South, where he felt at home "in a sense that I can be at home nowhere else. Anywhere in the South, I should be at home; anywhere out of the South, I shall be a stranger. And I had much rather labour & live among my own people; but there is no hope of making for many generations any innovations in the matter that concerns me against the strong Southern conservatism."[31]

Page's interest in the Unitarian ministry probably sprang from his frustrations in December 1879 and January 1880. He proposed to Alice Wilson around Christmas 1879. But, without work and still in debt, he was obviously in no position to marry her. The South and the limited future it laid before him occupied Page's mind more than religious reflections. Faced with dismal prospects, entering the Unitarian ministry may have looked like a grand gesture of principled defiance, by which Page might flaunt his unorthodoxy and depart the South forever.

For once, luck intervened. The owner of a newspaper in St. Joseph, Missouri, unexpectedly wrote to inquire whether Page would be interested in a trial position as editor. The young man's eager response elicited an offer on 17 January 1880 to work for the *St. Joseph Gazette* at a starting salary of fifteen dollars a week. At the end of January 1880, he left home. With fifty dollars in borrowed money, he made a trip that took him over a thousand miles, beyond the Mississippi River and to the edge of the Great Plains. For the third time in less than four years Page was journeying to the fringe of the South to face an unknown situation. At the time he probably felt only relief. The railroad journey from North Carolina to St. Joseph, Missouri, lasted nearly a week. It must have given the young man many hours to think about his future. More than once Page probably felt an anxious hope that his life might at last be getting under way.

"THE TRIUMVIRATE,"
Randolph-Macon College, 1875;
left to right: Wilbur F. Tillett, John B. Wardlaw,
and Walter Hines Page
(by permission of the Houghton Library, Harvard University)

CHAPTER 3

Journalist and Expatriate

St. Joseph, Missouri, had come a long way since serving as the jumping-off place for wagon trains heading for California during the gold rush. At the beginning of 1880, when Walter Page arrived there, "St. Joe" was a bustling, prosperous marketing and transportation center of about thirty-five thousand people— twice the size of any town in North Carolina. St. Joseph was situated on a bluff above the Missouri River and like its rival river towns, Kansas City, Omaha, and Leavenworth, it contained extensive stockyards and strove to become the commercial and cultural metropolis of the region. Some of those municipal aspirations apparently lay behind Page's job offer in January 1880. The *Gazette*, the only morning paper among the three St. Joseph dailies, had a new owner, James N. Burnes, a banker and prominent Democrat who wanted to make the paper a suitable vehicle for his political ambitions. Burnes disclosed what was uppermost in his mind when he promised to promote Page to editor-in-chief "as soon as you get 'the hang' of our Mo. politics and politicians."

Page quickly got the hang of both the political situation and the newspaper work. The *Gazette* appeared in eight-page editions, six days a week. Like most American newspapers of the time, it consisted of advertising, telegraphed reports from Washington, New York, and abroad, and notices about local events and agricultural prices. Three or four columns of editorials, containing partisan political comment, stale witticism, and curiosity items, comprised most of the paper's original writing. As editor, Page wrote editorials and presided over a staff of five or six sub-editors. Despite his lack of experience, the young man did well from the start. The *Gazette*'s previously limping editorials acquired polish and began to branch out into such novel subjects as biblical criticism and English literature. Politics and unrelenting Democratic partisanship still dominated the editorials, but Page did bend them toward a somewhat more detached consideration of issues. He managed the staff by deferring to more experienced hands and showing interest in everyone's work.

The duties were largely routine and hardly challenging. Page and the subeditors clipped pieces from magazines and metropolitan papers and stayed up until three o'clock every morning to receive the last telegraphic dispatches. But success compensated for drudgery. Page lived cheaply in St. Joseph and saved money toward repaying his debts. In the summer of 1880 he received the promised promotion to editor-in-chief. He felt so firmly launched on his career that he and Alice Wilson were married on 15 November 1880. The wedding took place in St. Louis at the home of one of Page's uncles. Afterward the couple left immediately for their new quarters in a boardinghouse in St. Joseph. Life did seem to be getting under way for the twenty-four-year-old literary southerner.[1]

Page liked to recall that he had started out in journalism at the bottom, as a reporter in the stockyards getting stories about the price of cattle. His recollection was faulty. If Page went down to the stockyards in St. Joseph, he either took the assignment voluntarily or filled in for someone else on the *Gazette*. His reasonably advanced start, as top man on a small city newspaper, was a fortunate way to break into journalism. Administrative duties as editor of the *St. Joseph Gazette* provided quick training in how a newspaper operated. Daily responsibility for writing two or three editorials furnished opportunities to express and develop his views on a variety of topics. The *Gazette*'s Democratic partisanship apparently did not disturb Page. As the state and national campaigns gathered force in the summer and fall of 1880, Page warmed to his partisan function. At one point, he condemned the opposing party as "this Caliban," the ill-begotten offspring of "Time, made pregnant by Anarchy, . . . an anachronism, a humpbacked bastard called Republicanism."[2]

Outside of party politics, the editor evidently followed his own interests pretty much as he pleased. Page's recent religious and academic concerns cropped up immediately after his arrival in St. Joseph. Between February and April 1880 editorials appeared in support of British efforts to revise the Bible in light of modern scholarship and on such varied British figures as William Ewart Gladstone and Beau Brummell. Several nonpolitical editorials emerged in response to readers' queries. Those responses to readers' interests showed that the novice editor was learning his way as a journalist. Page also experimented briefly with political cartoons. Many editorials revealed personal concerns. For example, a humorous essay on baldness in October 1880 probably owed something to Page's losing part of his formerly thick, curly hair. The most insistent personal interest in his editorials concerned the South, such as when he pleaded for a Democratic victory in the 1880 presidential election as the only way to liberate the energies of "the young men to whom the war of rebellion is as much a matter of the past as the war of the revolution. They are eager, ambitious, strong. They are full of hope, of energy, of promise."

On racial subjects, Page expressed moderate views. He believed that blacks had made impressive economic and political progress since 1865, and he scorned both ex-Confederates' disparagement and Radical Republicans' idealization of black people: "While all these theorists were busy making their little noises, the negro himself was working quietly along solving unconsciously the problem that vexed the wise so sorely." When the Republicans won in November 1880, the young editor observed that one issue had cut "incomparably deeper than all questions of mere party politics: it was the question of Southern education, the question of Southern thought." The South's best hope lay in the rising generation of whites, who had not inherited the "complacent lethargy of the old slaveowners." This group was "ambitious of knowledge, of a wider culture, and [had] great intellectual possibilities." Their emancipation required only "a recognition of the Southern ambition and capabilities without a destruction of Southern peculiarities."[3]

In his thinking about southern problems, Page developed ideas that he had sketched first in his letters to the *Raleigh Observer* in 1877. By hammering at the proposition that the South could develop culturally and intellectually only through selective adaptation of Yankee ways, he entered the mainstream of the New South movement. Like Henry Watterson in Louisville and Henry W. Grady, the newly influential editor of the *Atlanta Constitution*, Page urged southerners to get on with rebuilding their homeland by adopting certain Yankee skills. Unlike other New South spokesmen, however, Page did not yet stress industrial development and he did not parade his loyalty to the Lost Cause and white supremacy. Page's own background and upbringing had fostered such New South views, and he had first expressed his convictions before he had heard of Watterson or Grady. Walter Page's developing New South viewpoint expressed his Tar Heel perspective and exalted Frank Page's unsentimental, businesslike attitude. Already in his *Gazette* editorials, he was blaming slavery and slaveowners for the evils that had befallen his native region. The idea that slavery had perverted a humane, democratic development was one that Page repeatedly advanced in his career as a southern spokesman. That interpretation later became the hallmark of critical, reformist thinking among southern whites during the first half of the twentieth century.

Page expounded his southern views most fully in an article that he published in the May 1881 issue of *The Atlantic Monthly* entitled "Study of an Old Southern Borough." The essay described an unnamed community that was a composite of several North Carolina country towns but that drew most heavily on Cary. Page explained how "elements of two distinct civilizations" coexisted in such places. One civilization consisted of the remnants of antebellum society, represented by old southern gentlemen who leisurely supervised their lands and endlessly talked about the past. The other civilization flourished in the town, epitomized by laconic, hardworking storekeepers who had usually risen from a lower social and economic station. Overall, the community showed "little animation in man or beast. The very dogs look lazy." The worst effect of the prevailing torpor, in Page's estimation, was pressure on bright, ambitious youths to leave. Women were the only truly cultivated, large-visioned people in the place, and their chief influence lay in inciting sons and brothers to get out and enter a wider world.

Personal elements were plain in the picture. Page's mother furnished the model for the southern woman, "ready-witted and quick to catch ideas," keeping alive "a glow, a sort of intellectual life." His father typified the merchant with his "business air" and "more energetic step." The young people, for whom "an immediate departure" offered the "only successful rebellion," came straight out of his own experience. Page had written the article two or three years before its publication, at a time when he had keenly felt the pangs of searching for opportunities and having to leave North Carolina. Yet the tone was not bitter. About the South as a whole, Page remained optimistic. He noted that few young people left newer towns and cities. In depicting the old town, he dwelt on the fine manners and gentle womenfolk of the traditional type. Page's conclusion was harmonizing and buoyant. "The new South cannot build up its possible civilization merely by looking backward and sighing," he declared, "nor yet by pressing blindly forward in the new paths that are now open." Rather, through "the proper fusion of the old and the new," the South enjoyed a "chance for greatness that is almost unparalleled in history."[4]

The Atlantic Monthly was the country's most distinguished literary periodical. "It is the exponent of the *culture* of America," Page himself declared in the *Gazette*. His article confirmed his own successful entry into national journalism. "The papers, North and South, and many of my old friends," he told his mother, "have been good enough to be pleased with it." Appearing in the *Atlantic* nerved Page to make a break. Editing the *Gazette* had taught him how to run a newspaper. Editorial writing had not only helped him to develop his political and social views, but the daily diet of editorials had also established his distinctive voice. The *Gazette* pieces marked the point at which Page's published work consistently acquired the plainspoken pungency that characterized his mature style as a writer and public speaker. By the time the *Atlantic* article appeared he was itching to make his mark somewhere more significant than St. Joseph, Missouri. Years later Page recollected that he had gotten all the useful experience he could by steering the paper through one "rousing political campaign. . . . Why do two? Besides, I knew my trade." In May 1881 Page decided to strike out on his own. He wrote to leading northern newspapers, announcing that he was going to make a journey through the South and would be describing what he saw in weekly letters to those papers. "I prayed heaven," he remembered, "they'd print them and pay for them." Page had not lost his taste for betting on himself.

This time the gamble paid off. The young editor hedged his bet by taking a leave of absence, not resigning, from the *Gazette*. He also aimed his letters from the South at selected metropolitan newspapers, rather than barraging the entire northern press. Page had two prime targets and possibly a few lesser ones. One was the *New York World*, the most powerful Democratic journal in the United States. The other was the *Boston Post*, a highly respected New England newspaper and a voice of the Yankee literary establishment. Page wrote different letters to the two papers. His communications to the *World* carried no signature; those to the *Post* at first used the pseudonym "Atlantic" and later his initials, "W. H. P." According to Page's own recollection, "All the papers published all that I sent them and I was rolling in wealth. I had money in my pocket for the first time in my life."5

Page's southern letters succeeded, in part, because of good timing. Pure luck got his journey off to a promising start. Leaving St. Joseph late in June 1881, he chanced to be in a small town in Tennessee when the news came that President James A. Garfield had been shot. Page's first letter to the northern newspapers became a timely report of reactions in a "backwoods 'rebel' town of 500 slow Democratic inhabitants" to the attempted assassination of a Republican president and former Union general. "Every man of them expressed almost a personal sorrow," wrote Page. "'A national disgrace,' 'a scandalous shame' were their own phrases. Little was said of politics or of parties. Mr. Garfield was President of the United States—that was enough." Besides that lucky break, Page showed good journalistic judgment in making a swing through the South during the summer of 1881. Previous travelers' reports from the South in northern newspapers since the Civil War had come from northern journalists and foreign visitors. Page was the first native southern white to describe his homeland to northern newspaper readers. The time was ripe for someone with his background and views to write about the former Confederate states. By 1881 the largest segments of northern opinion wanted to forget about southern problems and were ready to hear reassuring tidings. At the same time, northern readers had taken up the antebellum South as their latest literary fad and were anxious to learn more about the writers who were enthralling them with romances of plantation life and quaint, local-color stories.[6]

Walter Page fitted the requirements of the situation perfectly. With his newly acquired journalistic polish, he wrote crisp, evocative descriptions of scenes and people, as he moved down through Mississippi to New Orleans in July 1881, then came back through Alabama and Georgia in August, and finally completed his journey in North Carolina in September. In substance, Page's letters read like an elaboration of his *Atlantic* article. Everywhere he contrasted decaying age with vigorous youth, and almost everywhere he noted energetic forces of the future making the Civil War a dim memory. On the first part of his journey, Jefferson Davis furnished the young observer with a convenient symbol of the changing South. Early in August 1881 Page visited the seventy-three-year-old former Confederate president at his home near Mobile, Alabama. Page found Davis living in solitude, taking no interest in current affairs. Though his host was alert and hospitable, the reporter asked, "Can the visitor escape a certain depression? Everywhere in the South men are looking to the future. Cotton mills and railroads are of more consequence than battlefields where the fathers of this generation fell."[7]

These travels provided Page with his first glimpse of most of the South. Before the journey, he had never set foot in any of the former Confederate states except Virginia and his native North Carolina. What he saw now reinforced already-formed opinions.

In Mississippi Page visited some of the once-great cotton plantations, which he disliked on sight. Blaming the planters for fostering the insidious systems of farm tenancy and sharecropping, he nevertheless detected hopeful signs in declining absentee ownership and larger numbers of small farms. Although race received scant attention in Page's letters, he did criticize slavery for its influence on whites. Page contrasted dynamic, commercial Atlanta with Oxford, Mississippi, by observing, "Oxford still slumbers from the narcotic influences of slavery." He likewise attributed Atlanta's rise to the Georgia "cracker," who, unlike other southerners, "had not quite so many aristocratic shackles." Seeing the rest of the South convinced Page that his Tar Heel perspective had been correct all along.[8]

These newspaper letters also showed the first sign of his sharing the avidity of other New South spokesmen for building factories and wooing outside, especially northern, capital. Atlanta and the clique of businessmen-politicians who ruled Georgia excited his admiration, while North Carolina presented a contrast between the somnolence of Chapel Hill and the bustle of neighboring Durham, the center of the burgeoning tobacco industry. Although tobacco was regarded as "a plebeian business," Page observed that Durham sported "no professional talkers and habitual loafers as at . . . every other old Southern borough." But not everything about the rush for industrial development pleased him. At one point he noted that genuine progress could come only through "the way of agricultural improvement." Page disagreed with those southerners who regarded "large railroad projects and mammoth manufacturing establishments as the only avenues of advancement." They had forgotten that "the citizenship of all these States is and must forever be composed of farmers, and that everything depends upon them more entirely than in any other section of the globe." This emphasis on agriculture foreshadowed a major difference that later separated Page from other New South advocates and their successors.[9]

Another difference surfaced elsewhere. The October 1881 issue of *International Review*, a New York–based journal, carried Page's second article in a national magazine, "The Southern

Educational Problem." Page asserted there that "popular and practical education" formed the South's greatest need: "Educators are needed more than capitalists; schoolhouses more than cotton-factories; a change in educational methods more than a change in politics." Page traced the South's educational deficiencies to a conjunction of pre– and post–Civil War white prejudices. Before the war, aristocratic notions about turning out socially graceful gentlemen had prevented the establishment of mass schooling. After the war, Reconstruction governments and idealistic northerners had fomented new hostilities by educating blacks and by sometimes mixing children of both races in schools. Southern education, asserted Page, required "these three things: (1) Money,—which means educational equipments; (2) a change of aim, and consequently a change of methods,—a more practical aim and a more thorough method; and (3) a public opinion which demands popular education." He applauded southern educators' patient efforts and he approved of separate schools for blacks and whites. Negroes were suited, he thought, "mainly for manual labor" and would "rarely need or desire higher training than can be got in the most elementary public schools."

The *International Review* article in the fall of 1881 rehearsed some of Page's most important subsequent arguments as a southern reformer. Like Thomas Jefferson, he anointed education as the one true path to social and economic advancement, and he blamed the region's shortcomings on the twin evils of the old slaveholding regime and northern interference. He reasoned that progress would come only through the perseverance of native whites who worked within the limits of local conditions. "An impatient zeal coupled with ignorance of the difficulties can do no good." Page's comments on black education offered an early sign of the mixed viewpoint that would continue to characterize his racial thinking. In the *International Review* article Page also affirmed that southern economic advancement must serve a higher goal. To him, "practical education" meant not vocational training, but an educational system that would employ the latest scholarship and pedagogy to lay the foundations for cultural development. Even more than schools, he concluded, the South required "an indigenous intellectual development." He observed, "The poets, the novelists, the magazines, and the newspapers have done more than all the schools to stimulate the intellectual life of New England."[10]

On his travels during the summer of 1881, commentary on public issues did not totally eclipse literary interests. In letters to the *Boston Post*, Page described visits with two southern writers who had recently achieved fame, George W. Cable and Joel Chandler Harris. Calling on Cable in New Orleans provided the traveler with a stimulating afternoon and evening. The slender, soft-spoken novelist discoursed at length on southern literature and culture, confirming many of his visitor's views. Little distinguished writing had emerged before the Civil War, Cable contended, because the "idea of literature's being the work of genius of inspiration and not of toil" had made southern authors pathetically amateurish. Southerners' lack of "the habit of reading" Cable attributed to the sloth-producing climate. Page's interview with Harris was more humorous but less diverting. The author of *Uncle Remus* turned out to be "a dingy looking individual," whom Page initially mistook for a printer's devil on the *Atlanta Constitution*. Harris shyly frustrated Page's best efforts to draw him out. The saddest part of Page's trip was a visit in Georgia with the family of his closest friend and erstwhile literary mentor, Jack Wardlaw, who had died a month earlier. A few months before, Page had assured Wardlaw that he had not forgotten their old resolutions about "what needs to be done in Southern literature. By heaven! It is a chance! I mean to live and die trying it. There is no second ambition in my soul."[11]

The southern journey opened new opportunities for Page. When he finished his travels in September 1881, he apparently intended to go back to St. Joseph; he had not resigned from the *Gazette*. While awaiting the birth of their first child, Alice had gone to stay with Page's aunt and uncle in St. Louis. Unfortunately, the new father could not be present when a baby boy, whom they later christened Ralph Walter, arrived on 2 October 1881. But his absence had a happy excuse. Shortly before his son's birth, Page received an assignment to go to Atlanta for the

New York World. He was to cover the International Cotton Exposition, which advertised the South's latest capabilities for cotton growing and manufacturing. Between reporting the exposition and getting to know the ebullient Henry Grady, Page received heady exposure to the gospel of industrial development. Not only did he tout the prospects of southern textiles in his reports to the *World*, but he also invited his father to come and view the technological marvels and make business contacts at the exposition. "I feel very confident of the future," the young man wrote to Frank Page.[12]

His confidence received a momentary jolt when the temporary assignment with the *World* expired at the end of November 1881. Still betting on himself, Page cut loose from the *St. Joseph Gazette.* At the end of the exposition he sought a post on the *Atlanta Constitution*, but the newspaper turned him down. Page's life might have taken a different turn if the *Constitution* had hired him in 1881. He might have succeeded to the editorship after Grady's untimely death eight years later, thereby falling heir to the Georgian's mantle as the prime exponent of the New South viewpoint. That was perhaps the only position in the South that might have satisfied Page. At the time, however, a different possibility arose. When Page had reached "the end of my rope," as he later remembered, a telegram unexpectedly arrived from the *World* asking him to join the staff of the newspaper in New York. In December 1881 Page traveled north to begin his new job. In less than six months the twenty-six-year-old southerner had risen from the editorship of a small Missouri daily to a place on one of the nation's leading metropolitan newspapers.[13]

In 1881 the *New York World* enjoyed a special but none-too-secure place among top-ranking American newspapers. Although the *World* boasted a circulation of around three hundred thousand, mainly among Democratic loyalists and wealthier New Yorkers, poor management and stiff competition made the paper a money-loser. However, those shortcomings did not prevent Page from finding congenial surroundings. Both the paper's political viewpoint and its journalistic spirit suited the new employee.

The *World* was the leading Democratic journal in the United States, speaking for respectable Northern Democrats who sought to swing politics away from the Civil War issues and toward other concerns, particularly the tariff. Likewise, even people who despised the *World*'s politics admitted that the journal possessed literary style. At night, after the next day's edition had gone to press, the editorial room often took on the air of a slightly madcap literary club, as editors and reporters animatedly discussed books, philosophy, and various forms of cultivated amusement.

Page worked for the *World* for a year and a half, from the end of 1881 until the middle of 1883. Those months furnished his first experience with both a major newspaper and the bustling metropolis of New York, which had taken over from Boston the role of publishing capital of the nation. Yet Page seldom mentioned this period afterward. Twenty years later he described working on the *World* as "an interesting experience," during which he wrote "literary matter chiefly, an editorial now and then." The customary journalistic anonymity of the time makes it impossible to identify most of what he wrote, although a book review dismissing *A Fool's Errand*, Albion Tourgée's novel about Reconstruction in North Carolina, as a "Caliban" of a book almost certainly came from his pen. Much of his time with the *World* Page spent away from New York, making several trips to Washington to cover congressional debates on the tariff in 1882 and 1883. During the late summer and fall of 1882, he trailed the Republican-sponsored Tariff Commission on its investigatory itinerary through the Northeast, Middle West, and South. Because the *World* disdained the commission for being stacked with high-tariff advocates, Page's reports obediently dripped with sarcasm.[14]

One of the most important events in Page's life took place when his travels with the Tariff Commission brought him to Atlanta, where he looked up a friend, a struggling young lawyer named Edward I. Renick. Renick had formed a law partnership with one of his classmates at the University of Virginia Law School—Woodrow Wilson. When the tall, gawky Page visited the sparsely furnished office of the firm of Renick and Wilson on 22 September 1882, he first met the prim, strong-jawed Wilson.

Most likely Page had already heard of Wilson, whom Wardlaw had known at Princeton. For his part, Wilson already knew Page by reputation. Renick's first letter to Wilson, in January 1882, had mentioned "that talented North Carolinian, and I am happy to say, my old & warm friend, Walter Page."[15]

Page and Wilson liked each other at once. In addition to a common friendship with Wardlaw and Renick, they shared similar outlooks as ambitious, educated young southern whites who chafed at the provincialism of their native region. Of the two, Wilson was then straining harder at the South's cultural bonds. He found himself bored with his legal practice in Atlanta. The talk of the two young men turned directly to politics and government. Page remembered years later that they had discussed Wilson's reading about British institutions. Wilson recounted soon after the meeting that Page's "smart ridicule" toward the Tariff Commission had led to a discussion of the tariff question. The reporter discovered the attorney's "deep interest and considerable acquaintance with the issues involved." Their talk inspired Page to suggest that Wilson speak before the commission the next day on the principles of protection versus free trade. Page induced him to appear, Wilson said, "by promising a good notice in his letter to the *World*." In his report, the correspondent praised the young lawyer's half-hour testimony as the only "argument of dignity" and "the only statement made here that in any way showed the sentiment of the people."[16]

The meeting began an acquaintance fraught with future consequences. Wilson seems to have made a stronger impression on Page than the other way around, which was in keeping with their different personalities. Wilson was a self-contained character, with intensely focused interests, who evidently remembered his visitor as someone who relieved the tedium of his days in Atlanta and gave him a chance to display his expertise. Page was a more outgoing personality, who thrived on drawing people out. In later years Page considered himself, with some justification, an excellent discoverer of talent. He regarded Wilson from their first meeting as an important discovery. Three years later Page wrote a laudatory review of Wilson's first book. He reportedly told

Josephus Daniels in 1885 or 1886 that Wilson "has one of the finest minds in America. Keep your eye on him!"[17]

Working for the *World* never occupied Page's full attention. In 1882 he submitted another article to the *Atlantic*, entitled "The Negro in American History," which the magazine apparently accepted but did not publish. On his travels that year Page scribbled underlinings and marginal notes in a volume of Keats, indicating that he had not yet renounced his poetic interests. Early in 1883 he contracted to write weekly letters to the *Boston Post*, in which two concerns, race and the urban scene, drew his greatest attention. Commenting on blacks in New York, Page pronounced them "a success." By prevailing where Irish and Italians failed, blacks proved "certainly that the thriftlessness which slavery bred is eradicable." In April 1883 Page started writing occasional reports to an Australian newspaper, and at the beginning of May he traveled to Cambridge, Massachusetts, to talk about the South to the Harvard Finance Club. His talk stressed the retarding influence of slavery, the need for manufacturing, and the prospects of the "negro problem . . . solving itself," except in former plantation areas of the Deep South.[18]

As soon as he returned from speaking at Harvard, Page's journalistic career took another unexpected turn. On 9 May 1883 a tall, dark, elegantly dressed man strode into the editorial room of the *New York World*. He was Joseph Pulitzer, the dynamic publisher of the *St. Louis Post-Dispatch*, who had just bought the *World*. To an assembly of his new employees Pulitzer announced that "a change has taken place" and that the staff would no longer enjoy a soft life and highfalutin' ways. Most of the editors and reporters answered his ultimatum by quitting, including Page. Why he left is not clear. Pulitzer asked him to stay. Unlike the old hands on the paper, Page did not completely resent the change. In a letter to the *Boston Post*, he heralded Pulitzer's accession as "the first great experiment to domesticate western journalism in New York." At the least, Pulitzer would make the *World* profitable and supply "its recent lacks as a newspaper."[19]

Page probably refused to work for Pulitzer, in part at least, because he recognized their differences in journalistic philosophy. The young southerner believed, in common with the editor whom he most admired—Charles A. Dana of the *New York Sun*—that a newspaper ought to educate the public through clear, lively writing. Joseph Pulitzer was a mass journalist; Walter Hines Page was not and never would be. Another factor may also have entered into his decision to resign. Augustus Long remembered asking Page not long afterward why he had left the *World*. His face colored a bit before he replied, "In the first place, I did not wish to work under Pulitzer; and, secondly, I thought I might get into North Carolina politics." Political leanings would have been out of character for Page, but he was open to the possibility of going back to his native state. For a change, lack of opportunity did not bar the way.[20]

The opportunity was his own newspaper, a weekly that Page started in Raleigh, called the *State Chronicle*. Little evidence survives to elucidate how the venture originated. The first issue simply announced on 15 September 1883 that the *State Chronicle* was "beginning its career at the request and with the cooperation of not a few of the most enterprising men in the State." Actually, the enterprising man behind the paper was Frank Page. Edward Oldham, who was associated with the *State Chronicle* at its founding, later recalled that most of the financial backing came from Walter Page's father. Although newspapers did not fit Frank Page's usual line of activity, he was able and most likely willing to finance his eldest son's venture. By 1883 the family's lumbering activities in Moore County had prospered to the point where they had begun to diversify into railroads. Frank Page built a seven-mile line from Aberdeen to Southern Pines, originally to haul logs. One railroad led to another and in the succeeding decade the Page lines extended over eighty miles of track. These railroads, in turn, opened that section of North Carolina to real-estate development, particularly the resort area of Pinehurst. Frank Page's willingness to finance the *State Chronicle* probably sprang from a desire to bring back to North Carolina the only one of his grown sons who was not in the family business.

For Walter Page, the *State Chronicle* had two main attractions. First, he could be his own boss and shape his own journal from the beginning. Second, he could strike a blow for southern progress. The paper's first issue promised "plain speaking editorials about living subjects, advocating honest democratic politics, industrial education, material development, money making and hearty living." Walter Page was still betting on himself. This time he was wagering, with his father's backing, that he could help transform his homeland into the right kind of place for everybody, including himself.[21]

During the American Revolution, North Carolina had conceived as its official motto the Latin epigram, Esse Quam Videri —To Be Rather Than to Seem. The motto possessed an ironic accuracy throughout the first century of the state's history: North Carolina had never put forward much in the way of appearances. Only in the late 1870s with the advent of manufacturing, especially in tobacco and textiles, did the state seem to be pulling out of its age-old poverty and backwardness. Both the capital city of Raleigh and the newspaper that Page founded in September 1883 reflected the balance in North Carolina between old drawbacks and new promise. Although Raleigh afforded few advantages of size or modernity, signs of change were present. The town had grown to over nine thousand in 1880, and by 1890 the population was more than twelve thousand. Twenty miles northwest, in Durham, tobacco manufacturing had erupted into a major economic force under such native leaders as the Duke family. Eighty miles to the west, in Winston-Salem, another band of homegrown capitalists was launching simultaneous ventures in tobacco, textiles, and banking.

Page started the *State Chronicle* with a dash and confidence to match North Carolina's new bustle. Throughout the first six months he publicly and privately claimed great success for the paper. In December 1883 the editor told his mother, "I have found the *Chronicle* plunging forward at better speed than ever before." New advertising and subscriptions made the paper's prospects "very rosy." The first issue on 15 September 1883 set the tone and content for the rest of the time that Page edited the

State Chronicle. The front page carried a county-by-county survey of the probable strength of various Democratic politicians in the coming year's gubernatorial contest. Stories on the inside pages included items of local news and social notes. Editorials boosted the paper, applauded industrial expositions, and called for defeat of the Readjusters, the dissident white faction that had fused with the Republicans in neighboring Virginia. A state exposition for North Carolina formed Page's greatest single editorial crusade. The *State Chronicle* set an example by subscribing fifty dollars to the exposition, and Page delivered one of the welcoming speeches at the opening in Raleigh in July 1884.[22]

The paper regularly carried stories about factories and businesses and put out special issues on North Carolina industries. Page attempted to cover the state by arranging for local editors and various correspondents to write for the *State Chronicle*. Again demonstrating his faculty for spotting talent, he enlisted three young men who later became successful in journalism and other fields. Edward Oldham, Page's original associate on the *State Chronicle*, supplied news from Winston-Salem and the western part of North Carolina. Oldham went on to become a newspaper correspondent and public-relations man in New York and Washington. Augustus—"Gus"—Long, who first sent material to the *State Chronicle* while he was still a student at Chapel Hill, worked as a full-time reporter and lived with Page and his family for several months after his graduation in 1884. Long later left journalism to teach English at Trinity College and Princeton and became a writer in New York. But Page's greatest discovery was Josephus Daniels. The twenty-two-year-old Daniels filed stories from his hometown of Wilson, in the eastern part of the state, and ran the *State Chronicle* while Page went away during the Christmas holidays in 1884. Daniels took over the paper after Page's departure in 1885, beginning his rise to eminence as North Carolina's leading newspaperman and a major force in southern and national politics.

For the most part, however, the paper was a one-man show. A visitor once found the *State Chronicle* office a disenchanting place. Instead of "the lordly Editor in a well furnished office, and surrounded by helpers and others at his command," he saw a single man writing at a littered, unfinished pine table. A couple of chairs and packing crates supplied the room's only other furniture. The *State Chronicle* occupied two rooms on the second floor of a two-story building owned by the printing firm that put out the paper. Besides the editor, the paper's other regular employees were a white printer in an adjoining composing room, a black pressman who worked downstairs, and a succession of boys who scurried around as printer's devils. The newspaper was Page's own product in the strictest sense. During long working days he sat in his shirtsleeves at the littered pine table, constantly puffing on a corncob pipe. He wrote feverishly, turning out nearly all of the contents of each issue, often including some of what was supposed to be correspondence from the rest of the state.[23]

As a periodical, the *State Chronicle* blended familiar elements with daring departures. The format resembled those of the papers on which Page had worked previously. Like the *St. Joseph Gazette* and the *New York World*, the Raleigh newspaper did not have an eye-catching front page, and headlines were descriptive rather than dramatic, rarely spreading over more than a single column. Page departed from usual newspaper practice, however, by printing the *State Chronicle* on a high grade of paper in order to present better illustrations. Both the illustrations and the smooth feel of the paper gave the *State Chronicle* a distinguished appearance, more like a magazine than a newspaper. Weekly publication likewise required the journal to provide information and analyze news, after the fashion of a magazine, rather than try to provide up-to-the-minute accounts of events. Page's editorials broke with North Carolina newspaper tradition by discarding "we" and referring to the periodical in the third person, which was the custom among magazines and big-city dailies. In tone and style, the *State Chronicle* anticipated some of the advanced techniques that Page later used as a pioneering editor of national magazines.

The newspaper also showed how much the twenty-eight-year-old Tar Heel had learned in his brief journalistic career, especially during his sojourns in Atlanta and New York. With the

State Chronicle, Page was attempting to perform two tasks simultaneously. On the one hand, with the paper's special industrial issues and Page's boasts of "ADVERTISING NORTH CAROLINA AT HOME AND ABROAD," the editor was plainly emulating Henry Grady's *Atlanta Constitution*. On the other hand, Page was moving ahead of all other southern editors by seeking to import metropolitan journalism through the device of a statewide newspaper. Although other dailies and weeklies sometimes circulated beyond their immediate areas, a paper deliberately designed to cover an entire state was a revolutionary idea anywhere in the United States. Statewide coverage and circulation represented Page's attempt to overcome the South's lack of large cities that could support metropolitan newspapers. In all, the *State Chronicle* marked a bold venture. As such, it ran the danger of being too far ahead of its time and too much out of harmony with its place.[24]

Despite the concern for business and the Gradyesque touches, the *State Chronicle* was not primarily a promotional organ. Page's interests ranged wider than boosting North Carolina, while his views on several critical issues kept him from becoming a model New South spokesman after the pattern of Grady. He did not lay his greatest emphasis on manufacturing as the route to southern progress, for agricultural improvement still struck him as critical. "The work we have to do in North Carolina now," he asserted in November 1883, "is to improve our farms, to build up waste places, and to turn our manifold wealth into articles of use." Page also continued to stress education as vital to building a better society, viewing education, industrial development, and agricultural improvement as related parts of the single problem of southern uplift.[25]

The editor lumped all three matters together in a significant campaign to promote industrial education. Apart from editing the *State Chronicle*, Page's only major activity while he lived in Raleigh was helping to form a group that lobbied for the founding of a state agricultural and mechanical college. The group originally comprised twenty-four white men, all but two of whom were native Tar Heels. Since none of the members had yet reached the age of thirty, they were, one of them recalled, "too young to have been in the war, and, therefore, with faces all to the future." Page first brought these young men together sometime during 1884, and their early meetings took place in the *State Chronicle* office. Others in the company included Henry Fries, a business-man friend of Page's from Winston-Salem; G. E. Leach and W. J. Peele, two Raleigh lawyers; Charles W. Dabney, a chemist work-ing for the state; and, for a time, Thomas Dixon, a gangly twenty-one-year-old just elected to the state assembly.[26]

According to Dabney's recollection, the editor served as the group's sparkplug. They dubbed themselves the Watauga Club, after a stream in the mountains of western North Carolina, be-cause the name seemed devoid of untoward implications. Though initially pretending to outsiders to be just a social gathering, the Watauga Club devoted its energies to establishing an industrial school. In February 1885 the club petitioned the North Carolina legislature for a school to be founded in Raleigh, offering instruc-tion "in wood-work, mining, metallurgy, practical agriculture and in such other branches of industrial education as may be deemed expedient." Dixon simultaneously introduced a bill em-bodying the proposal in the state assembly.[27]

Along with the petition, the Watauga Club submitted a twenty-six-page report on industrial education, which Page al-most certainly wrote. The club envisioned an industrial school for North Carolina comparable to sophisticated polytechnic in-stitutes in Europe and elsewhere in the United States. By being located in Raleigh, the industrial school could aid the state gov-ernment by investigating and publicizing opportunities for indus-trial and economic development. The school would also "diffuse a spirit for industrial development" by attracting ambitious young people away from "that pure literary culture" that dominated southern colleges and served only to swell "the already over-stocked professions of medicine, law and politics. The energies of the people should be chiefly directed towards the accumulation of wealth, not so much as an end in itself, but as a means to higher ends, for as Mr. Buckle says, 'Without wealth there can be no leisure, and without leisure there can be no knowledge. Great ignorance is the fruit of great poverty.'" Fostering culture remained Walter Page's main reason for pushing southern economic development.[28]

The editor also differed from other exponents of industrial growth on two critical economic questions. One was cheap labor. Most New South advocates sought to woo investment and factories with tales about low-paid, docile workers. Page disputed such arguments. Sometime in 1883 or 1884, he helped host a delegation of New Englanders who were inspecting economic conditions in North Carolina. Accompanying the party on the train to Cary, the editor climbed on top of a lumber pile by the railroad tracks and gave a speech. Page recalled years afterward that he used "all the stock arguments," one of which "was the cheapness of labor." After Page compared wages in North Carolina and Massachusetts to show how much less Tar Heel workers got paid, a grizzled Vermonter snorted, "Young fellow, that's just the trouble: we get too little for our work here." The workman's retort made Page feel like a fool, but it also set him to thinking. "I gradually began to get hold of the great truth that cheap labor is the curse of any country where it exists, because it means inefficient labor." Page did not raise the matter in the *State Chronicle*, but his work with the Watauga Club for an industrial school betokened an approach to industrial development different from those who expatiated on cheap southern labor.[29]

The other point of difference from most New South advocates was the question of attracting northern capital. Page did not regard outside investment as indispensable to southern progress. In January 1884 the *State Chronicle* declared that North Carolinians needed above all to make wise use of the money that they already had. The chief obstacle to economic growth in the state was not lack of capital but "old loose business methods." Tar Heels needed only to apply "the business methods of Chicago to the industrial problems and to the money that we have in North Carolina (and no more)," and they would witness undreamed-of results. "It is the men who are making money that help us most and not the men who have made it and are now called capitalists, lending cash on real estate."[30]

Such talk hardly suited someone who sought patronage from established wealth. Oldham later remembered that he could never dissuade Page from printing statements that antagonized important people. At one point, Oldham recalled, he had practically clinched a lucrative advertising contract, on condition that the paper tone down its comments on certain subjects. When Page scorned the proposition, Oldham decided that the *State Chronicle* would never become a money-making property and he withdrew from the venture. Whether Frank Page disapproved of Walter's remarks is not known, but such experiences may have added to his conviction that his son did not know a thing about a dollar.

Walter Page likewise decried big business and heavy industry. "Larger manufacturing establishments indeed are not as desirable as small ones," he asserted in December 1883. Distrusting the "lordliness about a concern wherein hundreds of thousands of dollars are invested," he wished instead for many small, independent shops and factories. "So far as benefit to the community is concerned, a craftsman who earns $2 a day is a more valuable citizen than an idle man who can clip $50 a day from his bonds." These differences from other New South spokesmen sprang from Page's fundamental ideas about social and economic progress, which contained Jeffersonian biases against both bigness and finance. In 1886, Page recommended reading the "nine great volumes of Jefferson" as the best way to "root and ground a man in those great doctrines which lie beyond the shifting sands of controversy." His vision of the good southern society was an adaptation of Jefferson's ideal to the industrial revolution.[31]

Despite criticizing his native region, Page did not want the South to be just like the North, especially not in giant factories and vast urban nodules of filth, tension, and poverty. Selective adaptation of Yankee ways remained Page's prescription for southern reform, and his goal was always to preserve the essentials of a cherished and distinctive way of life. Page envisioned a land of independent farmers and artisans, who used the latest technological devices and supported schools, colleges, libraries, newspapers, and magazines in clean, orderly towns. His was a utopia on a small-to-middling scale. Page anticipated later white southern social reformers in believing that such a society could have emerged from the antebellum South but for the baneful influences of slavery and plantations. Approaching Jefferson like a latter-day North Carolina Whig, Walter Page believed that in getting the South back on the right track he was taking up where his father and grandfather had left off.

Page tried hard to steer an orthodox course for the *State Chronicle* around most questions on which white Tar Heels might be sensitive. Only on racial matters did the paper depart from expected opinions. Unlike all but the most advanced northern journals, the *State Chronicle* capitalized the word "Negro" while Page edited the paper, a practice that his successors dropped. Page's gesture epitomized generally friendly pronouncements toward blacks. On 22 September 1883 the second issue of the *State Chronicle* carried an editorial entitled "Our Brother in Black," which observed, "The black men of North Carolina—the best of them at least—are setting their kinspeople in other States a good example. What they need most to do for themselves is to work slowly and hard for their elevation and improvement precisely as white men or any other men work." In other areas, Page went out of his way to avoid giving offense. Religion could have been a touchy subject, and apparently the *State Chronicle* occasionally did disturb some sensibilities among the denominational press in Raleigh. But in November 1883 the paper affirmed, "The same spiritual forces that have made us what we are yet work for our uplifting, and the vigor of our churches is cause for sincere thankfulness."[32]

More than anything else, politics strained the editor's resolve to avoid controversy. From the beginning Page paraded the *State Chronicle*'s credentials as "a broadly Democratic paper," and he faithfully discharged partisan duties in the 1884 election. His editorials lauded Grover Cleveland, the Democratic presidential nominee, and Alfred M. Scales, the party's gubernatorial candidate. Yet politics frustrated and disappointed Page. He vented political spleen in December 1883, when he judged the latest generation of southern politicians "small men," far below the standard of antebellum statesmanship. He blamed the decline on the war and Reconstruction, which had made the region defensive, withdrawn, and backward looking: "We have been the victims of sectionalism." He likewise regretted that the 1884 campaign took "the shape of a political fight between the races. The campaign cry here will be, 'This must be a white man's government.' And so, of course, it must. But the misfortune is that we are forced to make the battle along any such line." During the campaign the *State Chronicle* refused to refer to any candidates by Civil War military titles, pointedly calling the gubernatorial candidate, who had been a Confederate general, "Mr. Scales."[33]

Political frustration may have played a role in Page's decision to abandon the *State Chronicle* and leave North Carolina after only a little over a year. The young editor's disappointment involved more than simply the failure of Southern Democrats to discard outworn sectional issues. By not orienting themselves toward new national concerns such as the tariff, politicians were failing, Page believed, as he wrote in June 1884, to "turn on proper political pivots—be honorable, patriotic, high." Page started making plans to get out soon after the 1884 elections. He asked Daniels to run the paper while he traveled to New York over the Christmas holidays. Although Page did not say so at the time, he was making a job-hunting expedition. That trip was unsuccessful, but on 24 February 1885 he tendered his resignation from the *State Chronicle*, "to take effect immediately." Page gave the stockholders two reasons for his action. One was financial: "The paper has not paid me anything and has, of course, given me no time to make a living in other ways." He also claimed that he had just received a job offer from New York, "an unusually flattering opportunity to do higher and more profitable literary work than I have ever done—a chance to earn a comfortable income and build a reputation."[34]

Page did not exaggerate the financial difficulties. Raleigh was neither large nor wealthy enough to support more than one major newspaper. "I had hope of making one paper there out of the half dozen little personal organs," Page later explained, but unfortunately his competitors would not sell out. The journalistic situation in Raleigh did not stabilize until Daniels bought the principal daily, the *News and Observer*, in 1894 and combined several papers under its masthead. But economic limitations did not fully account for Page's departure. In his letter of resignation he noted that "we have kept the paper in good financial condition." Daniels kept the *State Chronicle* going for another seven years, until particularly hard times hit in 1892. Some of Daniels's success owed to his being a bachelor who could live more cheaply than his predecessor. He also turned the *State Chronicle* into more of a local newspaper with greater attention to gossip, sports, and household topics.[35]

Politics entered into Page's money troubles. During the nineteenth century, state and local government printing contracts, awarded for party service, formed the financial lifeblood for most American newspapers outside metropolitan centers. Yet when he founded the *State Chronicle*, Page eschewed political patronage. "Journalism is a jealous mistress," he insisted. "You can't serve her and anybody else." Page's viewpoint would have made sense in a different context. As he recognized, the rising force in American journalism in the 1880s was the big-city daily that made money through circulation and advertising. Even with the novel idea of a statewide paper, Page could not transplant metropolitan journalism to a sleepy town in a backward, rural area. According to Daniels, Page recognized the futility of his nonpolitical approach and tried unsuccessfully to get the state printing contract at the beginning of 1885. Those contracts became a vital source of revenue for the *State Chronicle* under Daniels.[36]

Page did not claim that the paper's poor earnings supplied his only reason for resigning. His complaint really stemmed from feeling tied down by the *State Chronicle* in several ways. Gus Long remembered the editor's normal day consisted of going to the office early in the morning and working steadily until late in the afternoon, usually lunching at his desk on a cold snack that he had brought from home. Dinner-table talk was rare at the Pages' house, since both he and his wife seemed tired out from their day's work. Except for the Watauga Club and the Methodist church, neither Page nor his wife joined any organizations, and the editor seldom went out to the offices, hotel lobbies, and capitol corridors of Raleigh. Almost the only times he left Raleigh were to visit his grandfather at the Old Place or to spend an occasional Sunday at Cary, staying at the hotel that had been his family's home. At Cary Page sat on the porch smoking and looking at the view but engaging in, Long remembered, "very little talk."

Whether his father's involvement in the *State Chronicle* played any part in his decision to leave is hard to judge. It seems unlikely that Frank Page would have felt either patient with the paper's poor earnings or shy about meddling in his son's business affairs. Walter's disinclination to seek the state printing contract and to involve the paper more in local matters may well have irritated him. Yet no correspondence between father and son about the *State Chronicle* has survived. Long also recalled, "I never met Page's father or his brothers. They were then busy with their sawmills in Moore County." But even if Frank Page did try to play the uncharacteristic role of a silent partner, his proximity might still have bothered his son. Walter Page could hardly have helped wondering whether he would ever become his own boss or make his own way when his father was putting up the money and hovering offstage, no matter how unobtrusively.[37]

As much as lack of money and possible paternal interference, narrow cultural horizons made Page anxious to get out of North Carolina. Although he mentioned "higher and more profitable literary work" in his letter of resignation, Page did not have a job offer when he left Raleigh at the end of February 1885. After arriving in New York, as he told his wife, "dead broke," he did fill-in assignments and free-lance work before he found a full-time job. At bottom, Page lacked patience and willingness to accept cultural and political shortcomings. His central character in *The Southerner* lamented "the suppression of one's self, the arrest of one's growth, the intellectual loneliness." Page resembled his new friend Woodrow Wilson, who had given up practicing law in Atlanta in 1883 to study at the Johns Hopkins. Wilson, too, had made little money, but his greatest discontent had been, he confessed in May 1883, "I can never be happy until I am enabled to lead an intellectual life, and who can lead an intellectual life in ignorant Georgia?" In 1885 Page in effect asked the same question about North Carolina. His answer was that he preferred to face the uncertainties of New York rather than strain at the cultural confines of his native state.[38]

Quitting Raleigh at the end of February 1885 did not mean that Page had finished with either the *State Chronicle* or North Carolina. He still felt an obligation toward the paper that he had started. For over a year, from the summer of 1885 until the fall of 1886, Page wrote almost weekly letters from New York. Although many of his reports described conditions in the city and discussed national political issues, his most important communications concerned North Carolina. Writing from a distance of five hundred miles, the former editor spewed out criticisms of politicians and preachers and ignorance and prejudice that he had previously kept to himself. Page's successors on the *State Chronicle* disavowed his views, but they gladly printed the letters, which stirred up public opinion and evidently boosted circulation. Page's letters from New York made his name a household word in North Carolina. Also, in his own eyes those letters burned his bridges back home.

Politics formed the area of his first trespasses. During the summer and fall of 1885 Page labeled politicians generally "warring, snarling, malodorous and pestilential little men," and he charged the North Carolina political crowd with having "had less to do with the progress [of the state] than any other set of men." In January 1886 he berated "all the preachers" for preventing constructive work with the problem of liquor "by preaching prohibition." Page spiced the letter about prohibition with a reference to "our ancestral monkeys in Africa . . . a million years ago." Yet Page had done himself no great harm if he had wanted to return to North Carolina. Since before the Civil War, Tar Heel journalists' hard-hitting language and strictures about the failings of the state and its people, popularly termed "jeremiads," had been standard practice.[39]

Only with a letter that he wrote on 1 February 1886 did the

former editor stray into serious controversy. Aroused by continuing opposition to the Watauga Club's renewed proposals for an
industrial school, Page blurted out his anger and frustration in a
long, sarcastically humorous diatribe against the whole climate
of opinion in North Carolina. This was his famous "mummy"
letter. It was the most controversial and, albeit in ironic ways,
influential piece of writing that he ever produced.

"It is an awfully discouraging business to undertake to
prove to a mummy that it is a mummy," Page began. Yet the
mummy's existence was "a solemn fact" and apparently "lasts
forever. They don't want an Industrial School. That means a new
idea, and a new idea is death to the supremacy of the mummies.
Let 'em alone. The world must have some corner in it where men
sleep and sleep and dream and dream and North Carolina is as
good a spot for that as any." Never mind that North Carolina
was "the laughingstock among the States." Why be bothered that
"the most active and energetic men born in North Carolina have
gone away?" It did seem sad that so many "bright and promising
men" in Raleigh had drunk themselves to death during the last
twenty years. "Why did they drink?" The mummies drove them
to it. "When every intellectual aspiration is discouraged, when all
the avenues that lead to independent thought and to mental
growth are closed ... there is absolutely no chance for the
ambitious men of ability, proportionate to their ability." And the
mummies would go on ruling as long as men of ability kept either
annihilating themselves or leaving the state. North Carolina was
backward "not simply because we are poor." Georgia, Tennessee,
and Virginia had progressed further since 1865 by "giving every
man a chance in making intellectual and social progress." Tar
Heels could do even better if only the best of them were not
stifled or driven away by the mummies.[40]

Page went on with some personal observations, but that was
the brunt of the mummy letter. The letter kicked up a furious controversy. For the next two months the *State Chronicle* carried communications complaining about Page's allegations and printed a
number of essays rebutting his charges. Other newspapers, both
inside and outside North Carolina, also condemned his utter-

ances. Several months earlier, in the *Atlanta Constitution*, Henry Grady had rebuked his erstwhile disciple for undue "pessimism" in a magazine article. Page replied to his Tar Heel critics by sniffing that "a man who dares differ with one of the ordained powers now is an enemy, and he that calls sap sap is a traitor." He produced statistics to show that North Carolina sent away many more white inhabitants than any other southern state. The explanation was, he concluded, "an intolerance in North Carolina that is oppressive. Men do not have the chance to rise in life that they have elsewhere."[41]

Page believed that he finished himself in North Carolina with the mummy letter. Afterward he pictured himself as a prophet without honor in his own land. As the years passed, he lumped together his critical letters from New York with what he had said while he was still in Raleigh editing the *State Chronicle*. Page portrayed his central character in *The Southerner* as a thankless advocate of such unpleasant necessities as forgetting the Civil War, educating Negroes, and questioning the churches and the Democratic party. Yet Page was hardly a heretic driven into exile for telling the truth. While he edited the *State Chronicle* he had not engaged in offensive criticism. Rather, he had usually put a positive construction on conditions in his home state and often began editorials with such phrases as "The cheerful fact is. . . ."

Even the mummy letter did not burn his bridges. Page received congratulations as well as abuse for the piece. One letter from North Carolina urging him to keep on speaking out came from Charles B. Aycock, a young lawyer and aspiring politician from Goldsboro. Aycock told Page that "fully three fourths of the people are with you and wish you God speed in your effort to awake better work, greater thought and activity and freer opinions in the state." He hoped that Page would come back to North Carolina and start a daily paper in Raleigh with Daniels. "—It would be worth more to North Carolina than all the living and dead 'mummies' have been in a quarter of a century." Page's mummy letter also strongly resembled the similarly sarcastic blast at provincialism and backwardness that William Allen

White wrote in 1896 called "What's the Matter with Kansas?" White stayed in Kansas, editing the *Emporia Gazette* for nearly fifty years after writing his attack and using his small-town editorship as a base for a national career as a political commentator and reformer.[42]

For Page personally, the mummy letter raised an embarrassing question. Why, if departures by bright young men only perpetuated the mummies' reign, did he leave? Two weeks after writing the mummy letter, Page insisted that he remained a Tar Heel and expected "to spend the greater part of the next fifty years in the State at an editorial desk playing the same cheerful tune." Yet he never returned to North Carolina and no evidence suggests that he made any serious effort to go back. Instead, Page told his father in May 1886 that New York was now his home. "There is no [use] in my trying to do anything down South any more. I have proved disastrous every time. Here is the place that we must live."[43]

In the mummy letter itself Page implied why he did not intend to return. After criticizing the general situation, he described two North Carolina newspapermen who could not "in the great centres of journalism earn $10 a week as a reporter." Both men had denounced Page for being "Yankeeized," yet they had secretly applied for jobs on New York papers. In spite of Page's glowing recommendations of them, neither one got anywhere. "Their work has killed their chances . . . because they are neither scholars nor men who know modern things." Why should Page want to return to a field dominated by such second-raters? Both professionally, as a man who wanted to practice metropolitan journalism, and culturally, as a person with refined literary tastes and enlightened ideas, he believed he had outgrown not only North Carolina but the whole South.[44]

Neither then nor later did Page realistically examine the motives for his departure. As a result, he never ceased to feel guilty about leaving the South. Unlike George W. Cable, who had trespassed on the taboo subject of racial inequality in the early 1880s, the young North Carolinian did not leave his homeland because he held unpopular opinions or feared for his personal safety. Page's problem was the opposite of Cable's. His reform message was patient uplift. He exhorted fellow southern whites to toil in their own vineyards. Yet if persevering, small-scale efforts would regenerate the South, then where was Page? Why was he not down there digging in? Would he not be merely preaching—preaching from afar? Such questions never stopped embarrassing him.

When he boarded the train northward in February 1885, Page felt mainly relief. Whatever rationalizations he might later construct around his departure, he had no doubt about where he was casting his lot. For all but the last five of the remaining thirty-three years of his life, he lived not only in the North but in two of the nation's biggest and most cosmopolitan cities, New York and Boston. The last five years of his life he spent in London, which was then the largest city and capital of the greatest empire in the world. Yet the South always remained Walter Page's spiritual home. The region continued to occupy his mind more than any other subject. Except during the last five years of his life, he managed to make at least one trip a year to the South. He built a house in North Carolina near where his brothers and sisters lived, to which he planned to retire, and he satisfied his last wish of going home to die. Yet after the age of twenty-nine Page was a southerner only in spirit. His year and a half in Raleigh had led him to the same conclusion as that other literary North Carolinian Thomas Wolfe reached almost half a century later—"You can't go home again." In the future, Walter Hines Page might fancy himself an exile, but he was really an expatriate.

PART II

The American Scene

1885–1913

CHAPTER 4

The Magazine Revolution

Going to New York at the beginning of 1885 was a desperate gamble for Walter Page. The twenty-nine-year-old North Carolinian joined a mass migration of millions of people, both native Americans and immigrants, who streamed into the cities of the United States during the fifty years between the end of the Civil War and the outbreak of World War I. Page belonged to a distinct group of youthful rural and middle-class Americans who flocked cityward from the farms and towns of the hinterlands. Often graduates of small colleges or local universities, they were consumed with ambition to succeed in business or a profession. Every year thousands of such young men and women invaded San Francisco, Philadelphia, Atlanta, Boston, St. Louis, Cleveland, Chicago, and, above all, New York. With two million people, the metropolis on the Hudson was the nation's largest city in 1885. New York's established position as the financial center of the United States drew hopefuls in business and law, while the city's recently acquired cultural primacy beckoned aspiring scientists, doctors, actors, artists, teachers, and—in probably the largest numbers—journalists.

Most of these youthful invaders found a chilling reception amid the novelties of paved sidewalks, six-story buildings, gaslighted streets, and steam-driven elevated trains. Page sadly recounted in the *State Chronicle* in May 1886 how so many of his southern friends had decided to "drift up to this Babylon and see what blind luck and pluck not so blind" might gain them. Few found anything. "There are no 'vacancies' anywhere. But there are men of all kinds, of learning, of character, of experience, who are eagerly waiting for work to do." Yet, despite having to wait months before landing a full-time job, Page flourished in this inhospitable environment. Thanks partly to his previous employment with the *World*, he quickly found a market for his freelance writing. Two newspapers—the *Boston Post*, for which he had written before, and the *Brooklyn Union*—soon accepted his contributions on a regular basis. Alice was able to join him three months after he left North Carolina. Their two small boys—a second son, Arthur Wilson, had been born in September 1883— stayed with the elder Pages in Aberdeen through the summer of 1885. At some point during the year the *Brooklyn Union* hired Page as an editorial writer at a salary of eighteen hundred dollars.

The job with the *Union*, which went to press in the afternoon, left plenty of time at night for outside writing, and Page turned himself into a literary gatling gun, firing articles at newspapers and magazines. As he related to Alice in April 1885, he wrote essays on southern subjects for submission to the nation's leading monthly magazines—*Atlantic*, *Harper's*, and *The Century*. In the space of four days he also produced pieces for the weekly magazine *The Independent* and for seven newspapers. Other writing included work on a book and correspondence for newspapers outside New York. Much of Page's output was hit-or-miss. "How many of the articles I have written will be published I shall not know for several days," he wrote Alice. A fair amount of his production probably found its way into print, and peddling his journalistic wares helped Page learn where reader interests lay.

The experience also confirmed his faith in salvation through activity, especially feats with the pen. "I find," he told Alice, "... that writing (and writing reasonably well, I think) is the easiest thing in the world to do." A friend remembered Page's writing habits. After the family had set up housekeeping in a small apartment in Brooklyn, Page usually wrote in the living room during evenings. While Alice chatted with visitors, he often looked up and joined the conversation, sometimes writing on without stopping. "There's nothing to this," he remarked. "Mere mechanical stuff—just like a trade. Anybody could do it." By

May 1886 he could boast to his father, "Besides the [*Union*] salary, I have made a good deal of money by other work and shall make more—perhaps $1,000 a year." Betting on himself once more seemed to be paying off for the Tar Heel.[1]

Most of Page's paid writing, like his free contributions to the *State Chronicle*, concerned the South and national political issues. Leaving North Carolina hardly banished the South from his mind. In an article in the *Independent* in June 1885, Page foreshadowed the message of the mummy letter: "Old Southern society had many virtues," he wrote, "but its ghost now has a prodigious vanity. Its virtues are not lost. But what a pity the old ghost will not rest!" In a fragment written in 1886, which apparently did not get published, Page restated his conviction that slavery had warped the South's development. In the pre–Civil War slave states, "the democratic idea suffered a contraction." In denying basic human rights to blacks, slaveowners had taken "a backward step from the ground that Jefferson held." They had shrunk "clear back to the dark ages, when according to the pulpit God sanctioned slavery." Also in 1886 Page compiled a survey of southern black leaders' opinions for the *Independent*.[2]

He began to see southern problems as national issues. In one of his *Boston Post* letters in 1885, Page denied the existence of a separate "Southern problem." The section's needs were simply part of "the general American problem," which was "to lift up the masses to the general republican height without taking away from them their local peculiarities." Page likewise remained convinced that tariff reform would disenthrall American politics from leftover Civil War issues and bring the South back into the political mainstream. Moreover, as the uprooted southerner viewed the miseries of New York City slums, he came to believe that "a much more important emancipation proclamation than Lincoln's" was required to break the shackles of urban poverty. "The first word of such a proclamation, I should predict, will be FREE TRADE." Page's views coincided in part with the outlook of the prominent northern political independents who had broken with the orthodox Republicans in the campaign of 1884 and were often derisively called "mugwumps." Page's agreement with mugwump views, such as it was, stemmed from his impatience with the mummies' rule in his native region.[3]

The southerner newcomer's political inclinations got a further push through his next step up in metropolitan journalism. In February 1887 he went to work for the *New York Evening Post* at a salary of two thousand dollars a year. At that time the *Evening Post* was the high altar of the mugwump creed. Edited by E. L. Godkin, the newspaper denounced bosses and machines, espoused clean government and free trade at home and abroad, and generally supported President Cleveland. For Page, joining the staff of the *Evening Post* constituted a personal experiment in sectional reconciliation. The principal stockholder in the *Evening Post* was Henry Villard, a cultivated German-American railroad magnate who had married the daughter of the abolitionist William Lloyd Garrison. Because Page's duties consisted mainly of editorial makeup and brief book notices, he worked directly under Villard's brother-in-law, Wendell Phillips Garrison. As editor of the *State Chronicle* in 1884, Page had celebrated the death of his new boss's godfather, the abolitionist Wendell Phillips, by wishing him "a pleasant passage over the Styx." Page's work also included writing news digests for the *Nation*, the journal that he had once called "Republican in politics and infidel in religion." For a southern white like Page to be on the *Evening Post* staff was a measure of both his own changing views and the profound political changes that had occurred since the 1870s.[4]

Sharing part of the mugwump viewpoint occasioned one of Page's earliest personal political involvements. This was through the Reform Club of New York, a distinguished body that sponsored speakers and published pamphlets in support of lower tariffs, unfettered private economic activity, and President Cleveland's unsuccessful reelection campaign in 1888. Page's contribution to the Reform Club lay in preparing low-tariff material in a ready-to-print form for newspapers throughout the United States. He remained active in the club after the 1888 election and at one time served as a vice-president. The Reform Club in turn provided Page with useful contacts in New York's legal, financial, and journalistic circles.

But the former North Carolinian did not swallow the mugwump viewpoint whole. In his letters to the *State Chronicle* in 1885 and 1886, Page displayed divergent strains in his political and social thinking. New York itself provoked varied responses. Like many other Americans of his time, Page found himself appalled by stark urban contrasts of wealth and power side by side with poverty and misery. Writing about Christmas in New York in 1885, he advised Tar Heel preachers to "discard brimstone and fire for filth and hunger, as materials to make a hell of. One half of the world has no idea how the other half lives." Page treated *State Chronicle* readers to some radical-sounding utterances. In April 1886 he sympathized with labor unions, declaring, "We are all socialists in the best sense of the word. . . . You are bound either to be a socialist (in the best sense—not an anarchist but a Democrat) or an egotist." Three months later he avowed that if anyone had a choice between being born in a New York slum and in savagery in Africa, "he would be a fool who should not choose to be a savage. As for being a slave—what is slavery if this be freedom?"

The divergence in his views was not extraordinary. For Page, as for other educated young Americans of the time, the mugwump persuasion marked an early stage in his political evolution, not the rigid dogma that it was for his elders. Page's ostensibly radical mutterings were not unusual, either. Many Americans at the time were apparently receptive to ideas about drastic changes in the economic and social order, as widespread popular interest in Henry George's Single Tax and Edward Bellamy's Nationalism disclosed during the 1880s. Nor was Page unique in the disparity between his perceptions of human misery and the remedies he could envisage. Fittingly, he said kind words about the Single Tax advocate, George, who ran for mayor of New York in 1886. Page resembled George in apprehending the inhumanities of existing industrial conditions and yet believing that some single, limited change could set everything right. George carried his thinking further and urged a stringent form of one-shot governmental intervention in the economy through his "single tax." But Page did not mislead the *State Chronicle* readers when he dubbed George "the foremost expounder of free trade in America."[5]

As earlier, the southerner found himself both thrilled and repelled by New York. Although such cultural and commercial riches as the opera and Fifth Avenue stores filled Page with excitement, he disliked the conditions that middle-class urbanites like himself and his family had to endure. In common with other city dwellers of his station, Page soon tried to recapture the advantages of a rural and small-town environment. During his first years after returning to New York, he sent his family away for the summer, to stay with his parents at Aberdeen. Then, as his journalistic career prospered and as his family grew, Page joined the trek to the suburbs. In addition to the two older boys, Ralph and Arthur, the Pages had two more children. A third son, Frank Copeland, was born in Brooklyn in March 1887, and their only daughter, Katharine Alice, was born in January 1891. By the time Katharine arrived, the Pages had moved to New Rochelle, a short distance outside New York in Westchester County. After three years of renting a house in "the country," as Page described New Rochelle, from the spring through the fall, the family decided to stay year-round, and Page commuted to work an hour each way on the train to Manhattan. Thereafter Page became exclusively a town and apartment dweller again only once for a few months in 1909.

Another change after going back to New York was a gradual decline in Page's literary ambition. During summers when his family was away he frequently spent evenings engaging in beer drinking and deep talk with several other young men with intellectual interests who had come to New York from elsewhere. Their chief topic of discussion was literature. Some of the other participants subsequently remembered Page's interest in the poetry of Walt Whitman. He particularly delighted in reciting "O Captain!" in his deep, southern-accented voice. But Page also mockingly read off some of Whitman's freer and more sexually suggestive verses, which he dismissed with the condemnation, "That's not poetry!" Those estimates prefigured Page's later literary tastes as a book publisher, when he championed homely, vigorous realism yet disapproved of anything that savored of naturalism, lurid elements, or formlessness.[6]

But though his flirtation with creative literature would continue throughout his life, the focus of Page's interests was shifting to journalism and public affairs. He clearly indicated this change when he left the *Evening Post* after only seven months. One day in October 1887, as Page remembered, "a man whom I did not know" came to ask him to join the staff of the *Forum*. The man was evidently Lorettus S. Metcalf, the editor of the *Forum*, a monthly magazine in its second year of publication. Page was offered the position of business manager at a salary of three thousand dollars a year, a position that was his only journalistic post that did not involve writing and editorial work. Dissatisfaction with the *Evening Post* may have helped make the job attractive, and the *Forum* offered both a better salary and an appealing challenge. Page wrote that he had one main reason for taking the business managership: "Notwithstanding the fact that no dignified nonillustrated monthly either in England or in America . . . has, I am told, ever paid a profit, I cannot bring myself to believe that the *Forum* cannot be made to pay." He likened himself to a member of the crew when "the ship comes in" and expected to enjoy a share in the profits. Page was warning that he did not plan to be a mere hired hand on the *Forum*. He was accepting the business managership because of the twin desires that he had carried away from the fiasco with *The Age* eight years before. Page wanted to get into magazines, and he meant to be his own boss.[7]

When Page joined the staff of the *Forum*, he enlisted in a journalistic revolution. In company with such periodicals as *Cosmopolitan*, *Munsey's*, and *Ladies' Home Journal*, the *Forum* transformed the character of magazines in the United States. Before the 1880s, magazines still operated after the manner of literary reviews, as high-priced, leisurely productions serving an elite readership. With the advent of these new-style journals, magazines encroached on territory previously reserved to newspapers. Technological advances, in the form of high-speed presses, less expensive paper, and the half-tone process for illustrations, allowed larger circulations at lower prices. At the same time, new mass-production industries with national markets required a medium to carry advertising to broader areas. To meet these new demands, a different breed of magazine editor came to the fore. In place of the scholars, poets, and critics who had produced such stately journals at the *Atlantic*, *Harper's*, and the *North American Review* emerged a group composed mainly of former newspapermen. Their magazines possessed qualities that better newspapers prized—lively stories and articles, illustrations and eye-catching formats, timeliness in topics covered, and low prices.

The *Forum*'s contribution lay in stressing contemporary problems. Unlike other innovative periodicals, it carried neither illustrations nor fiction and was far more serious in tone. The *Forum* served up a monthly offering of around 125 pages of articles on topics of current interest, with greatest attention devoted to political, economic, and social issues. In the first year after its beginning in March 1886, the magazine ran a number of articles on labor unions and anarchism, which were attracting attention because of widespread strikes and violence. Also from its early numbers the *Forum* carried articles by prominent people, either on public issues or about personal influences in their careers. Another distinguishing feature from the outset was the symposium, in which writers with divergent or opposing views addressed the same question. These symposia sometimes included political and social dissidents who rarely gained a hearing in other mainline magazines.

Page later claimed, erroneously, that he had formed the character of the *Forum*. In fact, by the time he became business manager at the end of 1887, the journal had already acquired its basic shape, thanks to the work of its two founders. One founder was the principal stockholder and financial backer, a New York lawyer and financier named Isaac L. Rice. A German-born Jew, Rice possessed a combination of cultural and commercial interests that had given him the original idea for the *Forum*. He and a few fellow German-Jewish businessmen friends had invested a hundred thousand dollars in the magazine. The other pioneer was Lorettus Metcalf, whom Rice lured from the editorship of the *North American Review* to become the first editor of the *Forum*.

Metcalf, a short, stocky, balding man of fifty in 1887, had begun his journalistic career on newspapers in his native state of Maine. Like Page, Metcalf was an incessant worker. By his own account, he put in thirteen or fourteen hours a day without a vacation during his five years as editor of the *Forum*. Clear, lively writing obsessed Metcalf, and he believed in soliciting articles rather than waiting for them to come in, often coaching contributors about how to write their pieces. In the fall of 1886, for example, Metcalf advised the sociologist Lester Frank Ward that in a *Forum* article "philosophical distinctions ought to be avoided and practical aspects presented as much as possible." It was, he told Ward, "the great middle class of intelligent, but not necessarily educated men, that I am anxious to reach."[8]

Metcalf's approach to editorship also contained a defect that eventually proved his undoing. Metcalf obsessively edited *Forum* contributions over and over, sometimes as many as a dozen times. His editorial assistant, Arthur Bostwick, admitted that Metcalf probably "set rather too high a standard" and neglected to search for new talent. Viewing himself exclusively as an editor, Metcalf scorned "dictation from the business end." His attitude might not have caused trouble if the magazine had turned a quick profit, but like most magazine ventures, the *Forum* consumed substantial capital outlays in getting started. Rice and his fellow investors wanted to see a return on their money, and they may have pressured Metcalf into hiring a business manager.[9]

Page left little record of his activities as business manager of the *Forum*. His duties evidently fell into three categories. One included attempts to lower production costs. Page must have effected some savings, since Rice congratulated him in August 1888 for "a substantial gain" in reducing expenses. His second set of responsibilities lay in trying to build up circulation. Page resorted to standard practices of employing subscription agents and giving special offers to subscribers. This work Page found frustrating; early in 1891 he complained, "We kept buying new subscribers and losing old ones." The third side of the business managership required Page to attract advertising. After he joined the *Forum*, the advertising pages began to carry better illustrations and became the most visually attractive part of an issue. Page also introduced school advertisements, which Nathan Bijur, Rice's principal associate, called "the best thing in ads. we have ever had." The new business manager must have done his job well. After a few months, Bijur regretted "that you had not undertaken this at the time the *Forum* was founded." Bijur and Rice expressed their appreciation by giving Page a one-thousand-dollar stock bonus in May 1888. The experience benefited him in other ways, too. Page learned both the technical and the financial aspects of magazine work. In particular, he grasped the critical value of advertising to a modern, large-circulation magazine.[10]

But Page was not happy as business manager. Although the magazine defied his efforts to turn a profit, his basic complaint was that he was not editor. Page deluded himself if he thought that he could be content with any position on the *Forum* besides the editorial chair. In February 1891 he composed a long letter to Bijur—which he neither finished nor apparently sent—in which he surveyed possible courses of action for the magazine, with all the alternatives pointing to a choice between himself and Metcalf as editor. Yet he made no move to force a showdown. Never in his career did Page develop ruthlessness, and he always remained chary about openly pushing his own advancement. Nevertheless, he soon occupied the coveted position. "The controlling board was becoming restive," Bostwick recalled, "and as Metcalf refused to modify his policy, he resigned and was succeeded by Walter H. Page, then the business manager." Bostwick believed that Rice and Bijur chose Page, after considering other possible editors, because they believed that he would show proper regard for business matters. Metcalf's health may also have played a part in his decision to step down. Shortly after leaving the *Forum*, he collapsed for several months from a combination of eyestrain and stomach ulcers. The change of command occurred with no outward acrimony. Metcalf remained friendly with his successor. He later sold Page his *Forum* stock and rented his New York home to Page.[11]

Becoming editor of the *Forum*, at the beginning of March

1891, at a salary of five thousand dollars, meant a dream come true for Page. He claimed that ever since childhood he had carried in his mind an exact picture of the editorial office, down to the details of pictures on the walls and pieces of furniture. The *Forum* editorial office was a cozy, dimly lighted set of rooms with a big table. It probably seemed familiar to Page because it reminded him of the *State Chronicle* office. The southerner's accustomed clutter quickly replaced Metcalf's neatness. Bostwick remembered that when Page first came into the editorial room, he sat on top of a desk and swung his long legs around as he talked and laughed heartily. Page followed the editorial philosophy that he had formed on the *State Chronicle*. An editor, he had declared in 1884, was "a dull fellow at best," whose only salvation lay in getting out among his readers. "For freshness and breadth one day among men of other occupations is worth a week among those of one's own craft." After some time as editor, he argued that "the *Forum* will be valuable and suggestive directly in proportion to the freedom of the editor from mere routine duties. He must know men and be out among men." The new editor's attitude wrought immediate changes on the *Forum*. "Page's first act, when he assumed the editorship," recalled Bostwick, "was to cut out most of what Metcalf would have considered the 'editing,' and concentrate on engaging new and conspicuous talent." The normally retiring Bostwick found himself out on the streets of New York and on trains to other cities, on assignments to get prominent people to write articles. Within a short time proofreading replaced meticulous editing.[12]

Page took over his new post with his usual drive and gusto, matching Metcalf in capacity for work. "How do I manage the *Forum*?" he responded to a questioner after two years as editor. "I'll tell you. I work. There is not much else to say. It is work here, and hard work." In April 1893 he complained to one of his erstwhile companions in beer drinking and literary talk that he was "rushed as I never was in my life." At that moment he had over two hundred letters to answer. "I have worked nights and Sundays, hardly had a dinner at home in a month, have four drawers full of manuscripts, have gone two days at a time without seeing my children when one was sick. I have spent a week of nights on sleeping cars and have been in the doctor's hands myself." Page had himself to blame in part; by his own choice, he was filling both his own and Metcalf's jobs. He continued to deal with the production end and spent a good bit of time with printers and paper suppliers. Much of his traveling for the *Forum* still involved circulation and advertising. Before long, Page gave up trying to manage all aspects of the magazine. In 1894 he hired a young advertising man, Frank Presbrey, to take over the business side, and he looked forward to "complete emancipation" from "this long time of double labor."[13]

Despite his complaints, Page thrived on the work. He spent the greater part of his days and nights churning with ideas for *Forum* articles. His main activities in the editorial office consisted of sending out letters and receiving callers. He dictated some letters and wrote others in his own hand. Page never learned to use a typewriter. Like many people at the time, he believed that handwritten letters were more personal, politer, and therefore more effective. In conversations with callers to the office, he again displayed his faculty for drawing people out. Page's heartiness and enthusiasm did not make him forward or familiar in manner. Although an excellent talker, he was an even better listener, with a gift for convincing others that he was interested in them. In addition, Page read widely in other magazines, books, and newspapers. All of these activities supported his cardinal rule of editorship—to keep in touch with events, people, and ideas.

The *Forum*'s contents began to reflect the new editor's handiwork. Two experimental sections appeared briefly in 1891. One, called "Financial," surveyed business conditions around the country; the other, "Books of the Month," reviewed new books. The September 1891 issue treated a number of aspects of education, including boys' schools, universities, technical training, and women's colleges. During the succeeding months, articles examined the silver issue, the Farmers' Alliance, state politics, an interoceanic canal in Panama or Nicaragua, and expansion of the navy. Many of the pieces came from big-name contributors, usually well-known politicians, businessmen, and academic experts. Promising new figures in various fields also appeared, including the social worker Jane Addams; two opposing young literary lights, Hamlin Garland and W. R. Thayer; and three younger men who had yet to make their names in national politics, Theodore Roosevelt, Woodrow Wilson, and Henry Cabot Lodge. Another thrust of the *Forum* was to show how major trends affected people's everyday lives. In March 1892, Page asked his fellow magazine editor Albert Shaw to write on a "typical factory town" in a way that would illustrate "the economic theories and social tendencies of the time." As the 1892 presidential election approached, he solicited from leading financiers, clergymen, and writers statements about how they planned to cast their votes. "It is a personal example and sharply-expressed reasons for personal preferences," Page explained to one potential contributor, "—of men who are not politicians but are representative of our best citizenship—that have effect."[14]

Building on Metcalf's beginnings highlighted Page's true accomplishment as a magazine editor. At this stage in his career, his gifts lay less in the originality than in the fertility of his ideas, in vigor and resourcefulness in approaching authors, and in recognition and exploitation of opportunities. If magazine editors can be compared to generals, Page was more of a tactician than a strategist. This is not to downgrade his achievements. The most successful operators in the new magazine field after the 1880s were not inventors but adapters who applied sensitive barometers of popular taste to other people's ideas. With the *Forum*, Metcalf had played the role of Moses, the prophet who was not permitted to enter the promised land. Page was Joshua, who took up where Metcalf left off and conquered.

Page did make departures that advanced both his own magazine and the larger journalistic revolution. One variation was an expansion on Metcalf's idea of running series of articles on single subjects, thereby attempting to carry reader interest from one month to the next. Whereas Metcalf featured different authors in all but one of his series, Page favored single writers for each series. A far more imaginative and significant innovation was the investigatory article. Page had conceived of the idea before assuming the *Forum* editorship, when he had proposed various series of reports to Metcalf. The most important investigation undertaken after he took command was the series of articles on education by J. M. Rice, a physician interested in child training and pedagogy. Late in 1891 Page commissioned Rice to visit thirty-six cities and probe conditions in urban schools during the first half of 1892. Rice spent the summer writing nine articles, which ran in the *Forum* from October 1892 to June 1893. The articles unearthed the indifference, incompetence, and political interference that plagued schools in most cities. Rice's exposures roused howls of protest and helped kick off a mighty reform movement in American education. Where the idea for the series originated is not known, but J. M. Rice was the younger brother of Isaac Rice, the principal stockholder, and himself later editor of the *Forum*.

The Rice series contained the germ of a larger journalistic concept. Those articles prefigured the investigatory reporting that flowered into the "muckraking" of the early 1900s. The large-scale investigatory report would become the American magazine's distinctive contribution to journalism. Page deserved credit for pushing magazines toward this broad investigatory role. He not only ran the Rice series and another one on education by G. Stanley Hall, but he also published a comparable set of articles on municipal sanitation by John S. Billings, together with several individual pieces that delved into municipal government, corporations, and railroad regulation. Page's innovations can in some measure be regarded as the transference of newspaper practices to magazines. Yet in another way the southerner had been a magazine man ever since his first venture with the ill-fated *Age*. His weekly paper, the *State Chronicle*, had resembled a magazine almost as much as a newspaper, and after returning to New York he had seized the first opportunity to get into magazines. The irksome tour of duty as the *Forum*'s business manager had probably helped Page most toward becoming a successful magazine editor.

Page's last and most significant contribution to both the *Forum* and the development of magazines came with a financial gamble at the end of 1893. Against his editorial assistant's advice and in the face of doubts expressed by Rice and Bijur, Page slashed the price of the *Forum* in half, from fifty to twenty-five cents a copy. Profits and circulation had grown little since the change of editors, and with the onset of a depression in 1893 the *Forum* began to run monthly deficits. By February 1893 the magazine had lost $1,500 on the basis of $66,500 in yearly receipts and $68,000 in operating expenses. After several months of deliberation and argument, Page moved to meet the crisis. First, he took advantage of lower wages and prices caused by the depression to cut manufacturing costs by about $8,000. Next, starting with the December 1893 number, the *Forum* cover ran at the top, in big red letters, "REDUCED—TO 25 cts. A COPY, TO $3.00 A YEAR."[15]

The combined reductions brought almost instantaneous improvement. The first two issues of the *Forum* at the new price recorded a big increase in newsstand sales, from five thousand for the preceding two issues to over seventeen thousand. At the same time, new subscriptions during November and December 1893 stood at 3,653, as opposed to 1,200 for the same period in 1892. By the middle of December 1893, Page could boast to his mother that "the reduction in price promises to be a very great success. It is a move that I have advocated for two years, but the others did not think it wise. The promise of success is a 'feather in my cap.' " When circulation hit forty thousand with the second issue after the price decrease, Page forecasted yearly earnings for the *Forum* in 1894 of $96,150. He projected $38,400 from newsstand sales, $39,750 from subscriptions, and $16,000 from advertising. Total expenses he calculated at $78,000. Thus, the magazine should yield a profit of $17,350. If business conditions improved, Page foresaw a circulation of fifty thousand. Advertising revenues might then rise to $25,000 and profits to $40,000. Those predictions proved overly optimistic, but not by much. During 1894, the *Forum* brought in gross receipts of $97,936.46. Circulation slipped back to around twenty-eight thousand per month, and the magazine earned $61,726.77 from sales and subscriptions. Expenses amounted to $96,275.12, which left a new profit of only $1,688.34. Page claimed that the price reduction had incurred unusual expenses that would not recur. But despite the failure to maintain the 40,000 circulation, the *Forum* earned $36,236.69 from advertising, more than $20,000 above Page's projection. In the face of the steadily worsening depression, the reduction in price had worked wonders.[16]

More than anything else, Page's coup in cutting the price of the *Forum* proved his importance in the magazine revolution. As Frank Luther Mott has observed, the biggest change in American magazines stemmed from the introduction of periodicals that were high in quality and cheap in price. Like other editorial innovators, Page located an untapped market of readers who could be reached at a lower price. What enabled him to spot that market was his sense of his readership. Having served as business manager of the *Forum* had sharpened his perception of who might buy the magazine and what they wanted to read. But more important, Page represented at least one of the kinds of people who bought magazines in the 1890s. His entire life—particularly college, the Johns Hopkins, and shuttling back and forth between the hinterland and the metropolis—made him epitomize the actual and potential readership of a periodical like the *Forum*.[17]

Neither subscription lists nor reports on the distribution of newsstand sales have survived to show just who read the *Forum*. But the magazine's contents, both articles and advertising, provide indications of the people to whom it appealed. By far the largest number of articles treated timely topics. Page said that he regarded the *Forum* as "necessarily being a sort of news magazine." Often, however, newsworthy articles analyzed trends and events less than they publicized views of prominent figures. Likewise, personal reflections by famous people gave the impression of letting readers in on secrets of success, an impression that Page wanted to give. Early in 1894 he contemplated a series of "confessions" by successful graduates ten years out of college. The series would "show their own judgment of their college experience" and compile views "as to the ideal training of an American lad."

Even more than contributions by big-name figures, the overall distribution of articles highlighted the *Forum*'s readership target. Except for newsworthy topics, the subjects that received the greatest space were education, the professions, and urban problems. Education was the *Forum*'s hobbyhorse. Page devoted his two best single-author series, by Rice and G. Stanley Hall, to educational topics. He also solicited many individual articles. On the subject of professions, *Forum* pieces, separately and in a series, considered pay, working conditions, and possibilities for advancement in law, medicine, university teaching, the ministry, and journalism. Page also wanted to update one of Metcalf's early series of articles by prominent figures, called "Formative Influences." Top men in different fields would write their "matured conclusions" in ways that would throw "the most instructive possible side-light on each profession or calling." Articles on urban problems concentrated on the quality of life in cities and on corruption in government. The distribution of articles suggests that the *Forum* was aimed at educated, younger, middle-class men and women whose ambitions to get ahead economically, socially, and culturally had brought them to metropolitan centers.[18]

Advertising reinforced the impression that the *Forum* sought a special middle-class audience. From its beginning the magazine had advertised the wares turned out by mass-production industries—soap, pianos, rifles, furniture, cameras, chocolate, and the like. Insurance and financial advertising occupied a good deal of linage, too, together with advertising for cigars, patent medicines, and whiskey. Those were advertisements that abounded in every magazine of the day. But after Page joined the staff, the *Forum* differed from other periodicals by specializing in advertisements for schools and hotels. Page introduced school advertisements while he was business manager. After he assumed the editorship, the magazine began running a monthly classified directory of private schools and colleges. Promotional articles in the advertising section described preparatory schools. Hotel advertising was part of the *Forum*'s emphasis on travel. The magazine ran promotional pieces on tourism and business opportunities in various areas and also printed classified directories of hotels and lawyers by towns and cities.

The *Forum*'s specialties in articles and advertising stressed mobility. Page was appealing to readers who not only traveled but also were moving up in the world through education, membership in professions, and financial success. With a circulation of forty thousand at its peak, the *Forum* was hardly a mass magazine. After the reduction in price, Page sometimes called the *Forum* "a popular magazine" and the readers "a popular audience." But he was really addressing a select, serious-minded, middle-class audience, as the magazine's unfailingly sober tone implied.

Page's success stemmed from understanding and representing the newer, mobile elite that was growing up in America. People like Page composed that elite. They had usually attended college and entered one of the occupations that increasingly demanded university education and great expertise. More often than not, such people came from small-town and rural backgrounds. Whether or not they lived in big cities, they tended to form occupational, political, and intellectual allegiances that were national in scope. Journalism occupied a central place in this congeries of newer elites, both as a means of communication among them and as itself one of the new professions. The shift of the *Forum* editorship in 1891 from Metcalf to Page typified the change in journalism. Most of the successful magazine editors and writers in New York during the 1890s and early 1900s resembled the former southerner. Like him, S. S. McClure, Lincoln Steffens, Ray Stannard Baker, Ida Tarbell, and David Graham Phillips had all grown up after the Civil War on farms or in small towns and had attended hinterland colleges. Page succeeded with the *Forum* by reaching his audience at the right time. He had gained a foothold with a critical segment of American society —the ambitious but questioning younger lawyers, teachers, journalists, clergymen, physicians, and businessmen who were about to play a much larger role in the life of the nation.

Success as a magazine editor agreed with Page. His four years in command of the *Forum*, from February 1891 to June 1895, formed one of the happiest periods in his life. Except for occasional brief illnesses Page's health remained good. He kept most of the weight that he had put on in Raleigh, and the added pounds made him better looking than he had been as a younger man, with a fuller, smoother face and a sturdier, less gawky frame. For a while after returning to New York, Page grew a bristly beard, but he soon reverted to the moderately flowing moustache that he had worn off and on since his early twenties. At the same time, he upgraded his heavy smoking from a corncob pipe to cigars. Family life reflected the editor's well-being. Alice, who had also grown stouter, presided over a substantial home in New Rochelle, with at least one servant. The atmosphere there was both fun-loving and purposeful. His children's education particularly concerned Page. His second son, Arthur, remembered his having "always in his mind a desperate desire for the best education possible." Like other busy men of affairs, Page regretted not spending more time with his family. He served as friend and counselor to his three boys, Ralph, Arthur, and Frank, and he doted on his little daughter, Katharine.[19]

The demands of the *Forum* did not prevent Page from joining a few organizations and enjoying some social life in New York. Besides the Reform Club, he belonged to the Johns Hopkins Alumni Association, which he helped to found, and the Nineteenth Century Club, a monthly discussion group on public affairs. On a normal day in the city, Page lunched at either the Brevoort Hotel, near the *Forum* office on Union Square, or the University Club, which he also joined. The clubs and the luncheons helped him develop the contacts that he considered vital to magazine editorship. The Johns Hopkins Alumni Association allowed Page to renew his acquaintance with Wilson, who was now teaching at Princeton, and with other academics whom he drew into the *Forum* orbit. Early in 1895, as president of the Nineteenth Century Club, he organized a series of discussions about New York City's schools, finances, public-health facilities, and beautification—all topics of interest to his magazine. Page usually lunched with newspaper and magazine friends and with visitors from out of town, to whom he listened carefully and talked enthusiastically, frequently telling North Carolina anecdotes.

The *Forum* editorship formed the hub for his expansiveness

and domestic contentment. At no other time in his mature years did Page harmonize his varied interests and ambitions so well. Not since his adolescent bent toward the ministry had he felt so sure that he was being simultaneously literary and socially useful. Page implicitly compared the editorship of the *Forum* several times to something like the pulpit. In a confidential memorandum in May 1894 he rejected the "making of a mere conventional magazine" as an unworthy task "that satisfies no philosophic yearning. I had as lief make shoes or plows; and I had rather build houses. The whole 'literary' superstition that buoys up the men who do this kind of thing is a juvenile illusion; or if they no longer have any illusion, they recognize it as a decent sort of craft—a craft like the making or selling of 'notions'—which yields a more or less easy living." He was still Frank Page's son. In a way, Walter Page was trying to erect the *Forum* into something even better than a pulpit. When he said he would rather build houses than turn out an ordinary magazine, he was associating himself with what his father did. Perhaps the only work that could have genuinely fused Page's threefold desire—to be intellectual and creative, to wield social influence, and to make money—was architecture. The editor depicted himself as an architect with words, and he implicitly likened his magazine to an artistically constructed, socially useful, and economically profitable building.[20]

Even the *Forum* did not totally absorb Page. Despite recurrent complaints about how much work he had to do, he plunged into other projects. Writing evidently attracted him less than at most other times in his life, since Page published almost nothing of his own during these years. Whether from scruple, modesty, or lack of interest, he contributed only one article under his own name to the *Forum*. He was more involved in business schemes and in southern affairs. Page had a number of brainstorms for making money. One was a newspaper in St. Paul, Minnesota; another was a new kind of cooking stove. Nothing came of either idea. Continued sensitivity to his father's attitudes helped push him toward such schemes. Right after lowering the price of the magazine, Page told his mother about the success of the move and how the *Forum* "has given us bread and meat now for six years, and shelter and clothes to boot. Father remarked once that that was the only good thing *he* knew it had ever done. Well, it seems now in a pretty fair way to make a fortune for its owners, and all my troubles now arise from my efforts to own too much."[21]

The remark about trying to own too much referred to Page's most important outside venture while he was with the *Forum*. At the end of February 1892 he acquired control of the *Manufacturers Record*, a weekly paper published in Baltimore. In the seven years since its founding, the *Manufacturers Record* had grown into a potent voice for southern industrial development. The founding editor was Richard H. Edmonds, a shrewd businessman and journalist originally from Virginia, who had partially filled Grady's shoes as the leading spokesman for the New South viewpoint. At the end of 1891 Edmonds's health had broken down, and he offered to sell the *Manufacturers Record* to Page. The former Tar Heel jumped at the proposition. He wanted not only to buy a valuable property but also, as he told one of his investors, to contribute to "a subject of Southern importance." Page brought in as junior partners the *Forum* advertising manager Frank Presbrey, Albert Fox of the *New York Herald*, and Edward Sanborn of the *Philadelphia Record*, who succeeded Edmonds as editor of the Baltimore paper. Each man put up money that he possessed or borrowed. Page turned to North Carolina connections to secure twenty thousand dollars for his share. Two members of the Duke family, the rough-hewn Buck and his more refined brother Benjamin, contributed five thousand dollars between them. Another five thousand dollars came from Frank Page, whose lumber, railroad, and real-estate enterprises continued to prosper and who evidently could not resist investing in another of his son's southern projects.[22]

The venture encountered difficulties from the beginning. As Edmonds later recalled, Page and his partners disagreed over the direction that the *Manufacturers Record* should take. The new owners might have worked out their differences except for the depression. Both the paper and an office building in Baltimore, which was part of the property, began to incur heavy losses. By the middle of 1893 Page in desperation asked Edmonds, who had recovered his health, to resume the editorship. In order to induce Edmonds to return, Page had to relinquish control to him. Page originally placed his stock under a trust agreement, to go to Edmonds after the *Manufacturers Record* had paid dividends for a certain period. But a clash developed and in 1896, on advice from his lawyers, Page sold most of his stock to Edmonds at about ten cents on the dollar. He retained eighty shares at a par value of eight thousand dollars. How much money Page lost in the venture is not clear, but he certainly suffered a great loss in pride. His effort to regain a beachhead in southern journalism had come to naught, and he had failed to make money in yet another enterprise in which he had induced his father to join.

Living outside the South in no way diminished Page's concern for his native region. As editor of the *Forum*, he solicited and published many articles about problems, particularly racial ones, below the Potomac. Sometimes Page had to restrain his own interest. In 1891, he returned to George W. Cable an article on southern education that he had previously requested. Page explained that "my own interest in the matter . . . got the better of the *Forum* editor that is in me." The rise of lynching in the 1890s prompted him to run several pieces on the problem and to contribute his only signed article to the magazine. The November 1893 issue of the *Forum* included "The Last Hold of the Southern Bully," in which the editor reiterated long-held opinions. Page once more blamed the South's troubles on the combined legacies of northern interference during Reconstruction and the crippling effects of slavery on both blacks and whites. He viewed the rise of such racist demagogues as South Carolina's "Pitchfork Ben" Tillman with alarm: "It has, indeed, reached that grotesque level where the bully plays the part of the moral reformer."

When he discussed possible remedies for lynching, Page again exposed the inconsistencies in his ideas about solutions for racial problems. He did not blink away the difficulty that blacks and whites had in living together. The South still labored under the results of "the colossal and continuous misfortune of modern

times . . . —the coming of the African to this continent at all."
Yet Page could sympathize with blacks. The Negro not only
lacked ancestry, "but its lack is proclaimed by his color and he is
always reminded of it." Page quoted James Russell Lowell's
remark that he was glad not to have been a born a Jew but, if he
had been, he would be prouder of that fact than any other. What
white man could honestly make the same statement about being
a Negro? "When you have found many men of this mind, then
this race-problem will, owing to some change in human nature,
have become less tough; but till then, patience and tolerance."
Page remained optimistic about southern progress. Industrial
development would, he maintained, cure lynching. "Let it be
proclaimed by boards of trade, by merchants, by bankers, by
manufacturers, that they will not have industry and commerce
hindered by lawlessness." Little more was needed to give permanent quietus to the southern bully.[23]

In airing those views in the *Forum*, Page began to carve out a
new role for himself. He was becoming a self-appointed but
recognized ambassador from the South to the North. Ever since
his *Atlantic* article and his letters to the *New York World* and
Boston Post in 1881, Page had been interpreting his homeland
to northern readers. Besides writing about the South, he took
some actions toward promoting sectional understanding. In 1892,
when the Nineteenth Century Club planned a debate between a
northerner and a southern white about race relations, Page objected strongly. "The true 'opposing side,'" he insisted, " . . . is
to get a Negro." Page arranged for his old friend George Winston,
who had become president of the University of North Carolina,
to speak on a program in January 1893 with Joseph C. Price, the
president of a Negro college in the same state. Price's appearance
raised delicate problems about arrangements, particularly finding
a New York hotel that did not turn away blacks. Page himself
decided not to invite Price, along with Winston, to dinner at his
home. He explained confidentially that his wife, though a northerner, "has a lingering race-prejudice in such matters. As for me,
who have . . . eaten and lived with 'em all my life—I'd like nothing better."[24]

Page also occupied a different position down South. Having become an important New York magazine editor, he carried more weight among the people whom he had left. In North Carolina, he was a local man who had beaten the Yankees at their own game and could, therefore, tell his people how they stacked up against the Yankees. Many Tar Heels might still dislike the author of the mummy letter, but henceforth they had a harder time discounting him. A clear sign of Page's changed status came less than a year after he assumed the editorship of the *Forum*. On 20 October 1891 he appeared as the principal speaker at Winston's inauguration as president of the University of North Carolina. Assessing the state and the university from the perspective of "changes even between my visits here," Page renewed previous denunciations of political and religious bondage to the past. "Renounce forever servitude to ecclesiasticism and partyism," he admonished the university, "and set out to be the ruling and shaping force among the energies that stir the people and are making of our old fields a new earth, of our long slumbering land a resounding workshop." The university must exert "dominating influence" over North Carolina's burgeoning industry, because without culture "men get punier as they grow richer."[25]

The speech at Winston's inauguration set a pattern that lasted for the next twenty-two years. Between 1891 and 1913, Page made at least two or three trips a year to the South. Some were to visit family and attend to business, as he had done annually since leaving Raleigh. But after he became editor of the *Forum*, he spent more time with public commentary and reform activities. He enjoyed a growing demand as a speaker, particularly at first in North Carolina and Virginia, at college commencements and special events connected with education. In his speeches, Page continued to view the South from the standpoint of a native son resident in the North and conversant with Yankee opinion.

One northern opinion in particular that Page agreed with and took pains to relay to southerners in the early 1890s was condemnation of the rising agrarian protest that culminated in formation of the Populist party. To Page, the farmers' concerns were not the most important issues facing the country. He opened the April and November 1894 issues of the *Forum* with two articles that he wrote but signed with the pseudonym "An Independent." In "Mr. Cleveland's—Failure?" he affirmed that lowering the tariff remained the paramount requirement for the American economy, and he blamed his one-time hero in the White House for having failed to carry out his electoral mandate to end Republican protectionism. Page likewise perceived dire threats to the country from unscrupulous political bosses, especially Senator David B. Hill of New York. In the "Political Career and Character of David B. Hill," Page reviewed the boss's sordid dealings and warned Democrats against the blandishments of such a demagogue, particularly because he had besmirched the party's commitment to a lower tariff. "The tariff-reform tide was the last tide in national politics," Page avowed. "The next will be a tide of municipal reform." Compared with those concerns, the issues of agrarian protest appeared minor and diversionary. Privately, Page, who had become a "gold Democrat," deplored southerners' attraction toward monetary inflation through the unlimited coinage of silver. A network of North Carolina businessmen, journalists, and lawyers kept Page posted on the growing free-silver sentiment, and the editor knew that he was drifting apart from many of his friends and relatives.[26]

Neither southern concerns nor anything else long diverted Page's attention from the *Forum*. Different aspects of the magazine constantly engaged him. Finding the right people for the *Forum*'s staff occupied his attention during most of the four years of his editorship. Page fired Bostwick, Metcalf's mild-mannered assistant, at the end of 1891. After trying another editorial assistant, who was more energetic but succumbed to tuberculosis, Page concentrated instead on divesting himself of the business management, which Presbrey took over during 1894, and brought in another rising advertising man, Robert Frothingham. More than administrative problems, the shape and character of his product weighed on the editor's mind. Page often uttered standard and not-too-serious complaints about the *Forum*'s low earnings and lack of distinguished literary material. But his most insistent complaint concerned the ways in which he believed that the magazine failed to shape public opinion. "Every periodical that you can think of has some limitation to its public service," he wrote in a lengthy, confidential memorandum in May 1894. Periodicals in America, he asserted, "but half serve the public." Magazines' principal shortcomings were "the limitation of ownership." That was the nub of Page's predicament—he did not own the *Forum*.[27]

In December 1893, as soon as the success of the price reduction could be seen, the editor tried to borrow fifty thousand dollars from Andrew Carnegie, in order to buy and reshape the magazine. "Of this $50,000," Page explained, "$25,000 would go into *The Forum*'s treasury as a reserve fund—working capital to enable me to carry out from time to time large and important investigations—in short to make *The Forum* the foremost Review in the world." When Carnegie turned down his request, Page next tried to gain control by selling a new issue of preferred stock to two different sets of acquaintances. One group consisted of a few wealthy men, principally lawyers and financiers, whose large purchases were to go toward securing a voting majority of stock. The other group contributed less money and served a different purpose. On 31 January 1894 Page traveled to Baltimore, where he discussed his plans for the *Forum* with Woodrow Wilson, Herbert Baxter Adams, and Henry Carter Adams. Besides getting financial control of the magazine, he wanted to nullify "the purely commercial interest in it by the new men of my own choosing." His second group of stockholders were men like Wilson and the two Adamses—bright, rising academic stars in such fields as history, political science, and economics. Page intended to use their financial stake in the *Forum* "as a sort of golden chain to bind a group of exceptional men to this institution— . . . who will help me take the thought of the country in hand and shape and mould it in ways that make for progress."[28]

This second group of stockholders formed the linchpin of Page's design for the *Forum*. Through them he was seeking to yoke together the intellectual revolution led by the universities and the magazine revolution that he aspired to lead. "The stuff to make a great periodical of is yet lacking," Page wrote in May 1894; "and this stuff is a prodigality of ideas—such as no one man has or can have." A great periodical required more than "good will and casual suggestions of fertile men; it requires, to a degree, the identification of their personalities with it." Page envisioned a magazine that would resemble a university, transcending "the usual limitations of ownership and editorship" and carried on "by the cooperation of many minds. Along the way I am working I verily believe there is a revolution in periodical literature."[29]

Making the *Forum* stockholders resemble a university faculty, with intellectual luminaries actually part of the magazine, was an original and exciting idea. Distinguished university professors could have helped to tap the huge market for self-improvement and adult education, while academic experts on public affairs could have constituted a board of consultants for investigatory journalism. Moreover, Page contemplated other changes to broaden the *Forum*'s appeal. In August 1894, he regretted that the magazine carried no fiction, which was proving to be the biggest draw for new-style periodicals. In April and November 1894 Page published his two "Independent" articles on the current political situation. Those articles prefigured use of the magazine as a personal platform. Editorializing later contributed to Page's achievement with the *Atlantic* and formed one of his most successful techniques with *World's Work*. Clearly Page was toying with a number of departures. If he had brought off any of the moves that he had in mind, he might have become a still more significant figure in the magazine revolution.

But Page's dreams went awry. Everything depended upon financial control of the *Forum*, and that control Isaac Rice refused to relinquish. In March 1895, a struggle for possession of the magazine began when Rice and Bijur decided to reassert their control. After prolonged but usually polite contention over voting rights for stock, the struggle ended on a day in June 1895 when Rice telephoned to inform Frothingham, the *Forum*'s advertising manager, that he was now editor. Frothingham did not take the offer seriously, but when he went into Page's office, the editor smiled, rose from his desk, and made a low bow. "My dear Frothingham," he replied, "I welcome you to the editorial chair. There may be more to this appointment than you realize. I hope you will have more pleasure in it than I have had." Page put on his hat and coat and walked out.[30]

Losing the *Forum* did not shatter Page, but the experience did shake him. Page admitted that he felt physically run-down, and his defeat left deeper scars than had the abandonment of the *State Chronicle* ten years before. Occurring so soon after his misfortune with the *Manufacturers Record*, the loss of the *Forum* hurt his self-confidence. Worse, he lost the magazine just when he seemed on the verge of such exciting departures. The break left him temporarily at loose ends and threw him back into his once-familiar quandary of what path to follow. The situation was easier than in the past. Although he still had to work for a living, he had accumulated some property and jobs came seeking him. Yet his old dilemma persisted. As Page told one inquirer about his plans early in July 1895, "I am divided in mind which road to take: a quiet way that leads through pleasant fields that please me but leads to little profit, or a rougher way where I may make more money and with greater ease educate my children."[31]

Luckily for his immediate peace of mind, Page did not have to dwell on his dilemma for long. The inquirer to whom he responded was Horace Elisha Scudder, the editor of the *Atlantic Monthly*. A week after making his inquiry, Scudder again wrote to Page, this time asking him to come to Boston for an interview. The unhorsed editor made the overnight journey northward on 15 July and spent the following day conferring with Scudder and meeting the partners of Houghton, Mifflin & Company, the distinguished publishing house that owned the *Atlantic*. On 2 August Scudder came to New York to spend the entire day with Page. When the two men parted at the corner of Broadway and Seventeenth Street, Scudder handed Page a letter that contained an offer of a position. Page was to be Scudder's assistant on the *Atlantic* and in the book-editorial division of Houghton, Mifflin; he was to get the same five-thousand-dollar salary that he had received on the *Forum*. Scudder recorded in his diary that Page "said his answer would be yes, but that he wished to sleep over it and would write on the morrow." He pondered the offer a little longer before accepting on 7 August 1895, eight days before his fortieth birthday. Page was joining the most respected magazine in the United States and a major book publisher. Both were pillars of the New England literary establishment. The former southerner's star still seemed to be rising.[32]

CHAPTER 5

The Seat of Culture

Houghton, Mifflin & Company and *The Atlantic Monthly* shared a former mansion at 4 Park Street in Boston, just half a block down Beacon Hill from the gold-domed State House. The location of their offices symbolized the eminence enjoyed by the firm and the journal. Houghton, Mifflin, often dubbed "the House," was the foremost outlet for New England writers. The firm's founder and patriarch, Henry Oscar Houghton, died at the age of seventy-two on 25 August 1895, just two weeks before Walter Hines Page started to work for the company. Houghton's successor as chief executive officer was the other name partner, George Harrison Mifflin, who had previously served as head of the company's imposing printing establishment on the banks of the Charles River, the Riverside Press. The founder's son, Henry Oscar Houghton, Jr., in turn assumed the management of the press.

The *Atlantic* enjoyed even greater renown. Started in 1857 with James Russell Lowell as the first editor, the magazine had swiftly emerged as the most respected organ of American opinion and writing. Page himself had written in 1880 in the *St. Joseph Gazette* that the *Atlantic* occupied "a place peculiarly its own" among periodicals. "It is the exponent of the *culture* of America." The editorial chair of the *Atlantic* had gained special distinction in the world of magazines. Only five men had held the editorship during the thirty-eight years before Page joined the staff. Besides Lowell and the current incumbent, Scudder, the editors had included James T. Fields, Houghton's predecessor as the leading New England book publisher, and two other outstanding men of letters, the novelist and critic William Dean Howells and the poet and short-story writer Thomas Bailey Aldrich. In short, the publishing company and the magazine formed a literary coalition that anyone with Page's tastes and aspirations would have felt honored to join.[1]

The newcomer entered the service of Houghton, Mifflin and the *Atlantic* with rank, salary, and responsibilities befitting a former New York magazine editor. Page became Scudder's right-hand man in editing both books and the *Atlantic*. "What you want, as I understand it," he wrote to Scudder during their negotiations in July 1895, "is editorial assistance, not routine assistance merely, but assistance from someone who also has a broad outlook on contemporaneous life, who knows a piece of literature when he sees it in the rough, and who may sometimes know where to look for a piece of literature before anybody else has found it." Page believed that he could provide that kind of assistance. But, he warned, if he worked out he intended to become "one of the real forces of the institution." Further, he demanded "a certain freedom" from routine duties so that he could follow his editorial philosophy of extending "my acquaintance among men who are bringing things to pass." Page was again serving notice that he would not be just a hired hand. He also came at a higher salary than the firm was accustomed to paying.[2]

From the moment he walked into the Houghton, Mifflin offices, Page stood out. His booming voice, hearty laugh, bustling manner, and ever-present cigar jarred the sedate atmosphere of the publishing house. The prevailing tone still reflected the ways of the recently departed founder, Houghton, who had risen slowly in publishing circles through unswerving devotion to good books and conservative business practices. His death had opened the way for important changes in "the House," but those changes had barely begun when Page arrived. The company's top officers gathered every Tuesday, as they had under Houghton's regime, in a meeting called "the Powwow."

Page attended his first Powwow on 10 September 1895. The newcomer, Scudder noted in his diary, "when called on made some sagacious remarks. It is pleasant to see the cordiality with which he is received." Five other men comprised the group that Page joined. Mifflin and "Harry" Houghton were expansive men, but the other three members resembled the firm's modest, self-effacing founder, who had hired them all. Devotion to literature distinguished Scudder above anything else. He was also a devout Episcopalian, and he often mixed his religious fervor with his ideals of literary service. In 1890, upon becoming editor of the *Atlantic*, Scudder had confided in his diary, "My heart beats quicker at the thought of serving God in this cause of high, pure literature." The other two members of the Powwow maintained the company's fastidious business practices. Stewardship over finances belonged to the treasurer, J. Murray Kay, a Scot who lived up to the tightfisted role expected from his background. The final member of the Powwow was Francis Jackson Garrison, administrative head of the book-publishing division, who could state from memory precisely how much money every book published by Houghton, Mifflin had earned or lost.

Page's southern background accentuated the separation from his new employers and associates. Except for Kay, the rest of the company's officers were all Boston-born. Mifflin came from a wealthy, socially prominent family and was a graduate of Harvard, where he had belonged to the Porcellian Club. Scudder had been a classmate of Henry Adams at the Boston Latin School. "Frank" Garrison was another son of William Lloyd Garrison, who likewise maintained the family heritage of supporting international peace and equal rights for blacks and women. Page seems to have capitalized on his differences. One staff member recalled that "in the rough give and take of daily life and office routine, he employed a rough and ready vernacular which sometimes had a disturbing effect on the tranquil precinct of 4 Park Street." Page emphasized his sectional background almost to the point of becoming a professional southerner. As in New York, he frequently larded his conversation with North Carolina anecdotes, many of which he called "nigger stories." Page delighted in twitting Garrison by using the word "nigger." One of the editor's acquaintances recalled that the first time Page uttered the word in the Houghton, Mifflin offices Garrison pointed to a portrait of his father on the wall and enjoined, "Mr. Page, we have never used that word in this office." Page shot back, "Well, we do now."[3]

Nearly everything about his encounter with "the House" made Page believe that he was the savior of the *Atlantic*, just as he had pictured himself with the *Forum*. He did not stand alone in that belief. A number of close observers later testified that Page jerked the magazine out of its torpor and made it livelier, timelier, and more profitable. MacGregor Jenkins, who worked as business manager of the *Atlantic* from 1890 to 1928, recalled, "The effect of his presence was felt immediately, . . . and I personally found myself associated with an editor who recognized the existence of a business department, and who became at once a source of inspiration to us all." Bliss Perry, Page's successor as editor, afterward described his predecessor as "a far better journalist than I," who shunned scholarly and critical articles as "sinkers" for the magazine. Perry's successor, Ellery Sedgwick, admired Page for laying "his revolutionary and invigorating hands" on the *Atlantic*, with the result that "the old magazine jumped forward a full century." The finest tribute came from Mifflin, who told Page in 1901, "We always think of you as having ploughed the way for a good and permanent future for the old magazine."[4]

In reality, the situation was more complicated. Behind the firm's old-fashioned exterior, changes had begun before Page's arrival. In fact, he owed his appointment to the convergence of several currents of dissatisfaction. The longest-standing complaint and the one that immediately occasioned the offer to Page stemmed from Scudder's heavy work load as editor of the *Atlantic*, chief book editor, and scout for new writers for both the magazine and the book department. Scudder had long wanted a competent assistant to handle routine work on the magazine and search out fresh talent. "Is there not some way by which I can be editor, strictly speaking?" he had implored Houghton in September 1894.[5]

Other factors entered into providing Scudder with such an

experienced, well-known, and high-priced assistant as Page. Two men had grown convinced that the *Atlantic* and Houghton, Mifflin needed new blood and fresh departures. One was Scudder himself. Many people judged the short, stocky, bearded, bald-headed man dull and stodgy and blamed him for the troubles of the *Atlantic*. "Why is Horace Scudder greater than Moses?" went one pun in the literary drawing rooms of Boston. "Moses dried up the Red Sea once only; Scudder dries up the Atlantic monthly." Actually, Scudder's manner belied aggressive policies of seeking out bright new writers and soliciting contributions on the timeliest topics. In both subject matter and contributors, Scudder's *Atlantic* had overlapped greatly during the early 1890s with Page's *Forum*. Yet Scudder's performance with the *Atlantic* was financially disappointing. The magazine showed a small profit at the end of 1892, but the depression that began the following year helped to create losses that averaged around ten thousand dollars annually over the next several years. By July 1895, Scudder contemplated a bold step. On his own initiative, he made the first contact with Page, "with the secret hope that he might be ready for a new place and we find him the man we want."[6]

If matters had remained solely in Scudder's hands, Page probably would not have received the offer. When Page and Scudder met for the first time on 16 July 1895, the *Atlantic* editor developed misgivings. "My fear would be that he would be impulsive, and restless, and perhaps bolt suddenly on some trivial matter," Scudder wrote in his diary, "or that he would find it hard to work in harness after his independent captaincy." The dying Houghton also disliked bringing in an outsider. After an interview during Page's visit to Boston, he told Scudder that he mistrusted "people who come in through the cabin window." But Houghton knew that his active career had ended, and he declined to try to sway the other members of the Powwow.[7]

Fortunately for Page, the company's new head, George Mifflin, also wanted to shake up the organization. Mifflin's succession inaugurated a new style of leadership. Houghton and Mifflin had little in common beyond devotion to their "House" and appreciation of sound business practices. The fifty-year-old Mifflin resembled Page in his large frame, infectious enthusiasm, and fondness for bold ventures. "He is delightfully headlong," Scudder wrote about Mifflin in his diary after one Powwow in April 1896, "but I sometimes sigh for the steady, strong lead of Mr. Houghton, even though he sometimes seemed to be agin [*sic*] all progress." For the previous twenty-five years, Mifflin had steadfastly deferred to Houghton and insisted on learning the business by working up through the ranks. But by 1895, when he assumed command, he was ready to run things his own way.[8]

Besides personal differences, two other factors prompted the new chief to depart from the founder's practices. One was a divergence in publishing philosophy. Success and eminence had never fully weaned Houghton, a self-made Vermonter, from viewing himself primarily as a printer and rather humbly deferring to men of letters in matters of taste and critical judgment. Mifflin, by contrast, regarded himself as a book publisher. To him that meant being both a businessman and a member of a jealously competitive fraternity. Later, Bliss Perry and Ellery Sedgwick each accused Mifflin of not caring about the literary merit of what he published. Both of them admitted, however, that the publisher delighted in beautifully produced books as aesthetic objects and prided himself on the prestige of his stable of authors. Mifflin's deepest concern lay with his company's standing in the publishing world. The tests of success in that world consisted of keeping established authors on the list, discovering and attracting fresh talent, and, above all, making profits.

Houghton, Mifflin's recent shortcomings suggested the need for new departures. For several years, the Boston firm had been slipping. It lost several major writers during the 1890s. Bigger advances and better royalties from New York publishers tempted away such stars as Howells, Gilbert Parker, and Paul Leicester Ford. Nor did "the House" fare well in uncovering promising newcomers. Most fledgling luminaries of the decade, including Stephen Crane, Harold Frederic, and Frank Norris, first published under New York imprints. Worst of all, the company's profits sagged, reflecting an unimpressive showing by the book department. Such poor profits made the *Atlantic*'s deficits even more irksome. Mifflin hoped that Page would supply the contacts and talents necessary to correct some of these deficiencies. Responsibility for bringing Page really belonged to Mifflin, who had ended all wavering by proposing that he be hired at the five-thousand-dollar salary. When Page accepted the job, Mifflin exulted, "In your own field, we shall look to you for substantial help, and I am full of high hope for the future."[9]

Curiously, the newcomer got off to a slow start. During his first months at the new job, Page's performance suffered from both poor health and outside pressures. Throughout the latter part of 1895, he wrestled with problems left over from disposition of his interests in the *Forum* and the *Manufacturers Record*. In November 1895 he missed several days' work because of an illness, and in February 1896 he suffered an attack of rheumatism that kept him away from the office for two days. Though not in themselves serious, those complaints marked the beginning of health problems that dogged him for many years.

Page also had to deal with an unclear, narrow definition of his responsibilities. Although he was supposed to assist Scudder on both books and the *Atlantic*, it was not until the middle of October 1895, possibly under prodding from Mifflin, that Scudder granted Page authority to select book manuscripts for publication, and Scudder still had to countersign Page's decisions. Scudder's idea of Page's pulling what he called a "laboring oar" on the *Atlantic* evidently consisted of his assistant's handling the administrative work, "leaving to me my more distinct function of editing." Once Page started showing his expected energy, he collided with those implicit limitations. In November 1895 he started commissioning articles for the *Atlantic*. "We do not merely want articles for the *Atlantic*," he explained to a prospective contributor; "we wish to accomplish a great result, and articles for the *Atlantic* are merely the instruments for that purpose." At the same time, he proposed a series of books by distinguished public figures on current problems.[10]

Page's growing initiative coincided with Mifflin's mounting dissatisfaction with the *Atlantic*. Matters came to a head in April

1896. The magazine's continuing deficits at first impelled Mifflin to criticize the situation to Scudder on 14 April. A week later, Page independently voiced his discontent to Scudder and suggested a number of changes. "He became much stirred," wrote Scudder in his diary, "and pronounced the weakness of the Atlantic to be a lack of moral earnestness, and I suspect that though he deprecates such a thing he would regard the Forum as nearer the mark than The Atlantic." Then on 25 April Page talked with Mifflin about the *Atlantic*'s small circulation and deficits. "Page took fire at this and came to me consumed with zeal for bringing up circulation," Scudder recorded on 27 April. The editor responded with a self-sacrificing move. He decided to "take the logical step and put the fortunes of the magazine largely, indeed so far as the shaping goes quite unreservedly into his hands." For the next two days, the pair debated the proposition, with Page protesting that he had never wanted to take over the *Atlantic*. Scudder stood his ground, and Page eventually "made up his mind to obey the behest and it only remains for us to see Mifflin."[11]

This outwardly smooth change of command marked strained behavior by both men. Page again recoiled from any notion of promoting himself at another person's expense, although his protestations about not wanting the editorship are hard to believe. Scudder's self-sacrifice likewise contained discordant notes. He clung to the title of editor for another two years, constantly eyeing Page for lapses in literary judgment. He worried that "Page with all his respect for literature and his perception of its artistic side nevertheless somewhat unconsciously is disposed to look upon it chiefly for what it accomplishes and will see in the magazine an instrument rather than a vehicle."[12]

That assessment of Page formed the basis for a gentle tug-of-war over the *Atlantic*, which persisted as long as Scudder retained the editorial title. In his diary Scudder frequently mentioned having "a long talk with Page" about the *Atlantic*. He also fretted about Page's growing "too indifferent to the statics of literature" and the *Atlantic*'s "being too much Forumized." Another confrontation occurred at the end of March 1897, when Mifflin again criticized the magazine's poor circulation. Mifflin hinted to Scudder "that I did not give Page his head sufficiently." The editor rejoined, "I am heartily in favor of giving Page all the swing he wants," so long as Scudder could exercise his own influence "as a conservative element."[13]

Scudder went abroad during the summer of 1897 to begin a long-planned year's leave of absence. At first, from London, Paris, Rome, Venice, and Florence the editor fired off lengthy letters of advice and criticism. But absence promoted detachment, and in January 1898 he hinted that he might retire from the editorship. His letters during the second half of his year abroad grew less frequent and less meddlesome. And promptly upon returning to America the following July, Scudder renounced the title of editor, while continuing as head of Houghton, Mifflin's book department. Even then, he confided in his diary, "I cannot give up the charge without real regret. I had an ideal of the magazine which I see is not the same as Page's."[14]

The prolonged but genteel hassle over the conduct of the *Atlantic* did not bother Page greatly at the time. Little overt friction occurred. Page gratified Scudder with his receptivity to advice and correction. Whenever he offered criticisms, Scudder noted in August 1896, Page bowed to them with "openness and reasonableness and we are able to discuss everything with perfect good nature." Such behavior was characteristic of Page, for throughout his life he took criticism willingly and he never liked conflict in personal relations. Scudder's suzerainty seems to have formed a drag on Page's forward motion, rather than a roadblock to any paths he wished to follow. Insofar as any one person was master of the *Atlantic* after May 1896, it was Page. Only later did the lack of real independence have an effect.[15]

Years afterward, Ellery Sedgwick recalled that Page's accession had "taken on the dignity of a legend." His first action supposedly consisted of replacing his rolltop desk with a big, flat table, which soon became littered with accumulations of books, papers, clippings, ashes, and cigar butts. As earlier on the *State Chronicle* and the *Forum*, Page found fresh working space by moving his chair around the table, leaving his previous clutter behind. Timeliness became the *Atlantic*'s lodestar. To that end Page tried, without success, to cut production time to three weeks. He brought his best material out as quickly as possible. Sedgwick remembered that he often exclaimed, "Never save a feature. Always work for the next number, forget all the others." In September 1896, Page responded to John Jay Chapman, "If I were a 'sensational editor,' you write, I am! . . . Now there is not a day in the calendar when I would not close my weary desk here and go to New York, or to San Francisco, or to Zanziber [sic]— anywhere—to get a first-hand, clear-cut sensational thing." The *Atlantic* was, he added, "stupid and merely traditional and dull," and he meant to make "an *Atlantic* so different and so much better that men would *see* what I mean."[16]

Page's plans for contributions proceeded mainly along two lines. The first was strengthening the *Atlantic*'s treatment of political, social, and economic questions. Page asserted to the historian Frederick Jackson Turner that "a statement of purpose of the Atlantic" might be to take "hold on the bases of our interesting civilization and . . . work towards an interpretation of the larger tendencies that are shaping us." He enlisted Turner to write a paper on the possible disappearance of regional peculiarities. He likewise induced E. L. Godkin to present his views on the progress of democracy throughout the world. Page's second line of planned articles constituted what he termed "an effort to bring the Atlantic a little in line with contemporary, and to a certain extent, with American literary interests." In proposing an article to be entitled "The Present Tendencies in Literary Production," he wanted the piece to deal with the lack of poetry, increase in historical writing, and poverty of criticism. He also tried to persuade several leading writers, including Howells, Aldrich, and Joel Chandler Harris, to contribute to a series of short personal statements on literary topics. As on the *Forum*, Page poured out suggestions to prospective authors, often practically telling them what and how to write.[17]

Page confirmed Scudder's fears that the *Atlantic* would become more journalistic and less literary. But the shift stemmed only in part from Page's predilections. Events themselves since

1890 had made public concerns more pressing to American magazine readers. On the *Atlantic* increasing attention to political subjects had already begun under Scudder. Page's contribution lay in accelerating the change of focus.

The election of 1896 presented a special opportunity to address the magazine to questions of national importance. In July the farm-based advocates of free coinage of silver money carried the Democratic convention and nominated William Jennings Bryan for president. Page hurriedly asked Turner to switch his projected article to an examination of the situation that had allowed forces of agrarian discontent to capture one of the major political parties. Writing against a deadline, the historian produced "The Problem of the West," which Page placed as the lead article in the September issue. In October the magazine contained an anonymous piece, "The Political Menace of the Discontented," that may have come from Postmaster General William L. Wilson, an anti-Bryan Democrat. The next month the *Atlantic* published "Causes of Agricultural Discontent," by the economist Professor J. Laurence Laughlin of the University of Chicago.

Nor did the passing of the 1896 election divert the *Atlantic* from public issues. During the next year, the magazine featured Godkin's articles on democracy, two pieces on the South by the literary historian William Peterfield Trent, three essays on various topics by Woodrow Wilson, and a contribution on the New York police department by Theodore Roosevelt. As Page settled into running the *Atlantic*, a variation emerged on the trio of concerns that had dominated the *Forum*. Education and urban life remained as prominent as before, but attention to professions gave way to treatment of rural and small-town life. Page's aim in those articles was, as he told William Allen White, "to secure fresh, first-hand social studies of the life of people in different sections of the country—studies that contain at once the observation of a sociological student and the work of an artist." From White he requested "a composite photograph of several interesting Kansas towns."[18]

The high point in the *Atlantic*'s attention to public affairs came during 1898, when the subjects of war and diplomacy dominated the magazine. Foreign policy did not represent a novel interest for either Page or the *Atlantic*. During the first half of the 1890s he and Scudder had independently warmed to rising sentiments of American nationalism. Tremendous industrial and agricultural growth had transformed the United States into a potential world power. Simultaneously, the interest of intellectuals in overseas expansion and periodic outbursts of popular jingoism had betrayed a widespread yearning to look abroad for both national adventure and solutions to problems at home. Page had earlier published articles in the *Forum* by Lodge and Alfred Thayer Mahan on naval power and expansion. The *Atlantic* had carried a two-part essay by Mahan in 1893. By the time Page moved to Boston, he had made foreign policy one of his major journalistic interests. During 1896 and 1897, he tried to solicit articles on Anglo-American relations and international arbitration, and he succeeded in getting former secretary of state Richard Olney to write "The International Isolation of the United States." Olney's essay came out in the May 1898 issue of the *Atlantic*, on the eve of the outbreak of the Spanish-American War.

Mobilizing the *Atlantic* for the war, Page evidently shocked some proper Bostonians with the June 1898 issue. A picture of the Stars and Stripes appeared on the cover, above the title. Lowell had done the same thing in 1861 at the time of the firing on Fort Sumter, and Page was copying the Civil War precedent. He further imitated Lowell by opening the issue with a rousing editorial in support of the government's action. But the imitations masked a departure from tradition. To the consternation of many in Boston, especially some of his associates on Park Street and some of the *Atlantic*'s most prominent contributors, Page jubilantly endorsed not only the war with Spain but also the prospect of American colonial expansion. Page filled the magazine with articles on the war and international problems. One of his coups was to elicit an essay from the leading British commentator on the United States, James Bryce, entitled "The Essential Unity of Britain and America." Other articles treated Anglo-American cooperation, naval strategy, conditions in Spain, and problems of colonial administration. The October issue featured a patriotic poem "The Old Glory," by James Whitcomb Riley. By November 1898 Page began to fear that he had overplayed the international theme. "We hardly dare go on with war papers," he informed one potential contributor; " . . . for I feel pretty sure that those magazine editors who are going to keep up bellicose literature will weary their readers."[19]

Page's literary thrust resembled his search for timely articles on public issues. In some cases, he merely wanted to print popular authors in order to boost circulation. For example, although he disliked *The Red Badge of Courage* as "a queer sort of impressionistic work," he tried to solicit stories from Stephen Crane. Page likewise dealt roughly with dullness in both authors and subjects. Having previously declined an essay by Henry James for the *Forum*, he rejected one of that author's ponderous stories for the *Atlantic*. Even Howells had a contribution returned, though gently. Page reacted warily to literary criticism, most of which struck him as lifeless and destructive. "It is never sympathetic," he asserted to a well-known critic, "and I am constantly tempted to try my own hand at an essay to show that the present dearth of American letters is due to the abnormal development of our smart critical faculty, and our lack of sympathy alike with writers and with people in the mass." Criticism continued to occupy a prominent place in the magazine, but the emphasis shifted to human-interest stories about famous authors and optimistic assessments of literary possibilities. Most important, Page sought fresh fiction for the *Atlantic* and Houghton, Mifflin. His own background and early interests gave him particular concern for discovering new southern writers. He befriended and cultivated the young Virginia novelist Ellen Glasgow; the New Orleans poet Albert Phelps; the black short-story writer Charles W. Chesnutt, who originally came from North Carolina; and the Alabama writer, Mary Johnston, whose novel, *To Have and to Hold*, was serialized in the *Atlantic*.[20]

Page's conduct with the *Atlantic* resembled his earlier career with the *Forum*. In each case, he succeeded a quiet, stocky, baldheaded New England Yankee about fifteen years older than himself. Each of his predecessors had, by turns, led his periodical to the verge of increased circulation and profits, only to have Page reap triumphs by continuing their policies. Yet, as with the *Forum*, the newcomer's actions did not bear fruit quickly. Circulation and advertising revenues evidently rose somewhat after Page took over. A comparison of November advertising figures showed $1,059 for 1896, $1,361 for 1897, and $2,441 for 1898. But those improvements did not keep pace with rising expenses. Net losses for the *Atlantic* mounted from $13,638.70 for April 1896 to April 1897, to $16,455.04 for the same period in 1897–98. Only after Page waved the flag during the Spanish-American War did the magazine make impressive gains. For April 1898 to April 1899, the loss fell to $9,490.91 and still further to $6,895.59 for the following twelve months. Circulation in 1898 and 1899 seems to have grown to seventeen or eighteen thousand, up from around ten thousand in 1895; total advertising revenues for 1899 amounted to $20,750. At last Mifflin found cause for satisfaction with the magazine. Early in 1900, he told one of the Houghtons, "It looks as if for the year 1899 we should successfully learn the Atlantic trick." By then, Page had left the *Atlantic*. For once in his magazine career, he suffered his predecessors' fate of having others reap where he had sown.[21]

Page did well with the *Atlantic* for largely the same reasons that he had boosted the *Forum*. Once again he displayed sensitivity to the interests of a readership composed largely of people like himself. He was trying to reach the same audience that he had sought for the *Forum*—that rising, diffuse, middle-class elite. His mixture of attention to pressing political and social issues and stress on education and urban conditions drew more of those readers to the *Atlantic*. Diminished attention to the professions reflected a partial shift of focus. Page seems to have viewed his new audience as more generally national than precisely metropolitan-oriented, and making the *Atlantic* a national magazine was his overriding concern. In March 1897 he told one southern friend, "I wish to get the magazine out of the New England rut." Page viewed himself as an invader from the great American hinterland who was breathing new life into effete Boston institutions. Writing to the naturalist John Burroughs about the divorce between literature and life, Page commented, "You have felt it, seen it, protested against it, gone to Whitman for relief from it, and felt the emptiness of the 'angel-cake' schools and methods."[22]

The reference to Whitman disclosed that Page was trying to fit a well-established image of a cultural folk hero. Since the early years of the nineteenth century, advocates of American intellectual independence had celebrated figures who would act like barbarian scourges in uprooting decadent, derivative standards and draw strength from native soil like homegrown versions of Antaeus. Whitman with his "barbaric yawp," Mark Twain, and many others had essayed to play such roles, with varying degrees of sobriety and humor. Those ideas were hardly new to the *Atlantic*. During the 1870s Howells had combated New England exclusiveness and East Coast gentility by seeking out writers from other parts of the country and encouraging realistic, homely fiction like his own. Under Aldrich, the magazine had reverted somewhat to serving a New England coterie, but Scudder had resumed Howells's efforts. Page played a less pioneering role on the *Atlantic* than he thought, but his mistake was understandable. The big, hearty Tar Heel relished picturing himself as an editorial Davy Crockett, and his achievements excused some of his fantasy.

Page had reasons to feel pleased with life in Boston. His family seemed to enjoy living there more than they had in New York. They rented successively two large frame houses off Brattle Street in Cambridge, where their neighbors included several Harvard faculty members and two eminent Houghton, Mifflin authors, John Fiske and Thomas Wentworth Higginson. The three-mile journey by streetcar to and from Park Street was more pleasant and less time consuming than the hour's train ride each way from New Rochelle to New York City. When the weather permitted, Page often walked home from work, chatting along the way with someone from the office, usually Scudder or MacGregor Jenkins, the *Atlantic*'s business manager. His acquaintances in Boston and Cambridge were more academic and literary than in New York, but such new friends as Higginson, W. R.

Thayer, the Harvard psychologist Hugo Munsterberg, and the historian James Ford Rhodes had keener wits and more stimulating thoughts than the newspapermen, lawyers, and businessmen of his former circle.

Shorter distances around Boston permitted the Page family to spend more time together. The two older boys, Ralph and Arthur, went away for part of the time to Lawrenceville School in New Jersey. Their youngest son Frank and their daughter Katharine attended classes at a private school in Cambridge. Alice and the children still spent summers away from their town home, but instead of going to North Carolina, they now went to Massachusetts's North Shore or the mountains of New Hampshire, where Page could join them on weekends. In Cambridge during the year Page and his wife frequently went out as a couple. They joined the Query Club, an organization of husbands and wives as well as single people, which met once or twice a month to read and discuss papers. Dinner parties also featured serious discussions. Years later Rhodes remembered a debate across the table about the Spanish-American War, with Page and himself on one side and Edward Everett Hale on the other. Contrary to their expectations of Yankee reserve, the southerner and his wife fitted in well among the intellectual lions and lionesses of Cambridge. "In some way I used to get an intellectual impetus from seeing you," Rhodes told Page after he had moved away. "You are such a confident and energetic literary fellow."[23]

Regaining some of his earlier literary vocation gratified Page, although he evidently did not do much writing of his own during his years in Boston. Page's renewed literary role stemmed from his positions with the *Atlantic* and Houghton, Mifflin. Besides seeking out and presenting fiction in the magazine, he had responsibilities in book publishing, a new field for him. The original division of labor with Scudder assigned Page the task of overseeing the editorial side of Houghton, Mifflin's book department. After taking over the *Atlantic* in May 1896, Page spent less time with book editing, but he continued to read manuscripts and seek out authors for books. While Scudder was abroad from August 1897 to July 1898, Page again supervised the editorial work on books.

The *Atlantic* may have outshone other parts of "the House" in cultural prestige, but the book division also enjoyed literary luster. More important, the book division made money. For the year April 1896 to April 1897, the profits on book sales accounted for $394,507.25 out of total company profits of $534,123.28. For the same period in 1897–98, book profits comprised $431,-214.17 out of $573,473.93. Moreover, the book department's work load was growing. Houghton, Mifflin usually limited acceptance of manuscripts to less than 50 a year in the late 1890s, yet the number of manuscripts submitted rose from 510 in 1895 to 622 in 1898.[24]

Page took to book publishing at once. At the beginning of 1896, he proposed the book series on major political, social, and economic problems by leading public figures. He also called on the historian John Fiske to discuss plans for future work, for historical writing remained one of Page's principal book-publishing interests. He cultivated Turner and John Bach McMaster, sharing ideas with them for a series of brief, popular histories of different periods of the American past. Timely treatment of public problems and literary values in books likewise concerned him. In February 1896 he counseled a prospective author in his series on public questions, "A book ought to have a literary quality—ought to be a work of art—as well as a record of facts." A book must exist "in a certain sense apart from the facts that it conveys." It was "not merely so much printed matter bound between covers, but an animate, artistic thing, having a real reason for existence."[25]

Page occupied himself more with fiction as a book publisher than as a magazine editor. He examined manuscripts sent to Houghton, Mifflin and scouted for promising novelists and short-story writers. One manuscript that he read in 1897 produced a spectacular boner. A massive, clumsily written tale about a small-town banker and his homey philosophies, entitled "David Harum," came to Park Street from an unknown author named Edward N. Westcott. The first reader was Susan Francis, a long-time employee of the firm, who rendered a mixed verdict on "David Harum." She found enough merit in the story to call it "a rough diamond," but she disliked its coarse language and vulgar subject matter. As second reader, Page threw his weight against publication, mostly because of the manuscript's excessive length. Mifflin then initialed their report and the manuscript was returned to the author. Westcott subsequently submitted the novel to D. Appleton & Company, a New York firm, which published the book after making cuts and revisions. *David Harum* became the leading best-seller in the United States in 1898 and amassed total sales of more than four hundred thousand copies over the next three years. Mifflin afterward chided Page several times by sticking his head through the door of the editor's office and asking, "Refused any David Harums today?"[26]

A year later Page redeemed himself as a picker of potential best-sellers. During the summer of 1898 an associate came into his office with a manuscript of a novel. "I think this is a good story," he told the editor, "a capital story." Page asked, "Who wrote it?" The other person replied, "I never heard of her." The author was identified only as Miss Mary Johnston of Birmingham, Alabama. Her novel was an adventure tale set in colonial Virginia, entitled "Prisoners of Hope." After reading the manuscript Page agreed with his associate, and Houghton, Mifflin published the book in the fall of 1898. *Prisoners of Hope* sold well, earning over two thousand dollars in 1898 and nearly nine thousand dollars in 1899—much better than any Houghton, Mifflin novel had done for several years.

Page had not finished with Mary Johnston. Sensing that he might be on the trail of more best-sellers, he stopped in Birmingham on his trip south in February 1899 to meet the author. "She is a shy, wee body, a mere child in appearance," he reported to Mifflin. But Johnston's intelligence and determination made him think that she had the makings of a major writer. Even more exciting, he discovered that she "has more prisoners of hope in her writing desk." Johnston allowed Page to take away with him the manuscript of her second novel, another romance set in colonial Virginia. That book, which came to be entitled *To Have and to Hold*, became almost as big a publishing sensation as *David Harum*. *To Have and to Hold* gave the first hint of its phenomenal appeal when stenographers in the Houghton, Mifflin offices borrowed galley proofs to read during their lunch hours. The book sold 275,000 copies and earned $76,660.64 during the first year after publication. Page had won his spurs as a commercial book publisher.[27]

But Page did not measure his accomplishments by sales alone. He held strong convictions about literature and culture. He wanted to combat artificiality in fiction and, as he told one novelist in September 1897, he wanted to make "a strong protest against the psychological novel." He favored "the novel of objective life—of action; even of adventure in some cases, of motion—the out-door rather than the indoor point of view and outlook on life." Page expounded his literary opinions when he gave a speech, entitled "The Making of Literature," in North Carolina in March 1899. Only through literature, he avowed, could men judge their lives and activities by standards that were not transitory or trivial; "the one great and stable thing whereby we may measure men and civilizations is great literature." Page believed "that all literature, especially English literature, is a thing that was made at home, of homely products, homely qualities, and not a thing that was separate from the everyday life of the people of the time in which it was made, or of any artificial thought."[28]

Howells had been preaching a similar catechism for nearly twenty years, and Page must have been familiar with his views. But he went much further than Howells in adhering to his *Atlantic* predecessor's well-known pronouncement about "the more smiling aspects of life, which are the more American." Page rejected stories for the magazine and novels for Houghton, Mifflin on the grounds that they did not treat "socially healthful people" and were "very far from cheerful." He eschewed mysticism as alien "to the rough and energetic race to which we belong." He disdained weird and morbid writers and subjects. In a speech entitled "Literature and Its Making," delivered at the University of Tennessee in June 1900, Page dismissed Edgar Allan Poe as a liar and a drunkard who had turned out "artificial stories and not at all in line with the literature of wholesome character, depicting wholesome American life." Among southern writers, he argued that Poe ranked far below such romantic storytellers as Johnston and his own Virginia namesake, Thomas Nelson Page.[29]

Howells's possible influence did not make Page's literary views derivative. Nearly twenty years before, in his pieces in *The Age*, Page had argued for "virility" and plainspokenness in literature. In his reaction against the Johns Hopkins he had stressed the need for popularization in art and culture. In his days of youthful searching Page had expressed the notion that great events produced great literature. His fragmentary essays and the review of Timrod in *The South Atlantic* in 1878 had predicted a literary flowering of the South, based upon the "heroic age" of the Civil War. As editor of the *Atlantic*, Page extended those ideas to the nation as a whole. In June 1896, he asked his historian friend Rhodes to write an article on the American Revolution and the Civil War as "Our Two Heroic Periods." Page's literary views sprang from his own youthful background, particularly his conflicts between worldly and literary callings and his mixed reactions to the Civil War and the Lost Cause.[30]

The moralistic element in Page's literary views was significant but also misleading. Although his strictures about cheerful, healthy writing made him sound like a priggish Pollyanna, he tolerated much writing about shocking and depressing subjects. He later knew and admired Frank Norris, and through Norris he played a part in the publication of Theodore Dreiser's *Sister Carrie*. Page's own novel, *The Southerner*, contained episodes of sadness and defeat and depicted sex, miscegenation, and illegitimacy. Violence evidently never bothered Page, since it abounded in many of the novels that he admired and in the one that he wrote. Nor did his moral standards prevent him from spotting able new writers. Page showed his appreciation of fresh talent best with Ellen Glasgow. Despite the flaws in her first novel, *The Descendant*, he recognized that Glasgow had great gifts. During 1897, Page advised her to set future works in the familiar terrain of her native Virginia. He also urged her to concentrate on writing novels rather than ephemeral stories. Page apparently did not worry, as others did, about alleged immorality in Glasgow's treatment of relations between men and women. Actually, Page compromised his literary taste more often through commercialism than through moralism. He overrated writers who sold well and underrated those who did not.

Page's literary moralism linked his cultural and political views. Wanting to promote culture in the South had stimulated his first interest in politics, and during the 1890s, especially after going to Boston, Page broadened his earlier southern objectives to encompass the entire country. His most important political stands came when he took issue with the Democratic party and many of his southern friends and relatives, first to oppose Bryan in 1896 and then to support imperialism in 1898 and 1899. Rejecting Bryan was a natural consequence of Page's earlier distaste for populism and free silver. During the summer of 1896, he solicited several articles for the *Atlantic* dissecting what he called "this pseudo-democratic movement" on the part of "the deluded and discontented." Page remained detached enough to ask whether the agrarian revolt was not "an unavoidable outcome of democratic institutions under the influence of recent economic tendencies? Agricultural depression is world-wide—necessarily so, since a smaller proportion of mankind can produce the food of the world." That condition had elicited "a vast rural discontent" that had stumbled blindly on "the old remedy of inflation."

Page's opposition to Bryan was not as momentous as it might have seemed. He did not announce his position publicly and never said whom he supported. Page probably voted, as did Scudder and Woodrow Wilson, for the splinter Gold Democratic ticket. Opposing Bryan's candidacy did not mean that Page scorned everything that the Nebraskan and his followers stood for. Right after the election, he asked John Jay Chapman to write an article for the *Atlantic* on the subject that he considered "the most important one in its direct and immediate moral import. . . . I refer to the thing that the populist demagogues mean when they talk about 'trusts and monopolies.'" Nor did disagreeing with fellow southerners mean that Page wanted to see his native region ape the North. "Commercialism is the evil of our land at this time," he declared in a talk to the Harvard Southern Club in February 1898, "and the fate of our land depends on the strength and principles of the south." Living among Yankees for a decade had not made him kneel at the altar of northern big business.[31]

Colonialism in 1898 brought an open break with most Democrats and southern whites. Ironically, Page became an imperialist out of the same considerations that led him to condemn northern commercialism. In his editorial accompanying the flag-waving *Atlantic* cover, Page predicted easy victory for American arms, but he asserted that postwar problems would be more difficult and important. Whereas Americans had formerly busied themselves with "the prosaic tasks of peace, . . . a nation to ourselves,—'commercials,' as our enemies call us in derision," they now faced "the management of world-wide empires. . . . Shall we still be content with peaceful industry, or does there yet lurk in us the adventurous spirit of our Anglo-Saxon forefathers?" Page obviously preferred harking to the call of the blood. "The race from which we are sprung, is a race that has done the adventurous and outdoor tasks of the world."

In the past, Americans had won their independence, expanded over a vast continent, fought the Civil War, and built great industries—all tasks equal in opportunity "for the play of the love of adventure as our kinsmen over the sea have had in the extension and management of their world-empire." Lately, however, a generation had "come to manhood that has had no part in any great adventure." Political horizons had narrowed to preoccupation with "routine, regulative duties," and able men refused to enter politics because of "the lack of large constructive opportunities." Literature, too, had suffered. Americans had nearly "lost the art of constructive writing, for we work too much on indoor problems." Politics and literature had meandered together into utopianism, romantic dreaming, crackpot schemes, and minor enthusiasms. "These things all denote a lack of adventurous opportunities, and indoor life such as we have never before had a chance to enjoy." But had Americans changed into something other than "the same race of Anglo-Saxons," with their "restless energy in colonization, in conquest, in trade"? Clearly not, since "it is the temperament that tells, and not schemes of national policy, whether laid down in Farewell Addresses or in Utopian books." Americans were keeping faith with their racial heritage, both by fighting Spain and by acquiring a colonial empire.[32]

That editorial expressed more than a passing enthusiasm. Besides filling the *Atlantic* with articles on colonial and diplomatic subjects, Page gave two speeches and published two more editorials applauding the United States's embarkation on the course of empire. In December 1898, he informed an audience at the Pratt Institute in Brooklyn that acquiring colonies posed the same question as preserving the Union had in 1861. Once again, "race instinct" had prevailed over timid rationalization. Page argued that acquiring the Philippines would test the strength of democratic institutions, and he declared that Washington's and Jefferson's warnings against alliances had become outmoded. Instead, "the two great English-speaking peoples" were joining in the task of civilizing and reclaiming the tropics. On his southern trip early in 1899, Page addressed students at Chapel Hill on "the Greater Republic." That meant, he insisted, not "simply an extension of territory, but of language, institutions, and in brief civilization."

Short editorials applauded the imperial venture in two other issues of the *Atlantic*. In September 1898, "The End of the War, and After" urged retention of Caribbean islands and at least part of the Philippines as a way to alleviate the inexorable "pressure of commerce for new markets." But economic considerations were not fundamental. The editorial concluded with the assertion that "larger and further-reaching political duties" would "appeal to the imagination rather than to the private greed of men," thereby restoring American public life "to the level of statesmanship." In the March 1899 issue of the *Atlantic*, "A Wholesome Stimulus to Higher Politics" approved the debate over empire as "evidence that we once more have a public subject that appeals to the imagination." Page obeyed his own preachment about activism by seeking an appointment to the Philippine Commission, the government body that was to study the problem of governing the new colony.[33]

His support for colonialism caused clashes in the North and South. In March 1899 Page reported to Scudder that whenever people in his native region disputed his stand he replied "that the home of Secession is naturally the home of 'Anti-Expansion.' Then they have reminded me that the home of Abolition is now of the same mind." The *Atlantic*'s flag-waving cover and imperialist contents flew in the face of many prominent Bostonians' opposition to the Spanish-American War and to taking the Philippines. Yet Page did not stand alone. Not everyone within the Bostonian elite opposed imperialism. The split between Massachusetts's two Brahmin Republican senators—George F. Hoar, a staunch antiimperialist, and Henry Cabot Lodge, an equally ardent imperialist—epitomized divisions in Back Bay and on Beacon Hill. The Adams family contained the divergent brothers, antiimperialist Charles Francis and imperialist Brooks. Nor was Page isolated in the Houghton, Mifflin ranks. Garrison and Mifflin denounced the war, but Scudder wrote to him from England in May 1898, "I am delighted with the unfurling of the flag. Nothing could be more fit." Scudder wanted the *Atlantic* to "throw its heart and soul not only into the war but also into an early contribution to the solution of the civil problems involved."[34]

The social and cultural perspectives that led Page to espouse overseas expansion resembled the views of Lodge, Brooks Adams, and Theodore Roosevelt. Like those men, Page welcomed the colonial enterprise because it seemed to offer a glorious alternative to the political predicaments of the 1890s. Roosevelt, Lodge, and Adams had denounced the populists and Bryan as dangerous radicals. At the same time, they disdained businessmen as crass, flabby, timid, and dull. They seized upon empire as a way to revive heroic, manly virtues, and they pointed to Britain as an example of imperialism's beneficent effects. Even though he came from a different background and held divergent ideological predilections, Page had no trouble joining those upper-crust northerners in formulating what was essentially an aesthetic, militarist critique of a business-dominated society.

Two factors probably influenced Page to adopt an imperialist perspective. One may have been his age. Much of the division between leading imperialists and antiimperialists, especially the split within the Boston Brahminate, was a conflict of generations.

Earlier mugwump fears of the country's being ground to bits between upper and nether millstones of sordid capitalists and radical masses formed a common starting point. The division over empire was a tactical disagreement over whether overseas expansion would worsen or alleviate the predicament that all deplored. Older figures foresaw only further disaster, while their juniors imagined exciting possibilities for escape. Page, who became forty-three in August 1898, belonged to the younger generation of men who adhered to the latter attitudes. So did Roosevelt, who turned forty the following October. Woodrow Wilson, who became forty-two in December 1898, also approved of the colonial experiment as a means of uplifting American politics, though he did not embrace imperialism nearly as fervently as did Page.

Page's passionate intensity in espousing imperialist views sprang from another source, the combination of boyhood experiences and memories associated with the Civil War. Page resembled Roosevelt in having a father who had not served in the war. Neither man ever professed anything but admiration for his father. Yet in his *Autobiography* Roosevelt commented, about his joining the army in 1898, "I had always felt if there were a serious war I wished to be in a position to tell my children why I did take part in it, and not why I did not take part in it." Page did not try to enlist. Unlike Roosevelt, he had been in poor health recently and he had no outside income. But his attempt to get on the Philippine Commission demonstrated how much he wanted to participate. His vehemence in supporting the Spanish-American War implied a sense of personal commitment. Another ardent imperialist whom Page resembled was the young Indiana Republican politician Albert J. Beveridge. His thunderous invocations of Anglo-Saxon destiny sounded strikingly similar to the *Atlantic* editor's. Despite coming from an even more provincial background than the Tar Heel, the Hoosier also scorned business and hankered after the glories of war and empire. With Beveridge, the critical influence toward such views seems to have been his father's romanticized tales of service as a Union cavalry officer. The examples of Roosevelt, Beveridge, and Page showed how widely separated men in the 1890s carried a powerful psychological imprint from having been children during the Civil War and having grown up afterward with pervasive legends of heroism on both sides.[35]

Page's foreign-policy views were also significant because he later became ambassador to Great Britain during World War I. At that time, he duplicated the ardor for both armed intervention and Anglo-American solidarity that he had shown at the end of the 1890s. Promoting better relations with Britain had concerned him since the Venezuela boundary dispute in 1895. During 1897, he attempted to initiate a series of *Atlantic* articles, "which shall try to eradicate the silly and unfortunate notion that England is our enemy." The war with Spain, in which Britain sympathized with the United States, quickened his hopes for concert between the two nations. In May 1898, Page admitted to Bryce that he was not "wholly sorry that the inevitable contest with Spain has come because of the important incidental results; and the most important incidental result is the radical (and I think permanent) change of feeling towards England." The victory at Manila made him hope that the United States might do even more than acquire colonies. "The possession of the Philippines & of the Hawaiian Islands will," he told Bryce, "bring an overwhelming reason for as close an alliance as possible with Great Britain."[36]

Page soon dropped the idea of an alliance, but he continued to advocate cooperation between the two English-speaking empires in ruling and uplifting tropical areas. After 1899, like most Americans, Page turned his attention largely away from foreign affairs. Even at the height of his imperialist outburst, Page never became a slavish Anglophile. Youthful admiration for classic English authors had not prevented him from becoming a robust literary nationalist. He did not share the envy common among cultivated Americans for British aristocracy and cultural refinement. The contemporary English author whom he admired most in the 1890s was Rudyard Kipling. Not only was Kipling an imperialist, but he also wrote stories and poems about common subjects in simple, vigorous language. At bottom, Page's Anglophilia always remained a function of his American nationalism.

Page also had reason to be pleased with life in Boston because of his undiminished interest in southern problems and reform. Moving two hundred miles further away in 1895 did no more to remove his native region from his thoughts than had leaving ten years earlier. Going to Boston enhanced Page's standing as a representative and interpreter between North and South. When such impeccably Yankee literary institutions as the *Atlantic* and Houghton, Mifflin elevated an outspoken southerner to prominent positions, they advertised their emancipation from New England exclusiveness. Especially after he assumed the title of editor of the *Atlantic*, Page gained still more impressive credentials as a southerner who had succeeded among Yankees. During his four years in Boston, he gained in importance as a spokesman for understanding and cooperation between the sections. His trips to the South continued at the rate of two or three a year and more of his time went to speaking engagements, principally at colleges and universities. A token of recognition from his people came when he received his first honorary degree in June 1899, from Randolph-Macon College. Page also spoke to northern audiences either on southern problems or on sectional aspects of national questions. But, increasingly, his importance to and in the South revolved around activities to improve educational, economic, and racial conditions.

Education remained Page's favored avenue toward progress. He kept in close touch with leaders in movements to improve schools, particularly in North Carolina. Starting in the late 1880s, a pair of native white Tar Heels, Charles D. McIver and Edwin A. Alderman, mounted a crusade for a stronger tax base for education and for founding a state normal college. Together and separately, the burly, genial McIver and the handsome, polished Alderman traveled up and down the state spreading their message. At length, efforts by them and others led to modest gains. Appropriations for school facilities increased; longer school years became required; and the North Carolina State Normal and Industrial School for Women at Greensboro opened in 1896. The two crusaders also reaped personal rewards in that year. McIver became the first president of the normal school and Alderman succeeded Winston as president of the University of North Carolina. Of the two, Page knew McIver well. He had first met McIver when he was editor of the *State Chronicle*. They had corresponded since the early 1890s, and McIver visited at Page's house in Cambridge during the summer of 1896. Although Alderman had attended Page's lectures at Chapel Hill during the summer of 1878, they had not met again. The new president of the university did know about the editor by reputation and probably through Winston and McIver. In August 1896, immediately upon taking office, Alderman wrote to Page soliciting advice "as to the aims, ideals, and policies of the university." Page replied by again urging independence of churches and political parties, and he admonished Alderman to unlock the grip of *"Dead Men's Hands."*[37]

Friendship with McIver led to an opportunity for Page to reinsert himself into southern educational reform. He did so by giving what was probably his most significant speech, "The Forgotten Man," which he delivered at Greensboro on 19 May 1897 to the normal school's first commencement. The educational campaign in North Carolina had reached another critical stage. Special elections were scheduled for August 1897. Educational leaders were trying to induce recalcitrant townships to levy school taxes and to get the legislature to increase state aid to townships that voted such taxes. McIver wanted a rousing speech to kick off the summer campaign that he and Alderman were about to mount. Having selected Page as the best man to give the speech, McIver coached his friend about arguments and facts to include in his address. The advice was unnecessary, since the former editor of the *State Chronicle* and author of the mummy letter could draw on a wealth of his own comment and observation. Page also wrote to the Census Bureau in Washington for the latest figures on native North Carolinians who had emigrated to other states.

In "The Forgotten Man," Page skillfully blended old arguments with fresh images and with his new pose as an expatriate. After comparing himself to "old-time wanderers" who carried pots of native soil on their journeys, he launched into his main argument. North Carolina must develop, he declared, "one un-developed resource more valuable" than all others, "and that is the people themselves," particularly "forgotten and neglected men." Those people were more important than anyone else be-cause they formed the foundation of society. "When you build a house, you make the foundation the strongest part of it, and the house, however ornate its architecture, can be no stronger than its foundation." So, too, in a community: "Its few rich men, or its few cultivated men" did not "really make the community what it is" or determine "the soundness of its social structure, its economic value and its level of life. The security and soundness of the whole body are measured at last by the condition of its weakest part."

Page pursued the argument by again describing how the antebellum aristocratic ideal of education for a privileged few and the ecclesiastical ideal of sectarian education had combined to stifle the growth of public schools. "What," he asked, "have the aristocratic system and the ecclesiastical system to show for themselves?" They did not even provide "their own favoured classes" with colleges and universities that measured up against northern institutions. "Make another test: there are no great libraries in the State, nor do the people yet read, nor have the publishing houses yet reckoned them as their patrons." Page likewise revived his device from the mummy letter, "the test of emigration from the State. In 1890 there were living in other States 293,000 persons who were born in North Carolina. One in eight of every native of the State then living had gone away." Giving the device a new twist, Page noted, "If a slave brought $1,000 in old times, it ought to be safe to assume that every emigrant from the State has an economic value of $1,000. This emigration therefore had up to 1890 cost us $293,000,000—a fact that goes far to explain why we are poor." True, thanks to "twenty years of organized effort to induce immigration," 52,000 outsiders had moved to North Carolina by 1890. But counting them at $1,000 each, too, "we had still lost $241,000,000 by the transaction. This calculation gives a slight hint of the cost of ignorance and of the extravagance of keeping taxes too low."

The masses who remained paid the price many times over, Page asserted. "In 1890, twenty-six per cent of the white persons of the State were unable to read or write. One in four was wholly forgotten. But illiteracy was not the worst of it; the worst of it was that the stationary social condition indicated by generations of illiteracy had long been the general condition. The forgotten man was content to stay forgotten." Not only did he become "a dead weight" on social progress, but he served as the willing dupe of preachers and politicians who opposed all new ideas and improvements. Even worse off was "the forgotten woman." Page described these creatures, "thin and wrinkled in youth from ill prepared food, clad without warmth or grace, living in untidy houses, working from daylight till bedtime at the dull round of weary duties, the slaves of men of equal slovenliness, the mothers of joyless children." Still worse, these women had no escape. "Some *men* who are born under these conditions may escape from them; a *man* may go away, go where life offers opportunities, but the women are forever hopeless." These men and women were the people whom "both the politician and the preacher have failed to lift." Plainly, the time had come "for a wiser statesmanship and a more certain means of grace."

Evidently mindful of his reputation for pessimism and disloyalty, Page devoted the last part of the speech to upbeat comments. "But now the story brightens," he added. The efforts of Alderman, McIver, and their kindred were achieving miracles. "In my judgment there has been no other event in North Carolina since the formation of the American Union that is comparable to this new educational progress." Page slipped in additional criticisms by observing how far the state still had to go. "According to the last published report of the Commissioner of Education, the total sum spent per year per pupil was still lower in North Carolina than in any State except South Carolina." Only one or two North Carolina cities had established free high schools, whereas other states maintained tax-supported secondary-school systems. Nor did the state have a network of free libraries like the ones that graced the village greens of every New England town. In higher education, Tar Heels needed to adopt "the wholly free

University and Industrial Schools" that Texans were inaugurating. But, Page concluded, the future looked bright. "Great changes come as silently as the seasons. I am no more sure of this spring time than I am of the rejuvenation of our society and the lifting of our life. . . . The neglected people will rise and with them will rise all the people."[38]

"The Forgotten Man" hit the mark. "Praise of your Greensboro speech is still heard in every direction," reported his brother Robert. Page received many congratulatory letters. Most North Carolina newspapers acclaimed his utterance, except for the denominational press, which assailed his allegation that sectarianism had impeded public education. In the *News and Observer*, Daniels published the entire speech and included a signed editorial report. He called "The Forgotten Man" the "product of an honest heart and an honest brain," and he noted that fifteen years' experience and reflection had gone into the speech. Daniels did add, however, "Mr. Page always speaks in extremes." The drive to increase tax levies failed in 1897, although McIver insisted that "the educational effect of this campaign will be tremendous." Later improvements gradually bore out McIver's estimate. North Carolina made further educational advances after 1900. A new element subsequently entered the situation in the form of organized aid toward the whole South by an interlocking directorate of white southern educational leaders, southern expatriates, and northern philanthropists, principally through the Southern Education Board. Page owed his own appointment to this board in 1901 to his prominence not only as an editor and publisher but also as a spokesman on southern education. Much of his reputation in educational matters sprang from "The Forgotten Man."[39]

Meanwhile, other work also kept his native region close to the center of his thoughts. As in the *Forum*, Page devoted space in the *Atlantic* to southern topics, and the magazine's literary character supplied an added dimension to his southern interests. Among established writers, Page cultivated authors from every part of the country, but the fledgling and unknown authors whom he encouraged were nearly all southerners. Assisting writers from his homeland was an area in which Page made no racial distinctions. The black novelist and short-story writer Chesnutt appealed to him because he wrote about southern subjects. Page urged W. E. B. Du Bois to write a series of nonfiction sketches on Negro life in the United States. He also reportedly told a black writer who submitted an essay to the *Atlantic*, "I know what you are thinking of. You are thinking of the barriers we set up against you, and the handicap of your lot. If you will write what it feels like to be a Negro, I will print that." In seeking articles about the South, Page discovered a trenchant native white critic in William Peterfield Trent, who taught at the University of the South, where he had founded the *Sewanee Review*. When he criticized an article by Trent in the fall of 1896, Page urged the professor to stress "the effect of religious dogma upon intolerance of liberal opinion in general." He asserted that "any discussion of religious influences in the South which does not say strictly, point-blank and with emphasis, that the intellectual life of the people has been hindered unspeakably by the narrowness of religious opinion falls short of the most important and significant fact that needs to be said about the South."[40]

Living and working among descendants of abolitionists did not change Page's racial attitudes. Although Frank Garrison always deplored Page's use of the word "nigger," the two men frequently discussed racial topics. Privately, Page regarded people like Garrison as addlebrained on the subject of blacks. In *The Southerner* he described a Harvard man who became indignant at alleged discrimination against a Negro, while admitting that discrimination against other groups did not bother him. "The Negro-in-America, therefore," observes Page's central character, "is a form of insanity that overtakes white men." That remark referred to latter-day abolitionist types, not southern whites. Garrison and Page did find a bond in their admiration for Booker T. Washington. Page solicited an article for the *Atlantic* from the black leader during the summer of 1896. Later in the year, the former North Carolinian met the principal of the Tuskegee Institute in Boston and took him to dinner at a hotel. Page evidently had no objection to dining with some blacks in public places in the North. A few years later, he remonstrated with McIver and

Alderman when they refused to join him for lunch with Washington at a hotel in Saratoga Springs, New York.[41]

Events in the South highlighted Page's conflicting attitudes. During the 1890s race relations below the Potomac took an ominous turn. Successive states enacted laws disfranchising and segregating blacks, while violence and Negrophobic demagoguery exploded. North Carolina in particular witnessed spectacular campaigns of violence and intimidation, through which in 1898 and 1900 white Democrats overthrew the Populist-Republican fusion regime that had attained power during the earlier agrarian discontent. Page's erstwhile protégé Daniels and his one-time admirer, Charles B. Aycock, helped spearhead those drives. Many of his friends joined them in expressing racist reform sentiment. These men, like others in the South, urged disfranchisement as a way to clean up southern politics. Eliminating black votes would, they argued, end the fraud and violence previously employed to nullify those votes. Legalized segregation would likewise improve race relations by clarifying the black man's "place" and reduce friction by promoting greater separation between blacks and whites. Because he no longer lived in the South, Page could avoid taking a stand on such matters. Although he could also plead ignorance of rapidly changing conditions as an excuse for silence, he did betray some of his thoughts. Writing to Chesnutt directly after the November 1898 election in North Carolina, Page admitted that "occurrences there have given me also very deep concern." Yet a month later, in his imperialist speech in Brooklyn, he noted that "race instinct, greater than logic, has disfranchised him [the Negro] in Georgia and South Carolina and will soon also in North Carolina—against the law more is the pity." Where Page stood was hard to tell, most likely because he did not know himself.[42]

His uncertainty probably played an important part in his decision, in February 1899, to make a six-week trip through the South to study the racial situation. Part of the journey went to public speaking, but Page's major reason for revisiting his native region was to write about race relations for the *Atlantic*. He arranged his itinerary and secured letters of introduction in order to gain firsthand acquaintance with attitudes on both sides of the color line in several parts of the South. As soon as he arrived in Washington at the beginning of the journey, Page informed his wife, "I threw every subject out of my mind but the Negro." He vowed "to think about, talk about, read about" nothing else until he returned. "I may turn black before I'm done!"

This trip was Page's first extended journey through the South since his 1881 trip. He followed much the same route as before: after stopping in Washington, he went first to Tennessee, then dropped down through Mississippi to New Orleans, and came back through Alabama. But this time he did not stay in Atlanta. He traveled instead to South Carolina and paid his first visit to Charleston. Finally, he stopped over in his native state on his way back to Boston. Many of the same conditions struck him as they had in 1881. The Deep South states of Mississippi and Alabama once more repelled him. Not even booming industry in Birmingham could overcome the prevailing sloth, disrepair, and ignorance. "Don't you see the trail of slavery in all this?" Page wrote to his wife. " . . . It is the sloven who sets the public fashion, the thriftless wretch who takes no pride in his work, who mends nothing, who saves nothing." Yet Page's observations in 1899 differed radically from his newspaper reports in 1881. Now he was examining the racial situation rather than trying to avert his eyes or minimize problems.

From the start, Page found himself torn in his reactions. Visiting prominent blacks and whites in Nashville, he was continually impressed by their similarities to each other. Yet he realized that only a white outsider like himself could visit homes and families of both races. "I have lost my own identity a time or two," he wrote to Mifflin. "Several times I have checked the impulse to weep by the sudden & saving thought, that if Garrison could see these things he'd drop dead! Both the pathos and the humor of it go beyond anything in literature." Page felt compassion for blacks. "I'd rather be any other man in any other country than a nigger in Louisiana," he wrote Scudder. "It is pathetic—his situation; to say nothing of the tragic aspects of it." From Charleston, he sent back a similar observation to Scudder,

"So far as the negro is concerned, I'd rather be an imp in hades than a darkey in S.C. One decided advantage that the imp has is—personal safety." As the comment to Mifflin indicated, Page did not want to get depressed and he strained to find humor. But on this trip optimism and humor found few outlets. In New Orleans, for example, he marveled to Alice at "a sunny cheerfulness, with only hints here and there of the tragic possibilities always beneath the surface."[43]

Page's best occasion for hope and the emotional high point of the journey came when he visited Booker T. Washington at Tuskegee. The black leader offered encouragement by confirming much of what the white editor already thought. In a long discussion, Washington explained some of the attitudes behind his program of industrial and agricultural training. The freed black had too often, he told Page, "caught the usual white man's error —that an educated man ought not to work, certainly not to work with [his] hands. This misconception has been bad enough for the white man; but when the negro once got it into his head, it worked havoc with him indeed." Page could hardly have heard more welcome words; Washington was repeating his own argument of fifteen years before for an industrial school in North Carolina. Page and the black spokesman also apparently shared similar views on certain racial problems. Both men agreed that relations between the two races would improve if both blacks and whites forgot about politics and agitation and concentrated on economic activity. Speaking at a chapel service on 5 March 1899, the *Atlantic* editor admonished the Tuskegee students about the value of "practical" work. "Be a better farmer than any other man in Alabama. Be a better nurse than any other woman. Then the whole problem, not only of your life, but of every life is solved." Later in the visit Page listened to the student body sing spirituals. Washington asked the visitor to request his favorite hymn, and the former Tar Heel Methodist thrilled to hear two thousand voices fill the chapel with "O, Lord, What a Morning!"[44]

The southern trip in 1899 bared Page's inner conflict about race. He lacked neither perception nor compassion toward blacks.

Yet he remained willfully optimistic that, left alone, southern whites would make things better. In common with other prominent whites, Page embraced Washington and the Tuskegee approach as justification for his own hopes. Page certainly missed an opportunity to write a timely treatment of an important subject, for as soon as he returned to Boston at the end of March 1899, he fell seriously ill and had to go back to North Carolina to recover. Then, during the summer of 1899 he left the *Atlantic* for fresh ventures in New York. Yet, over the next three years Page kept insisting that he was on the verge of producing the long-awaited articles. Finally, the May 1902 issue of the *Atlantic* carried an article by the former editor entitled "The Rebuilding of Old Commonwealths."

The article advanced slightly beyond earlier arguments. Page began by revisiting the scene of his first *Atlantic* article in 1881, noting signs of progress everywhere in the village and again worrying whether old-fashioned leisure and courtesy could survive. Outside towns and villages, however, people remained "essentially like the men and women who lived there fifty years ago, or eighty years, or even a hundred." Life had stagnated in the countryside because of three influences: "first, slavery, which pickled Southern life and left it just as it had found it; then the politician and the preacher." Page once more related how theological timidity hampered southern colleges, and he noted the persistence of reactionary ideas about race and class. Yet he was not pessimistic. Page predicted gradual but inexorable progress through education. "The problem that the South presents has at last become so plain that thoughtful men no longer differ about it. . . . It is simply the training of the untrained masses." He no longer "doubted whether a democracy could absorb two different races thus living together and yet apart." Right training would assure mutual advancement. "Training to economic independence is the only true emancipation."

Although "The Rebuilding of Old Commonwealths" did not spark controversy and repeated many of Page's well-worn arguments, it did state more boldly than before that slavery had perverted the growth of an equalitarian, balanced, antebellum society. Anticipating a point later made by W. J. Cash in *The Mind of the South*, Page asserted that the South had "a state of life that keeps permanently the qualities of the frontier civilization long after the frontier has receded and been forgotten." Page also foreshadowed such later native white interpreters of southern society as Cash, William E. Dodd, and Howard W. Odum when he declared, "There is no undemocratic trait in the Southern people that is not directly accounted for by slavery and by the results of slavery." Page anticipated a common stand of subsequent southern white racial reformers, too, when he invoked Jefferson as a symbol of legitimacy. The current public-school crusade he labeled "native" and "nothing different from Jefferson's creed and plan." One of Page's last comments in the essay was "to speculate on the effects of Jefferson's plan for public education if it had been carried out. Would the public schools have prevented the growth of slavery?" Although he rejected a simple answer, he affirmed that with mass education "a stronger economic impetus might have been given to diversified pursuits than cotton-culture gave to slavery, and the whole course of our history might have been changed." In "The Rebuilding of Old Commonwealths" Page helped to shape the mainstream of twentieth-century white southern social-reform attitudes.

The article also supplied the title for Page's first book. In May 1902, at the time of publication of the *Atlantic* piece, a hardcover volume appeared under the same title. Besides "The Rebuilding of Old Commonwealths," the book included two of Page's speeches, "The Forgotten Man" and an address entitled "The School that Built a Town," delivered at the Georgia State Normal College in December 1901. The Georgia speech comprised an extended fable about a sleepy southern village that found itself transformed into a neat, prosperous town through the influence of a public school. Page reiterated two of his pet educational arguments: that schools constituted an economic benefit rather than a burden to a community and that truly comprehensive education must offer industrial as well as academic training. As a book, *The Rebuilding of Old Commonwealths* was a small, thin volume, with 153 pages of large print and wide margins. It was the only book that Page ever published under his own name. At the time of publication, however, *The Rebuilding of Old Commonwealths* appeared to mark a long-overdue beginning of a writing career. The book also made some of the statements about the South and race that Page had promised from his journey in 1899. Except for the one article, however, the *Atlantic* gained nothing from Page's achievement, nor did Houghton, Mifflin. By the time the book was published, Page had long since left Boston. He had also helped start the publishing company that brought out *The Rebuilding of Old Commonwealths*.[45]

Despite reasons for satisfaction, Page was not happy in Boston. His closest colleagues sensed his deep discontent. In April 1896 Scudder recorded in his diary, "There is a smouldering volcano in him, and I don't know but that he may burst forth some day. . . . I suspect now and then that he suffers from the depression which overtakes a man who dreams of high things and finds himself called back to petty routine." Jenkins, the *Atlantic*'s business manager, later recalled that "the outstanding impression which he made upon me was that of intense intellectual restlessness." Page seemed to be "a man who had not found himself—a man who was hearing some call at the time that he did not quite know how to answer." Jenkins remembered Page's having "for days on end periods of abstraction and one of my most familiar recollections of him is his figure as he stood with his hands deep in his trouser's [sic] pockets and a cigar in the corner of his mouth, looking out of the windows of our old Park Street office across the Boston Common, in utter forgetfulness of anything about him. Those were the days and hours when I knew it was best to keep away from him."[46]

Some of Page's unhappiness was unavoidable. After he moved to Boston in 1895, his health took a long turn for the worse, and every few months he missed work because of an illness. Some complaints were minor, but two were more serious. One threatened his livelihood and the other, possibly, his life. In January 1898 Page developed a problem with his eyes, probably some form of inflammation. For more than a week he had to stay in a darkened room during daylight hours, forbidden to read or write. The threat of blindness was frightening in itself, and eye trouble had forced his predecessor as editor of the *Forum* to abandon his career. Sometime in the 1890s he began wearing eyeglasses, at first for reading but by the early 1900s nearly all the time. Page's most serious illness struck at the beginning of April 1899, right after his return from the southern trip. He suffered a severe attack of erysipelas, a skin and facial infection. The disease left him delirious with a fever of 104 degrees for several days, during which the doctors may have feared for his life. As it was, Page recuperated slowly and did not resume his duties at the office until the middle of May 1899.

Overwork and strain may have helped bring on that illness and some of the others. It seems likely that psychological factors, such as depression over his work, played some part in Page's repeated breakdowns from 1895 to 1899. But age probably counted most in his worsened health. Having turned forty in August 1895 Page was losing the youthful resiliency that had protected his constitution from the exactions of his driving ambition. The pattern of periodic minor illnesses persisted with Page for much of the rest of his life. After he returned to New York in 1899, two chronic conditions developed, a stomach ulcer and what he called "catarrh," a chronic cough and shortness of breath. He endured more or less constant inflammation and congestion of the throat and lungs, perhaps caused and certainly aggravated by his heavy smoking. By the end of his life, he had developed a mild form of emphysema. In short, from his late thirties on, Page showed the telltale signs of being a middle-aged man whose health was gradually declining under the combined impact of advancing years and his own habits and working conditions.

Additional unhappiness stemmed from the deaths of his parents. Page's mother died first, on 21 August 1897, at the age of sixty-five. Except for a brush with pneumonia in 1889, Kate Page had enjoyed vigorous health until a few months before her death, when a long illness beginning in the spring of 1897 warned the family of her deterioration. Walter's three sons spent the summer with their grandmother, and he was present himself at the end. Her departure, Page told Scudder, removed "a living presence" from his life, "and I could not have guessed at the kind of loneliness I have felt." Frank Page lived for another two years. He moved back to Raleigh, remarried, and indulged his penchant for speculation in the hotel business, at which he evidently lost a good bit of money. Walter spent some time with him on trips to Washington and North Carolina during 1898 and 1899. The old man recovered from one serious illness at the end of 1898, but several months later another lengthy malady overtook him. Frank Page died on 16 October 1899 at the age of seventy-five. "What we have been fearing for several years came at last," wrote Page, again to Scudder, "—leaving me lonelier than I have ever felt before." Frank Page's death must have hurt, too, by coming just when his son had gone back to New York and at last seemed on the verge of financial triumph.[47]

Scudder and Jenkins guessed right when they thought that Page's deepest discontent lay with his work. In his own view, the problem remained his desire to be his own boss. "I should probably have spent the rest of my life as editor of the *Atlantic*," he explained in an interview in 1903, "but for one reason. I wanted a magazine of my own. I did not see why I should always edit other persons' magazines." Page also told his Cambridge friend W. R. Thayer in December 1900, "I couldn't afford to take permanently the risks that a hired editor must take." Page claimed that the magazine's previous editors had been fired or pensioned off to make way for new blood. He was wrong about his predecessors' fates. "The House" hardly ever fired anybody, least of all *Atlantic* editors, who all either stepped down voluntarily or found themselves gracefully eased aside. But insecurity haunted Page. "If I was a 'magic editor,' " he protested to Thayer, "I confess I didn't see the magic; and there is no power under Heaven or in it that can prove to me that I ought to keep on making magazines as a hired man—without the common security of permanent service for lack of which nearly all my predecessors lost their chance."[48]

Page never did gain a free hand over the *Atlantic*. The two-year penumbra of authority from 1896 to 1898 left doubts about how much independence he would ever enjoy. When Scudder prepared to go abroad in 1897, the firm agreed to hire an assistant for Page, but the choice rested almost entirely in Scudder's hands. Overlapping duties with the magazine and Houghton, Mifflin's book-editorial department wore Page down the same way that they had earlier exhausted Scudder. "If I had seen any chance of disentangling the editorship of the Atlantic from the drudgery of considering third-rate novels *et al. et al. et al.*," Page complained in 1899, " . . . nothing on earth could have tempted me to leave it." Page declared that "the only way to have a good *Atlantic* is to have a man who is absolutely free—not approximately free—to give his whole constructive thought to it—absolutely free—so free that he is not responsible for any routine office duties."[49]

Yet Page did not try to gain as much freedom as he wanted and might have gotten in directing the magazine, nor did he display the same resourcefulness with the *Atlantic* as he had with the *Forum*. His only new departure in technique lay in broadcasting editorials. He used his own voice more on the *Atlantic*, acting somewhat like a newspaper editor—a practice that he continued on his own magazine, *World's Work*. But Page did not pursue his earlier ideas about investigative reporting, and he showed less spark in his plans for series in the *Atlantic* than he had for series in the *Forum*. Even though Page interested himself more than any previous editor in the business side of the *Atlantic*, he displayed little of the alertness to advertising, circulation, and profits that had characterized his editorship of the *Forum*.

The oddest contrast between Page's conduct of the two magazines lay in the matter of financial control. The *Atlantic*'s basic trouble was its connection with Houghton, Mifflin. As Ellery Sedgwick later noted "what the magazine suffered from was its position as the very small fifth wheel of a very cumbersome coach." The *Atlantic* did not begin to fulfill its potential for garnering a broader circulation until Sedgwick became editor in 1909. With aid from Jenkins, he effected a separation and later a divorce from "the House." As his complaint to Scudder indicated, Page recognized the trouble. At one point in 1897 he implied that he might seek the same combination of intellectual and financial backing for the *Atlantic* that he had sought for the *Forum*. "In a word, I am going to make the *Atlantic* a kind of power that we haven't now," he informed John Jay Chapman. " . . . Well, the Atlantic in two or three years will be another sort of thing—provided I can find half a dozen men like the two or three that I've already found." That vague hint offered the sole evidence that Page thought about taking over the *Atlantic*. It seems strange that he did not make an active bid for control, especially after the way he fought for the *Forum*. Even stranger, Page apparently did try to buy the magazine about two years after he left. In May 1901 he conveyed a cryptic offer to Mifflin, who pretended to treat the request as a joke.[50]

At heart, Page probably did not want to run the *Atlantic*. His subsequent offer to buy the magazine seems to have been a gesture of concern rather than a serious attempt to gain control. He evidently wanted to show his interest in literary culture, just as he had earlier attempted to maintain a foothold in southern journalism through ownership of the *Manufacturers Record*. In both cases, Page intended to remain at a safe distance in New York. Besides lack of independence for himself, the southerner's most frequent complaints about the *Atlantic* involved its limited audience and small budget. And he clearly missed the excitement of New York, which was now the country's undisputed cultural capital. Once, when he was visiting in Boston after leaving the *Atlantic*, he remarked to a southern friend, "New York is everything. Boston is Boston."[51]

The circumstances under which Page abruptly left the *Atlantic* in the summer of 1899 exposed the roots of his discontent. Rather then seeming restless when he resumed work after his illness on 15 May 1899, Page showed signs of settling down. Early in June he and Alice inquired about buying a house in Cambridge. His summer plans included a bicycle trip with his sons along the Maine coast, lecturing at Chautauqua, and camping in New Hampshire. Then, without warning, late in June 1899, Page found those prospects shattered by a barrage of communications from S. S. McClure. The meteoric editor of

McClure's Magazine first wrote from an ocean liner. "I have greatly enlarged my borders," he apprised Page. "I want very much to see you." As soon as his ship docked on 24 June McClure telegraphed, "Should see you immediately. Have biggest thing on earth. Several in fact." The same day he sent Page a letter urging him to come to New York the following week. "I have got the earth with several things thrown in," he announced, "and am anxious to see if you don't want one or two kingdoms for yourself." McClure added, "I regard you as the one indispensable man in the world for our enterprises at the present time."[52]

Page traveled to New York on 29 June 1899 to learn what realms were being offered. A heat wave sent temperatures on Fifth Avenue as high as 106 degrees, but hot weather never enervated "Sam" McClure. The irrepressible editor disclosed that he and his associates had taken over the nation's leading publishing company, Harper & Brothers. The "house of Harper," as that firm was known, enjoyed unequaled eminence. It was both America's oldest and largest book publisher and the owner of four distinguished magazines, *Harper's Magazine*, *Harper's Weekly*, *Harper's Bazaar*, and *Harper's Round Table*. The venerable house had fallen on bad times in the late 1890s, principally because of mismanagement by a third generation of the founding clan. Only substantial loans from the magnate J. P. Morgan had saved the company from bankruptcy. In February 1899, Morgan had invited McClure and his partners to assume control under an arrangement by which they would try to repay the 2.5 million dollars he had advanced to the Harper firm. McClure had leapt at the proposal because, for once, a project fulfilled even his grandiose visions. Between his own enterprises, which included *McClure's Magazine* and the book-publishing firm of Doubleday & McClure, and "the house of Harper," he would command a publishing empire.

The *Atlantic* editor's prospective part in the venture fell somewhat short of McClure's advance billing. He wanted Page to edit an encyclopedia, which he envisioned as an American equivalent and competitor to the *Encyclopaedia Britannica*. Page must have doubted the significance of the job, since McClure protested soon afterward, "But the encyclopedia *is* a worthy work for you." Finances offered added inducement. Over the Fourth of July, Page conferred with McClure's second in command, John S. Phillips, at his summer home in Duxbury, Massachusetts. According to a telegram from McClure on 7 July, Phillips made a "proposition equivalent for first ten years service of half million dollars. Phillips suggests encyclopedia royalties could be used by you in securing additional stock." In that telegram McClure offered Page a salary of fifteen thousand dollars a year, fifty thousand dollars in stock, and a royalty on each set of encyclopedias sold. McClure presented one further enticement— the prospect of a place in the magazine side of his empire. In the same telegram on 7 July he stated, "Want you immediately on account partly five great periodicals and tremendous reorganizations going on." Writing a letter the same day, McClure insisted upon the importance of the encyclopedia but added, "However as I said we are a band of independent brothers & you can pick out your own planets to rule." He hoped, too, that Page would go "with John & me into the great magazine work for the next few months."[53]

Page's reservations quickly crumbled. On 5 July, after he had met with Phillips, Page warned Mifflin that he might resign. Two days later, when McClure's telegraphed offer came, he wired back his acceptance within a few hours. Thus two weeks after first being approached by McClure, Page threw aside the most distinguished editorial chair in the United States. His action did not surprise Scudder, who attributed Page's departure to "the consciousness he would have of playing in a large game and of employing his powers in a large enterprise." Scudder accurately assessed the project's attractions for Page. Money probably loomed larger than he cared to admit. In a long letter to Scudder, Page denied that money had led him to resign from the *Atlantic* and Houghton, Mifflin. Yet he concluded the letter with the assertion, "It is only when a man is reduced to the work that tires and fags one out & never ends & becomes a dull routine of a thousand kinds—only then that he necessarily becomes a hireling and thinks of money or can be tempted by money."[54]

Page's decision also reflected his state of mind during the summer of 1899. Several conditions made him regard McClure's offer as a now-or-never proposition. His complaint to Scudder about being tired and fagged out indicated how much his illness the preceding April had shaken him. When Bliss Perry came for an interview in July, he thought Page looked much older than he had in the days with the *Forum*. Indeed, he was older. His forty-fourth birthday came in August 1899. His illness, together with his mother's recent death and his father's failing health, all served as reminders of his own mortality. When he later explained his resignation from the *Atlantic* to Thayer, Page asserted that there were "many easier & better & more influential things to do—yet; ten years hence I might have been too old." Frank Page's declining condition may have had a particular influence on his son. Not much time remained for Walter to show his father that he could make a great business success. When he talked with Perry during July 1899, Page made his remark, "A man who won't bet on himself isn't worth a damn."[55]

This gamble nearly ended badly, not because of what Page had given up, but because of what he had taken on. If he had examined McClure's project with any care, he could have seen that the takeover of Harper & Brothers was not a sound venture. Observers in New York publishing circles doubted that anyone could relieve the old firm from its heavy indebtedness. Fortunately McClure's business manager, Albert Brady, had inserted an escape clause into the agreement with Morgan. At least the undertaking did not carry the risk of total financial disaster. For Page, the venture soon developed snags. Several persons who knew S. S. McClure commented on the vagary of his promises. Page got his first taste of his new chief's unreliability when he began making arrangements to join the McClure organization. McClure had sailed off again early in July 1899 on another of his ceaseless peregrinations. As was customary in his organization, the top lieutenants, particularly the quiet, steady John Phillips, had to execute the chief's proposals. When Page discussed the terms of his position shortly after accepting, Phillips began to hedge with generalities.

Once Page arrived in New York at the middle of August, he encountered further disappointments. First, Phillips insisted that the Harper book department required direction, so that Page again found himself wrestling with book editing and manuscript reading. Still worse, Page learned that he was being frozen out of the magazine side of the venture. McClure's flattery had been another example of his effusive insincerity. Actually, McClure did not hold a high opinion of Page's ability as a magazine editor. His main reason for recruiting Page apparently was to use the former *Atlantic* editor as window dressing and then groom him to head the Harper book department. In the combined Harper-McClure venture, all but one of the magazine editorships went to people who had an inside track with the chief. Two *McClure's* staffers, Ida Tarbell and Ray Stannard Baker, edited that magazine and *Harper's Round Table*. Henry Mills Alden retained the editorship of the monthly *Harper's*, but McClure brought in his old friend John Huston Finley to become editor of *Harper's Weekly*. The assignment of the *Weekly* must have come as a blow to Page, because the resignation of the previous editor was deliberately kept secret from him until after Finley's appointment.

Page was not the only dissatisfied party. McClure's bid to control the house of Harper began foundering in the fall of 1899 on the predicted reef of the firm's debt. The top people in the McClure and Harper offices grew tense and fatigued. Some of the strain found a focus that soon benefited Page. One member of the McClure team who hung back from the Harper venture was Frank Doubleday, the partner in the book-publishing side of the McClure enterprise. Doubleday was reluctant to submerge his new and relatively small publishing house within an enlarged version of the already-mammoth Harper firm. Friction had occurred earlier between Doubleday and McClure's principal associates, Phillips and Brady, over the allocation of stock. The original nucleus of McClure's organization consisted of himself and those two, who had known each other since student days at Knox College in Illinois. The organization had not remained entirely inbred, since Baker and Tarbell had also risen to important positions on *McClure's*, yet it was hardly coincidental that Finley, the new editor of *Harper's Weekly*, was president of Knox. Doubleday and Page, who were alumni of neither McClure's college nor his magazine, remained outsiders. As the financial situation worsened for the Harper venture, McClure put pressure on Doubleday to amalgamate his operation with the rest of the enterprise. The chief demanded both additional working capital and an undivided effort.

Page maintained an unruffled appearance during these months. At the beginning of November 1899 he told Scudder, "I enjoy the new freedom that I have found—freedom from having to read millions of poems & stories & to make up magazine schedules and the freedom to go out & try to find out what people are writing." Page may have been dissembling, but he was not just keeping up a brave front. By that time he and Doubleday had almost certainly laid plans to break away from McClure and start their own company. The two men had first met soon after the North Carolinian came to New York in 1885, and they had renewed their acquaintance in the spring of 1898, when Page had dealt with Doubleday and McClure over disputed publication rights for some Carlyle letters. How and when Doubleday and Page decided to split off from McClure are not known, but their joining forces was natural. Both were outsiders who harbored grievances against McClure. By the middle of November 1899 they were confiding to friends and prospective authors that they were about to start a new publishing house.[56]

Events moved swiftly. Late in November 1899 McClure finally bowed to Phillips's and Brady's demands that they withdraw from the attempt to take over Harper & Brothers. Despite their efforts, the firm had lost four hundred thousand dollars under their management. Everyone except McClure felt lucky to have escaped with his financial skin. Then on 8 December Doubleday informed McClure of his and Page's imminent departure. On 18 December 1899 came the public announcement of the formation of Doubleday, Page & Company, with offices at 34 Union Square East. Page had passed through an incredible six months since resigning from the *Atlantic*. He had recouped an error in judgment into partnership in his own publishing firm. Moreover, most publishing houses at that time regarded a magazine as a necessary adjunct. The new firm announced no plans for a magazine, but both custom and Page's background suggested that a new periodical would soon emerge under his editorship.

In a sense Page had come full circle in the four and half years since he had left the *Forum*. His time in Boston represented a detour in his career, even though he had gained important experience. Working for Houghton, Mifflin had introduced Page to book publishing, which, despite his complaints, would continue to be his second most important occupation. The *Atlantic* had helped him develop his political and social views further, and editing the magazine during the Spanish-American War had stimulated him to use a journal as his own platform. Equally important, Page took away from the *Atlantic* the aura of having held the country's most prestigious editorial chair. Best of all, Page could at long last become more or less his own boss, and he would soon have a magazine of his own creation. On 14 December 1899 Page was back in Boston on business. Stopping in at 4 Park Street to see Scudder and Mifflin, he naturally informed them about his forthcoming venture. "Everything looked big to Page," Scudder remarked in his diary. That comment could have served as Page's epitaph. It certainly described his experience in Boston, especially his coming and going.[57]

CHAPTER 6

Publisher

Doubleday, Page & Company did not start out big. The third floor of an older building on Union Square housed the entire concern when it began in December 1899. Editors, clerks, executives, and stenographers worked side by side in one sparsely furnished room. Only the company's five partners had cubicles for private offices. Besides Page and Frank Doubleday, the partners included Samuel A. Everitt, the firm's treasurer; Herbert S. Houston, who had formerly worked on newspapers and magazines; and Henry W. Lanier, the son of the poet Sidney Lanier and himself experienced in the advertising side of book publishing. None of them except Page had turned forty by the end of 1899. Everitt and Lanier were still in their twenties. Only Page enjoyed any renown outside New York book-publishing circles. None of the partners except Doubleday had much money to stake in the new company. The firm's original capital totaled twenty-five thousand dollars, nearly all of which evidently came from Doubleday's wife, who belonged to a wealthy Chicago mercantile family. Thanks in part to the beginnings made by the Doubleday and McClure firm, Doubleday, Page & Company put out in its first year of publication about 60 books as compared to 120 for a leading New York firm such as Charles Scribner's Sons, or 90 for Page's former employer, Houghton, Mifflin.

But the firm's relatively small size and slender capital were deceptive. Doubleday deserved his reputation as a shrewd commercial publisher. From the McClure connection he took away exclusive American book rights for the work of his friend Rudyard Kipling, who was then at the height of his popularity on both sides of the Atlantic. Doubleday also brought with him Booth Tarkington as an author and Frank Norris as both author and employee. Page contributed to the firm's stable of proven popular novelists early in 1900 by luring Ellen Glasgow away from Harper's and Mary Wilkins from Houghton, Mifflin. Among nonfiction works, Page had been arranging in December 1899 to publish Booker T. Washington's autobiography before either the black leader had written the book or the company had opened its doors. Doubleday's and Page's efforts turned their firm almost at once into a major book publisher. During its first year the company cracked the best-seller lists with Glasgow's *The Voice of the People* and Tarkington's *The Gentleman from Indiana*, as well as with the memoirs of a scandalous Polish countess and the dog story *Bob, Son of Battle*. During its second year Doubleday, Page added to its best-sellers Norris's *The Octopus* and Washington's *Up from Slavery*, together with three romantic novels.

Sales continued to climb throughout the next few years, with the volume for 1910 amounting to $1,800,000. Profits followed apace. For the three-year period from 1905 through 1907, yearly net profits averaged $64,442. During the following three years, 1908 through 1910, the average annual net profit stood at $184,572. The gains in sales and profits also reflected expansion of Doubleday, Page's operations. The annual number of titles published grew to over one hundred within a few years, while the company's physical size mushroomed. In 1903, the firm forsook its original quarters on Union Square for its own new six-story building a few blocks away on East Sixteenth Street. The number of employees had by then grown to over a hundred, not only because of book sales but also because the firm had entered the magazine field and had begun to do its own printing. In October 1910, Doubleday, Page & Company moved again, this time twenty miles to Garden City, Long Island. A sprawling, three-story, Tudor-style structure, christened the Country Life Press, housed a work force of nearly a thousand and turned out five thousand books and between fifteen and twenty thousand magazines a day. In a decade, Doubleday, Page had become one of the giants of American book publishing.[1]

Book publishing came first with Doubleday, Page & Company. During the initial months of the firm's existence the new partners busied themselves with signing up authors and bringing out books. Not until the spring of 1900 did either Page or Doubleday start thinking about magazines. Even after the company's magazines became profitable, books continued to earn the bulk of its revenues. Books were Doubleday's forte, just as magazines were Page's. A division of labor eventually arose between the two senior partners. But that division, which always remained flexible and informal, developed later. At the outset Page plunged into book publishing as deeply as Doubleday, and he contributed almost as much to their firm's rousing start.

Now that he was working for his own company, Page stopped complaining about being entangled in the book field. Most of his attention went to authors with whom he had dealt previously at Houghton, Mifflin and Harper's. In December 1899 and January 1900 Page also tried to pry loose Woodrow Wilson, James Whitcomb Riley, and James Ford Rhodes from Harper's and Joel Chandler Harris from D. Appleton & Company. Of those four, he succeeded only with Harris. His wooing of Glasgow and Harris showed that he had not sated his appetite for southern fiction. Later he secured novels and volumes of short stories from Thomas Dixon, Sara Beaumont Kennedy, and James Branch Cabell, and he tried to add Mary Johnston to the firm's list of established stars. Page did not lose interest in black authors, either. Besides Washington, he attempted to get Charles Chesnutt to publish his new novel with Doubleday, Page. His approaches to Wilson and Rhodes indicated that history still formed one of his major emphases in book publishing. From Harper's he took away the project he had conceived there for a series of biographies of major figures in American history.

Page also transferred his previous working practices and literary opinions to the new publishing house. He continued to seek after promising authors and manuscripts. His cultivation of

*Presumed to be a self-caricature of Walter Hines Page,
executed ca. 1905*

COUNTRY LIFE PRESS, *September 1910;*
left to right: F. N. Doubleday, Theodore Roosevelt,
and Walter Hines Page

(*by permission of the Houghton Library, Harvard University*)

Washington for his life story foreshadowed further efforts to elicit autobiographies from well-known people. Some whom he later approached included such diverse figures as Jane Addams, Helen Keller, Andrew Carnegie, Robert M. La Follette, and William Howard Taft. Page still usually dealt with authors on a cordial personal basis, and he soon gained a reputation for skill and tact in handling some notoriously prickly writers. His courtesy extended to authors whose work he rejected as well as to those whom he published. "Every letter of declination ought to be written by a skillful man," Page wrote in his anonymously published work *A Publisher's Confession*, "—a diplomatist who can write an unpleasant truth without offence." He filled his own bill so well that his fellow Tar Heel O. Henry supposedly quipped, "Walter Page could turn down a story so neatly that you could take that letter to a bank and get money on it."[2]

In accepting and declining manuscripts, he maintained both his literary moralism and his commercialism. In February 1901, for example, Page turned down a novel because it was *"an unrelieved study of the most distressing form of disease."* To the rejected author he delivered the dictum, "One thing counts in art, in literature, in life, as nothing else; and that is health." Nor did Page modify his disdain for destructive criticism and precious writing. As a corollary to his literary democracy, he partially accepted commercial standards in judging a book's value. Page seldom had compunctions about refusing manuscripts on the ground that they would not sell, and he defended popular novels in his *Publisher's Confession* for having "construction" and "substance," which were "qualities that are rarer than the merely literary quality."[3]

Moralism and commercialism each occasioned the two most famous incidents involving Page and novels published by his firm. The first incident arose a few months after Doubleday, Page's founding. In May 1900, a twenty-nine-year-old journalist submitted a novel that Harper's had just rejected. An earthy, occasionally profane work, the novel told the story of a promiscuous woman, her thieving lover, and other amoral characters among the lower strata of society, all of whom the author depicted without blame, as creatures caught up in a web of impersonal forces. The title of the manuscript was "Sister Carrie," and the author was Theodore Dreiser. Doubleday, Page's chief reader, the novelist Frank Norris, erupted with enthusiasm for "Sister Carrie" and urged publication. Next, Page read the manuscript and echoed at least some of Norris's acclaim. On 9 June he wrote to Dreiser congratulating him on "so good a piece of work" and telling him that "we are very much pleased with your novel." The two men met a few days later to discuss the manuscript, and Page promised that his firm would publish "Sister Carrie."[4]

Nothing untoward occurred until mid-July, when two of Page's partners attacked the novel. On 13 or 14 July Henry Lanier announced that he disliked the novel and thought some other firm should publish it. Then on 18 July Frank Doubleday returned from a three-month business trip to Europe. Stopping at the office immediately after his ship docked, Doubleday learned about the Dreiser novel and probably about the disagreement between Page and Lanier. He took the manuscript home to read. That night he and his wife went through "Sister Carrie" with mounting dismay. The Doubledays agreed that the novel was a bad risk for the company. According to the recollection of Doubleday's lawyer, the publisher thought that "the book would be a flop commercially," while Mrs. Doubleday "knew it would not be allowed in the homes of her friends who were rearing young children." The following day Doubleday came back to the office bent on stopping his firm from publishing Dreiser's book.[5]

Doubleday did not succeed, but his attempt created an incident that fostered a fable about the suppression of a great novel. Dreiser, with Norris's continued backing, demanded that the firm go through with publication. Doubleday, on advice from his lawyer, felt compelled to honor Page's earlier promise, and he signed a contract with Dreiser on 20 August. But, true to the publisher's prediction, the book sold badly after its publication on 8 November 1900. The publishers disposed of only 650 copies, including those distributed to reviewers; Dreiser earned less than one hundred dollars in royalties. Worse, *Sister Carrie* did badly despite special promotional efforts by Norris, who retained his faith in the novel. The book's poor showing never ceased to rankle Dreiser, who insisted for the rest of his life that Doubleday, Page had refused to sell any copies and had thrown them in the cellar. Much of Dreiser's bitterness sprang from his own legendary insecurity. The firm actually gave *Sister Carrie* more attention than most of the books it published in the fall of 1900. The novel evidently failed to sell because the reading public was unready, not so much for its subject matter as for its ungainly style and utter absence of moral judgment.

Page's role in the incident did him little credit, but it did reveal some important facts about his new business, his personality, and his literary views. The incident showed unmistakably who was boss at Doubleday, Page. Doubleday did not hesitate to try to break Page's promise to publish *Sister Carrie*. Of the people in the firm, only Norris stood up to Doubleday. Page wrote to Dreiser on 23 July trying to renege on the commitment. When Dreiser refused to budge, Page again tried to wriggle out. He suggested that not publishing *Sister Carrie* with Doubleday, Page was of no great consequence and that not publishing the novel at all might be better for Dreiser's literary career. Page's knuckling under to Doubleday furnished an early sign of his subordinate place in the publishing house. His behavior toward Dreiser showed how weak he could often become in attempting to avoid personal unpleasantness.

For Page's literary views, however, the incident again demonstrated that he was nowhere near so priggish as he sometimes seemed. Page had a mixed attitude toward *Sister Carrie*. In his first meeting with Dreiser he claimed to have criticized the "choice of characters." Yet even while he was trying to get out of publishing *Sister Carrie* in July 1900, he confessed to Dreiser that he found "the vivid workmanship of the book exceedingly attractive." In accepting the novel for publication Page probably got swept up in Norris's enthusiasm. But even so, he could never have gone along with Norris if he had been a complete prig. Several years later one of Norris's successors in the firm, another bright young writer with advanced tastes, reportedly complained about Arthur Page, "I wish I could get past Arthur and win his father's ear. He's not so hide-bound and conventional."[6]

Commercialism undermined Page's principles more than fin-ickiness about subjects. The other renowned incident involving him and novels published by his firm showed how much he could betray cherished views for the sake of selling books. A year after the *Sister Carrie* incident, in August or September 1901, Page received a manuscript in the mail from an address in Virginia. It was a novel set in North Carolina after the Civil War, a lurid tale of Negro bestiality curbed by white men resorting to violence and political repression. The novel bore the title "The Leopard's Spots," and it came from Page's onetime Watauga Club friend, Thomas Dixon. In the intervening years, Dixon too had left North Carolina and had tried his hand at law, acting, the minis-try, and graduate study at the Johns Hopkins, before deciding to write novels. "The Leopard's Spots" was his first effort. Dixon later claimed that the novel had made such an impression on Page that the publisher had stayed up all night reading the manuscript and had gotten knocked down by a trolley the next morning as he crossed a street, still engrossed in the story. Ac-cording to Dixon, Page had wired him immediately, accepting the book and asking the author to come to New York to sign a con-tract. Much of Dixon's story sounds apocryphal, particularly because Page secured a reading from Norris, who urged the firm not to publish the novel. But Page went ahead with the book, and *The Leopard's Spots* quickly became a best-seller. During the next six years, Doubleday, Page published three more novels by Dixon, *The One Woman*, *The Clansman*, and *The Traitor*, each of which sold several hundred thousand copies.

Being Dixon's publisher caused Page embarrassment as soon as *The Leopard's Spots* appeared. Dixon's book seemed in singu-larly bad taste because it was published by the same house that only a few months before had brought out Washington's *Up from Slavery*. Doubleday, Page compounded the lapse of taste by advertising the two books on adjoining pages in *World's Work*. Garrison, Page's former associate at Houghton, Mifflin, later wrote to upbraid him for publishing Dixon along with Washing-ton. The black leader himself reportedly complained in a personal interview with Page after the publication of *The Clansman* in

1905. Page supposedly rejoined that *The Clansman* "stood for a point of view in the South and that the surest way to overcome that point of view was to bring it into the light." About the same time, in June 1905, Dixon embarrassed his publisher among moderate northern and southern whites by publicly attacking the Southern Education Board. The board's head, Robert C. Ogden, confided to another member, "It is difficult to see how our friends, Doubleday, Page & Co., can give to Dixon the moral standing created by the character of their house as his publisher."

Except for Washington and Garrison, almost none of Page's friends confronted him with objections to Dixon. The publisher, in turn, rarely said anything about the author. But Page's few comments indicated that he recognized how badly he had compromised his literary and social views. The thinly veiled lasciviousness of Dixon's novels offended moral scruples. A Doubleday, Page employee later remembered that Page rejected another author's story on a sexual subject with the remark, "Even 'The Leopard's Spots' (for which may God forgive us) does not go the length of this." Page likewise held a low opinion of Dixon's talents as a writer. In 1913 he observed about a flashy English author, "I thought he'd play out as Tom Dixon did." Nor was Page always able to satisfy himself with his own rationalization to Washington that giving exposure to Dixon's racism was the most effective way to combat such prejudices. During World War I, while he was in London as ambassador, he attended a showing of D. W. Griffith's film, "The Birth of a Nation," which was based on *The Clansman*. Page wrote in his diary, "Gott Strafe Tom Dixon! I saw 'The Birth of a Nation' tonight."[7]

Misgivings about Dixon did not entail doubts about the commercial aspects of publishing. Defending the need for books to make money formed the strongest argument in Page's own book, *A Publisher's Confession*. Page spun many writing plans between 1900 and 1903, including ideas for short stories and novels, proposals for New York letters to the *Boston Transcript*, and promises to dramatize Mary Johnston's *To Have and to Hold* and to do articles on the South for the *Atlantic*, the *Outlook*, and the *Encyclopaedia Britannica*. Except for the 1902

Atlantic piece, none of the plans came off. In 1904, however, Page finally carried through with one of his writing projects—a series of ten anonymous letters about book publishing, which appeared weekly in the *Boston Transcript* between September and November 1904. Doubleday, Page reprinted the letters, still without the author's name, as a short book in the spring of 1905, under the title *A Publisher's Confession*.

Page wrote his second book almost by accident. *A Publisher's Confession* was a defense of the book trade from the publisher's standpoint, prompted, he said, by conditions against which a "self respecting worm would have turned long ago." Page described and criticized the whole publishing process from manuscript to sales. He produced figures to show that on a $1.50 book that paid a 20 percent royalty to the author, the publisher's earnings were only 50 cents. The figures signified two things to Page: first, that the author was getting too big a royalty, and second, that the book was priced too low. He advocated both smaller royalties and higher prices. Upholding a strictly businesslike approach to publishing, Page declared that "a book is a commodity," "novel-making is an industry," and publishing "is, after all, only a piece of machinery." He admitted that publishing "has for the moment a decided commercial squint," but he maintained that authors, by gouging ever-higher royalty advances and percentages, had done more than publishers to commercialize the trade. Page also argued that commercialization did not mean that publishing had become degraded. "Bad" novels he defended as a legitimate form of entertainment, although they might offend "literary" sensibilities. "But the 'literary' view of fiction is no more trustworthy than the 'literary' view of politics or of commerce; for it concerns itself more with technique than with substance."

Such iconoclasm was bound to stir up controversy. A number of newspapers and publishing trade journals in the United States and Britain took issue with the *Transcript* letters. After the book *A Publisher's Confession* appeared, several observers guessed at Page's authorship, and a few commentators praised the book. But in June 1905 George Bernard Shaw acknowledged receiving a copy by suggesting that the title should read "Confessions of a Thundering Liar." The following November, the *Atlantic* carried a long rebuttal to *A Publisher's Confession* by Henry Holt, one of the most old-fashioned New York publishers. Most of the book's detractors misread its defense of commercialism. Page called for lower royalties and higher prices as ways to put publishing houses on a more secure financial footing. That way, he believed, publishers would not have to depend so heavily upon the huge volume sales that only the most popular novels could assure. Page sneered at "the writers of romances for kitchen maids and shop girls," who treated "the publisher as a mere manufacturer and 'boomer.'" He looked forward to a better day when authors and publishers would once more enjoy close personal relations, cease to "imitate the manners of tradesmen," and join hands again in mutual service to culture, learning, and literature. "Here is a chance for reverence, for something like consecration." In the end, *A Publisher's Confession* preached an old-fashioned, idealistic sermon.

As with his other occupations, Page regarded book publishing partly as a secular equivalent to the pulpit. In *A Publisher's Confession* he called publishing "the least profitable of all the professions, except preaching and teaching, to each of which it is a sort of cousin." He also affirmed that "a publisher who is worthy of his calling regards himself as an educator of the public." After the first year or two of Doubleday, Page's existence, Page devoted less of his attention to fiction and more to nonfiction works that related to public affairs or had educational purposes. The change continued his earlier shift of interests away from literature. Although Page did not forsake fiction as either a publisher or a writer, his main activities went into nonfiction. Page's two pet projects demonstrated both what really interested him and what ends he most wanted to serve as a book publisher.[8]

The first project originated while he was still at Harper's. In the fall of 1899, Page proposed to publish a series of English texts and grammars under the editorship of Mark H. Liddell, a professor at the University of Texas. The core of the series was to be a new edition of Shakespeare, based upon the latest scholarship, "with a *copyrightable text*" that would earn royalties for all reprintings and play productions. The series was also to include grammars for Shakespeare and Old and Middle English, low-priced editions of English classics, and a book by Liddell on the structure of English poetry. "These several enterprises all hold together as a definite unit," claimed Page, because the "complete revolution . . . in the study and the teaching of English" had brought "the matter to the point of scientific and systematic organization." Taking the project with him to Doubleday, Page, he negotiated a contract in April 1900, under which Liddell quit his Texas post to work full time on the series. Liddell's book, *An Introduction to the Scientific Study of English Poetry*, came out in 1902. An edition of "Macbeth," the first volume in what had come to be entitled "The Elizabethan Shakspere [*sic*]," appeared early in 1903. Other volumes in the Shakespeare edition were scheduled to follow at the rate of three to six a year.[9]

These plans came crashing down soon after publication of the first Shakespeare volume. Liddell had insisted upon Elizabethan spelling and an elaborate format of printing in which annotation appeared all around the play's text on each page. As a result, not even the handsome typography that he had also demanded could make the book easy or pleasant to read. The format and typography also made production outrageously expensive. None of those conditions boded well for the "Elizabethan Shakspere" to become the standard edition that would find its way into every school, library, and theater of the English-speaking world. At the end of May 1903, when sales had proved disappointing, Doubleday intervened, refusing to commit the firm to more than two further volumes unless those sold better than the first one. Two months of bitter argument ensued before the series was scrapped.

Like the *Sister Carrie* incident, the Liddell venture showed who called the shots at Doubleday, Page. When Doubleday decided to scuttle the project, Page did not oppose him; rather, he tried to minimize the difficulty, as he had with Dreiser. In July 1903 he urged that Liddell "trust to my judgment, my ability, [and] let me manage the publishing problem as best I can."

Liddell preferred Doubleday's frankness to Page's reassurance. "Doubleday's conversation," he replied to Page, "admitted a different situation—the business one—that that situation was not new—that both you and I had been mistaken." Doubleday, Liddell added, "intimated the other day that you were too generous in business dealings." The main difference between the Liddell project and the *Sister Carrie* incident was that Page had gotten carried away with his own enthusiasm as much as someone else's. To the end he protested to Liddell, "We set out in a great enterprise—. . . one of the most important things that can perhaps ever come in my publishing life." But Doubleday prevailed and the series never resumed.[10]

The collapse of the Liddell project evidently chastened Page's notions about simultaneous pursuit of culture and profit through a book series, for he never again attempted anything on such a grand scale. The experience did not, however, completely change him. He made a second stab at the same sort of educational commercialism five years later. Starting in the spring of 1908, he urged another professor of literature, C. Alphonso Smith of The University of North Carolina, to undertake a series of "what may be called self-culture books." Page wanted to reach "the great audience for books about literature in the United States," people who had no specialized training and little formal education but who were nevertheless ambitious "to know how to go about making their culture higher and finer." He warned Smith that writing for such "an audience that is not trained but that is exceedingly intelligent" was difficult. The task was "really the teaching of intelligent adults. Yet it is not an easy Chautauqua-sort of shortcut to learning or culture."

Page let the idea lapse until April 1911, when he suggested a two-headed project to Smith. One part was a book explaining literature to ordinary people in simple, appealing terms. "He said that he had in mind," Smith later recalled, "a laboring man coming back from his daily tasks with money in his pocket and with willingness to give his children better opportunities than he himself had." The suggestion led Smith to write *What Can Literature Do for Me?*, which Doubleday, Page published in 1912.

The second part of the project was an attack on, as Page put it, "the problem of getting good literature into the hands and homes of the masses." Low-priced editions of classics still intrigued him, although he admitted that "the trouble lies in the difficulties of distribution. The bookstores do not reach enough of the masses of the people." Page urged Smith to keep thinking about it. "Put this problem before you: What machinery could you use to instruct the whole American people in Literature?"[11]

Nothing came of the project's second part. By 1912 when Smith's book appeared, Page had become even more deeply absorbed in public affairs, particularly in the Wilson presidential campaign, and in 1913 he left for the ambassadorship in London. But the 1911 proposal to Smith indicated how important schemes for the profitable promotion of culture through book publishing remained for Page. The Liddell and Smith projects provided him with opportunities to try to implement some of his strongest convictions about American society. In June 1904, just before he wrote *A Publisher's Confession*, Page delivered a speech at the University of Chicago entitled "The Cultivated Man in an Industrial Era." In the speech he contended that the nation's new industrial wealth presented not a threat but an opportunity for cultural growth. Economic development had, he believed, reintegrated cultivated people into national life. "Your cultivated man is not a man apart. He does not affect a manner of living or of speech or of work that betrays a dislocation from the life around him." A money-making way to reunite culture with practical affairs was what he wanted to achieve through his book-publishing projects.[12]

Yet before he aired his ideas to Smith, Page had turned his major attention away from book publishing. *A Publisher's Confession* in a sense represented his valedictory to primary concern with the book trade. After his early efforts to attract authors and his involvement in the Liddell project, he seems to have detached himself somewhat from the book side of Doubleday, Page, although he still interested himself in that part of the business and he did plan other book projects besides the one with Smith. With Upton Sinclair's *The Jungle*, Ray Stannard Baker's "David Grayson" books, and Woodrow Wilson's *The New Freedom*, he later attracted other best-sellers. But those books came to Doubleday, Page as by-products of Page's magazine work and his involvement in public affairs, not because he hustled for authors and manuscripts the way he once had done. The firm owed most of its best-sellers after 1904 to Doubleday's cultivating popular authors and snatching up the rest of McClure's stable when that great editor's enterprises foundered in 1908. The successful launching of the firm's first magazine, *World's Work*, at the end of 1900 with Page as editor began the division of labor between him and Doubleday. After 1904 the two men apparently staked out semiautonomous provinces. Magazines formed Page's greatest concern in the company and his principal avenue for pursuing his interests and aspirations.

In 1898, while he was straining at his bonds on the *Atlantic*, Page had given a speech in which he had compared a magazine editor to a locomotive engineer: "He does not make the machine, he only guides it, he cannot make it go on any track except the track which was originally designed for it." Coming from Frank Page's son, the comparison was revealing, and it was probably more than coincidence that railroads and railroad building became perennially favorite topics in the magazine that Page started in the fall of 1900. Founding *World's Work* gave him the long-awaited chance to break through the limitations that had hitherto hampered him as a magazine editor. With *World's Work* Page could be not only the engineer but also the railroad builder.[13]

Although they waited until Doubleday, Page got well under way in book publishing, the new firm's partners assumed from the outset that they would start a magazine. In 1902, Page recalled that because they had all had experience with magazines they had agreed, "We must make a magazine, *must* for the sheer love of it." Doubleday and Page began laying plans as early as April or May 1900. While he was in England, Doubleday discussed their ideas with Kipling, who reportedly suggested the name "World's Work." By midsummer, the project had taken shape. Someone, probably Doubleday, decided that the firm would not sink a huge sum of money into the venture. Too many magazines, Page later commented, drained "men's pockets and vitality" in pursuit of the "enticing and deadly fallacy" that they would pay next year. "If ours doesn't pay quickly," he remembered himself saying, "it will never pay." Some disagreement arose over whether to shoot for advertising or circulation first. The partners agreed, predictably perhaps, to go after both. In late July Page began seeking contributors for the first issue. By the middle of September, the contents were nearly complete. Page spent the first two weeks in October with the printers overseeing makeup and typography. On 13 October 1900 the first copy of *World's Work* came off the press. A week later the first issue of the hundred-page monthly, dated November 1900, hit the newsstands. Page at last had his own magazine.[14]

World's Work paid its way promptly. The magazine began with a press run of 35,000, and by May 1901 it had garnered 16,000 subscriptions. Total circulation pushed steadily, though not spectacularly, upward. In 1907 *World's Work* reached 100,-000, which was then considered the threshold of truly successful magazines; circulation eventually peaked at around 125,000 in 1909. It was a fine achievement. A number of people, including Andrew Carnegie and Mark Twain, had warned Doubleday and Page that they were courting failure by running a fresh entry in the already-crowded magazine field. Moreover, *World's Work*'s twenty-five-cents-an-issue price, serious tone, lack of fiction, and absence of artwork in illustrations all flew in the face of the formulas that had boosted the big-circulation periodicals that had emerged in the 1890s—*McClure's*, *Munsey's*, and the *Saturday Evening Post*. Those departures were intentional. Page later recalled, "There was a field that was vacant or at best partially occupied" that he wanted to fill. Before the first issue appeared he told Joel Chandler Harris that he was starting "a bully good" magazine. "It is not going to publish fiction, but it will be rather a practical, man's magazine, handsomely illustrated, as well written as possible, a thing of serious purpose and broad scope." Page had his own formula, which accounted for both the success and the shortcomings of his magazine.[15]

The first Doubleday, Page office on Union Square, where *World's Work* began, stood only a few hundred feet from the building that had housed the *Forum* when Page had been editor. The proximity was appropriate, because Page took up with his new magazine where he had left off with the other periodical five years before. The same focus of attention and viewpoint prevailed on *World's Work*. Public affairs dominated as much as or more than in the *Forum*. Educational, cultural, and economic topics likewise figured prominently. The opening number of *World's Work* revealed the basic mix of the magazine, with articles on the Catholic church in politics, nature photography, business conditions in Nebraska, America's position in international affairs, and new methods of teaching English. Page also tried unsuccessfully to get an article on the status and pay of teachers for the first issue. But *World's Work* initially differed from the *Forum* in three major ways: a lengthy section of editorial commentary entitled "The March of Events" opened each issue; articles did not follow the symposium format; and profuse illustrations graced the pages. In *World's Work*, Page was pursuing most of the departures that he had been contemplating at the time he had lost the battle for control of the *Forum*.

"The March of Events" started with an untitled, one-page statement on a subject of particular concern at the time of publication. Next came between twelve and twenty titled comments on other topics, varying in length from two hundred to fifteen hundred words. Often, one or more unsigned essays of two or three thousand words followed those pieces, elaborating on the opening statement or subjects in the shorter comments. This section of the magazine was pure Page. Not since the *State Chronicle* had he written so much in any publication that he edited. For the first eight years of *World's Work*, he produced nearly everything in the "March of Events." After 1908 or 1909 he delegated some of the writing to his son Arthur, who had joined the staff, but he continued to contribute substantial portions until 1913.

"The March of Events" provided Page with an ideal editorial platform. Each month, he delivered an informed, wide-ranging commentary that put the news in perspective. American politics loomed largest in the section, with business, agriculture, and the society also attracting much comment. Special attention frequently went to Page's own concerns, such as education, the South, black people, and foreign affairs. "The March of Events" also reflected the editor's peculiar style, and these commentaries contained Page's most effective writing outside his letters. His highest compliment to anyone else's writing was that the author made him hear "the very sound of your voice in my ears." "The March of Events" broadcasted Page's voice. His brother Henry exulted at the end of *World's Work*'s first year of publication, "The part of it that is so fine is the *you* that's in it. Your treatment of the live questions of the day not only has my hearty approval—without a single exception—but you say the very thing I would say if I only knew how."[16]

Henry Page's remark conveyed more than brotherly gush. He was the first of many to praise Walter Page for giving lucid expression to their own thoughts. His brother hit upon the quality that formed not only the secret of Page's success with "The March of Events" but also one of his greatest contributions to the development of American magazines. As in the *Forum*, he showed his sensitivity to a readership of educated, middle-class, mainly urban people like himself. "The March of Events" provided him with his best medium for reaching that audience.

Opening an issue of a magazine with views on current issues was a long-established practice among such political weeklies as *The Nation* and *Harper's Weekly*. Nor was the practice new to monthlies. Ten years earlier, Page's friend Albert Shaw had inaugurated a similar section, called "Progress of the World," in his *Review of Reviews*. With "The March of Events" Page once again improved on a good thing. But his improvement contributed to the development of magazines, for in borrowing the device Page made two adaptations. One was to put the imprint of his personality on his commentary, which not only made "The March of Events" livelier than similar features in other magazines but also provided a readily discernible viewpoint with which readers could identify. That was one reason why people could say that

"The March of Events" expressed their own thoughts. For example, one comment in the first issue expressed standard middle-class beliefs about initiative and education: "There is not a successful man, engaged in any active pursuit, that will read this paragraph who does not need a young man, or a dozen young men, of the right mettle and training. . . . There are, moreover, more brilliant chances in the professions for the best-trained men than our society ever before offered."

Page's other adaptation in "The March of Events" was to abandon direct advocacy. His comments left no doubt about where he stood, but he did not come out and tell people what to think or do. The first issue of *World's Work* appeared a few days after the 1900 election, which had rematched Bryan against President McKinley. "The March of Events" stated that the gold standard had played the decisive role in McKinley's victory because "almost every community that has a highly organized and responsible commercial life voted for it." In the second issue, "The March of Events" observed that the election had hinged on the question: "Should we maintain our commercial honor and credit, should we accept our international responsibilities, and should we go forward in our natural and fairly won commercial progress to supremacy?" Such postures of blatant commendation without formally endorsing parties and candidates sustained the impression in readers' minds that *World's Work* was viewing events just the way they would if they were better informed. In its ostensibly detached yet forcefully opinionated discussion of the news, "The March of Events" employed the same technique and style that Britten Haddon and Henry Luce began using on a weekly basis in the 1920s in *Time*. Page had developed the basic device of the twentieth-century newsmagazine.[17]

Not only "The March of Events" embodied the newsmagazine concept. So did a second distinctive feature of *World's Work* —the absence of fiction. In eschewing fiction Page was rejecting the most popular magazine feature of the time. Practical considerations may have played a part in the original decision not to publish fiction. McClure retained serial rights to several of the best-selling authors, including Kipling and Tarkington, whose book rights Doubleday had brought to the new publishing house. Also, at the time of the founding of *World's Work*, Page was overseeing *Everybody's Magazine*, under a contract with its owner, John Wanamaker. *Everybody's* devoted the bulk of its space to short stories and serialized novels, and either Page or Doubleday decided to make that magazine the principal outlet for the firm's new fiction authors. However, Page did lower the bar once on fiction in *World's Work*. During the first year, the magazine ran a monthly observation on the passing scene by "Colonel Billy Sanders," an imaginary cracker-barrel philosopher created by Joel Chandler Harris. "We want Billy Sanders to keep the thing from being unnaturally solemn," Page told Harris. That was another way of admitting that humorous stories by a famous author would help sell the magazine.[18]

But Page's underlying reason for steering clear of fiction was his conception of *World's Work* as a newsmagazine. In a "March of Events" comment in 1910 he divided magazines into three categories: the "class" periodical, which presented the finest in thought and literary art; the "general" one, which purveyed entertainment and "mild and easy instruction"; and a "newer kind . . . that concerns itself chiefly with the present activities of the world and is interpretative of contemporary life." *World's Work* belonged to that third category, which had "come into existence chiefly because of the geographical and other limitations of the newspapers." The magazine seemed to confirm even further Scudder's earlier opinion that journalism mattered more to Page than literature. Although Scudder apparently never discussed *World's Work* with Page, their mutual friend W. R. Thayer criticized the magazine after the second issue by asking, "What opening does it afford for *best* work?" Page responded to the criticism both by explaining to Thayer why he had left the *Atlantic* and by asserting in the third issue that *World's Work* cared "about literature and its production more than it cares for all other things put together." The magazine sought to encourage literature by reporting men's activities, because it was "out of action, hope, achievement, the doing of things—that the independence of mind comes that feels the creative impulse." In short, Page believed that an

exciting newsmagazine served the democratic, activist requirements of American literature.[19]

A third distinctive feature of *World's Work* lay in its illustrations, which formed another facet of Page's idea of a newsmagazine. Unlike virtually every illustrated periodical, *World's Work*
used only photographs. The sole artwork came on the cover,
which experimented for the first ten years with various designs
before resorting to a plain listing of leading articles under a small
globe. Inside, *World's Work* abounded with photographs. A gal-
lery of full-page portraits of men and women in the news appeared
regularly in "The March of Events." Pictures of scenes, people,
buildings, and activities ranged throughout the magazine and
varied in size from full pages to small insets. Seldom more than
two or three pages passed without a photograph. Besides carrying
far more photographs than any other magazine, *World's Work*
often used the text as a vehicle for the illustrations. Articles on
advances in photography, especially by naturalists and scientists,
afforded opportunities for presenting striking pictures of plants,
animals, volcanoes, and stars. Such subjects as railroad building
in remote areas and difficult terrain and construction of bridges
and skyscrapers presented occasions for spectacular photographs
of natural and man-made scenes. In all, *World's Work* photographs conveyed the most vivid impressions of the contemporary
world of any American magazine.

The photographs likewise reflected Page's basic viewpoint.
Except for portraits of newsmakers, the most common subjects
for pictures were feats of technology and faraway places and
exotic peoples. Those illustrations made *World's Work* look strikingly like the format that Gilbert Grosvenor introduced in 1901
to *The National Geographic*. Though probably accidental, the
resemblance was fitting. The two magazines were the only periodicals of the time that made extensive use of photographs, thereby foreshadowing *Life* and other picture magazines of the 1930s
and 1940s. Both *World's Work* and *The National Geographic*
also conveyed a sense of excitement and wonder at the technical
achievements of modern Western man in mastering the environment and making every part of the world accessible. That was

the spirit espoused by Page in *World's Work*. In the statement of purpose at the beginning of the first issue, he celebrated modern American industry for "changing the character of men," bringing to workers and businessmen the same joy and sense of accomplishment that only artists used to find. *"It is with the activities of the newly organized world, its problems and even its romance, that this magazine will earnestly concern itself, trying to convey the cheerful spirit of men who do things."*[20]

World's Work embodied the basic idea and method that Page had pursued throughout his journalistic career. He was still seeking through magazines a fruitful, harmonious synthesis of culture, business, and public affairs, and he had the same way of going after that aim. *World's Work* gave him expanded scope for practicing his editorial credo of getting out among people and keeping in touch with events. In the Doubleday, Page offices in New York he received his usual stream of callers, and he resumed his earlier custom of lunching at a hotel or the University Club with visitors and steady companions. It probably never occurred to Page to separate home life from work. He frequently invited guests for dinner and to stay overnight at his home, where they engaged in earnest conversation until after midnight. His neighbor when he lived in Englewood, New Jersey, remembered that Page constantly read books, magazines, and newspapers on their daily train and ferryboat rides to and from Manhattan. The *World's Work* editor also managed to see a bit of the world. His several yearly trips south of the Potomac now included regular attendance at the Conference for Education in the South, along with the other members of the Southern Education Board. In 1905 Page visited the West Coast for the first time, in connection with a special issue of *World's Work* on the Pacific Northwest. During the summer of 1909 he spent two months with his wife and daughter in Britain, Ireland, Germany, France, and the Netherlands.

Page continued previous practices, too, in getting material for *World's Work*. He once more fired off volleys of letters imploring prospective authors to write articles, telling them what and how to write, and evangelizing them about the importance of their subjects. A classic Page exhortation came in July 1908 when he asked Ray Stannard Baker to do a piece *"at once"* on wheat and corn. He suggested at length how Baker could convey a feeling for life on a typical farm, include sketches of successful farmers, and describe colors, sounds, and smells of wheat and corn, rain and drought, and great harvesting machines. He wanted "photographs (by pen and lens) of typical men who are great farmers. . . . I keep coming back to individual experiences. Everything interesting reduces itself to that at last—doesn't it?" Page was prescribing the same formula as he always had for the successful magazine article—it should be, as much as possible, a story of individual people. "In this magazine game," he told a friend in 1911, "we have got to have stories. That may be regrettable, but nevertheless it is a fact. Essays don't do the trick." Page continued to advocate presenting a subject "sensationally," by which he explained again that he meant "in personal, graphic ways, in a way that is polewide from the essay form."[21]

For the first ten years the *World's Work* staff numbered just four people besides Page himself. A managing editor handled administrative work, a financial editor wrote the regular business features, and two editorial assistants did a variety of jobs. These staffers were all young men who eventually moved on from *World's Work*. In them, the editor again demonstrated a faculty for spotting talent. The editor and his young staff functioned as a close-knit team. They had frequent, freewheeling luncheon conferences and for a while they organized a dinner club to exchange ideas with other journalists. The editor often acted as a fatherly tutor, and one staff member lived with the Pages in Englewood for a year. Page's son Arthur joined the magazine in 1905, upon graduation from Harvard. The situation changed in later years, with the addition of established writers to the staff, while the magazine relied less on outside writers. In 1910 Page hired William Bayard Hale from the *New York Times*. Hale wrote some exciting features for *World's Work*, but he proved unreliable and left in 1912. When Page departed in 1913, Arthur Page brought in the veteran magazine writer Burton J. Hendrick as managing editor.

No publication except the *State Chronicle* ever mirrored Page's ideas and character so fully. *World's Work* was a curious blend of the new and the old. The manifestations of the newsmagazine concept in "The March of Events" and the illustrations placed the periodical ahead of its time. The technology of rapid communications and photographic reproduction had not yet advanced to the point that allowed the flowering of the modern newsweekly. Yet articles in *World's Work*, which comprised two-thirds of every issue, read like an updated version of the *Forum*. Although he did not use the symposium format, Page still sought the same type of articles as he had for the *Forum*, with identical recipes for attracting readers. When he was planning the *World's Work* in September 1900, Page described the new periodical as "half magazine and half review." He was unintentionally confessing that the magazine was half ahead of and half behind its time.[22]

Page's most significant and oddest departure from the *Forum* came in his response to "muckraking." Despite his having earlier pioneered with the investigative series, he rarely used the device in *World's Work*. The magazine did carry some investigatory series, including one on urban schools in 1903 and 1904 by Adele Marie Shaw, which retraced the steps of the Rice articles. Page also went in for some exposés, including articles and series on railroad safety, featherbedding in Civil War pensions, big-business high-handedness, and municipal corruption. The most famous exposé in *World's Work* came in connection with Upton Sinclair's novel *The Jungle*, which was published by Doubleday, Page. Recognizing *The Jungle*'s news value, Page decided to coordinate the book's publication with a trio of lead articles on meat packing in the May 1906 issue of *World's Work*. By confirming and amplifying Sinclair's account, the magazine gave important added publicity to Sinclair's charges and aided the passage of the Pure Food and Drug Act in Congress.

Page was a reluctant muckraker, and he often apologized for the few exposés that *World's Work* did run. His statement accompanying the meat-packing articles was symptomatic of his attitude: "Reform by exposure is the detective method for the correction of criminals—a necessary method for police and grand juries, but it makes dreary literature." Page disliked muckraking for the same reasons as Theodore Roosevelt, who coined the term. He found it negative and destructive and he believed that true reform must come from a positive, constructive outlook. The editor also resembled the president in liking the financial and industrial power that big business had brought to the United States. Page personally admired leading tycoons as forceful, large-visioned men. In his view they were American counterparts to European empire builders. After 1906, *World's Work* published laudatory articles by and about such magnates as Carnegie, Rockefeller, E. H. Harriman, and James J. Hill.[23]

Yet despite those temperamental and ideological reasons for disliking muckraking, Page's aloofness was odd. An editor whose credo was activism let the biggest journalistic crusade of his time pass him by. A man who justified his magazine career largely through his impact on public affairs declined to join the movement that established that medium as a major force in American politics and society. An early discoverer of the potential of investigative magazine reporting declined to exploit the greatest opportunity for establishing and extending the practice. A long-standing believer in the curative powers of publicity disdained the strongest application of his own prescription.

Perhaps Page's deepest motives for avoiding muckraking were journalistic and financial. On the one hand, exposé journalism did not fit in comfortably with his conception of *World's Work* as a fast-moving newsmagazine. On the other hand, the magazine's avoidance of muckraking probably did not hurt its circulation. Contrary to some estimates, the leading muckraking journals such as *McClure's* did not boost sales and subscriptions through spectacular exposés. *World's Work*, by contrast, grew steadily throughout the heyday of muckraking. Although apparently no figures have survived to indicate revenues, the magazine usually seems to have turned a decent profit. In prosperous years nearly half the income came from advertising. A normal issue carried between fifty and a hundred pages of advertisements, and Page resumed the earlier *Forum* practice of running articles in the advertising section. During the first year these articles became a regular feature called "The World's Work Advertiser." As in the *Forum*, advertising in *World's Work* emphasized travel and schools as well as books and consumer goods. Together with the subjects of articles and illustrations, the types of advertising indicated that Page was aiming his magazine at the same readership as before—those mobile, middle-class groups.

Both profits and the newsmagazine idea suggested seeking a larger audience. Of the three magazines that Doubleday, Page came to publish, *World's Work* evidently made the least money. The one available set of figures shows that in January 1908, during a business recession, *World's Work* lost eleven hundred dollars, while *Country Life* made four thousand and *Gardening* one thousand dollars. Page must find that showing "simply gruelling to the last degree," observed Herbert Houston, " . . . to have the *World's Work* No. 3 in our magazine family and with a marked tendency to drop down to No. 5 or 6 if there were intervening magazines to take the places before it." Page and Houston experimented with a number of circulation-building gimmicks at different times, including selling subscriptions through railroad agents and seeking fresh territory in the South and West. Gaining readers in the hinterlands also suited both the editor's continuing desire to address a nationwide audience and his wish to make his periodical a national news medium. *World's Work*, he declared in 1911, "tried always to be national both in the subjects it has taken up and the treatment of them. For this is the particular and peculiar province of such a magazine—its opportunity for service such as the daily press cannot give."[24]

Page never succeeded in reaching a big readership. The main reason that he never expanded *World's Work*'s readership probably lay in a fundamental division of purpose within himself. Like all his enterprises, Page's magazine reflected the three-way divergence of his aspirations. If making money and exerting influence argued for big circulation, fostering culture pulled in other directions. Page may have shelved his literary interests on *World's Work*, but he had not forsaken his conviction that a magazine could pursue an educational mission. He does not seem to have hatched any grand schemes for enlisting professors behind *World's Work* as he had with the *Forum*, but he did try to hire Frederick Jackson Turner away from the University of Wisconsin in 1905. In speeches, Page compared his editorial role less than in the past to preaching—although he certainly used "The March of Events" as a pulpit—and more to teaching. Arthur Page recalled long afterward that the contents of the *World's Work* covered "about the same things that you have in the curriculum of a liberal arts college."[25]

With his magazine, Page faced a variation of the conflict in book publishing between commercialism and moral and cultural uplift. At one point he perceived the fundamental issue. In May 1912 he discussed the possibility of an endowed magazine with Hamilton Holt, the editor of the weekly *Independent*. Page confessed that after having once "doubted the wisdom of an endowment" he had changed his mind as he had learned "about the difficulty of really effective public education and leadership by periodicals." He believed that the magazine's "true analogy is the college or university. The editor is a teacher who is constantly acquiring information and passing it on." But "commercial conditions" hobbled even the best periodicals. Having to attract advertisers and subscribers meant that "we simply can't get certain kinds of information to the public." Page deplored the fact that "the teaching of men and the shaping of opinion in our democracy is left to the hap-hazard [*sic*] work of a merely commercialized business." He proposed further discussion with Holt and planning for an endowed weekly magazine; "it's a task that would call to its doing the very highest type of men. It would be better than any university that ever existed."[26]

Nothing came of those discussions. Holt and Page made a golf date with Andrew Carnegie soon afterward, but they evidently failed once more to pry open Carnegie's pocketbook. The first endowed weekly did not begin until late in 1914, when Willard and Dorothy Straight subsidized *The New Republic* under the editorship of Herbert Croly, Walter Lippmann, and Walter Weyl. When Croly sent Page a copy of the first issue, he responded, "Strength to your elbow!" The endowed-magazine idea offered further proof of Page's perceptivity. Between his features in *World's Work* and his other schemes, he anticipated practices carried out successfully by such diverse periodicals as *Time*, *The National Geographic*, and *The New Republic*. Even *World's Work*'s least original part, the articles, anticipated the direction toward timely, lively nonfiction in which the highbrow monthlies *Harper's* and the *Atlantic* subsequently moved. By pursuing most of the departures that he had first conceived for the *Forum*, Page showed how to expand the circulation of a basically educational magazine. In the end, despite shortcomings, *World's Work* turned out to be his most successful handiwork.[27]

Publishing brought Page financial comfort and security, if not wealth. He drew a salary of ten thousand dollars a year, and by the end of 1906 he could estimate his interest in Doubleday, Page at two hundred thousand dollars. By the time of his death in 1918 those holdings were worth close to half a million dollars. The family's residences reflected his affluence. The Pages spent their first two years back in New York living in apartments in Brooklyn and Manhattan, and each summer they rented a house in Westchester County or on Long Island. From 1902 to 1909 they became suburbanites again when they leased "a quiet country house," as Page described it, on the edge of Englewood, New Jersey. By 1909 Page had had his fill of commuting, and he bought a two-floor cooperative apartment on East Sixty-seventh Street in Manhattan, the first home that he owned. When Doubleday, Page moved to Long Island in 1910, Page briefly tried commuting again before deciding to rent a house in Garden City. Both the Englewood and the Garden City houses were imposing places on extensive grounds, while the East Sixty-seventh Street apartment featured a front hall with a sweeping staircase that reminded one visitor of "a spacious southern home." Also, in 1912 Page began planning to build a house at Pinehurst, North Carolina, near his brothers and sisters. An architect drew sketches of variations on a pillared, plantation-type dwelling.[28]

Page maintained a style of living to match his residences. The family always had several servants, including a cook, maids, and often a gardener and butler. Sometime after returning to New York, Page took up golf. In 1904 he bought an automobile, a twenty-five-hundred-dollar machine that the manufacturer sold him at a discount in return for advertising in *World's Work*. All four Page children attended private schools: Lawrenceville for Ralph and Arthur, Milton Academy for Frank, and a girls' school in Englewood for Katharine, who spent the year following her graduation traveling in Europe with two of her classmates and a chaperone. The children all attended college, Harvard for the three boys and Bryn Mawr for Katharine. Only Frank failed to graduate, while Ralph also received a degree from the Harvard Law School.

Page remained a devoted family man and still shared ideas and plans with his wife. For her part, Alice Page persisted in giving him hard-hitting criticism and independent advice. Yet she remains an elusive figure. After Page's death Alice admonished his first biographer, "Don't put me in the book. I have a strong feeling against it. I know that I must appear as a person now & then [but] let it be please the person who comes on the stage to change the chair to a convenient place & then off again." Alice Page's modesty did her a disservice, since from every indication she played a significant role in her husband's life.[29]

Page gave his children as much time and attention as his schedule permitted. When Arthur found himself accused of cutting classes at Harvard, his father accepted his denial without question. "That degree of confidence stuck in my mind," Arthur remembered long afterward, "so that there was nothing on earth that he ever expected of me that I wasn't going to do." Frank's recurrent academic troubles gave Page many anguished hours, as he corresponded at length with the Harvard authorities and arranged a job for his son when Frank was finally dropped early in 1909. Page delivered the commencement address at Katharine's school in 1908, and she joined her parents on their European trip during the summer following her year abroad. Katharine later accompanied the elder Pages to London, where she was married in 1915.[30]

With his sons Page shared business, too. The publishing

house turned into a family concern for both senior partners, as Doubleday's son Nelson and Page's son Arthur became their fathers' right-hand men and later succeeded to their places in the company. Frank later worked for the firm, and Ralph wrote several articles for *World's Work* during World War I. Between 1910 and 1913 Page joined Frank and Ralph, who had quit practicing law after a brief try, in a real-estate venture in North Carolina. He invested, made contacts, and did publicity for a scheme with them to develop a twenty-six-thousand-acre tract near Pinehurst. The development was to be a combination resort community for wealthy northerners, a model farming area, and an experiment in social organization. Although the three made some money from land sales, their overall plan broke down in the fall of 1912. The failure stemmed in large measure from the behavior of Frederick T. Gates, an associate of Rockefeller's whom Page had brought in and who drove sharp bargains with the young men. "This man is the living image and exponent of overbearing monopolistic business," Ralph told his father. "And I'm all ready to believe most anything they say about his gang, in the business world."[31]

The real-estate venture typified several enterprises in which Page mixed profit-making motives and idealistic concerns. Despite his earnings, money never ceased to be a problem for him. In 1901, presumably to pay debts, he sold for nine thousand dollars the half interest in a Raleigh building that his father had left him. During 1906 and 1907 he borrowed over twelve thousand dollars to defray personal and medical expenses. In 1912 he sold eight thousand dollars of his share in the Page family enterprises to invest in the scheme with Ralph and Frank. Page remained as much on the lookout as before for outside business deals. But now nearly all of his schemes resembled the one with his two sons: they involved agriculture and southern uplift. In 1909 and 1910 Page participated in an effort by a Dutch agrarian reformer, Frederick van Eeden, to develop a cooperative farming and industrial community near Wilmington, North Carolina. Also in 1910 he plunged into a venture to develop a mechanical cotton picker, which he hoped would revolutionize southern farming as mechanical harvesters had done in the Middle West and West. These schemes, like book publishing and magazines, betrayed a strain of utopian capitalism in Page's thinking, in which social betterment and private profit would march forward in total harmony.

Public affairs occupied Page more than money-making schemes. Education and the South continued to be his foremost concerns. Most of his memberships in social and philanthropic organizations revolved around one or both of those. His educational services included, as Page noted in a memorandum to himself in 1910, membership on the Johns Hopkins Alumni Council and the board of trustees of Columbia University's Teachers College, together with the Southern Education Board and the General Education Board, the boards of the Jeanes Fund and the Slater Fund, which were concerned with Negro and rural education, and the Rockefeller Sanitary Commission, which was mounting a combined medical and educational campaign to eradicate hookworm in the South. A year earlier, Page stated that he tried to divide his activity between business and efforts "pro bono publico. Now, this second part is getting very full." The educational boards were not, he added, "mere dead-head or ornamental activities, but real work which take my time and energy." Each board met several times a year. The Southern Education Board's schedule included an annual spring trip below the Potomac, together with a joint gathering with the General Education Board at George Foster Peabody's estate on Lake George every August. Governmental and political activities from 1908 through 1912 further deepened Page's involvement in public affairs.[32]

Speaking engagements continued to claim much of his time. He became one of the most sought-after college and university commencement speakers not only in the South but also, as his fame spread, in the Northeast and Middle West. Educators' conventions likewise vied for him. By 1909 these demands had grown so persistent that for several months Page "delivered no lectures or speeches anywhere because the thing got to be a nuisance." Experience did not make speaking easy for him. "I am one of those slow and methodical persons," he complained in

1910, "who can speak only when there is really something that must be said—on occasions that make the subject; and the Lord knows, it's halting enough then!" Page's speeches remained simple, direct statements on issues or problems and he still delivered them without gesticulations and with an almost conversational tone to his deep voice, which never entirely lost a southern accent.[33]

In some of his speeches Page defended the money-making side of publishing to literary folk, and he extolled advertising as the lifeblood of magazines and, thereby, an important subsidy to literature. The 1904 speech at the University of Chicago, "The Cultivated Man in an Industrial Era," marked Page's broadest attempt at reconciling culture and commerce, and he put forward at least one concrete plan for joining the two spheres. From the mid-1890s onward, he had been urging schools and colleges to teach writing. In June 1907 in another address at the University of Chicago, "The Writer and the University," Page proposed the establishment of "post-graduate professional schools for writers at our universities." Writers suffered comparable drawbacks, in his view, to lawyers in the days before law schools and doctors before medical schools. University training would give writing the same higher standards and solid professional definition as law and medicine. Such professional education would benefit society by rescuing writers from "the forces of commercialism" and by bridging "a great gap between our scholars and the rest of the community." At bottom, he was proposing to institutionalize the role that he had sought to play during the nearly thirty years since he had left the Johns Hopkins—a kind of symbolic bid for readmission to the university.[34]

Page lived at an extraordinary pace between 1900 and 1913. Nearly every other book publisher and magazine editor, except S. S. McClure, found his job too time consuming to pursue such a plethora of private business schemes and public-service involvements. Nor did those activities exhaust Page's range. He also wrote, publishing several articles in *World's Work* and other magazines, as well as his three books. His dynamism and versatility did not escape notice. At the beginning of 1902 Ellen Glasgow wrote him, "When I hear—as I do now & then—of the many forms your amazing energies acquire, I begin, indeed, to regard you as a kind of animated Colossus, or a second Theodore Roosevelt." The comparison was apt. Page did possess the same sort of preternatural vitality that distinguished such famous figures of his generation as Roosevelt, McClure, and Albert Beveridge in the United States, and David Lloyd George in Britain.[35]

But Page's activity did not spring solely from superabundant energy. Both the variety and the frenetic pace of his involvements betrayed inner disquiet. Despite his successes, he was not happy. His literary, public, and commercial ambitions still pulled him in different directions, and from 1900 until 1913 his health made it more difficult than before for him to find satisfaction or fulfillment. Although nothing so dramatic as the eye trouble of 1898 or the illness of 1899 again befell him, a number of complaints, including a stomach ulcer and rheumatism, highlighted a general decline. Despite much attention to his health, Page seems to have been oblivious to its most serious threat—his heavy smoking. Though he rarely smoked cigarettes, he sometimes consumed as many as twenty cigars a day. "He smoked cigars as most men smoke cigarettes," recalled one associate on *World's Work*, "inhaling every puff, if anything more deeply than most cigarette smokers. It was a constant source of wonder to those around him that he could stand the shock of those inhalations of strong tobacco smoke or survive the continued process." In fact, Page did not survive it. His smoking almost certainly aggravated the high blood pressure and hardening of the arteries that eventually caused his death at the age of sixty-three.[36]

Between 1900 and 1913, the chief significance of poorer health was to remind Page of advancing age. A streetcar accident in 1904 and back trouble in 1910 occurred as he neared his fiftieth and fifty-fifth birthdays. Passing those milestones of mortality and approaching the even bigger one of sixty disturbed Page. Another circumstance that deepened his disquiet was his relationship with Frank Doubleday. Whenever they appeared together, the two senior partners presented an arresting sight. Doubleday, too, was a big man with a forceful manner. He and

Page had lively brown eyes, moustaches, and dark complexions that conjured up Near Eastern images to some who knew them. But those images suggested more about contrasts between the two men than similarities.

After 1900, as age and poorer health made his features homelier and craggier, Page's large bulbous nose, heavy eyelids, glasses, and now scraggly moustache gave him the slightly comic appearance of a Syrian or Armenian merchant. A friend who once saw him wearing a fez as a joke thought that Page looked "completely the Unspeakable Turk." Doubleday, by contrast, enjoyed the nickname "Effendi," the respectful term of address to sheikhs and pashas. Kipling had dubbed him "Effendi," both as a pun on his initials, F. N. D., and because of his looks. The poet Christopher Morley, who was another junior book editor with the firm, remembered that on the wall of Doubleday's office hung "a photograph of him taken in the burnous [sic] of an Arab chief." The part fitted Doubleday perfectly, according to Morley, thanks to his darkly handsome features and aura of command. "It was a thrill for us youngsters when we saw him coming into the office with his long swinging stride. One was instantly aware of power."[37]

Effendi's authority equaled his image. He not only owned the controlling interest in Doubleday, Page, but he also exerted his dominance freely, often without consulting Page or the other partners. The decision to move to Garden City, for example, reportedly popped into Doubleday's mind as he gazed out over the railing of the ship on which he was sailing to Europe in the spring of 1910. He wired back to New York to engage an architect and have the plans ready upon his return. He then selected the site, arranged the financing, directed the construction, and managed the move, all within less than six months. Doubleday relished the commercial side of publishing. "I am a merchant," he was supposed to have announced. A book had to "have good selling stuff in it or I am not interested." Other publishers might worry about "artistic stuff," but they were "very often hard pressed to pay their rent. I don't run that kind of shop." Fittingly, Doubleday's firm has led the publishing industry for over fifty years in volume of trade-book sales and still holds a commanding lead in the record for best-sellers. The company has been called the "General Motors of book publishing." Frank Doubleday belonged to the same breed of tycoons who built corporate empires in commerce and manufacturing.[38]

Partnership with Doubleday hardly fulfilled Page's dream of becoming his own boss. Arthur Page later mentioned "a divergence of opinion between the Doubledays and the Pages that was always there." He and his father "were more concerned with the success of certain ideas than we were with the maximum of sales. . . . I don't mean we were not commercial—we were. But Doubleday wanted to leave out the more serious side of the magazine job." A comparable difference extended into their book-publishing efforts. The Pages concentrated more on nonfiction—"serious" books, Arthur called them—while Doubleday and his son devoted their attention to novels. Those divisions marked a natural specialization of interests, but they left the Doubledays in command of the more profitable side of the business. Not only did their magazines, *Country Life* and *Gardening*, earn better returns than *World's Work*, but also by Arthur Page's estimate, fiction accounted for four-fifths of the firm's book list. Moreover, the two and a half decades from 1890 until World War I witnessed a "fiction boom" in which novels formed the growth area of the trade.

How the two senior partners regarded each other is not entirely clear. In the late 1920s, Doubleday mentioned Page cursorily in his privately printed memoirs, remarking that public service took up most of his partner's time. George Doran, who later had an unhappy experience as a partner of the Doubledays, maintained that Effendi "chafed at the apparent inaction of his editor-partner," while Page endured the "near-humiliation of being reduced to a mere machine in a great factory-like organization." It should be noted that Doran was notorious for the untrustworthiness of his statements and recollections. Arthur Page probably came closer to describing the original relationship when he recalled that his father's and Doubleday's differences were "not of any particular importance. You need different kinds of people to make a team anyhow."[39]

The two partners did complement each other. In the early days of the firm they and their families saw a good deal of each other, and the men and their wives remained friends until Mrs. Doubleday's and Walter Page's deaths in 1918. The partnership carried over into a second generation of both families, with the connection lasting almost fourteen years after Page's departure for London. The ultimate dissolution of the partnership in 1927 resulted from changed conditions in the magazine field and Doubleday's growing irascibility in his old age. Even then, Doubleday struggled to keep the Page name as part of the company's title. Commercial cunning and an imperious manner did not make Frank Doubleday unrefined. The publisher whom he resembled most among his contemporaries was Mifflin. Despite coming from a modest background and having gone to work at the age of fifteen, Doubleday shared the Boston Brahmin's conception of publishing as a select, competitive fraternity. Doubleday's literary taste at least equaled Page's. He preferred to publish good books that sold well, and the two most renowned writers on the Doubleday, Page list, Kipling and Joseph Conrad, came to the firm through Doubleday's efforts. In short, Doubleday and Page were not polar opposites. Effendi may have sometimes pushed his partner around but he still liked and valued him.

Page apparently had more complicated attitudes. Business ability represented one of the most sensitive spots in his personality, and that sensitivity made him regard Doubleday as more than just a strong partner. His submissiveness toward and admiration for the other man's commercial ability recalled attitudes that he had held toward his father. Frank Doubleday seems to have filled part of Frank Page's place in Walter Page's mind. Page revealed the depth of his deference when he evidently let his partner sway some of his views of public affairs as a magazine editor. On issues regarding capital and labor Doubleday held fiercely antiunion and pro–big business opinions. Page had previously sympathized with labor organizations and worried about the concentration of private economic power. Yet both areas received ambivalent, sometimes inconsistent treatment in *World's Work*. Toward unions, the magazine wavered between a detached perspective and an impassioned defense of the open shop. On the trust problem, comments varied from sharply criticizing irresponsible financial power to extolling the accomplishments of men like Rockefeller. In part, these postures reflected Page's own divided mind, regardless of any influences from his partner. Yet it does seem noteworthy that Doubleday apologized to a financier friend in 1911 for a statement in *World's Work* about a certain corporation. "I will get after Mr. Page for his indiscretions," he promised. Page evidently could not be completely his own man even with his magazine.[40]

Becoming a publisher seems to have intensified Page's pursuit of his first love—writing. In 1899 he hatched the most unusual of his many writing projects when he secured Mary Johnston's permission to do a play based upon her novel *To Have and to Hold*. The scheme came to naught, however. Resignation from the *Atlantic*, involvement with McClure, and the founding of Doubleday, Page kept him much too busy. When Page bowed out in March 1900, he vented a sigh of regret. "For years I had given all my time to other people's work—in the awful, unspeakable drudgery of a magazine-editor (the galley slave is a free man in comparison); and now when I had become master of my own time, I was happier in trying my own constructive powers on this task than I had been since I was a boy." Although the remark smacked of disingenuousness, since Page had done almost no work on the play, he did speak from the heart when he wished for "trying my own constructive powers." Page still yearned to be not just a writer but a creative one—no longer a poet, perhaps, but a playwright, a story writer, or a novelist.[41]

Another five years passed before he produced any fiction. In March 1905, when he spent three weeks in St. Augustine, Florida, convalescing from the aftereffects of a streetcar accident, he wrote a story. Several circumstances evidently combined to bring Page's literary yearnings to fruition. Besides enforced rest and reminders of advancing age, a prod may have come from having met Thomas Nelson Page for the first time in January 1905. Except for praising his Virginia namesake's storytelling gifts,

Page seldom said much about him. Yet he could not help being aware of the other man's greater literary fame and widely differing view of the South. In 1902 one of Page's old journalistic enemies in Raleigh, *The Presbyterian Standard*, drove the point home by contrasting the "two Southern literary men by the name of Page" and observing that the former North Carolinian had produced no real literature and offered only carping criticism of the South. "Mr. Walter H. Page," concluded the *Presbyterian Standard*, "is a page that needs to be turned down." When he finally met "Tom" Page in January 1905, they discussed southern history and racial problems. The encounter could hardly have failed to recall to Walter Page the contrast between their opinions, reputations, and accomplishments.[42]

He spent the three weeks in St. Augustine in March 1905 "on a jag of hard work." The effort took Page back, he wrote Alice, "to the old, old days, before you were mine, when I had the world to conquer." Doubts sometimes infected him, especially about trying to turn out a whole novel in three weeks. "The audacity of the thing at least is splendid." Audacity, together with his capacity for fast writing, enabled Page to do enough to offer the story for magazine serialization the following fall. Bliss Perry snapped up the story and "The Autobiography of a Southerner since the Civil War" ran in the *Atlantic* from July through October 1906, under the pseudonym "Nicholas Worth." Three years elapsed between magazine serialization and publication of the book. Despite pleas by Perry for additional chapters and a gratifying competition between Houghton, Mifflin and Doubleday, Page for book rights, Page did not get back to "Nicholas Worth" until early in 1908. He finished the book during the summer of 1909, on the eve of his European trip. Doubleday, Page's fall list for 1909 included *The Southerner: A Novel: Being the Autobiography of Nicholas Worth*. At the age of fifty-four, Page published his first novel, under a pseudonym.[43]

The 425-page book was a revised but not much expanded version of the *Atlantic* serial. The word "autobiography" in the title of both versions indicated that it was a fictionalized life story. The narrator and central character, Nicholas Worth, recounts his experiences. He starts with his boyhood during the Civil War; he proceeds through his education at a military school, a denominational college in a neighboring state, and Harvard; and he finishes with his unsuccessful reform work as a school superintendent, college professor, and candidate for public office in his native state. Besides Nicholas, the characters include the other members of the Worth family—his parents, brother and sister, aged grandfather, and beautiful cousin Margaret, whom he loves but eventually loses through his skepticism about orthodox religion, the Lost Cause, and the ideal of southern womanhood. Outside the family the most prominent characters are "Professor Billy" Bain, another educational reformer; "Captain Bob" Logan, the disillusioned white Republican boss; Tom Warren, a handsome young Democratic politician; "Uncle" Ephraim, the devoted and humorously wise black manservant to Nicholas's grandfather; and Louise Caldwell, a strong-willed, activist southern woman who has been educated abroad and whom Nicholas finally marries. The setting is an unnamed coastal state in the Upper South bordering on Virginia. Major public events swirl around efforts at educational and economic uplift, race-baiting politics, and agrarian discontent. More personal lines of the story encompass three different romances, including an interracial love affair between Tom Warren and Uncle Ephraim's light-skinned adopted daughter, 'Lissa.

The novel drew transparently on Page's own life. North Carolina obviously provided the setting. The name Worth belonged to a prominent Tar Heel family, and a number of characters were recognizable public figures in the state. Big, genial, infinitely patient Professor Billy was McIver. Minor characters such as the Democratic boss Senator Barker; the demagogic editor of the newspaper *The White Man*; and the farmers' spokesman, "a harebrained, energetic, oratorical man of long whiskers and long tongue," resembled Senator Matt W. Ransom, Josephus Daniels, and the Populist leader Marion Butler. Equally clearly, Nicholas Worth and his family represented the author and the Pages. Such alterations as having Nicholas's father killed when the boy was young and sending him to Harvard did little to disguise the story's autobiographical foundation. Family and friends immediately recognized the military school, the Old Place, and the Confederate soldier's coffin from Page's conversations. The major difference between character and creator is that Nicholas Worth does not leave the South. Braving "the suppression of one's self, the arrest of one's growth, the intellectual loneliness," he resolves to stay and fight. Nicholas Worth embodies Page's musings about what his life might have been if he had remained in North Carolina.[44]

As an autobiography, *The Southerner* contains plenty of self-criticism. Nicholas Worth is not the novel's hero. He acknowledges that Professor Billy possesses essential qualities for an effective reformer, which he lacks himself. Likewise, Nicholas recognizes that his shrewd, progressive businessman brother Charles, based on both Page's father and his brother Henry, is a more constructive citizen than himself. Even the outwardly cynical Captain Bob Logan receives a backhanded compliment for having a political toughness absent in Nicholas. Curiously, in the book version, Nicholas never says what work he pursues after failing as a schoolmaster, professor, and political candidate. In the *Atlantic* serial, Charles Worth dies, and Nicholas takes over the family cotton mills, which provide employment, industrial discipline, and education to local people. In *The Southerner*, however, Charles lives on and Nicholas does unspecified good deeds. Although he alludes to puttering at a history of the state, that endeavor hardly constitutes meaningful public service. Even in his imagination, Page could not solve the problem of what he would have done if he had stayed in the South.

Nicholas Worth naturally serves as a mouthpiece for his creator's ideas about southern problems. That role for Worth introduced a serious weakness into both versions of the story. "Maybe it's a lot of people only preaching sermons at one another," Page wondered while he was writing in Florida. The story frequently becomes a vehicle for speeches, as Nicholas wins the college oratorical contest, writes the manifesto for a reform organization like the Watauga Club, campaigns for state education commissioner, and explains the South to northern audiences.

Revisions between versions entailed pruning the narrator's editorial intrusions and introducing more plot, humor, and romance. Yet even Nicholas's courtship of Louise Caldwell, which does not appear until the book version, features oratorical exchanges between the soul mates. The one social view that enlivens the story is Page's ambiguous attitude toward blacks. Throughout the story Nicholas and Professor Billy usually present moderate views of the Negro. Yet in depicting the comical but insightful Uncle Ephraim, Page came closer than any white writer since Albion Tourgée to presenting an honest view through a black man's eyes. His treatment of the affair between Tom Warren and 'Lissa and of their illegitimate daughter bared the most tragic and feared aspect of racial discrimination. Page had touched on a subject that almost no white novelists, northern or southern, would confront frankly until 1943, when Lillian Smith published *Strange Fruit*.[45]

Creating a few interesting characters and presenting some enlightened opinions did not make *The Southerner* a good novel. Page displayed faults common to expository writers who try their hand at fiction. One fault was didacticism. Later, such noted literary critics as Van Wyck Brooks, Edmund Wilson, and Bernard De Voto would fumble similarly as novelists when they failed to subordinate argument to artistry. Also like those later critics, Page wrote too much according to formula. As an editor and publisher he held strong views about what subjects and approaches made good literature. He tried to plug those subjects and approaches into *The Southerner* almost mechanically. He was neither the first nor the last editor or critic to mistake the ability to judge and inspire literary performance with literary artistry itself.

The flaws in *The Southerner* also highlighted a fundamental limitation in Page's writing. As several of his contemporaries observed, he expressed himself best in letters. His next most effective utterances came in newspaper pieces, most notably the "mummy" letter, and in such speeches as "The Forgotten Man." His editorials in the *Atlantic* and *World's Work* usually conveyed comparable pungency, simplicity, and vigor. Page's more formal writing, including magazine articles or the novel, suffered a precipitous decline in style. Page succeeded as long as he was addressing a person or a known audience—when he was, in effect, talking on paper. As soon as he had to address an unknown reader through an article or book, his talent shriveled. In that sense, Page was hardly a writer at all. Although he always despised talkers, especially southern ones, as inferior to doers, he remained a prime specimen of that breed himself. Small wonder that *The Southerner* is a talky novel or that the talk in it, which has to be uttered through mouthpieces, seldom reflects the author's vivid personality.

Those shortcomings doomed the story commercially. Bliss Perry later recalled that the *Atlantic* serial did not arouse the interest that he had hoped for in the South. Page's revisions did not make the book much better. Although the relatively few reviews of *The Southerner* tended to be favorable but lukewarm, even the most complimentary of them commented on the thinness of the plot and most of the characters. Page launched several promotional schemes, including mail-order coupons and a twelve-page brochure for booksellers. He also allowed a southern businessman friend to distribute free copies to "a thousand of the most important school people in the Southern states." The efforts were to little avail. *The Southerner* attracted scant attention and sold badly. In the first three months after publication, sales totaled 2,692 copies, earning $323.04 in royalties. During the remainder of the first year of publication, only another 192 copies were sold, yielding an additional $23.04 to the author. Overall, the book posted a net loss of $238.70 for Doubleday, Page.[46]

Page took the disappointment philosophically, maintaining to several friends that he had never expected commercial success. His biggest regret, he told a colleague on the Southern Education Board, was that almost no one "seems to have seen the main matter that I had in mind. . . . that was, the insistence on the Union point-of-view in the South—on the continuity of history, with the war as a mere interlude, a nightmare—and the linking on of the present and of the future with the ante-bellum past."

Claiming primarily didactic intent masked an unsuccessful novelist's disappointment. In his promotional pamphlet for *The Southerner* Page insisted "It is a story and not a history." Page could have presented his viewpoint toward the South much more effectively in a nonfiction volume with his name on the title page. A straight autobiography, pitched in his own voice, would probably have served both his cause and his talents better than anything else he could have written.[47]

As it was, the pseudonymous novel stirred up some of the same controversy as an openly acknowledged tract. The disguises fooled nobody in North Carolina. Friends and relatives guessed at Page's authorship after the first installment in the *Atlantic*. After *The Southerner* appeared, several reviewers again punctured the pseudonym. What opinion there was of the book in the southern press divided along ideological lines. Such latter-day New South exponents as the *Richmond Times Dispatch*, the *Birmingham Age-Herald*, and the *Louisville Courier-Journal*, which was still owned by Watterson, praised the novel for presenting truthful views and expounding a sound message. The sharpest attack came from Daniels's *Raleigh News and Observer*, which ran a scathing review by J. G. de Roulhac Hamilton, professor of history at Chapel Hill. Hamilton scored the book as a "fairy tale" with a "holier than thou" attitude based upon "misrepresentation" and fawning upon the "sectional aspirations and aims of New England or some other segment of the Union." Three and a half years later, aspersions of disloyalty returned to haunt Page. In July 1913, a Confederate veterans' magazine discovered his authorship of *The Southerner* and condemned his appointment as ambassador to Great Britain, thereby creating a minor tempest among a few southern papers and politicians. "All that 'Southerner' business is stupid," Page wrote to his son Arthur from London. " . . . I hope it will start the book to selling. No such luck."[48]

Nicholas Worth's fate chastened but did not destroy Page's literary aspirations. In 1907, between magazine and book versions, he sketched ideas for short stories, a different novel, and a nonfiction book on the American character. In January 1911 he resumed writing notes and outlines to himself. One note read, "Novel of Present So. Life. Sequel to N. W." Later in 1911 he scribbled ideas for history and travel books and for a trilogy of novels about man's temptations. Around the end of 1912 he started keeping a series of notebooks in which he jotted down ideas for a number of stories and wrote several fictional sketches. One sketch was a preface to "my own autobiography," in which he declared, "It occurs to me that I am for the first time in my life doing what I have always wished to do. . . . I recall that I set out to write: that was what I have always wished to do. (Describe my own disappointment & the same—of the many town-wrecks!)"[49]

Page wrote those sketches at an important juncture in his life. Between 1906 and 1908 he tried fitfully to keep a diary. From 1910, when he turned 55, through 1912 he collected a haphazard journal of notes to himself, sometimes in Greek script, about his thoughts, hopes, aspirations, and accomplishments. In October 1912 Page remarked in a speech, "What is a man to do when he has reached the age of 55 or 60?" A man had to begin a new way of life both because "you have reached the ripened age of experience" and because a man's health at sixty required him to be "either his own doctor or a fool." Moreover, his old acquaintance Woodrow Wilson was elected president in November 1912, and Page was advising him on agricultural policy and appointments.[50]

At the end of 1912 Page confided to friends that he might go back to North Carolina to join his sons and brothers in land development and rural regeneration. "I have reached a curious stage in life," he told Edwin Alderman, "and by far the most interesting that I've yet come to. On one side is Wilson with his zest for action. . . . Action, action to stir one's blood—mingling with men, managing men, using men, inspiring men, wearing one's life away dealing with men and nations." On the other side was a healthful life close to the soil and improving society down South. Page did not say whether he preferred high politics or grass-roots uplift, but either sphere would furnish fine material about which to write. Since his youth Page had believed that great events produced great literature. His two main avenues of activity outside his business after 1901 or 1902 were southern reform and politics. Each represented in part a roundabout pursuit of his literary vocation. The aspiring writer was still seeking his subject.[51]

CHAPTER 7

Reformer

Despite what he thought, Page never made an irrevocable choice between serving his southern homeland and seeking opportunities elsewhere. As in most important conflicts in his life, he tried to reconcile opposing elements and have matters both ways. Interpreting the North and South to each other continued to furnish one of his most important tasks both as a writer and speaker and through his book-publishing and magazine enterprises. With the novels of Thomas Dixon and Ellen Glasgow and such nonfiction works as Washington's *Up from Slavery* and Ray Stannard Baker's *Following the Color Line*, Doubleday, Page & Company published most of the widely read books on southern and racial topics between 1900 and World War I. *World's Work* carried far more material, pictorial and written, on the South and Negroes than any other leading magazine. Moreover, much of what Page published in books and in his magazine reflected not only his interests but also his involvements through the Southern Education Board and other philanthropic agencies.

After returning to New York in 1899 Page expanded his role as a self-appointed intersectional ambassador. The Southern Education Board, which he joined in 1901, brought together northern philanthropists and resident southern white educational leaders, while well-known southern expatriates such as Page served as a symbol of cooperation. The Southern Board also formed the nucleus for a set of agencies involved in improving education and public health, mainly in the South. An integral part of the network was the General Education Board, which was established in 1902 to furnish the principal means for dispensing John D.

Rockefeller's massive benefactions. These boards gave concrete meaning to Page's ambassadorial role, plunging him into some of the most dramatic reform efforts of the time. Working with these organizations augmented his knowledge of rural problems. The contacts that they provided with business and political leaders, including Rockefeller, Carnegie, and William Howard Taft, deepened his involvement in public affairs and raised his prestige. Page mistook himself when he believed that he had to choose between the South and the world. Trying to combine the two did more than anything else to open the world to him.

Page and the Southern Education Board represented a near-perfect match. Education had long been his favored avenue for southern progress, and with "The Forgotten Man" speech in 1897 he had emerged as a major spokesman on southern educational problems. In the meantime, northern philanthropists interested in the South and southern white educational leaders had been moving toward a new basis of accommodation and cooperation. The founding of the Southern Education Board in August 1901 joined these two reform elements in one institution. The board's founding occurred mainly as the result of efforts of two men. One was its president, Robert C. Ogden, a wealthy New York merchant, prominent Presbyterian layman, and philanthropist for many causes. The other was its executive secretary and only full-time, paid official, Edgar Gardner Murphy, a brilliant, humanitarian Episcopal priest from Montgomery, Alabama.

Ogden's interest in the South, like that of most socially concerned northerners, had started with black education. During the 1890s, however, various influences had begun to shift his and others' attention toward a broader attack on southern problems. In July 1898 the Conference for Christian Education in the South had assembled at Capon Springs, West Virginia, native white educational leaders and other whites hitherto concerned primarily with black education. Additional meetings of what was renamed the Conference for Education in the South followed at Capon Springs in the summers of 1899 and 1900. Meanwhile Murphy independently organized a larger and better publicized Conference of the Southern Society for the Consideration of Race Problems in the South, which convened in Montgomery in May 1900. All of these conferences aired a common argument—that racial progress could come only through improving education for all southerners under responsible native white leadership and without outside criticism or interference. The Capon Springs and Montgomery gatherings merged into a single, enlarged Conference for Education in the South, which met at Winston-Salem, North Carolina, in April 1901. That conference voted to establish an executive committee, which began meeting in June under Ogden's chairmanship and became, in August 1901, the Southern Education Board.

Page took part in several of the steps that led to formation of the Southern Education Board. In the spring of 1899 Hollis B. Frissell, the principal of Hampton Institute, invited him to speak on "Cooperation" to the second Capon Springs conference: "Knowing both sides as you do, you are peculiarly fitted to give such an address." Illness and work made him decline. Page first met Ogden the following November, after his return to New York, and in April 1900 he traveled with other special guests in Ogden's private railroad car to the thirty-fifth anniversary celebration at Hampton Institute. About the same time, Page accepted Murphy's invitation to address the Montgomery Conference, but he withdrew when he learned that another speaker planned to call for repeal of the Fifteenth Amendment. "I regard its [the Amendment's] adoption, when it was adopted, as a grave mistake," Page explained to Murphy, "but I should regard it a much graver mistake to repeal it now, even if it were possible to repeal it." This was the first instance of the friction that persisted between Murphy and Page. The following year, the editor did speak at the Winston-Salem conference, and only absences from New York during the summer of 1901 prevented him from joining the board at its inception. At the next series of meetings, on 5 November 1901, the Southern Education Board elected Page as one of its first additional members.[1]

Belonging to the board and its allied agencies for the next twelve years provided Page with possibly the most satisfying sustained experience of his life. The Southern Board normally met three or four times a year, for several days at a time. The General Education Board, the boards of the Slater and Jeanes funds, and later the Rockefeller Sanitary Commission met concurrently, inasmuch as roughly three-quarters of the members of each body served on all or most of the others. During the winter the boards met in January at Ogden's offices in lower Manhattan. In the spring the members and other guests journeyed in Ogden's railroad car to the Southern Education Conference, which met in a different city or town in the South each year. They usually made additional stops to visit schools, colleges, experimental farms, and other facilities. During the summer the combined boards customarily met for a week on Lake George at the estate of George Foster Peabody, another native southerner and millionaire financier who was the southern board's treasurer. Sometimes, too, brief meetings occurred in the fall. Frequent correspondence, telephone calls, and luncheon or dinner meetings likewise kept members in touch, especially the ones who lived in New York, principally Ogden, Peabody, Murphy, and Page. The editor relished these gatherings, particularly the summer meeting at Lake George. "There we leave our smaller, private affairs and moods at home," he told Peabody in 1904.[2]

Fellow members and the work of the Southern Education Board equally gratified Page. He enjoyed warm personal relations with nearly everyone. Old North Carolina friends made up the core of the board's original southern contingent, including McIver, Alderman, and Page's onetime Watauga Club comrade, Charles W. Dabney, who had become president of the University of Tennessee. After McIver's death in 1906, Page raised a scholarship fund to send his daughter to Vassar. When Alderman had to be hospitalized with tuberculosis in 1912, his fellow Tar Heel wrote him long weekly letters, full of comment and information. Among the northern representatives on the board was another magazine editor and longtime acquaintance, Albert Shaw. Mutual respect and affection grew between Page and Ogden and, to a lesser extent, between him and two other northerners, the railroad magnate and philanthropist William Henry Baldwin and

the former Baptist minister who supervised the Rockefeller benefactions, Wallace Buttrick. Through the General Education Board
Page also entered into an acquaintance with John D. Rockefeller,
Jr. The only strain occurred between him and Murphy, with
whom he disagreed on fundamental issues, and, less so, with
Peabody, who privately deplored "the material view of life that
the *World's Work* signifies." Consideration and decorum, however, kept board gatherings almost invariably free from argument
and acrimony. Page took special pride in acting as host to the
summer meeting in 1912 at Garden City, where he provided
various entertainments and showed off the new Doubleday, Page
headquarters.[3]

More than fellowship with other members, the accomplishments of the boards heartened Page. The Southern Board functioned as the planning, coordinating, and propaganda center for
a series of public-school campaigns in the former Confederate
states after the model of McIver's and Alderman's efforts in
North Carolina. Partly as a result of the board's evangelism,
southern education took a huge leap forward in quality, expendi-
tures, and facilities during the first decade of the twentieth century.
At the same time, the General Education Board dispensed several
million dollars to the Southern Board and to colleges and universities in the South. Rockefeller funds through the General Board
and other agencies also underwrote extensive farm-demonstration projects and a spectacular public-health campaign to rid the
South of hookworm. Benefits from these efforts did not descend
equally on every area below the Potomac, much less on the two
races. Despite limitations and inequities, however, the phalanx of
philanthropic ventures led by the Southern Education Board
brought more than enough progress to justify what Page in 1908
called his "continual encouragement in trying to be of some little
help."[4]

What help Page personally rendered is hard to judge. He
does not seem to have become a major force on the Southern
Education Board. Surviving minutes of board meetings and other
correspondence indicate that most initiatives and decisions came
from Ogden and Murphy. Predictably, most of the editor's con-

tributions involved publicity and speaking. *World's Work* had begun calling attention to efforts to improve southern education even before the board's formation. Frequent comments in "The March of Events" and a steady stream of articles described the activities of the board and other educational reformers. Also, by the end of 1912, the magazine had carried full-page pictures of every board member except, modestly, Page himself. From 1901 through 1905 he delivered a speech at every meeting of the Southern Educational Conference. Despite attempts to beg off afterward, he addressed most of the conferences from 1906 to 1913. Page's other speaking engagements likewise featured educational reform as his leading topic, especially at colleges and universities. In 1902 he distributed a number of copies of *Rebuilding Old Commonwealths* to philanthropists and educators at his own expense, and in 1909 he allowed *The Southerner* to be sent to southern school superintendents. These activities helped establish Page as probably the nation's foremost educational propagandist.

For the Southern Board and Page himself, his role had the added dimension of intersectional ambassadorship. Ogden's main reason for appointing the former North Carolinian, aside from his reputation and editorship, was his status as a native southerner who had achieved a national reputation. "Northern men cannot afford to say plain things to Southern people," Ogden explained to another Yankee philanthropist in June 1901. "They have the hypersensitivity of general ignorance, and plain things should be said by their own people." But Page and Dabney, he believed, "have a standing in discussion which circumstances deny to us." By working simultaneously to improve the South and avoid the stigma of outside meddling, the board's approach offered an important place for such expatriates as Page, who had both greater familiarity with their own people than northerners and greater latitude than resident southern whites.[5]

In bridging the sections, Page sometimes gave the board more than it bargained for. The one important incompatibility with another member was his clash with Murphy, which broke out openly twice during 1903. The first skirmish occurred in

March, when Page and Baldwin attended a banquet in New York, at which two blacks came in after dinner to listen to the speeches. Several southern newspapers printed distorted stories about two members of the Southern Education Board dining with Negroes. The incident spread fright in the offices of the Southern and General boards. Murphy immediately had an earnest talk with Ogden about Page's behavior, and he wrote to McIver to urge him and Alderman to reprove their friend "in a frank and brotherly spirit." Meanwhile, Buttrick, who was secretary of the General Board, spoke to Page. According to Murphy, Page told Buttrick "that if it were any other man he 'would be shown the door.' That he, Page, was prepared to dine with negroes at any time and that it was nobody's business but his own." The whole affair distressed Murphy because, he told McIver, "Mr. Page is supposed to be upon the General Education Board as a representative of the South." In fact, Ogden struck him as "a great deal more of 'a Southern man' than either Dr. Page or Mr. Peabody." McIver's friend was neglecting "elementary statesmanship, and it is a question which, if Dr. Page persists in his present attitude, will certainly involve the gravest consequences."[6]

The incident turned out to be trivial. Whether any of Page's other associates mentioned the matter to him is not known, but nothing comparable happened afterward during his service on the boards. As a revelation of underlying attitudes, however, the incident was important. Murphy's reactions exposed the everpresent fear of arousing white prejudice. The Southern Education Board believed that the best way to combat racial injustice was to ignore it and stress positive accomplishments in other fields. "While its principle is for the education of all the people," Ogden admitted to Carnegie in 1906, "its efforts are primarily for the benefit of the white people. To educate the white is indirectly and powerfully to aid the Negro." From the perspective of several generations, that conviction may have been correct, but during the period of the board's activity it proved to be highly misleading. As Louis Harlan has demonstrted, the Southern Education Board not only failed to blunt the contemporary onslaught of white discrimination and violence against blacks but also sanctioned grossly inequitable allocation of educational resources between the races.[7]

Page's differences with Murphy surfaced again in December 1903, when the two men clashed directly over the proposed appointment to the board of Chancellor James H. Kirkland of Vanderbilt. Because Vanderbilt was a Methodist institution and Kirkland a Methodist bishop, the suggestion inflamed Page's resentment toward southern churches and preachers. He objected to such an appointment in principle, he told Ogden, because people could no longer say of the board, "Here is a broad and free force—free from political and church and sectional control." He also noted the abysmal racial record of southern Methodists and Baptists. "No Negro is welcome in one of their white churches. Now this is the kind of religion that cannot stand up straight before God or man." But Page did not touch the heart of his objection until he asserted, "I doubt if there has come a week in twenty years but some Southern man has told me or written to me of his sense of suffocation—his longing for fresh air; and their troubles have come oftener from church parties than from political parties."[8]

Murphy vigorously rebutted Page's opinions about churches and Christianity. Turning the intolerance argument around, he accused the editor of restricting freedom by seeking to exclude representatives of religious institutions. "I think I ought also to say," added Murphy, "that with my whole soul I dissent from . . . the suggestion that organized Christianity is in opposition to freedom and democracy. All that I know of freedom and all that I know of democracy I learned from the Christian church." Murphy's disagreement made Page respond, as he often did, by seeking harmony, and at one point Page tried to insist upon Kirkland's appointment. But his original objection, coupled with similar arguments from Dabney, prevailed because Murphy and Ogden wished to avoid dissension. Four years later, after Kirkland had severed Vanderbilt's Methodist ties, he joined the board without controversy.[9]

Page and Murphy continued to disagree during most of the

decade following their initial clashes, until Murphy's death in 1913. The two men held fundamentally different perspectives toward their native region. In 1909 Murphy criticized *The Southerner* to Page by commenting, "There is certainly a different South in every State." In Alabama he had found that the Confederate veterans and old leaders were "the strongest public school and *un*-'anti-nigger' force. . . . Our bad times are now with us, largely because the older men are gone or going—and the crude new fellows who know nothing (but who will be all right twenty years hence) are on the top." Murphy also observed, "I often feel (especially in 'religion and politics') that in your reaction from formulas you have only exchanged one set for another."[10]

That was probably the most perceptive criticism of himself that Page ever heard. He did view the whole South through the eyes of a middle-class white North Carolinian burned by personal experiences with the Protestant denominations. Many things looked different from Murphy's standpoint as an Episcopal clergyman from the Deep South who identified with the descendants of the planter class. Murphy espoused a creed of humanitarian Christian paternalism, while Page hewed to a materialistic, democratic viewpoint. Both men's attitudes prefigured important and frequently conflicting strains in twentieth-century white southern racial moderation.

In November and December 1903, while he was clashing with Murphy over sectarian influences, Page was also battling his erstwhile protégé, Josephus Daniels, over his other great southern bugbear—political meddling. The two journalists struggled against each other in the Bassett affair at Trinity College, a battle that afforded Page the opportunity to perform his most effective single service as an intersectional ambassador. The previous October, Professor John Spencer Bassett of the Trinity history department had stated in *The South Atlantic Quarterly* that Booker T. Washington was "the greatest man, save General Lee, born in the South in a hundred years." That remark had stirred up the wrath of North Carolina's leading white supremacists and Democratic politicians, particularly Daniels in the *News and Observer*. They demanded Bassett's scalp, at least symbolically, through his dismissal from Trinity.

The controversy could hardly have aligned the sides more to Page's liking. During the eighteen years since he had left Raleigh, his onetime friendship with Daniels had curdled into enmity, at least on Page's side. He had come to despise his successor on the *State Chronicle* because of his racist demagoguery and his championship of Bryanite agrarian radicalism and, perhaps, for having succeeded where he, Page, had failed. Now, through Bassett, Daniels was attacking not only Trinity, but also the Duke family, who had contributed heavily to the college, and indirectly Page's brother Henry, who was a Trinity trustee and a political foe of the *News and Observer* over railroad issues. Ironically, some of Trinity's Methodist supporters had hampered the growth of public education in North Carolina. But for the state's most prominent expatriate, academic freedom overrode any such irony.

Page rose to the occasion with a campaign on several fronts. He corresponded at length with Bassett, whom he already knew, both to encourage him and to get his side of the story. He solicited a separate, confidential report from another friend on the Trinity faculty, Edwin Mims of the English department. Then, having satisfied himself that Bassett's cause was just and that the trustees would probably support the professor, the editor arranged for Mims to rush a report to him for the January 1904 issue of *World's Work*. With minor changes, Mims's dispatch appeared as a long, unsigned editorial piece entitled "A Notable Victory for Academic Freedom." Page kept fellow members of the Southern Board, especially Ogden and Baldwin, apprised of developments. Perhaps his best contribution came with his handling of Benjamin Duke. During November, before the trustees met to decide on Bassett, Page sent three handwritten letters to his old acquaintance. The first two were brief notes, expressing confidence in the outcome of the affair and mentioning that he had just returned from conferring with President Roosevelt at the White House. The third letter, written on Thanksgiving Day, filled eight pages. "When you win this fight," he exulted to Duke, "you may forever afterwards be sure that *Trinity College will be free*—and *everybody will know that it is free.*" Page recalled a similar case the year before involving Professor Andrew Sledd of Emory College, in which the trustees had not resisted demands for his dismissal. "Well, Emory College is now held in pity & contempt at all the great institutions of the land." He congratulated Duke in advance on "so beautiful a chance for Trinity to show that it is free & the home of free men."[11]

Page's tactics demonstrated how the yearnings of some southern whites for respectability in northern eyes could be used to promote tolerance and decency. This sort of experience, together with the Southern Board's apparent successes, convinced the editor for a while that his native region had at last started to make progress. The apogee of Page's optimism came in June 1907 when his magazine ran its "Southern Number." In "A Journey through the Southern States," he retraced the steps of his 1899 trip, delightedly discovering, "Everything is different." Material progress and "the coming of cooperation, the unifying of forces, of energies, of interests" had put southerners back on the right track, "doing the very work that their fathers would have done long, long ago but for slavery and the war and all that followed those." This renaissance was bringing the South for the first time in a century "into the full current of the life of the Republic."[12]

Page's views of the South and race relations after 1900 contained plenty of wishful thinking and credulity. But when he occasionally took time to reflect on southern conditions, he often did not like what he saw. Page apprehended the glaring twin failures of the Southern Education Board and its allied agencies. They had not halted the rampage of white violence and repression, and they had not secured anywhere near equitable allocation of educational funds and facilities for blacks. In May 1911, he called southern progress "a very ziz-zag thing, . . . full of tragedies at every step." Over a year earlier, in a letter marked "confidential" to Wickliffe Rose, the secretary of the Hookworm Commission, Page had asserted, "There is overwhelming testimony that the Negro in some parts of the South—I fear in many parts—

does not receive anything like a square deal in the distribution of public school money, particularly in the country. In most places the poor devil is simply forgotten; in some places he is deliberately swindled." Page insisted, "I have no sentimental stuff in me about the Negro, but I have a lot of economic stuff about the necessity for training him." He wanted to see the situation exposed in a way that would not rile white demagogues but would produce constructive action. Only an agency of overwhelming prestige, he believed, such as the Hookworm Commission, the General Board, or the federal government's Bureau of Education, could safely publicize the problem. Nothing came of the suggestion. Rose, Buttrick, and the commissioner of education all refused to touch the idea, and the editor let the matter drop.[13]

In wishing to avoid provoking southern suspicions, Page remained loyal not only to the strategies of Ogden and the Southern Education Board but also to the convictions that he had formed in his youth. In January 1908, he had confided to another southern white educational reformer, Samuel Chiles Mitchell, "If we *publicly* grant that Southern sentiment stands in need of nationalization we seem to give away the very case we fight for. . . . I believe that this is a subject which can best be treated indirectly. What I was really driving at, for instance, in the Southern number of the World's Work in emphasizing industrial development was to show that this form of activity is nationalizing Southern thought. Of course, in that effort I was at a great disadvantage, for the shallower people took it for granted that I was merely booming money-making. . . . "[14]

At the same time, Page followed his convictions about the power of positive publicity in regard to race relations. *World's Work* devoted far greater attention to blacks than did any other leading magazine. Articles by and about Booker T. Washington appeared regularly, together with other pieces on achievements of individual Negroes and their enterprises. Unlike Ogden and Murphy, who regarded Tuskegee and its principal as "vulgar" and given to "showiness," Page never wavered in his admiration for the black leader. He sang Washington's praises in *World's Work*, and Doubleday, Page published all of his later books.

Thanks to Page, the firm also published the most widely read book on race relations by a white author, Ray Stannard Baker's *Following the Color Line*. During his 1907 southern trip the editor encountered Baker, whom he advised extensively about people to interview, material to include, and interpretations to follow. This advice evidently reinforced Baker's support for the Washington program and his optimism about growing white tolerance. *World's Work* likewise continued to accept contributions from W. E. B. Du Bois, despite the editor's private distaste for Du Bois's criticism of Washington and the civil rights militancy of the newly formed National Association for the Advancement of Colored People (NAACP).

Page took a position on disfranchisement similar to Washington's, that there could be no objection so long as literacy tests and other requirements applied with equal stringency to both races. In 1902 he predicted a gradual reentry of blacks into southern political life; "as their disfranchisement is gradually overcome by their education and their thrift, they may also divide and some become members of one party and some of the other." Before that happened, he believed that southern whites would have abandoned their Democratic fealty and become part of the national two-party system. Page sometimes talked like other southern white progressives in viewing black disfranchisement as a necessary step toward restructuring southern politics. Yet the editor enjoyed a good reputation among blacks and northern white civil rights advocates. Early in 1913 when Oswald Garrison Villard, Du Bois, and other NAACP leaders planned to ask Wilson to appoint a presidential commission on race relations, Page was their choice to head the group. His departure for Britain probably killed whatever slight chance the plan might have had, by removing the one man who might have sold Wilson on such a commission.[15]

From shipboard on his way to London Page wrote to Villard about the commission. "Leave off the martyrs," he counseled. "Martyrs & traitors—they lack balance. Get just men, plain men, straightforward men, who have no grievances. God made this world pretty well after all. I trust those most who as a rule approve it." From his post as ambassador, Page refused to comment privately on attempts to segregate the federal government under Wilson, and in his correspondence he revealed little concern with southern and racial problems. In April 1916, however, Page broke his ban on neutral ambassadors' making public statements during wartime, to eulogize Washington, who had recently died. "I should say without hesitation," Page declared, "that the work of this one man has been the strongest single influence toward taking the negro [*sic*] problem out of the region of angry controversy and into the region of useful helpful work." That statement also described what Page had tried to do.[16]

Page held unclear, sometimes contradictory opinions on a number of the most important issues that faced the country between 1900 and 1913. Writing his monthly commentary, "The March of Events," during those years would have introduced variations and contradictions into almost anyone's pronouncements on public affairs. *World's Work* resembled other leading magazines and their middle-class readership in espousing shifting views about the seemingly inexorable growth of big business, the efforts of organized labor, proposals for governmental intervention in the economy, and moves to make politics and government more directly democratic. Magazines stood near the center of the burgeoning national reform mood known as progressivism, which grew after the turn of the century. Page may have been loath to involve *World's Work* in muckraking, but he could hardly avoid the concerns that were swirling through public consciousness. As a good journalist attuned to his audience, Page made *World's Work* a fairly typical voice for a certain brand of reform opinion, and the main divisions in his thinking reflected his representative role.

Page's attraction to reform sprang from the perspective toward southern and national politics he had held since the 1880s. In November 1901 he reiterated in *World's Work* his conviction that the period since the Civil War ranked "as the most insufferably dull era in our political annals." Although he still claimed that politics "is and ought to be but a small segment of American life," he hoped that the time had arrived when constructive tasks would reinstate politics as "a noble and worthy expression of national life." Page initially pinned his hopes for such a revival not on domestic reform but on the colorful, dynamic new figure in the White House, Theodore Roosevelt, and on the building of an interoceanic canal in Central America and the expansion of foreign trade. The editor had not really changed his thinking since his advocacy of imperialism in 1898. Nor did he turn his attention toward issues at home readily or enthusiastically. Big business was becoming a matter of broad concern, but Page only gradually came to share some of the widespread apprehension. "The truth is," he announced in November 1900 in the first issue of *World's Work*, "the aggregation of capital in large enterprises is a phase of economic development that was as inevitable as the gold standard or the growth of our exports. . . . Productive combinations are part of the machinery in the better organization of the world whereby we have quickened our pace."[17]

That statement set the tone of approval for large-scale enterprise that never left Page's discussion of big business. The viewpoint antedated the editor's association with such tycoons as Rockefeller in philanthropic ventures, although those contacts later reinforced his sympathy for big businessmen. Two considerations lay at the heart of his approval of big business. One was his abhorrence of the agrarian radicals, particularly Bryan and his southern followers, who had first raised the trust issue. "It would be hard to say on which side greater hurt has yet been done," commented *World's Work* in April 1901, "by the corporations' improper influence on legislation or by the wild and hindering legislation provoked in opposition to corporation influence." His second consideration in approving of big business was what he implied in the phrase "machinery in the better organization of the world." Page never lost his fascination with the expansion of man's power wrought by the industrial revolution. He simply could not regard huge aggregates of organizational, technological, and financial might as all bad.[18]

Yet the editor had worries. He conceded that large corporations exercised undue political influence, and in his November

THEODORE ROOSEVELT,
speaking at the cornerstone laying of the Country Life Press,
September 1910; Page is standing to the left

(by permission of the Houghton Library, Harvard University)

JOHN BURROUGHS *and* WALTER HINES PAGE,
September 1910

(by permission of the Houghton Library, Harvard University)

1900 statement he also granted that big business "must be regulated" and "must be required to work with publicity." His disquiet grew during the next four years. In November 1902 he envisioned simultaneous pushes toward monopoly of capital by the corporations and of labor by the unions. "The whole question is: how can the public defend itself?" He expatiated on the paramount "public" interest, which he equated with the lot of unorganized operators and consumers who appeared threatened from above and below. In March 1904, when the "domination of our politics by industry and commerce" aroused him, Page finally called for governmental actions against big business. "The reign of industrialism brings into the public mind a lower conception of politics, a less keen appreciation of the higher type of public man," with the result that the two parties "bid simply for the support of industrialism." Like kindred reformers of the time, Page wanted to prevent divisions between the upper and lower classes that might lead to social upheaval, just as he wished to elevate politics above the crass pursuit of economic interest.[19]

After 1904 Page became a moderate, circumspect, but committed reformer. He found himself once again in company with Roosevelt, who campaigned for reelection in 1904 on the square-deal platform. When the president followed his triumph at the polls with proposals for railroad regulation and attacks on corporate influence, *World's Work* applauded: "What a relief it is to turn from the old policies of reminiscence and obstruction to positive tasks! The problems of industrialism are now becoming clearly defined, difficult as their solution is; and sooner or later the general government must solve them." During Roosevelt's second term, the magazine supported his programs at the national level, together with a variety of state and municipal reform movements throughout the country. Page pointed with particular pride to such business-minded, anti-machine, pro–public school southern governors as Aycock in North Carolina and Andrew Jackson Montague in Virginia. As Roosevelt's presidency wore on, the editor warmed to his new reform allegiance. "*We are going to have in this Republic a standard of financial and corporate morals that will square with the moral sense of Americans in their private conduct,*" his magazine avowed in October 1907; "and we are going to have it at any cost."[20]

Yet Page's reform enthusiasm, even at its height, retained a strain of skepticism. In April 1906, for example, he called the outcry against big business "a sort of revolution," yet he doubted "whether a time will ever come when Industry will loosen its hold on public affairs." The most that he expected was an unremitting struggle "to weaken this hold, at least to the point of lessening corruption and open tyranny." *World's Work's* tougher stance toward corporations did not entail any softening toward labor unions. Instead, the magazine wobbled toward unions in much the same way that it did toward the corporations, between denunciations and resigned or understanding acceptance. Nor did Page equally favor all current reform proposals. Measures such as direct primaries and popular election of senators left him cold, because he believed that moneyed interests and political machines could control those processes just as easily as conventions or state legislatures. He never contemplated stringent remedies for economic or social problems. The editorial of October 1907, in which Page thundered about *"corporate morals,"* concluded by recommending "more honest conduct of corporations," loosening "the grip of the financial kings on the surplus capital of the whole country," and "reform of the tariff." In viewing industrial America after 1900 Page displayed the same disparity that he had in the 1880s between acute perception of injustices and limited conception of redress. Similarly, lowering tariffs still beckoned to him as a principal cure of economic ills.

Toward social problems, Page demonstrated comparable dilemmas and confusions. More than twenty years' residence in northern cities had not reconciled him to urban life. On this subject his views hardened considerably. After 1900 he displayed mounting hostility toward the denizens of the slums, particularly the immigrants from southern and eastern Europe. Although Page did not openly advocate immigration restriction, he did worry about "the new immigration from the least desirable part of the European population," which was adding "incalculable difficulties to our city life." Some of the editor's enthusiasm for agricultural reform and conservation of natural resources sprang from his revulsion toward cities. In May 1908 *World's Work* affirmed "that the United States is, and always will be mainly an agricultural country." The combined influences of the idle rich, ill-led labor unions, yellow journalism, and rotten city government seemed to be "making a large part of city-dwellers hopelessly degenerate." Americans must grasp anew "the old truth that the normal life is the life of the soil . . . whereas American cities ought to be chiefly market-places for American farmers and manufacturers in smaller towns." Those opinions sounded strange in company with the magazine's frequent apologetics toward big business.[21]

Page generally agreed with Roosevelt. Except for his unconcern about lower tariffs, the president held views on most major issues, especially the problem of the trusts, that had an almost uncanny correspondence with the editor's. Their affinity did not spring from any particular influence on each other. Although the two men had been acquainted since the early 1890s, they did not become close friends. The congruence in their political views derived from similarities in temperament and personal outlook. Several of Page's friends besides Ellen Glasgow likened him to Roosevelt. Both men crackled with nervous energy, gave fairly loose rein to their emotions, and delighted in using vivid, hard-hitting language. Despite differences in social and sectional background, they had faced similar personal problems of reconciling intellectual leanings with a life of action and had contracted compulsive concerns about "manliness." Similarly, despite differences in occupations, both men had long scorned "commercialism" as unheroic and had preached first colonial adventure and then governmental economic regulation as ways to avert social conflict and to uplift politics. The full extent of their similarities in foreign-policy views would become evident during World War I.

But these fundamental compatibilities did not bring them together. The editor first attracted Roosevelt's attention as an interpreter of the South. The president conferred with Page in December 1901, the day after his dinner with Booker T. Washington at the White House had triggered a wrathful barrage from white supremacist editors and politicians. "Do you think this is going to hurt Mr. Washington's influence in the South?" he asked Page. Thereafter, Roosevelt summoned the editor to the capital periodically to seek his advice on such diverse matters as lynching and conservation. These conferences did not make Page a presidential confidant, although unfounded rumors once popped up about his receiving a cabinet post. The only appointment that Page got from Roosevelt was to the Country Life Commission at the end of 1908. The appointment came at the suggestion of the president's intimate friend Gifford Pinchot, who knew Page through *World's Work*'s support of conservation. The editor received the appointment because the commission required a member who was at least nominally a southerner and a Democrat.[22]

Acquaintance with Roosevelt meant a great deal to Page. Except for one or two brief interviews with Grover Cleveland long before, he had never met an incumbent president, much less conferred with one on a fairly regular basis. Cultivation by Roosevelt confirmed Page's importance as a journalist, publisher, and southern spokesman. The president's initiatives and example may also have hastened the editor's becoming a reform advocate. Yet Page admired Roosevelt less than might be expected. *World's Work* displayed more mixed sympathies in the 1904 election, when the Democrats nominated the anti-Bryanite Alton B. Parker, than in any other presidential contest during Page's editorship. Curiously, temperamental similarities did not raise Page's esteem for Roosevelt. In July 1908 *World's Work* praised William Howard Taft for not having the "excess of vitality" that made Roosevelt appear "rash when he was merely energetic." In 1912 Page privately damned Roosevelt for "Vanity and Egotism" for having opposed Taft's renomination and then having bolted to run as the Progressive, or "Bull Moose," party candidate. Yet at the same time, he congratulated a friend, "Bully for you! This is Bull Moose language, but I sent it also with Bull Moose vigor." If Wilson had not emerged as the Democratic candidate in 1912, Page might have found himself in the Bull Moose ranks. If he had, his political involvements might have turned out more happily than they ultimately did, for he tried to invest both Taft and Wilson with qualities and views that their predecessor had possessed. This failure to appreciate how close Roosevelt had come to embodying his ideal of statesmanship left Page with a certain mistaken political identity.[23]

The Country Life Commission appointment epitomized the editor's relationship with the president. Becoming one of the commission's seven members conveyed prestige, but the assignment brought neither power nor pay nor much immediate reward of any kind. The Country Life Commission owed its establishment principally to the work of Liberty Hyde Bailey, the head of Cornell University's College of Agriculture, and, to a lesser extent, to the influence of Sir Horace Plunkett, the Anglo-Irish agrarian reformer. Between them and through their friendships with Gifford Pinchot, Bailey and Plunkett had infected Roosevelt with concern about the plight of rural people. Although their efforts met resistance from the aging, conservative secretary of agriculture, James Wilson, Pinchot's perseverance finally moved the president to set up a five-man Commission on Country Life on 10 August 1908. The original members included Bailey, as chairman; Pinchot; Henry D. Wallace of Des Moines, Iowa, who was both a leading farm editor and a close friend of Secretary Wilson; Kenyon L. Butterfield, president of the Massachusetts State Agricultural College; and Page. Later Roosevelt added a second, resident southerner, C. S. Barrett, of Union City, Georgia, and a representative of the Far West, William Beard, another agricultural journalist from Sacramento, California. Dr. Charles W. Stiles accompanied the commission as a staff expert. The terms of their appointment directed the commissioners to investigate "the question of securing better business and better living on the farm, . . . by any other legitimate means that will help to make country life more gainful, more attractive, and fuller of opportunities, pleasures, and rewards for the men, women, and children of the farms."[24]

But the scope of the assignment hardly squared with the means for carrying it out. Besides having to complete their work by January 1909, the commissioners received no pay or expense allowances. Page made his first contribution to the group by using his philanthropic connections to get a five-thousand-dollar grant from the Russell Sage Foundation to defray travel and investigatory costs. The commission conducted two tours, through the Middle West and West in October 1908 and through the South in November, staging over two hundred hearings in thirty cities and towns. Page made only the second trip. In operation, the commission functioned smoothly, although members sometimes pursued divergent interests. When the commission gathered in Washington during December 1908 and January 1909 to draft a report, the agricultural business spokesmen, Butterfield, Barrett, and Beard, concentrated on such economic problems as credit, marketing, and technology. The evangelical chairman, Bailey, along with Pinchot and Page, envisioned a sweeping regeneration of rural life through education and a variety of new cooperative and cultural institutions. Wallace, like his son and grandson after him, amiably embraced both the businesslike and the visionary tendencies. The members also differed over how to present the commission's findings. Page dissented from the plan to submit a lengthy report by Bailey for government publication. He wanted a "short, smart, and snappy" paper that would get "real publicity." "Official publication is not publicity," he told Bailey. "It is generally burial." The commissioners compromised on a comprehensive survey of rural conditions by Bailey, together with specific recommendations and a brief introduction by Page and Pinchot. All were embodied in the commission's report, which went to Congress on 21 January 1909.[25]

The commission's efforts got a frosty official reception. In Congress foes of Roosevelt, abetted by undercover sabotage by the secretary of agriculture, refused to appropriate money either to continue recommended investigations or even to print a large number of copies of the report. Secretary Wilson commandeered the commission's research materials, and the report received only limited circulation as a Senate document and in a couple of privately published editions. But it still had immense influence, particularly in universities. These troubles left Page undismayed, both because he believed any publicity was better than none and because membership on the Country Life Commission had presented him with his most spectacular opportunity to aid the South.

The commission's southern tour in November 1908 had brought Page in contact with the staff expert, Dr. Charles W. Stiles, a government scientist who had earlier discovered the parasitic cause of hookworm, the intestinal infection that was rampant in the states below the Potomac. According to one story, Page was sitting in the smoking car of the train with Stiles and Henry Wallace early in the journey. When Wallace noticed a listless, emaciated white man on a station platform, he asked whether the man was an example of "white trash." "Yes," Page replied, "though it is better not to use the expression south of the Potomac." Stiles then interjected that the man was simply a victim of hookworm. "Can that man be cured?" asked Page. "About fifty cents worth of drugs will completely cure him," rejoined Stiles. Following that conversation, Page used the commission's hearings as a vehicle for publicizing Stiles's views on the cause and cure of hookworm. On several occasions, they ran afoul of the old charge of defaming the South. A session in Raleigh roused Daniels to lambast Page in the *News and Observer* for again running down his native state. Back in New York after the conclusion of the commission's work, Page informed Rockefeller's principal philanthropic agents, Buttrick and Frederick Gates, about Stiles's work. Largely through Page's persuasion, the Rockefeller Commission for the Extermination of the Hookworm Disease officially began work on 26 October 1909. Page and other Southern Board and General Board members served as directors and managed an endowment of one million dollars.[26]

The Hookworm Commission achieved fantastic results. Employing the Southern Education Board's techniques of stimulating local campaigns and soft-pedaling northern influence, the Hookworm Commission's teams moved through the South during the next four years, examining and treating over a million people. They likewise kicked off a series of sanitation and public-health campaigns in towns and states, after the model of the education crusades. For the Rockefeller philanthropies, the Hookworm Commission began their entry into tropical medicine and sanitation work, which became a worldwide venture. Later, as ambassador in London, Page made contacts between Buttrick and British colonial officials, paving the way for Rockefeller work in Africa and Asia. Before that, he believed that the South had found the key to unlock the chains of backwardness. In September 1912 Page declared in *World's Work* that hookworm, "not the warmth of the climate, . . . not the after-effect of slavery, . . . not a large 'poor-white' element," had shackled the region. "The hookworm has probably played a larger part in our Southern history than slavery or wars or any political dogma or economic creed." Just as he had grasped at free trade in the 1880s, Page still seemed to be seeking one-shot remedies to social ills.[27]

Service on the Country Life Commission also sharpened the editor's thinking about rural problems. Before 1909 Page's interest in rural life had been strong but diffuse. For almost thirty years, he had regarded improved farming as more important to southern progress than attracting manufactures. More recently, through the Southern and General Education boards, he had learned about the phenomenal results achieved by Seaman A. Knapp through farm-demonstration techniques. Page also knew Bailey, who had once edited Doubleday's magazine, *Country Life in America*, and, possibly through him, he had become acquainted with Plunkett's work in Ireland. After 1909 these interests intensified. The main object of Page's transatlantic trip during the summer of 1909 was to visit Plunkett and to study rural cooperatives in Europe. Even before that journey, the editor became convinced that a nationwide program of agricultural extension held the key to revitalizing country life. "I do not think of extension work as a particular scheme, or device," he declared in January 1909, " . . . but as a fundamental underlying method of popular propaganda, by which such problems as the hookworm disease, cooperative demonstrations, and a hundred other things may be systematically put before all the people." Similarly, Page believed that only the federal government could carry out that program. He told Plunkett in May 1909, "It is perfectly clear to me that we shall do nothing (do, as distinguished from agitation and talk) in the United States until the Department of Agriculture takes up the work, and the Bureau of Education." Unfortunately, the political failings of Roosevelt's successor in the White House, Taft, and the office-holding tenacity of Secretary Wilson prevented any action for another four years.[28]

Right after the 1912 election, Page started working to convince Woodrow Wilson of the importance of a comprehensive, educational assault on rural problems through the Department of Agriculture. At the same time Wallace, with whom the editor had become particularly friendly, was drumming up support for Page's appointment as secretary of agriculture to carry out such a program. Clearly, the Country Life Commission had furnished Page with valuable connections. The experience also broadened and focused his southern reform ideas. After 1909, rural America became for him an extension of the South. In May 1913, Page observed in his last *World's Work* editorial, "When you come to think of it, the essential difference between the town and the country is this: one is organized and the other is not. The town is organization." Obviously, the task was to extend organization to the country. Speaking in North Carolina in December 1912, he predicted a flight of people from overpopulated cities to the countryside. Simultaneously, the organization of rural life would create "equilibrium between the town and the country," when "neither will have undue advantage over the other; when in a word American life will cease to be lop-sided." This change would bring, he added, "something better than literature; but literature will come along with the other arts." Walter Page had come full circle, back to his starting point as a literary southerner who sought to lay a material foundation for culture in his native region. Rural organization, together with sanitation, provided the most clearly defined materials that he ever found for such a foundation. In that way, like Roosevelt, the Country Life Commission had brought him closer than he realized to fulfilling his ideals.[29]

The cause of agricultural uplift in turn permitted Page to

swallow some of his long-standing distaste for political participation. During 1911 his stress on getting the Department of Agriculture into rural organization involved him with opponents of Secretary Wilson in efforts to shake up the department and depose the aging chief. Nor did those moves constitute Page's first personal political involvement. His conceptions of southern reform impelled him to take part in a movement to break the region's Democratic solidarity during and after the 1908 election. Possibilities for political change below the Mason-Dixon line had formed a perennial topic in "The March of Events" since the founding of *World's Work*. In 1901 and 1902 Page had welcomed signs that pro-business Southern Democrats might loosen their ties to the national party. In 1904 he wished that Republicans would carry a southern state as a way to loosen "the superstitions that overgrow all creeds when they are held without change for generation after generation."[30]

Wanting to see the Solid South break up did not make Page a Republican. An independent posture came naturally to *World's Work*, inasmuch as the editor disdained the Republicans' "standpat" subjection to big business as much as the Democrats' Bryanite "insanity." In 1907 he commented, "Both the old parties, merely as parties, are moribund." Before 1908 Page still cared about his old party. How to revive the democracy became another favorite subject in "The March of Events." Right after the 1904 election, he urged the Democrats to find "some vital issue," and he suggested that they had inherited "two great duties ... to reform the tariff and to regulate the trusts." Fresh leadership offered another opportunity, and in that connection *World's Work* made its first venture into the political function that magazines were taking over from newspapers—the booming of presidential candidates. In February 1903 *World's Work* mentioned Alton Parker as a good Democratic nominee for 1904. Page did not pursue that initiative, because he also admired Roosevelt and the president looked unbeatable.[31]

With the approach of the 1908 contest, the editor was ready for a more strenuous inning in the game of president-making. The magazine published an editorial and a well-illustrated article on Governor John B. Anderson of Minnesota, calling him a potential winner. An article on Bryan, by contrast, carried no pictures and dismissed him as "a vent for public discontent." After the Great Commoner captured his third Democratic nomination, the magazine barely mentioned him except to rejoice at his defeat in November.[32]

Page made his most serious plunge into presidential politics in 1908 on the Republican side. The editor not only promoted Taft's candidacy through his magazine, but he also made private efforts to improve the Republican candidate's showing in the South. William Howard Taft combined two main attractions for Page. One was that the secretary of war was the first potential presidential candidate whom he knew personally. The two men served together on the board of the Jeanes Fund. This acquaintance gave Page a sense of discovery with Taft that he could never feel about Roosevelt. The second attraction lay in Taft's needing the kind of publicity that as a magazine editor Page could provide. Although Taft had been regarded as a possible successor to Roosevelt since the 1904 election, he had the handicap of never having run for office and not being well known politically. *World's Work* helped remedy the situation by boosting Taft for the presidency from October 1906 until the election. Almost monthly comments in "The March of Events" praised his qualifications and training for high office, and from July through November 1907 an illustrated, serialized biography recounted the man's exemplary life and enumerated his noble qualities.

Promoting Taft through *World's Work* marked a development in Page's role as a magazine editor, showing that he had grasped the possibilities of using the medium for political influence. But his biggest departures occurred outside the editorial office. Privately Page tried to persuade several southern politicians and newspaper editors to support Taft if Bryan won the Democratic nomination. In April 1908, he urged former governor Montague of Virginia to lead such a movement. "The old solidity will crack of its own weight before very long," he told Montague. "It ought to be led, therefore, and not hang on longer in a stupid fashion." Although no one took up his challenge before the election, the lack of response to his overtures did not overly disappoint Page. He confessed to Montague in July, "Perhaps it is practically certain that there will be no break this year; but I do mean at an early time; and when it comes, it is going to come with a vengeance and I can't keep from believing it's going to be a good thing."[33]

Page did his part to precipitate the break directly after the 1908 election. At some point in the fall, he joined William Garrot Brown, a scholarly, semiinvalid expatriate from Alabama, in an effort to get Taft to make the Republican party more attractive to southern whites. At Page's urging, Brown traveled to Cincinnati to discuss the southern situation with the president-elect a few days after the election. The editor invited Taft to address the annual dinner of the North Carolina Society of New York early in December. The dinner's program, he explained, would concern "Industrial and Educational and Social, and (in a broad way) Political Progress, in a frank and outspoken way." The audience would include prominent natives of all the southern states who were now living in New York—"your friends and friends of your Administration, men who stand ready to help in the liberalization of the South and who confidently expect to see an end of its political solidity under your Administration." Page offered to come to Hot Springs, Virginia, where Taft would be vacationing, to talk further. He and Brown also convinced the president-elect to consider appointing conservative Democrats from North Carolina and Virginia to federal posts and to give public assurances that his administration had no intention of interfering with disfranchisement or segregation.[34]

Taft accepted Page's invitation to use the North Carolina Society dinner as the occasion to beam reassuring signals toward the white South. On 7 December 1908 six hundred men and women gathered in the ballroom of the Hotel Astor for a dinner, after which came a series of brief speeches, with the president-elect last. Around ten o'clock, the tall, craggy Page, who was president of the society, introduced the guest of honor. Predicting the swift "breaking of the Solid South," Page called for the region to embrace "a Democratic party of tolerance and a Republican party of character; and neither party must be ranged on lines of race." He urged the South to recapture its pre–Civil War role "in the great constructive work of the government," adding, "If it cannot regain its old-time influence through one party, it will regain it through another." Then the massive man with the twangy voice who had just been elected president delivered a ponderous but manifestly friendly speech. Taft affirmed that he had no objection to election laws, "which square with the 15th amendment, to prevent entirely the possibility of a domination of Southern state, county, or municipal governments by an ignorant electorate, white or black." He dismissed the notion of federal interference in social relations: "The federal government has nothing to do with social equality." Taft concluded by endorsing the conviction "that the solution of race question in the South is largely a matter of industrial and thorough education." His speech received a standing ovation. A Republican president-elect could have hardly aimed more welcome words at a white southern audience.[35]

The occasion appeared to portend dreams coming true for Page. The Republican vote in the Upper South in 1908 and prospects for further gains there particularly gratified him. "North Carolina is ripe for plucking," he had assured Taft in November. Earlier, during the campaign, he had asserted in *World's Work*, "The upland part of the South was a stronghold of the Whig party, and the Republicanism of Mr. Taft is closely akin to the old Whig party. There would, therefore, be no violent change for the men of this generation to go back to the faith of their fathers." The Taft departure seemed a step toward restoring the kind of southern politics that Page claimed had flourished before the slavery crisis and the Civil War. As earlier, he thought that bringing the region back into the nation's political mainstream meant resurrecting a more genuinely southern situation. In contrast to William Garrot Brown, Page did not believe that the South had to alter its essential character and become indistinguishable from the North. Nor did he believe, like other advocates of republicanism south of the Potomac, that he was selling out blacks. "I have talked this subject over with Mr. Booker T.

Washington, who heartily seconds its purpose," he also told Taft in November 1908. To Page's mind, the breakup of the Solid South would bring proper political alignment for both blacks and whites.[36]

Unfortunately those dreams rested on a shaky base. Taft's southern strategy came to naught in the general foundering of his administration. Although he did appoint a few anti-Bryan Southern Democrats to lesser federal posts, Taft discarded the broader strategy of wooing white support. The more pressing problem of internecine conflict between reformers and conservatives in his own party distracted him from the South. By 1912 he had slipped so badly that his renomination depended in large measure upon heavily black southern delegations to the Republican convention. "Lily-white" Republicanism became instead the property of Roosevelt and his insurgent backers. The departure that Page had envisioned in 1908 would not bear fruit until 1928, when Herbert Hoover made inroads in exactly the areas of Dixie that the editor had predicted. Further development toward a two-party South would wait until the 1950s and 1960s, and by then race would have reemerged as the central political issue in ways that Page never contemplated.

Having staked his faith in Taft, the editor did not grow easily disillusioned. The president's early failure to carry through on tariff reform failed to shake him. In September 1909 *World's Work* blamed congressional obstructionists for the fiasco of the Payne-Aldrich tariff, insisting that Taft had won "a moral victory" and cautioning against unfair comparisons with Roosevelt. Page declined to lash out even at Taft's firing of Gifford Pinchot, refusal to cross Secretary Wilson, and support of a rise in postage rates for magazines. As late as July 1910 the editor still clung to a few private hopes. "He's 'coming up' in public favor," Page told Ray Stannard Baker, "but he can't change radically." In September, Page seems to have participated in a behind-the-scenes effort to bring about a reconciliation between Taft and Roosevelt, who was now openly critical of his successor.[37]

It is hard to say whether the editor showed worse political judgment in underestimating Roosevelt or in overestimating Taft.

Page's reluctance to break with the man whom he had promoted for the presidency testified to his personal involvement. Actually, he became no more intimate with Taft than he had been with Roosevelt. Page conferred at the White House no oftener after 1909 and, although he secured book rights to the president's speeches for Doubleday, Page, their sale was embarrassingly small. *World's Work*'s part in boosting Taft's candidacy mattered less to the editor than his personal engagement in the southern departure. Page had at last let down his guard against politicians and parties in an effort to help his native section. Both the politician and the party failed him. During 1910, despite the many exciting events of the intensified insurgent Republican revolt, *World's Work* carried less political material in "The March of Events" and fewer articles about politics than at any other time. Page's occasional comments betrayed a fresh edge of bitterness, bordering on radicalism. Agitation against special privilege was, he warned in July, "a ground-swell, not a mere passing mood of discontent. The old political parties are losing the moral hold because they have lost moral earnestness, and the moral earnestness of the people continues to become greater and to show itself in new forms." Page's bruised feelings did not last long, however, because a new and far more thrilling opportunity for political involvement and belief was about to come his way.[38]

At seven o'clock on the evening of Friday, 24 February 1911, the fifty-five-year-old *World's Work* editor joined two fellow southerners at the Aldine Club, the book publishers' social organization. One of the people with whom Page met was Walter L. McCorkle, a native of Virginia, corporation lawyer, and president of the Southern Society of New York. The other was William F. McCombs, an Arkansan who was a graduate of Princeton, also a lawyer, and a dabbler in New York Democratic politics. They were meeting to organize a presidential campaign for their common acquaintance who had been elected governor of New Jersey the previous November—Woodrow Wilson. They gathered, at McCorkle's proposal, to commence such "practical work" as drumming up news coverage, appointing a publicity manager, arranging a speaking tour in the West for the governor, consulting with Democratic senators and representatives, and raising money. Page noted in his appointment book, "W. H. P.—find publicity man—who?" He also planned to contact the editor of the *New York World*, which was still the country's leading Democratic paper, and to "call crowd together again." That meeting started the Wilson presidential movement. For Page, its location had a fitting symbolism. The Aldine Club stood just six blocks up Broadway from the street corner where fifteen years earlier Horace Scudder had offered him a job with the *Atlantic*. The 1911 meeting would also lead eventually to a memorable job for Page.[39]

The editor had concerned himself with Wilson's presidential prospects well before the 24 February meeting. Stories about his having envisioned Wilson in the White House many years earlier sound apocryphal, but *World's Work* had recommended the Princeton president in January 1907 as a long-shot possibility for a Democratic nomination, a fit beneficiary of "a political miracle that might produce a new face." Another member of the Southern Education Board later remembered Page's predicting in the summer of 1908 that Wilson would succeed Taft. Page never ceased to regard his old acquaintance as a man to watch. In October 1902 he had run a full-page photograph of the new president of Princeton in *World's Work*. Over the next few years he had published a highly sympathetic article and several comments in "The March of Events" on Wilson's reforms at the university. Around March 1910, Page wrote in one of those personal stock-taking notes to himself, in Greek script, "Write a letter every year to W. Wilson." In July 1910, after Wilson accepted the New Jersey Democratic gubernatorial nomination, Page went to see him about his political plans. Democratic state-house victories the following November prompted *World's Work* to urge the party to seek its next presidential candidate "outside of Congress; for the greatest need of the party is national leadership." The magazine named several governors as possible contenders, stressing "the great qualities in Mr. Wilson's character and methods which the public has not yet become aware of." At the beginning of February 1911 Page set out to remedy that lack of awareness by detailing his top staff writer, William Bayard Hale, to do an article on the governor. The piece would, he explained to Wilson, apply "some corrective influences" to his budding national reputation in order "to keep the witches off and to restore a proper balance."[40]

The initiative for Page to involve himself personally in the campaign came from Wilson. On 10 February the governor wrote to inform the editor that McCorkle "and other Southern friends of mine in New York" seemed bent upon "getting up some kind of organized movement to advocate my claims." Wilson had advised McCorkle and the others to contact Page "for hard headed advice." Page jumped at the opportunity. He replied that he had "some very definite notions about such work. . . . They are very simple and very old-fashioned notions, but they are based upon a life-long study of the fickle thing called public opinion." He offered to come down to Trenton and talk further. After 24 February Page, McCorkle, and McCombs pursued the tasks they had outlined at their meeting. Among themselves, apparently, they put up three thousand dollars, and they started seeking other contributions. Early in March Page chose the publicity manager, a writer for *World's Work* and former Cincinnati newspaperman named Frank Parker Stockbridge. The venture plainly excited Page. "I feel impatient about the enterprise that we are engaged in," he told McCorkle, suggesting that the three of them meet regularly. According to Stockbridge's recollection, however, the trio met only twice after hiring him. Priority went to arranging a speaking tour of the West for Wilson, who met to discuss the trip with his backers on 25 March 1911 at Page's apartment on East Sixty-seventh Street.[41]

The editor oversaw Stockbridge's arrangements for the western tour. At one point he soothed McCorkle's and McCombs's jitters about possible harm in Wilson's speaking in Bryan's hometown, Lincoln, Nebraska, while the Commoner was away. Page also arranged for texts of Wilson's speeches, which he and Hale edited, to be prepared before the trip began, for advance distribution to the reporters. To their dismay the governor discarded those texts and insisted upon giving most of his speeches extemporaneously. "He is not yet fully educated up to the value of publicity," wailed Stockbridge. However, the snag did not prevent Wilson from getting good coverage in western papers and attracting attention from the magazines. Stockbridge sent Page extensive reports on the trip. The editor arranged for Stockbridge to distribute proofs of Hale's article, "Woodrow Wilson: Possible President," which appeared in the May issue of *World's Work*.[42]

Page made two further contributions to kicking off the Wilson campaign during the spring of 1911. One was financial, at least indirectly. From April through June he practiced his persuasions on the financier Henry Morgenthau, who subsequently became one of the biggest donors to Wilson's candidacy. Page's other contribution was organizational. Starting early in May, he urged the appointment of a campaign manager. When Wilson returned from his western tour, Page arranged a conference on 4 June at the Willard Hotel in Washington. The candidate met with the campaign organizers and a few others, including Page's brother Robert, who was now a representative from North Carolina. All of them pressed Wilson to mount a full-fledged campaign. "My reason for it is this," Page reiterated to McCorkle shortly afterward: "delegates must be got. If he were nominated and the election were coming on, I should have great confidence in trusting simply to public opinion; but delegates don't vote according to public opinion always." Wilson resisted those entreaties. He told Page that by appointing a campaign manager "we would seem to have descended into the arena and would create some very unfavorable impressions." Wilson preferred to keep the organization limited to a publicity bureau headed by Stockbridge, with McCombs assuming responsibility for additional fund raising. Yet the campaign did move closer to what Page advocated. During the summer of 1911 a tighter organization took shape through the efforts of McCombs and a fresh recruit, still another native southerner and successful New York businessman, William Gibbs McAdoo.[43]

Publicity remained Page's major contribution to the Wilson movement. Stockbridge's work on the western tour and Hale's article helped stir up national political interest in the New Jersey governor. *World's Work* proceeded to boom Wilson in the same way that it had Taft four years before, but with greater effort and even less pretense of detachment. Each month from the spring of 1911 until the election in November 1912, "The March of Events" contained some favorable comment or comparison with other candidates. In August 1911 the magazine ran both a report by Stockbridge on the western trip and the results of a preferential mail ballot of fifteen hundred voters, which purported to show Wilson in the lead, ahead of both Taft and Roosevelt as well as rival Democrats. The October 1911 through March 1912 issues of *World's Work* carried a serialized, profusely illustrated, eulogistic biography of Wilson, also by Hale. Only three other candidates became subjects of even single articles, Judson Harmon and Oscar Underwood on the Democratic side and Robert La Follette on the Republican. The Hale biography and several of Page's "March of Events" comments saw extensive circulation as pamphlets and leaflets by the Wilson organization, especially before the Democratic convention at Baltimore in June 1912. Page had once more demonstrated his grasp of the opportunities for political influence through his magazine editorship.

Yet except for providing publicity in *World's Work* and helping set up the original organization, the editor's part in the Wilson campaign did not extend much further than his earlier involvement with Taft. Page's diminished role in the campaign evidently stemmed from several circumstances. One was simply time. When he pressed Wilson to appoint a campaign manager, he apologized to McCorkle, "I heartily wish it were possible for me to take the time to get out and hustle on this matter; but it isn't." As the tempo of the campaign quickened, active participation required the kind of free time that was available to men of established means, such as McCombs and McAdoo, but not to a busy editor and publisher. Personal incompatibilities probably loosened Page's ties, too. McCombs, who became campaign manager in October 1911, resented anyone whom he suspected of rivalry for Wilson's confidence. According to Stockbridge's assistant, by July McCombs "had succeeded in pushing Page out of it together with Walter McCorkle and some others." In December he fired Stockbridge, who was Page's man in the organization, for supposedly coming between himself and the candidate. In addition, Page's antagonist Daniels became one of Wilson's most effective backers in North Carolina and the South, and after the convention he came to New York to head the Democratic National Publicity Bureau.[44]

Another reason for the editor's stepping aside was that by the summer of 1911 he had already performed his most useful function. Page's warning to Wilson about not "trusting simply to public opinion" contained an implicit confession of his own limitations. Publicity was his forte, and the critical period for publicity passed with the western tour and Wilson's emergence as a national figure. As Page said, lining up delegates now took priority over everything else, and that job required skills the editor did not possess. In December 1911 William Garrot Brown, who had also shifted allegiances from Taft to Wilson, cautioned Wilson's newfound confidant Colonel Edward M. House against relying too much on Page in North Carolina. "Walter Page himself is very radical in some lines & distinctly antagonistic to very powerful Democrats. He is not the best man to *head* the Wilson movement here."[45]

Those circumstances did not, however, completely explain why Page backed so far away from the campaign. The deepest reasons for his withdrawal lay with himself. Exercising political influence as a magazine editor had not erased Page's distaste for parties and politicians. Rather, the disappointment with Taft had rekindled his old mistrust. During the 1912 campaign Page restricted his enthusiasm to Wilson himself, viewing the Democrats with unabated suspicion. "I think it very probable that the party can't live up to this high water mark," he told Henry Wallace in August 1912, "and that there will be a row and a split and a falling back to the old level." A month later, he commented that he was worried, not about Wilson's getting elected, but about what would happen after he entered the White House. "The hungry hordes that will beset him—Good Lord! Save him! He will not surrender. I am not afraid of that. But I am afraid that

they'll turn on him and rend him asunder." Personal traits reinforced repugnance toward politics in holding Page back from the
campaign. Staying active after the summer of 1911 would have
required him to push himself forward, at least to some extent,
and most likely to clash with such people as McCombs. Page's
behavior in the Wilson campaign resembled his earlier confron-
tations with Metcalf on the *Forum* and Scudder on the *Atlantic*.
In each case he had plunged in with enthusiasm but abruptly
drawn back when faced with the prospect of shoving someone
aside and getting into a personal conflict. This pattern would
repeat itself again after the 1912 election.[46]

Absence from the later phases of the campaign did not
prevent Page from taking pride in his earlier role. On the evening
of 2 July 1912, he stood in Times Square with Stockbridge,
watching the electric news ticker on the *New York Times* building
flash the report of Wilson's nomination. "Well, Stockbridge,"
Page remarked, "it looks to me as if we started something." Even
without personal involvement Page could hardly have avoided
enchantment with Wilson, since his old acquaintance seemed to
be the answer to all his political prayers. Before the Taft departure, *World's Work* had advocated Democratic nomination of a
national-minded southerner for the presidency as the surest way
to bring the section back into the mainstream of politics. As a
fellow expatriate southerner, Wilson filled the bill perfectly, and
he enhanced his attractiveness by drawing fire from various
southerners who impugned his sectional loyalty. The governor's
performance in New Jersey likewise meshed with the editor's
own sharpening reform sentiments. Best of all for Page, Wilson
combined literary grace with forceful action. Immediately after
his nomination Page exulted, "Sound economics, right social
ideals, even an impulse toward sincerity and human sympathy in
literature—all these will have a new impetus under your leadership." *World's Work* hailed Wilson's success in November with
the declaration, "We have never had a President who expressed
himself in such vigorous pure English, nor a man with better
mental furnishing."[47]

Page displayed his newfound faith best in his behavior in

November 1912. On election day he congratulated Wilson for a victory "fairly, highly, freely won, and now we enter the Era of Great Opportunity." He urged the president-elect to do three things: call an immediate session of Congress to revise the tariff and institute agricultural reforms; put trusted friends to work preparing analyses of the biggest national problems; and revive the practice of addressing Congress in person. Ten days later, on 15 November 1912, Page drove to Princeton to confer with Wilson about the "Big Change and Great Outlook." The editor "went at my business without delay. The big-country-life-idea, the working of great economic forces to put its vitalization within sight, the coming equilibrium by the restoration of country life—all coincident with his coming into the Presidency. His administration must fall in with it, guide it, further it." Then the president-elect asked his visitor, "Who is the best man for Secretary of Agriculture?" Page demurred, "May I look about and answer your question later?" Wilson assented, and Page offered to draft memoranda on the Department of Agriculture, rural credits, and conservation. "I shall be very grateful, if it be not too great a sacrifice," answered the president-elect. After an hour's talk, Page took his leave and drove back to New York.[48]

The editor threw himself into advising the president-elect with a flurry of writing. Over the next twelve days he sketched a number of notes to himself about possible appointees to important jobs and about agriculture and conservation. He produced several drafts of memoranda on farm-demonstration work, the Department of Agriculture, and the Bureau of Education. He also set down an account of his meeting with Wilson, which he placed among his journals. Page was not forgetting the possible literary value of the events in which he was participating. Memoranda on agriculture and conservation, together with short estimates of several men who might be considered for posts in the new administration, went to Wilson on 27 November. In his covering letter Page stated again, "The building up of the countryman is the big constructive job of our time. When the countryman comes to his own, the town man will no longer be able to tax, and to concentrate power, and to bully the world." The letter also answered the president-elect's question about "who I thought was the best man for Secretary of Agriculture." Page named David F. Houston, the chancellor of Washington University in St. Louis, who was a native North Carolinian, a member of the Southern and General Education boards, and the former president of the University of Texas.[49]

Recommending someone for the agriculture secretaryship placed Page in a delicate position. The editor knew that others were booming him for the job. Strong support for him had gathered in two quarters, one among friends in his native state, some of whom hoped that between Page and Daniels North Carolina might gain two seats in the Wilson cabinet. James Y. Joyner, the state education superintendent, and Clarence Poe, the editor of the state's leading agricultural paper, *The Progressive Farmer*, orchestrated a stream of letters and telegrams to the president-elect to recommend Page. The other source of support lay with the editor's connections from the Country Life Commission. As early as September 1912, O. B. Martin, one of the rebels against Secretary Wilson in the department, contacted Wallace Buttrick about Page's becoming the next secretary. Martin and Buttrick enlisted Henry Wallace and, through him and Poe, a substantial segment of the agricultural press behind Page.

Page acquiesced in those efforts to promote his appointment, but he did not actively seek the post. His behavior toward the agriculture secretaryship duplicated his earlier role in the campaign. After his initial burst of enthusiasm, Page hung back. He saw the president-elect just twice more before the inauguration, once at Wilson's request, and wrote him only a few brief notes. Wilson's responses did not encourage him, either. Page told Alderman that he had received notes "of almost abject thanks. . . . Yet not a word, what he thinks. The Sphinx was garrulous by comparison." With Alderman, Page shared his first doubts about Wilson, who struck him as "very shy, having lived far too much alone and far too much with women (how I wish two of his daughters were sons). . . . Wise? Yes. But does he know the men about him? Does he really know men?" In the past, Wilson had also had occasional misgivings about Page. When Page had left the *Atlantic* in 1899, Wilson had asked his wife, "And what *has* happened to Page? Has he made himself obnoxious, as I feared he might?"[50]

Those comments pointed toward the temperamental gulf between the two men. Where the president-elect valued self-control and emotional restraint, the editor believed in self-expression and giving vent to his emotions. The remark about living "far too much with women" disclosed Page's persistent concern with virility, unwittingly underscoring how much better Roosevelt had fitted his model of leadership. This temperamental difference would later have important effects on the relationship between the new president and his old acquaintance.

Page's characteristic way of drawing back probably cost him a place in the cabinet. Not wanting to appear to push himself made Page violate the first rule for aspirants to office: always be on the scene. In February 1913 he took a month-long vacation in North Carolina, leaving New York just when Wilson was making the final decisions about who would enter the cabinet. On Saturday, 22 February, the president-elect informed Colonel House that he intended to offer a place to Page, and he asked the colonel to sound the editor out. Because Page was away, House had to telegraph for him to return from North Carolina. By the time Page arrived on Monday, 24 February, political reconsiderations had knocked him off the cabinet list. Three weeks later House recounted the incident at lunch with the editor and McAdoo. "Page was told how nearly he was conscripted for the Cabinet," House recorded in his diary. "It was merely the fact that he was not at home on a certain Saturday afternoon that saved him." It would have been more accurate to say that Page's old attitudes toward politics and self-assertion had helped to trip him up.[51]

The editor may have contributed even more directly to his own undoing. The post for which Wilson slated him on 22 February was the secretaryship of the interior. The agriculture post had already gone to Houston, whom Page had recommended. Whatever Houston lacked in recognition among agricultural leaders, he more than made up through the sponsorship of his old friend from his days as president of the University of Texas,

Colonel House. During the preceding October, House had determined to place Houston in the cabinet. When he first mentioned Houston to Wilson in December, agriculture somehow emerged as the spot for him. It is possible that House did not choose that department for his friend but simply seized upon his having already been recommended for it by Page. When Wilson next discussed cabinet appointments with House on 8 January 1913, he asked the colonel's "opinion of Walter Page for Secretary of the Interior and of Houston for Secretary of Agriculture." House wrote in his diary that he "gave Houston unqualified praise but was somewhat guarded in regard to Page." They then tried switching departments for the two. Later in the conversation House pointed out to Wilson "that he was taking too many men from New York," including Page. That conversation evidently settled Houston's appointment, since on all future cabinet slates the agriculture post went to him. On 11 February 1913, on Wilson's instructions, House notified Houston that he would be the next secretary of agriculture.[52]

After 8 January the editor's chances for the cabinet dimmed, as his name disappeared from most subsequent slates. His insertion in the interior slot on 22 February came at House's suggestion. A. Mitchell Palmer's refusal to become secretary of war required shuffling posts once more. House recommended that Wilson "offer Walter Page the Interior and put [Franklin K.] Lane into War. He authorized me to interview Page and see whether he would take it." The next day House changed his mind. Talking with Joe Tumulty, Wilson's secretary, the colonel noted in his diary that "neither of us thought that Walter Page should go into the Interior Department." Tumulty's objection and House's second thoughts sprang from the circumstance that the interior department administered Civil War pensions to Union veterans, which seemed to dictate that no southerner should hold the position of secretary. When House telephoned Wilson in Princeton, the president-elect "thought Page had been living in the North long enough to bar that objection. I disagreed with him." The colonel consulted with other Democratic leaders later in the day and then telephoned back to Wilson, who "decided to keep Lane in the Interior and pick out another man for War." That was the end of Page's consideration for the cabinet.[53]

When the editor reached New York the following day, House explained the summons by saying that Wilson wanted additional advice on cabinet appointments. "Page was very earnest in his belief that Daniels should not go into the Cabinet," House recorded in his diary. "He thought he was not big enough." The prospect of his fellow Tar Heel's appointment upset Page so much that he left at once for Trenton on a vain errand to dissuade Wilson. Those encounters contained several ironies. Daniels was already in the cabinet, having been offered the secretaryship of the navy the day before. House knew that, but he did not tell Page and thus save the editor a useless trip. Nor did House let Page know that he had just missed an appointment. Politics was rewarding Daniels's liking and practice in the same measure that it was disappointing Page's distaste and avoidance.[54]

If the editor felt hurt at not getting an appointment, he concealed his wounds well. Page attended Wilson's inauguration on 4 March as an honored guest. *World's Work* hailed the new administration as "a brilliant opportunity." The editor not only defended Houston's appointment to Wallace and other skeptical agricultural spokesmen, but he also took the lead in raising a guaranteed thirty thousand dollars a year from private sources to defray the secretary's expenses in Washington. On 25 March he asserted that he was glad that "the President did not tempt me by the offer of a place in the Cabinet." He realized that "I could not go into political or public life at all—without first selling my interest in the *World's Work*. That must be kept absolutely independent, for its independence constitutes its value—is its very life."[55]

On 26 March 1913 Page had to start eating his words about wanting to remain a private citizen. That morning he answered the telephone at his desk in Garden City, to be greeted, "Good morning, your Excellency." Colonel House was calling to inform him that Wilson wanted to name him ambassador to Great Britain. The proposal took Page by surprise, but he liked the idea.

When he went to House's apartment on East Fifty-seventh Street in the afternoon to talk further, his host found the editor "excited over the news" and "immensely pleased with the compliment." Page raised ritual objections about inconvenience to his family and business associates, which House promptly brushed aside. In the evening, he discussed the offer with his wife and his sons Frank and Arthur.

Only Frank welcomed the news. Alice said that she did not know enough about it and, as Page later remembered, Arthur said, "No: the things that I was most interested in were all in the U.S., I wd be thrown among people whom I did not know & wd have duties that I cared little about—what real substance was there to such activities." Actually, Arthur Page was warning against what appealed to his father most. Page believed that he and his wife "had suffered from an insufficient social life because of my habits (and necessities) of work." He felt overworked and recalled "a sort of vague purpose to leave off active work at 60. This diplomatic task wd bring change, obligatory social duties and I cd test myself against men of consequence." Page's eagerness to accept the post attested to the restlessness he had felt increasingly in the last few years. On 28 March he telephoned House to say, "I have decided to turn my face towards the East." In his letter of acceptance to Wilson, he added, "Thus even things never dreamed of come true—in this glad year."[56]

Page judged correctly when he conceived of the post as a form of dignified semiretirement. Wilson had previously offered the ambassadorship to Britain to two men in their seventies, former secretary of state Richard Olney and the president emeritus of Harvard, Charles W. Eliot. Arthur Page also guessed right when he doubted the importance of the job. On two occasions Wilson had contemplated offering the ambassadorship to Bryan, as a way to render the Commoner harmless. On the eve of his departure for London in May 1913, Page called upon the president "to ask his instructions. He had none," Page remembered. "He knew no more about the task that awaited me than I knew. This is not to be wondered at; but I recall a feeling of (no doubt foolish) disappointment as I came away—that the whole outlook

seemed so vague." That feeling did not set in for a while, however, and Page would also learn that other influences would work
to make his diplomatic assignment more consequential.[57]

The editor probably owed his appointment less to his old
acquaintance with Wilson than to his newer one with House.
The colonel was the person who first suggested Page for the
London post, and he seems to have hatched the idea, like most of
his schemes, for a complex of reasons. Page had known House, a
wealthy Texan who resided in New York, since 1909. They had
become fairly good friends through their interests in southern
and rural reform. Sometime around 1912 House had begun to
concentrate on international affairs and to concoct plans for
reducing tensions between Britain and Germany. These plans
made him want competent, sympathetic American ambassadors
in the major world capitals. Wilson, too, desired "to lift up the
standard" of representation abroad, as he told House. But the
president meant appointing men of intellectual and literary distinction, such as Eliot and his former Princeton colleagues Henry
van Dyke, who became minister to the Netherlands, and Henry B.
Fine, who declined to become ambassador to Germany. The
name Page first came up in connection with the London post
when House insisted that Thomas Nelson Page was not fit for the
job. Walter Page did not occur to anyone as a possibility until the
colonel mentioned him to McAdoo on 17 March. The two of
them urged him on Wilson on 20 March. Five days later, the
president swung around, telling House "he thought that Walter
Page was about the best man left for Ambassador to Great
Britain."[58]

The editor's selection aroused no strong feelings either for or
against him in the United States. Page may have been an unusual
choice for the post, but he was neither a brilliant nor a controversial one. He had no diplomatic experience, and two summer trips
to Europe, thirty years apart, had hardly made him a cosmopolitan figure. As Page noted afterward, he had never set foot in an
American embassy. Nor had the success of Doubleday, Page &
Company brought him anywhere near the wealth that seemed
requisite for an ambassadorship to a great European capital. His

immediate predecessor in London, Whitelaw Reid, had been a millionaire, as had the ambassador before him, Joseph H. Choate. Before he left for Britain, Page informed House that he was worried "lest he might not be able to maintain himself, and yet he said he had enough sporting blood to undertake it."[59]

The editor did have some qualifications for the post. *World's Work* devoted more space to international affairs than any other leading magazine and Page retained some awareness of American involvements overseas. His business had given him a number of contacts among British authors, editors, and publishers, while his country-life involvement had introduced him to Sir Horace Plunkett, who was a well-connected aristocrat and member of Parliament as well as an agrarian reformer. The only minor complications about Page's appointment involved two matters unconnected with diplomacy. One was the flap over *The Southerner* after he had left, and the other was a protest by the British printers' union in May 1913 because of Doubleday, Page's open-shop practices.

The new ambassador started testing the amenities and distinctions of his post even before his departure. A whirl of official conferences and social engagements filled the month of April and the first half of May. The Pages spent several days in Washington at the middle of April, lunching at the White House with the Wilsons and attending dinners in their honor. In New York, the Doubleday, Page staff, the Periodical Publishers' Association, and a group of wealthy friends honored Page with large testimonial dinners. These functions gratified his wish to hobnob with the socially desirable. Besides the first family, he and Alice met Choate and Reid's widow, who briefed them on the domestic and social aspects of the London embassy. Page conferred with both the retiring British ambassador in Washington, Lord Bryce, and his successor who had just arrived, Sir Cecil Spring Rice.

Those activities left little time to prepare for the more serious side of diplomacy. Page made a second trip to Washington at the end of April to study recent correspondence between Britain and the United States, especially concerning the dispute over exemption of American coastal vessels from tolls in the soon-to-be-completed Panama Canal. He found the material "very dull stuff; and, after wading through it all day, on several nights as I went to bed the thought came to me whether this sort of activity were really worth a man's while." Calling at the White House on 30 April for final instructions disclosed the disappointing vagueness of Wilson's expectations. Page also remembered that "the President seemed to have in his mind only this idea—that he wanted somebody in London whom he knew upon whose judgment he could rely. That was complimentary, but it lacked definiteness." House filled in the dearth of instruction to some extent. On 2 May the colonel wrote in his diary that "I had gone over the matter [Anglo-American relations] myself with Page, and had given him the reasons for having the good will of the British Government constantly on our side." House also seems to have planned to depart for his annual summer vacation in Europe with Page, most likely intending to take advantage of the week-long voyage to initiate his friend into his international designs. The plan went awry when the British government informed the embassy in London that the king wished to receive the new ambassador on 30 May, thus requiring him to advance his sailing date.[60]

On 15 May 1913 Page left New York aboard the Cunard liner *Baltic*. His son Frank and Harold Fowler, a young man who was to be the ambassador's personal secretary, accompanied Page. Alice stayed behind to attend their daughter's graduation from Bryn Mawr and finish the chores of packing and moving before she and Katharine joined him in London. Neither last-minute rush and disorganization nor indefinite prospects marred Page's enthusiasm. The day after his departure, he wrote from shipboard to his sister Mary, "As Katharine said when she read the letter I have to the King of England, 'We're taking part in a play: it isn't real at all.' Here I am going to London to talk international affairs with the men who rule the British Empire; and I am to dine with the King and Queen on May 30." He confessed that he had "a sort of under-feeling that I'm going to enjoy it. One had just as well see the big world, now the chance is come. I feel as if I were going on a great adventure." On the day that he sailed from New York, Page was three months short of his fifty-eighth birthday. Yet he was embarking on the same kind of journey that he had made in his youth to Baltimore, St. Joseph, and New York. Once more, he was putting his homeland behind him in pursuit of glamor and distinction. Thanks ultimately to the South, a whole new world was opening for Walter Hines Page.[61]

PART III

The Venture Abroad

1913–1918

———

CHAPTER 8

The Patterns of Peace

The new United States ambassador to Great Britain looked nothing like the popular image of a diplomat. Walter Hines Page's large, raw-boned figure and homely, big-nosed face made him a conspicuous sight among the handsome, elegantly attired figures who made up most of the representatives to the Court of St. James's. For the ceremony at which he presented his credentials to King George V on 30 May 1913, Page had to wear knee breeches with silk stockings and carry what he called "a funny little tin sword." The ceremony and costume attracted some attention in the American press, and one of Page's old southern friends quipped, "I hope you stood the scrutiny of the King and showed him what a North Carolina farmer looks like." At most other court functions Page wore normal evening dress, but that, too, made him stand out. He and the Portuguese minister were the only foreign representatives who did not appear, as he told Colonel House, "arrayed like Solomon in all his glory." Sometime during Page's first year in London the caricaturist Max Beerbohm drew a cartoon of him gazing at a covey of his uniformed and bemedaled fellow diplomats and thinking, "I wonder if any of them has ever edited a good magazine."

Those initial appearances conveyed an accurate impression of what the first year of Page's ambassadorship would be like. From the start, the former editor could see that the post represented the desired break with his past. Since June and July were the height of the social season in London, the new American ambassador found himself swept up in a round of banquets, receptions, balls, and presentations. An official evening at the

India Office for the diplomatic corps on 4 June struck him as "the most brilliant affair I have ever seen." He and his son Frank gaped and laughed at the liveried, powdered footmen of the dukes and duchesses who invited them to dinner during their first two weeks in London. On these occasions Page sometimes committed a minor breach of etiquette, and he often found aristocrats "hard sledding" as conversationalists. But political and literary figures fascinated him, and he in turn delivered a graceful speech at his first public appearance, on 6 June before the Pilgrims, an organization of notables for the promotion of Anglo-American friendship. Eschewing "makeshifts and make-believe in our intercourse," the ambassador promised frank talk between "the two great nations of the English-speaking folk. . . . In our dealing blood answers blood, and our fundamental qualities of manhood are the same."[1]

The month after Page arrived in Britain on 24 May 1913 revealed nearly all the main features and problems of his first year as ambassador. At the royal audience on 30 May the king remarked that he could not understand why "a great and rich country like the U.S." did not buy a residence for its ambassador. Page had already gotten an inkling of his government's parsimony and inattention. The day after his ship landed, he visited his new place of work, the chancery of the United States embassy in London. He discovered a dingy, poorly lighted, converted apartment in an unfashionable commercial neighborhood. "I knew that Uncle Sam had no fit dwelling there." He could not understand how his predecessors had endured "that cheap hole" or why the American embassy in the leading world capital should not be "as good as a common lawyer's office in a country town in a rural State of our Union."[2]

The disparity between the prestige of his post and the means provided for the ambassador cut deeper than lack of an official dwelling and a tawdry embassy. The lavish scale of entertaining quickly confirmed earlier forebodings about expenses. When Alice joined Page at the end of June, she took alarm. "She sees financial disaster staring them in the face," noted House, who had also arrived in London. "She said if she had known before coming over what she knows now, nothing could have tempted her to give her consent for Mr. Page to accept the place." But Page did not want to let financial strain dampen his enthusiasm. He insisted to House that "if he can make a success of his work he will be content." Several signs during his first month in London convinced Page that he could not only do a good job but also find more than dignified leisure.[3]

"I've got this far," Page told Alice after his first two weeks. "I've pleased the King, it seems. I've got pretty well acquainted with Sir Edward Grey, the main man with whom I must deal during the lifetime of this Government; & I've made a good impression, if the papers tell the truth, by my first public speech." Of those contacts, the most important was with Grey, the foreign secretary in the Liberal government of Prime Minister H. H. Asquith. Page's first meetings with Grey disclosed the need to improve relations between Britain and the United States. On 27 May, even before being received at court, the ambassador called informally on the foreign secretary. Besides exchanging pleasantries, Grey mentioned the dispute over tolls on the soon-to-be-completed Panama Canal, a dispute regarded by the British as a serious controversy. Two weeks later, in their first official discussion, the two men touched on the tolls question again. The matter was not pressing, since Grey agreed to Page's request to wait until President Wilson could give it greater attention. The dispute also showed, Page told Arthur, that his "official job . . . is far from being a mere formality, as many suppose. There's a good deal of real work & some pretty difficult work."[4]

Page's idea of "real work" encompassed more than patching up Anglo-American relations. Considering his earlier ardor for partnership between the two nations, he could hardly have escaped viewing his ambassadorship as an opportunity to influence world politics. However, the meagerness of his personal and official establishment did not square with such a role. The State Department further vexed him both by failing to supply information and by broadcasting the nostrums of Secretary Bryan. But two other factors more than offset those drawbacks—admiration for Wilson, whose performance in the White House soon infected Page with another case of hero-worship, and friendship with House. House spun even grander visions than Page of reshaping international relations. On 19 June 1913 the colonel wrote in his diary that the ambassador "asks me to aid him in formulating some constructive policy that will make the President's administration and his notable in the annals of the embassy. He said of all men I could help him most in this regard."[5]

For Page, taking the ambassadorial post in London in 1913 recalled his joining Houghton, Mifflin and the *Atlantic* in Boston eighteen years before. Once more he pictured himself as a simple, vigorous democrat invading a preserve of aristocratic sophistication. After several months in Britain he told his sister Mary, "I fail to see how real men and women can do this sort of thing all their lives, as a business. For a few years it is an interesting experience to green backwoodsmen like us." The Tar Heel again exaggerated his rawness and novelty. His manner was direct and hearty but not overly familiar. The favorable impressions that he soon made in London, particularly on the king and Sir Edward Grey, showed that he was well suited to be an American ambassador to the Court of St. James's. One of Wilson's instructions before he had left the United States had been, he remembered, "Go, and be yourself." That turned out to be good advice.[6]

Assuming command at the embassy resembled Page's takeover of the *Atlantic*. He lost no time in pressing the State Department to reshuffle the staff. The first secretary, Irwin Laughlin, was an experienced career foreign service officer who had served as chargé d'affaires during the year and a half since Whitelaw Reid's death. Despite what Page found a "finical manner," Laughlin impressed him as "an ornament to the service and most efficient." Laughlin remained the number two man in the embassy throughout Page's ambassadorship. The military and naval attachés likewise seemed competent, but the embassy's second and third secretaries did not measure up to Page's standards, and he got them transferred. In their places came Edward Bell and Eugene Shoecraft, both career foreign service officers. Bell, at thirty-two, had served previously at posts in Africa, Asia, and

Latin America. The twenty-one-year-old Shoecraft was on his first assignment. Both men also stayed for the rest of Page's tenure as ambassador.

The former editor ran the embassy like one of his magazines. As in his New York and Boston offices, he received a stream of callers and used luncheon meetings to make contacts. Both practices were customary with ambassadors. Unlike his predecessors, however, Page continued his *World's Work* practice of holding regular staff meetings. "I have organized my staff as a sort of Cabinet," he explained to House in January 1914. "We meet every day. We go over everything conceivable that we say or try to do. We do good team work." The embassy operated smoothly, and the ambassador gained the loyalty of the people under him. "How I wish I had even a small fraction of your father's talent for getting work out of his subordinates without asking for it," Bell later told Arthur Page. "We were all ready to tear our shirts to accomplish anything he wanted." As on *World's Work*, Page took an interest in the younger members of his staff, especially Bell and the other junior foreign service officers who came to London after the outbreak of the world war. Fittingly, too, for a former journalist, Page soon established good relations with the press, both the correspondents for American papers and the nabobs of Fleet Street.[7]

Unfamiliarity with high society and diplomacy apparently presented few obstacles. Rubbing shoulders with royalty continued to thrill Page. "Mrs. Page, being sensible, is bored," he informed Wilson in January 1914, after a visit to Windsor Castle. "I am frankly—delighted, being historically frivolous." By contrast, the more exposure Page got to the ways of the State Department the less he regretted his lack of diplomatic experience. He kept up a volley of complaints about the department's failure to keep him informed. "Washington is a deep hole of silence towards Ambassadors," Page told House in November 1913. The following month he asked the president to have someone in the department, preferably the able career man William Phillips, who had just been appointed third assistant secretary, keep him informed about policies and decisions. Otherwise, "the vast silence across the ocean and the rhetorical indefiniteness at the other end of the line give a feeling at times of a vast vagueness."[8]

The crack about "rhetorical indefiniteness" referred to having to serve under Bryan. Distaste for the Great Commoner had formed a fixed point in Page's politics since 1896. The ambassador befriended Bryan's daughter Ruth, who was married to an Englishman and lived in London, and he corresponded amicably with the secretary. But Page never believed that the long-winded, teetotaling Bryan did any good on the world scene. He repeatedly sneered to House about the Commoner's plan for promoting peace through compulsory delay or "cooling off" in international disputes. Page hooted about the troubles between the United States and Mexico, "since a war under his Administration of the office, would make him as unhappy as if he had to have Scotch whiskey on his table." He also resented the way that the State Department under Bryan's management continually leaked confidential material to newsmen. The most serious leak during Page's first year in London occurred in January 1914, when a delicate item came out regarding Britain's involvement in the Mexican imbroglio. "It's hard to keep my staff enthusiastic under these conditions," Page protested to House. Their demeanor implied, "Oh, what's the use of our bestirring ourselves to send news to Washington when they use it to embarrass us."[9]

Page's worst vexations with his new post involved money. Entertainment and housing requirements quickly uncovered the enormity of the financial drain. Custom dictated that the American ambassador give an annual Fourth of July party for his countrymen in London and other guests. Even with the simplest arrangements, Page's 1913 affair attracted three thousand people and cost $1,250. Since the ambassador also had to reciprocate invitations, including those of the royal family, he needed a large house with a retinue of servants for such events. At the end of August, after spending three months in a hotel, the Pages leased a twenty-room townhouse at 6 Grosvenor Square for $10,000 a year. Salaries of house servants cost another $8,000, which did not include paying for either a chauffeur or an automobile. "It is an enormous thing and, of course, bankrupting," Page told Arthur.[10]

The ambassador soon made up his mind about how far he would go toward bankruptcy. On 25 August 1913 Page sent a memorandum to Colonel House outlining his expenses. Around $50,000 a year was the bare minimum the post required. With his $17,500 salary, that left between $30,000 and $35,000 to come out of his own pocket. "I'm willing for Wilson and for Uncle Sam and for the fun I'll have," Page insisted—for one year. "But I'll be damned if I'll go any further." He planned to resign on 1 September 1914 "if proper provision isn't made before that time. And, if it end then, I shall quit smiling, not complaining. But I'll quit." House let Page know in November and again in January that he and the president were discussing the possibility of a special fund. Although nothing was definite, a solution to Page's plight seemed to be in the works.[11]

By the fall of 1913 the ambassador could devote more attention to diplomacy. When he returned to London from a holiday in Scotland at the end of September, Page was ready to tackle the two main controversies between his country and Britain. One was the long-simmering dispute over the Panama Canal tolls. The matter had arisen during the summer of 1912, when Congress had passed a measure exempting American coastwise shipping from the tolls. The British had immediately protested against the measure, which would discriminate against one of their major industries, as a violation of the Hay-Pauncefote Treaty of 1901, under which the United States had promised all nations equal access and treatment on the canal. Because earlier discussions in Washington had gotten nowhere, the initiative fell to the new American ambassador in London. Page's main task lay not in changing minds at home, but in overcoming inertia. Although many leading Americans, including President Wilson, sided with Britain, political obstacles stood in the way of a settlement. The 1912 Democratic platform had called for favored treatment for American ships, while the party's important Irish constituency added to the difficulty of appeasing the British. Besides, since the canal had not yet opened, there seemed no need to hurry. To stimulate action, Page employed his talents at epistolary persuasion and dramatization. In August he sent a memorandum about the tolls dispute to House. "Whatever the U.S. may propose till this is fixed and forgotten will be regarded with a certain hesitancy," Page warned. " . . . This is the most important thing for us on the diplomatic horizon."[12]

By the time the ambassador began prodding his government about tolls, troubles in Mexico had complicated matters. In February 1913, while Taft was still president, General Victoriano Huerta had overthrown President Francisco Madero, who was killed during the coup. Both the outgoing and the incoming administrations had declined to grant diplomatic recognition to Huerta, while Britain became the first major country to recognize the Huerta regime. That action caused some awkwardness during the next few months as the Wilson administration's attitude toward Huerta hardened into hostility after learning more about conditions in Mexico. Then, in July 1913, the British blundered by appointing as their new minister Sir Lionel Carden, a career diplomat who had repeatedly clashed with Americans on earlier assignments in the Western Hemisphere and who championed Huerta even before he went to Mexico. As soon as he arrived in Mexico City in October, Carden publicly expressed his admiration for the Mexican leader and pledged continued British diplomatic recognition. Thanks to him, Britain and the United States appeared headed for a collision over Mexico.

Also in October Mexico mushroomed into Page's most pressing piece of business. Continued turmoil excited fears in the Foreign Office about the fate of British holdings in Mexico, which included Viscount Cowdray's vast oil fields, the principal fuel source for the Royal Navy. Charges meanwhile circulated in the United States that Cowdray's interests called the tune for British policy and used Carden as their mouthpiece. Grey summoned Page to the Foreign Office frequently during October and November 1913, to deny the allegations about Cowdray's influence and to press for American guarantees of the safety of British lives and property in Mexico. This situation confronted the ambassador with the reverse of his task in the canal-tolls dispute. Directing his persuasions at the British, he had to convince them of both the seriousness of the controversy with Huerta and the nobility of American motives. "I am delivering a series of well-thought-out discourses to Sir Edward," he informed House at the end of October "—with what effect I don't know." By mid-November, Page believed that he had succeeded in bringing the British around.[13]

Besides working on the British, Page engineered some meetings in the United States that probably did more than anything else to relieve the strain. When Spring Rice fell ill in the fall of 1913, his friend Sir William Tyrrell, who was Grey's private secretary, crossed the Atlantic to fill in for the ailing ambassador. Page seized upon Tyrrell's visit as an opportunity for an exchange of views about the tolls and Mexican controversies. "His going gives you and the President and everybody a capital chance to help me keep our good American-English understanding," Page informed House, urging him to have Tyrrell "fall into the right hands in New York and Washington." House picked up Page's cue through his own discussions with the Englishman and with a conference between Tyrrell and the president at the White House on 13 November, a meeting that improved relations at once. Wilson disclosed equally his intention to seek congressional repeal of the tolls exemption and his irrevocable opposition to Huerta, which Tyrrell at once cabled to Grey. The foreign secretary replied by instructing Tyrrell to tell Wilson "how cordially I appreciate what he has said to you" and to show the Americans his telegrams warning Huerta that Britain could not support him against the United States. From that time on, tensions relaxed. In January 1914 Wilson initiated legislative moves to repeal the tolls exemption, while Grey overrode Carden and other pro-Huerta spokesmen in the Foreign Office and reasserted the paramount British policy of deferring to the United States in the Western Hemisphere. Clearly, the activities of the new American ambassador in London had facilitated both moves.[14]

The tolls controversy and Mexico provided additional minor problems for Page during the first half of 1914. The first incident arose in January when the State Department leaked to the American press Page's confidential news that Carden was to be replaced. This was the incident that Page told House demoralized his staff

and required him "to make an humiliating explanation to the
Foreign Office." In February, when a British subject was murdered
by anti-Huerta rebels, the ambassador had to brave the British
wrath and the State Department's silence. He conferred with
Grey, Page complained to House, "as if I *knew* what the United
States government's position was." The ambassador's final trouble with the canal-tolls controversy was his own fault. On 11
March 1914 Page delivered a rambling, humorous speech to a
British businessmen's convention in which he noted, "I will not
say that we have built the Panama Canal for you, but I will say
that it adds greatly to the pleasure of building that canal when we
realize that it is you who will benefit most by it." Congressional
and editorial opponents of repealing the tolls exemption pounced
on that sentence as proof that the measure was a sellout to
Britain and that the ambassador was a tool of the British. Humiliated, Page twice apologized to Wilson and offered to resign.
The president brushed aside his self-reproach and reassured him
about "how thoroughly and entirely you are enjoying my confidence and admiration."[15]

Those incidents were minor. Mexico remained a diplomatic
sore spot for the Wilson administration, but events there caused
little further friction between the United States and Britain. The
tolls dispute faded away, as the House of Representatives passed
the repeal bill on 31 March and the Senate followed suit on 11
June. "Hearty congratulations," Page cabled Wilson, adding that
"there are expressions of gratification on all sides." Page, too,
had reason to feel gratified. He had helped foster mutual calm
and understanding in Anglo-American relations. "I am glad to
report that the docket here is remarkably clear," he also reported
to Wilson in June 1914. It was an agreeable summing up for his
first year as ambassador.[16]

Clearing the docket hardly provided Page with sufficient
justification for his ambassadorship to Great Britain. He did not
overestimate his impact on relations with the British. He assessed
his role accurately when he told House in February 1914, "A
year ago, they knew very well the fat failure [Taft] that had

saddled them with the tolls-trouble & the failure of arbitration, and an unknown President had just come in." The British had come around, he explained, as soon as they had seen a strong hand again at the helm in Washington. The new ambassador's task consisted of repairing communications within the framework of Britain's generation-old commitment to appeasement of the United States in the Western Hemisphere. Page's talents and personality qualified him admirably for that job, which did not require the skills and perceptions of a professional diplomat.

The former editor never thought of himself as a professional diplomat or of his post as one that called for professionalism. His notions had strengths and weaknesses. The historical heritage and common language shared by Britain and the United States placed special demands on an American ambassador in London. For example, he had to become a public figure and move outside official circles. Page did so by cultivating leaders of the press, business, and Parliament and by giving speeches. But lack of respect for the professional side of diplomacy led him to misjudge some of his functions. His worst misconception involved his relationship with Sir Edward Grey. Page found the tall, handsome, often melancholy foreign secretary easy to get along with, particularly because they shared a love of nature and the poets Wordsworth and Shelley. "Sir Edward is become a good personal friend," Page also remarked to House in February 1914. Yet Grey later regretted not having "been less reserved and more frank" in his pre–World War I dealings with Page. The ambassador did not appreciate the necessary constraint and manipulation in his discussions with a cabinet minister of a foreign power. Nor, despite contacts with others in the Foreign Office such as Tyrrell and Sir Arthur Nicolson, the permanent undersecretary, did Page apprehend the divisions within Whitehall over policy toward the United States and other major nations. Those oversights caused little trouble in peacetime Anglo-American relations, but they could become severe handicaps in more trying circumstances.[17]

Page's lack of diplomatic professionalism stemmed not only from inexperience but also from his conception of the ambassadorship. "The idea of diplomacy as a necessary quarrel," he wrote in a memorandum to himself early in 1916, " . . . that idea, put in practice between two friendly Gov'ts, such as the U.S. & G't Britain, puts their intercourse back on the old Machaevellian [*sic*], Bismarckian basis and greatly weakens the frank, sincere attitude that each nation has come to have towards the other." Page envisioned his ambassadorship through two sets of preconceptions. One was his earlier imperialist enthusiasm. Within three months after arriving in Britain, he resurrected most of his earlier convictions about Anglo-American partnership on the course of empire. On 15 August 1913 he delivered an address at Plymouth in which he celebrated "our destiny-led race" and the English "impulse of mastery," which the original colonists had transplanted to America. Two weeks later he informed House that a joint Anglo-American intervention in Mexico would be "a mere police duty that all great nations have to do. . . . It's merely using the British fleet and ours to make the world understand that the time has come for orderliness and peace and for the honest development of backward, turbulent lands and peoples."[18]

Also in August 1913 Page sent House, David Houston, Wallace Buttrick, Wickliffe Rose, and his son Arthur a memorandum in which he outlined a plan for promoting world peace through cooperation in uplifting tropical regions. Appalled at the spectacle of the European powers "spending their thought and money . . . in maintaining their armed and balanced *status quo*," he thought that the only path to disarmament ran through finding "some common and useful work for these great armies to do. . . . Is the cleaning up of the tropics not such a task?" He pointed to "what we did in Cuba" as a model for future multinational ventures of "conquest for the sole benefit of the conquered, worked out by a sanitary reformation." The ambassador showed that he could spin grandiose schemes unmatched by any other important figure, except House, whose example may have inspired the proposal. Actually, Page's idealistic imperialism placed him closer in his thinking to Theodore Roosevelt than to Woodrow Wilson.[19]

In that memorandum Page also bared his other set of preconceptions toward his ambassadorship: he equated Anglo-American solidarity with sectional reconciliation in the United States. He cast Britain in the same role as the South, as the more backward, though also gentler partner. "This island is a good breeding place for men whose children find themselves and develop into free men in freer lands," he asserted to House in September 1913. By the same token, the United States was an extension of the energetic, commercial, democratic North. "The future of the world belongs to us," Page announced to Wilson a month later. "A man needs to live here, with two economic eyes in his head, a very little time to become very sure of this." As in America, progress required both complementarity between the two partners and uplift of the less advanced one. Page wrote to Alderman in December 1913 that "the progress of the world lies along this union of institutions & of aims—I mean our working together." He identified strongly with the Liberals in Britain, not only because they were in power but also because David Lloyd George, the chancellor of the exchequer, was fighting for reforms aimed at reducing the wealth and power of the aristocracy. "The whole Liberal fight here," Page declared to Wilson in March 1914, "is confessedly to bring this Kingdom, as far as they know how and dare try, up to the economic level and practice of the United States: that's their standard and aim."

Anglo-American unity replaced southern reform as Page's fondest cause. "I can't get over the feeling, and life here intensifies it," he also told Alderman in December 1913, "that the English-speaking folk must rule the world." As for himself, he valued "the opportunity to be of some service to our country in this most interesting time. And an Ambassador to *this* Kingdom really has such an opportunity. Other posts are routine or ornamental. This is in addition full of hard labour & now and then of first-rate importance." Page had found the justification that he needed for his ambassadorship.[20]

Page's sense of mission about his ambassadorship supplied an outlet for his writing talents. First to House and later to both him and Wilson, he dispatched long, frequent letters and memoranda during his first year in Britain. Page described scenes, urged and deplored actions and policies, and constantly affirmed the significance of Anglo-American solidarity. Those papers contained some of his best writing. The president repeatedly praised the ambassador for his communications before the war. "Your letters are a lamp to my feet," he wrote to Page in March 1914. "I feel as I read that their analysis is searching and true." However, Wilson's commendation was not wholly warranted. Despite the vividness of Page's descriptions, his reports overlooked critical aspects of the British political situation. He came nowhere near grasping the gravity of British domestic political conflicts. By the summer of 1914, strife over Lloyd George's reforms, woman suffrage, and Ireland threatened to tear the country apart. Underestimating those divisions might seem an odd error for a former journalist, but Page's career had been almost entirely editorial rather than reportorial. His oversights and wrong estimates flowed mainly from the stance of commitment that he had transferred from the editorial chair to the embassy. Like advocacy of southern reform in his magazines, promotion of Anglo-American unity caused him to ignore and explain away inconvenient facts. Like his editorials, Page's reports from London usually stated compelling arguments, but they did not always present the most accurate picture.[21]

Another importance of the ambassador's missionary self-concept lay in solidifying his friendship with House. During his first year in London, Page grew closer to the president's confidant than to anyone else in administration circles. The two southerners made an odd pair. The Texan was small in stature, dapper in dress, precise in habits, and shy and soft-spoken in manner. He preferred to exert influence behind the scenes, through subtlety and flattery. Several who knew the colonel later remarked on his way of making delicate gestures with his little hands while murmuring, "I know it," or, "Yes, yes, I know." House often conveyed an aura of intimacy and secrecy to companions by putting his hand on the other person's and whispering, "This is between you and me and the angels," or "This is graveyard." The lanky, booming-voiced Tar Heel operated partly in public and mixed dignity with almost bullish straightforwardness. The two men's views of international politics likewise contained differences.

With his broader perspective toward the great power system, House did not pursue Anglo-American solidarity with anything like Page's single-minded intensity. The colonel sympathized to a degree with Germany's desires for a more favorable naval and colonial position in relation to Britain. Page resembled Roosevelt and many of his British hosts in regarding the Germans as the chief troublemakers of the international scene.[22]

The differences between them shrank in importance, however, in the face of their common devotion to Wilson and their sense of making history. The Pages entertained House and his wife a number of times in London during June and July 1913. The two men talked at length about both the colonel's diplomatic designs and the ambassador's financial and official difficulties. Those talks encouraged Page's already-present tendency to regard himself as other than an ordinary diplomat. For his part, the Tar Heel helped the Texan by introducing him to Grey. "There is an American gentleman in London, the like of whom I do not know," he told the foreign secretary. "Mr. Edward M. House is his name. He is the 'silent partner' of President Wilson—that is to say, he is the most trusted political adviser & the nearest friend of the President." When Grey responded with an invitation to lunch on 3 July, Page informed House, "Put it down. Particulars when we meet. Just we 3, you know." The colonel and the foreign secretary had a wide-ranging discussion of Mexico, the canal-tolls problem, and tensions between Germany and Britain. A few days later, Grey thanked Page for bringing him and House together: "I was much interested in what he told me—a man that I'm glad to know." Relaying that comment at once to House, Page added, "I send you this while it's still hot in my mind."[23]

That visit established another lasting pattern in Page's ambassadorship. After House sailed home in July, the two men continued to share both Page's personal problems concerning money and the State Department and sweeping ideas about world politics. Although House rejected Page's tropical sanitation scheme, he replied to most of the ambassador's communications with enthusiasm and ingratiation. During his first year in London, Page wrote to House more frequently, at greater length, and less guardedly than he did to anyone else in the Wilson administration. Unlike his letters to Wilson, the ones to House did not go through several drafts before being sent, and they contained blunter comments, especially about Bryan and the State Department. The pair likewise maintained by mail the tone that they had evidently established during House's visit—a schoolboyish air of conspiracy and adventure in their schemes to remake the world.

The bond between the two southerners waxed strongest in the spring and summer of 1914, when House made his first peace mission to Europe. Ever since his return to the United States in July 1913, the colonel had been laying the groundwork for a grand disarmament overture. House's immediate object was to secure a joint moratorium by Britain, Germany, and the United States on new battleship construction. But his larger designs stretched much further. "The general idea," House wrote Page in January 1914, "is to bring about a sympathetic understanding between England, Germany and America, not only upon the question of disarmament, but other matters of equal importance to themselves and to the world at large." During the latter part of 1913 and the first months of 1914, the colonel deftly worked to sell his ideas to the president, while simultaneously setting up a network of contacts with the British and the Germans. His principal contacts were three men: Sir William Tyrrell, when he visited the United States; Count Johann von Bernstorff, the German ambassador in Washington; and, closest of all, Ambassador Page in London.[24]

The colonel found his friend an eager accomplice. "You have set my imagination going," Page responded in January 1914. Suppose, he asked, there existed "the tightest sort of an alliance, offensive and defensive, between all Britain, colonies and all, and the U.S., what would happen? Anything we'd say would go. . . . That might be the beginning of a real world-alliance or union to accomplish certain large results—disarmament, for instance, or arbitration—dozens of good things." Sailing for Europe at the middle of May, the colonel proceeded first to Berlin, where he found, he told Wilson, "militarism run stark

WALTER HINES PAGE,
arriving at Euston Station, London, as ambassador, May 1913

(by permission of the Houghton Library, Harvard University)

ALICE WILSON PAGE, *ca. 1913*
(by permission of the Houghton Library, Harvard University)

mad." But he still believed that well-timed American moves might save the peace. House informed Page on 28 May that he had done "enough to open negotiations with London." Arriving in Britain on 9 June, he met with Page the next day to determine the proper procedure in London. "We decided to approach Sir Edward Grey first," House recorded in his diary, "and leave it to his judgment whether to bring in Asquith and the King."[25]

On 17 June 1914 House and Page held their first discussion with Grey and Tyrrell. "We talked from 1.30 until 3.30 and I feel I have made a beginning," the colonel wrote in his diary. "Sir Edward and I did practically all the talking, Page and Sir William only occasionally joining in." The ambassador's silence indicated interest, not disapproval. He confided to House after the meeting that he was sure that Grey would convey the proposal to the prime minister and the rest of the government. Page was right. House spent the next five weeks in London, engaging in friendly and evidently fruitful talks with Grey, Asquith, and other Liberal ministers. Page attended many, but not all, of those discussions. Other duties often occupied him, and House thought that the ambassador's presence might detract from the unofficial character of some talks. Page made contacts for House, and he and Alice frequently entertained the colonel and his wife. Page also advised, House recorded in his diary, "as to the best procedure in communicating with the Kaiser in furtherance of the 'great adventure.'" On several occasions the ambassador was the one who reported back to the president. "Page writes so well," House explained to Wilson, "that I have asked him to send you a more detailed account."

The House mission marked the apogee of Page's ambassadorship. At the beginning of July 1914, the colonel was able to tell the Germans that Grey was willing to seek a better understanding between their two governments. Page swelled with pride. On 5 July he wrote to Wilson that House's "most excellent work leaves the situation the best possible in this way: the future negotiations of almost every sort whatsoever between Germany and England and between our country and either of them can proceed on the very friendly understanding that has been reached." Naturally, the ambassador contemplated a central role for himself in pursuing the colonel's initiative. "An enormous amount of constructive work," Page added, "can be done along the way that he has opened." In another letter to the president the same day, the ambassador likewise noted, "I am keeping House's ball rolling (slowly) with Sir Ed. Grey." The "great adventure" appeared to be fulfilling the dreams of both the quiet little colonel and his big, hearty lieutenant.[26]

Beneath the cordiality of their partnership, however, signs of strain were appearing. The earliest discordant note had come the previous September when House had squelched Page's tropical sanitation idea. "What you are thinking of," the colonel had stated, "and what you want this Administration to do is beyond its powers of accomplishment at the moment." In part, House simply brought Page's dreams down to earth. Yet the colonel himself broached similar ideas about cooperation in the tropics to Grey the following June. House in effect pulled rank on Page as the Wilson circle's leading author of international grand designs. The ambassador took his own turn at playing a skeptical part when House put forward his naval disarmament idea in December 1913. "I doubt it; but let him try," Page wrote in his diary. During the early part of 1914 Page took a less hopeful view of the Germans than House, and at one point he warned, "I do not expect you to produce any visible or immediate results."[27]

When House reached London in June, Page at first doubted whether the British would want to negotiate with the Germans. Nor did Grey's cordial reception dispel all his doubts. "Sir Edw is wholly sympathetic," Page wrote to Wilson in July; "he will be even enthusiastic. I know my man. But how powerful he'll be— we'll see." For the most part, however, the ambassador's reservations dissolved in his ardor to make House's mission a success. Now House cooled toward Page. When the ambassador was unable to attend one of his meetings with British leaders, the colonel declined to invite anyone else from the embassy. "As a matter of fact," he wrote in his diary, "I would rather be with them alone anyway, for they will talk more freely and I will be more upon my mettle." House seems to have thought that Page was getting in his way, and he apparently wished to keep the "great adventure" more to himself. House also displayed irritation when Page sent a telegram rebuffing a request by two visiting Democratic politicians to speak at the ambassador's upcoming Fourth of July party. "I told Page his message was very impolitic, and that he should not have sent it," House recorded in his diary. " . . . I mention this incident to show how little discretion Page has, and how likely he is to get into trouble before his term of office expires."[28]

Those signs of strain did not bode well for the ambassador's relationship with the colonel. House had repeatedly demonstrated that he considered Page a subordinate who was not to be accorded too big a role. The Texan was expecting a meekness and docility that were not in character for the Tar Heel. On his side, Page showed some impatience and doubt, and he had not acquired the colonel's facility for intricate maneuvering among the great powers. Yet Page played along eagerly with House's game, and he contributed his share of excitement and fantasy. The ambassador may have eschewed "makeshifts and make-believe" in his first British speech, but he practiced plenty of both with his closest American associate.

Still another aspect of Page's ambassadorship that appeared during his first year in London was his singular relationship with the president. Starting in the fall of 1913, he sent Wilson a long letter almost weekly. Always handwritten, these letters were strictly private and did not go through regular embassy channels. Laughlin, the first secretary, subsequently believed that Page may not at first have even used the diplomatic pouch but simply dropped the letters in a postbox. He remembered convincing the ambassador that only by using the pouch and by writing on embassy stationery could he insure that his communications would go directly to the president without being opened by others at the White House. Afterward, Page usually showed Laughlin what he wrote to the president, but he rarely let the first secretary see what he received in reply or what he sent to Colonel House. Still later, after the outbreak of World War I, Page's personal secretary sometimes had a chance to copy the letters to Wilson on the embassy's newly installed photostat machine, without the ambassador's knowledge. All those procedures were extraordinary.

Page took greater pains with his letters to Wilson than with probably anything else that he ever wrote. He composed most of them late at night, sitting by the fireside of his study in the house on Grosvenor Square. He frequently first jotted notes to himself, then set down one or more preliminary drafts, and finally produced a smooth copy in his own hand, which he dispatched to Wilson. Taken together, those letters, Page's official communications by wire and pouch with the State Department, and his extensive correspondence with other people in the United States, particularly Colonel House and his son Arthur, made him do almost as much writing as he had done as a magazine editor. As with his commentaries in *World's Work*, Page carefully calculated the likely impact of what he said to Wilson. He exercised circumspection in touching upon such sensitive subjects as the shortcomings of Bryan and the State Department. He mentioned his own troubles with finances and the department only after having discussed them more fully and candidly with House.

The ambassador toiled over his correspondence with the president for two main reasons. First, he obviously wished to exert influence. Flattery and exhortation abounded in the letters. One of the first of them, in September 1913, opened with a fusillade of praise for the new tariff act. "Score one!" cheered Page. "You have done a great historic deed and demonstrated and abundantly justified your leadership." Succeeding letters continued in the same vein, and such communications plainly hit their mark. "Your private and confidential letters to me are invaluable," Wilson wrote back in December. "The one I just read, dated November twenty-second, clears up a great many things in my thought." Several months later, when Laughlin was in the United States on home leave, he reported to Page that the president "spoke repeatedly of your letters to him which have the valuable—& unusual—quality of imparting important & serviceable information in a diverting form! In speaking of them he said it was this quality that used to compel him in the past to yield to your requests when you wanted him to write something for the World's Work." The other reason for Page's epistolary labors was literary. He continued to believe that he was observing superb material about which to write. After his ambassadorial appointment, Page again tried to keep a diary. In January 1914 he recorded in one entry, "Why shouldn't I write a book about & bring it out the day after my ambassadorship ends?" In fact, Page began building a literary monument to his ambassadorship in his letters to Wilson. As much as influence, the likelihood of future publication prompted him to invest so much effort in descriptions, phrases, and interpretations.[29]

Literary leanings also deepened Page's admiration for Wilson. The ambassador could hardly have failed to admire the president. Apart from feeling gratitude and pride of discovery, Page held the new chief executive in awe for his stunning performance as a legislative leader. "There comes from Washington in private letters the feeling that the men in harness there all have," he wrote in his diary in January 1914, "—that great things are taking place about them." Page's admiration flowered into near idolatry when he once more depicted Wilson as a literary man. Addressing the Author's Club in London in December 1913, the ambassador identified the president as "one of my oldest and best friends" and himself as one of the few people who years before "had ever thought of his being a man of action." Wilson, in Page's view, was a man of many parts: "He might be a lawyer, he might be a great expounder, he might be a man of action. Having those careers to choose from, he chose all three." Further, the president had long ago perceived "that a man of literature must first of all have something to say, and then, that he cannot hope to say it in a way that will attract and convince men unless he become a great artist in the use of speech." Changing a single word in that portrayal of Woodrow Wilson—substituting "businessman" for "lawyer"—would have yielded an idealized self-image of Walter Page.[30]

The ambassador also practiced "make-believe" in his relationship with the president. Besides exaggerating the closeness of their friendship and projecting his own personality onto Wilson, Page overlooked profound differences in their foreign-policy views. Those differences showed up most strikingly in their divergent attitudes toward Mexico. Page never seemed to appreciate Wilson's desire to foster democratic self-rule below the Rio Grande. Rather, he read the president's opposition to Huerta as a step toward establishment of an American protectorate. He liked that idea, both for America's sake and as a possible boost to Anglo-American solidarity. After suggesting joint intervention in Mexico to House in August 1913, Page discussed such a project in detail for two and a half hours on 8 January 1914 with the oil tycoon Lord Cowdray. The ambassador insisted, as Cowdray reported to the Foreign Office, "that he had merely been speaking as a private individual and not as a representative of a nation." But the circumstances of the conversation demonstrated Page's lack of discretion, and what he said would have been far more acceptable in the sight of Theodore Roosevelt than of Woodrow Wilson.[31]

Exaggerating intimacy between the two men cut both ways. Wilson's reserve did not prevent him from believing, too, that he and Page were close friends. The ambassador nurtured personal ties by insisting that the president's daughter Jessie and her husband Francis Sayre stay at his house during their honeymoon in England in December 1913. Yet the strongest influence in creating the notion of closeness was, ironically, long-distance correspondence. Letter writing was Page's literary forte. "I have known Page for many years," Wilson said to Laughlin in May 1914, "and I have never known anyone more compelling on paper." Communicating by mail allowed the ambassador to insinuate himself with the president in a way that no one but House was able to do in person. The long letters written in Page's neat, attractive handwriting stood out in the flow of usually brief, typewritten correspondence and memoranda that crossed Wilson's desk. Their contents—vivid descriptions, humorous anecdotes, and reminders of opportunities for world leadership—all contrasted with the terse and drably official material that the president mostly saw. One of Wilson's many compliments on Page's letters was the comment in February 1914, "You have a great faculty of making things real about which you write." In view of the president's habit of avoiding personal contact, the ambassador had hit upon an ideal way to reach him.[32]

Wilson proved his esteem for Page in two actions during 1914. One was to consider his old acquaintance again for a cabinet appointment. In January and April the president contemplated naming Houston to head the newly established Federal Reserve system, with Page to take his place as secretary of agriculture. Wilson authorized House to sound the ambassador out. Page expressed willingness, though not eagerness. "But between you and me," he explained to House, "I know this job better now than I'd know the Washington job at first." The proposal went by the boards in a protracted struggle that developed over the powers and membership of the Federal Reserve Board. Wilson's second display of regard came when he solved the ambassador's financial problem. At the beginning of April, Page spelled out his predicament directly to the president. He protested that he was *"most reluctant* to burden you with such a subject; but I think, in fairness, you ought to know the facts in due time." When that letter apparently elicited no action, Page wrote again at the beginning of June. Wringing that second letter through five separate drafts, the ambassador started to recount how his old North Carolina friend "Buck" Duke, the tobacco magnate, had offered to subsidize him. Ultimately, he decided just to state that he wanted to resign and perhaps "tell the public the whole truth, that we can have only rich men as Ambassadors." The president wrote back, "I feel confident I can make arrangements. I could not in any circumstances think of losing you at that all-important post."[33]

Wilson's "arrangement" consisted of asking his millionaire Princeton classmate Cleveland Dodge to contribute twenty-five thousand dollars a year. In July 1914 the president explained the ambassador's situation to Dodge, calling Page "an indispensable man in the right management of our foreign relations. I would not know what to do if I were obliged to part with him. My relations with him are intimate, and he has furnished me with more light on difficult foreign matters than all my other informants and advisers put together." Dodge immediately responded with a pledge to supply the money for the duration of Page's ambassadorship. The president delegated the matter to House, who acted as a relay for payments between Dodge and Arthur Page. "I have told Arthur some of the arrangements," House informed Page, "but please do not discuss it with him. Just let us do it our way." The ambassador was happy to let them do it their way, even after he eventually learned the identity of his benefactor. Having a private financial angel added another extraordinary element to Page's ambassadorship, but the arrangement instilled pride rather than embarrassment in the recipient. The special fund constituted a tangible token of the president's favor.[34]

Financial relief was just one of several favorable omens during the early summer of 1914. The transcending significance of House's mission made the frustrations of dealing with the State Department seem relatively minor nuisances. In fact, Page was able to remove another frustration by hoodwinking the department. In March 1914 the owners of the building on Victoria Street that housed the embassy served notice that they planned to raise the rent when the lease expired in September. "No raise in rent ever came so welcomely," Page later recalled. After cabling the department, the ambassador got authorization to pay the new amount. But instead of renewing the lease, Page found a four-story building for the same rent. The new embassy was located two and a half blocks away from the old one, at Grosvenor Gardens, just behind Buckingham Palace. "It's a beautiful, big residence," Page rejoiced to Arthur; "and the place is worthy of the U.S.—dignified & spacious, full of light." To rent the new embassy, Page had to sign a seven-year lease. He "conveniently forgot," as he subsequently put it, the State Department's rule against leasing property for longer than one year.[35]

Moving the embassy symbolized the pattern that Page had established during his first year as ambassador. He had proven himself a resourceful, energetic amateur diplomat, who frequently employed unconventional practices. Behind his actions lay the thrill of participating in great events and the satisfaction of intimacy with the men who mattered most. However, this pattern had several weak spots. His disdain for diplomatic professionalism and ignorance of divergent views and temperaments held potentials for trouble. Moreover, Page operated under long-established conditions of peace and mutual appeasement. His strengths might not outweigh his weaknesses under more stressful circumstances. World War I was about to test Page's ambassadorship under just such conditions.

Yet almost nothing seemed amiss in July 1914. On the diplomatic horizon, peace prospects looked good, thanks in part to House's effort. As Grey later remembered, "In the early months of 1914 the international sky seemed clearer than it had been." Personally, Page was doing splendidly. He and Alice took the London social season more in stride than the year before. When the season ended, they closed the Grosvenor Square residence and moved to "the prettiest little country place you ever saw," the ambassador told his brother Robert. The "little country place" was an estate in Surrey, within easy commuting distance of London, from which Page planned to go to the embassy two or three days a week. He anticipated "a very happy, quiet time for three months," during which he would play golf and read. He likewise intended to use the vacation to hatch long-range projects. "I see plenty to do here," he wrote to Arthur from Surrey, "—a vast deal in fact; I'm going to use the time we have down here to lay out a year's work that will, I hope, count for more than this first rush-&-hurry year when we were learning the job."[36]

From every standpoint the situation seemed perfect. In August Alice Page wrote to Arthur, "Yesterday was your father's birthday. He is 59, and he looks younger today than he did five years ago. He is heavier now than when you were here, not much a pound or two, but it tells in the freshness of skin, and his general bearing." No one knew it then, but Page's life had reached its pinnacle. By the time his wife described him to their son, World War I had begun. In his own way, the United States ambassador to the Court of St. James's would become one of the war's casualties.[37]

CHAPTER 9

The Strains of War

World War I caught the American ambassador in London by surprise, along with everybody else. Page's first inkling that all Europe might be swept into a conflagration came when Austria declared war on Serbia on Tuesday, 28 July 1914. Toward the end of the day, he called on Sir Edward Grey at the Foreign Office to offer his country's assistance in the widening diplomatic crisis. "I think I shall never forget yesterday," Page wrote afterward to Wilson. "There sat this always solitary man—he and I, of course, in the room alone, each, I am sure giving the other his full confidence. He looked ten years older than he looked a month ago." Amid the late afternoon shadows in his ornate office, Grey struck Page more than ever "as a sort of sad and wise idealist, . . . a grave philosopher who feels the prodigious responsibility he carries." The foreign secretary's pessimism about averting a general war shook the ambassador. "Throughout his frank talk I felt the possibility of a sort of crack of doom for Continental Europe."

Page judged the situation correctly. During the next week the major European powers took up arms, with Britain the last to enter the conflict. On Tuesday, 4 August 1914, Grey issued an ultimatum: unless the kaiser's armies withdrew from Belgium by midnight and promised to respect Belgian neutrality Britain would go to war against Germany. At three o'clock in the afternoon, Page again saw the foreign secretary, who spent nearly an hour explaining Britain's obligation to defend Belgian neutrality. "If we give up such solemn compacts," Grey asked, "on what does civilization rest?" Standing up, he murmured with tears in his eyes, "Thus the efforts of a lifetime go for nothing. I feel as a man who has wasted his life." Page recorded in his diary that the interview "was most affecting . . . & I came away with a sort of stunned sense of impending ruin of half the world." The ambassador went to hear the declaration of war announced at midnight in the House of Commons. Then he went back to the embassy to await official notification, which quickly came. "I have received at this moment, one forty a.m., August fifth," Page cabled the State Department, "a note from the Foreign Office dated August fourth informing me that a state of war exists between Britain and Germany."

Depression over the war was only one of Page's reactions. The indisputable momentousness of the conflict swept away any lingering doubts about the importance of his ambassadorship. "Events here alone seem to me likely to make your Administration historic," he wrote to Wilson on 2 August. Page could not help feeling excited at having an opportunity to witness happenings that were about to change the history of the world. "Upon my word," he told the president a week later, "if one could forget the awful tragedy, all this experience would be worth a life-time of commonplace." It seemed as if Page had found his life's supreme occasion, in which he might satisfy his longings to take part in and observe and describe great events.[1]

The war at once dispelled the old leisurely atmosphere at the United States embassy in London. The embassy had not yet been moved to its new location, and on the morning of Monday, 3 August, Page found the cramped quarters on Victoria Street jammed with American tourists, who feared being stranded by the hostilities. He got up on a chair and addressed the throng, telling them that he had already wired Washington for ships and money to help them get home. "I made a speech to them several times during the day," he told Wilson, "and kept the Secretaries doing so at intervals." But the hordes kept coming and made the outer offices look to Irwin Laughlin like "a theatre lobby at a fire." Hysterical people shouted at embassy personnel, "What are you here for?" and "Why don't you stop this war?" Sometimes they burst into the ambassador's inner office. Disruptions in trade, finance, and communications likewise consumed Page's time. "I was at work from waking time till 2 or later every morning last w'k," he wrote his son Arthur the following Sunday. " . . . Think of it: a new problem every 10 minutes 20 hours a day for a straight week."[2]

The ambassador rose to the challenge. None of the turmoil in the embassy's outer offices ruffled him, Laughlin remembered. Another staff member, Emily Bax, described Page's inner office as a haven of quiet and concentration. "His long body was hunched over his desk," Bax recalled, "and at his side in a cheap tin tray a cigar was still smoking fitfully. His expression was anxious and careworn, and he seemed absolutely unaware of the noise outside." The pace and volume of the tasks may have fatigued Page, but he plunged into them with his usual zest. On his own initiative, he made the first tender of American good offices on 28 July. The ambassador met with the foreign secretary almost daily, both before and after Britain went to war, and he called upon the king to transmit President Wilson's formal assurance that the United States stood ready to assist in bringing the belligerents together to make peace.[3]

Page brought off a feat of organizational initiative in handling the swarm of anxious American tourists. He secured funds and ships and enlisted the services of several fellow countrymen to administer the relief operations. Chief among the volunteer helpers was a wealthy American engineer who was engaged in international business enterprises and made his headquarters in London. His name was Herbert Clark Hoover. The ambassador had gotten to know Hoover during the previous year. Under Hoover's direction the American Residents' Committee expedited the departures of forty-five thousand people between 5 and 29 August 1914 and had assisted around sixty thousand by the middle of September. Despite the strain, the effort gave Page the satisfaction of launching a big practical enterprise and helping such diverse friends and acquaintances from earlier days as Edwin Alderman, James Ford Rhodes, and W. E. B. Du Bois. Moreover, in Hoover the southerner made another of his discoveries.

A more lasting source of responsibility arose from Page's position as the leading neutral ambassador. During the first week of the war he was asked to take over the embassies of Britain's principal enemies. Handling German and Austrian affairs in London added to the embassy's burgeoning labors, for which the State Department provided extra personnel, most of whom were talented younger foreign service officers. The most trying aspect of assuming the belligerents' interests emerged from the carnage that was soon spawned on the western front. The American embassy transmitted a continuing stream of inquiries about whether British soldiers listed as missing in battle had been taken prisoner by the Germans. Often people of high position and others who knew Page approached the ambassador personally. In October 1915, for example, Rudyard Kipling asked him to try to locate his only son, John, a lieutenant with the Irish Guards who was reported missing in Flanders. Only rarely did the inquiries result in ascertaining that the soldier was a prisoner.

A happier side of serving as a neutral go-between developed early in the war, when Page helped set up the Committee for Relief in Belgium. During September 1914 Herbert Hoover relayed news of near-starvation among the civilian population of Belgium to the ambassador, who at once opened discussions about relief possibilities with the Foreign Office. The main difficulty lay in British fears that food and supplies might wind up in German hands. According to Hoover's recollection, Page decided at a meeting with him and three Belgians that the only way to overcome British objections was for the ambassador to give the United States government's guarantee of the distribution of relief materials. Such an arrangement would require a capable director who enjoyed Page's confidence. Who, asked Hoover, could fill the bill? Page flashed back, "Hoover, you're it!" The story sounds apocryphal, but the ambassador evidently was responsible for choosing Hoover to head what quickly became renowned around the world as the "CRB." Thereby, Page helped create one of the most substantial American reputations to come out of World War I.[4]

American dealings with Britain also multiplied the tasks of

the ambassador and his staff. Allied war orders in the United States and trade restrictions against the Central Powers each generated fresh duties for the London embassy. These duties required constant additions of staff and began to cause over-crowding in the new chancery on Grosvenor Gardens. At the end of 1915 Page wrote to his sister Mary, "Of all sorts of workers, I now have about 80—so far as I know, the biggest embassy in the world." Page continued to find his embassy's expanded activities exciting and exhausting. In September 1914 he estimated to Arthur that "the diplomatic work proper is about 6 times as much as it was 6 months ago. Nobody in his wildest dreams cd have thought of the questions that come up every day." The ambassador had fewer distractions. Since the royal family ceased entertaining for the duration of the war, social life settled to a drastically reduced level. Ironically, Page needed Cleveland Dodge's special fund less than he had before, although his expenses remained high. He also stopped making speeches in deference to the delicacy of his position as a neutral ambassador in a country at war. The reduced outside activities caused Page mixed relief and regret. In January 1915 he told Alice that "one day hardly differs from another, every one being filled with dispatches and errands and protests."5

Page's strongest complaint about the work load involved neither exhaustion nor lack of diversion. "I wish I could write about this Eternal Smash," he lamented to Arthur on 23 August 1914. "But I haven't time to put pen to paper." Page's conviction that great events produce great literature made him regard his post now as his heaven-sent opportunity as a writer. He affirmed to Wilson in September 1914, "You may be dead sure the story will be told well, and therefore, it will become history, and sung well, and therefore, it will become literature." The ambassador meant the remark to apply to himself. At different times during the first year of the war he stated that after retiring from the embassy he wanted to write a personalized, interpretative history of the United States since 1870. He had other plans, too. His duties during the first weeks of the war did not prevent him from keeping his diary and from starting to write a memoir

entitled "The Consecutive Story: The Ambassadorship." He likewise wrote to the president, as before, with an evident eye on
posterity. "I have these months only the hours around midnight
to write anything," he informed Wilson in October; "and it's
come to be a joke in my household—that when I'm writing
anything I'm writing to you." As much as for any other reason,
Page valued being ambassador in London during World War I for
the chance to write about great events.[6]

Everything seemed to go well for the ambassador during the
first two months of the war. Page boasted to Wilson in August
1914 that "the diplomatic work proper" went forward, despite
all the difficulties, "without error and without fumbling. . . . The
saving fact is (and the importance of this cannot be exaggerated)
that I have dealt so candidly and frankly with Sir Edward Grey
and so completely given him my confidence that his candour and
confidence in me are now my shield and buckler." The ambassador believed that the foreign secretary "has told me every fact at
every stage in this troublesome journey so far." That was hardly
the case, and Page was naive to think so. But he viewed the
present state of Anglo-American relations as a vindication of his
prewar nonprofessional diplomacy. America's having "kept faith
in the Panama tolls controversy" had put relations with Britain
on the best possible footing, he told Arthur in August.[7]

Page maintained remarkable equanimity at the beginning of
World War I. His initial reaction was to stress moral and ideological contrasts between Europe and America. "Monarchy and
privilege and pride will have it out before they die," he wrote to
the president on 29 July, "—at what cost! If they have a general
war they will set back the march of progress in Europe as to set
the day forward for American leadership." As the conflict wid-
ened, Page dwelled further on potential advantages for the United
States. He advised Wilson on 2 August to bide his time until the
belligerents wanted peace. That would furnish "*your* opportunity
to play an important and historic part. Ours is the only great
government that is not in some way entangled. (How wise our
no-alliance policy is!)" Page also believed that American "shipping and foreign commerce will gain immensely." A week later,

he reiterated to the president, "Now, when all this half of the world will suffer the unspeakable brutalization of war, we shall preserve our moral strength, our political power, and our ideals."[8]

Page did not long sustain such uncharacteristic detachment. The spectacle of World War I soon appalled him. "Think of it," he wrote to Arthur in September, "—there are piles of dead men 150 miles in Eastern Germany; 200 miles in Austria. A man's life is not worth a dog's anywhere there." The war's likely future consequences also disquieted Page. "Then think of the next generation in all these stricken countries," he continued to Arthur in October. "The men who die become the fathers of no more children. Chiefly the scrub-stock is left to breed. That's to a degree what happened in the Southern States, you know, after the civil war; and that's what's been the matter down there for about 50 years." The grim scenes on the continent often dampened the ambassador's excitement about the significance of his work and the opportunities for his country. As he told Wilson, "I myself, as detached from it as a man here can be, find myself, when I ought to be in bed, sitting alone silently looking into the fire, not thinking but dumbly brooding on it, wondering in what world I live. For it is not the same world it was last July—nothing is the same." Page seldom lost his horror and dismay at the slaughter and destruction throughout the next four years of war.[9]

How soon pro-Allied sympathies displaced the ambassador's detachment is not completely clear. As early as 2 August he wrote in his diary, "Germany has staked everything on her ability to win primacy. England & France (to say nothing of Russia) really ought to give her a drubbing." Two weeks later Alice Page informed Katharine that her father was "absolutely strict in his neutrality, the more so that we really are in full sympathy with England." Yet Page also believed that an Allied victory might not be an unalloyed blessing. On 9 August he told Wilson that he worried "that England will gain even more of the earth's surface, that Russia may play the next menace; that all Europe (so much as survives) will be bankrupt." But on 6 September the ambassador declared to the president that the Germans were "another case of Napoleon—even more brutal; a dream of universal conquest." Democratic ideals would never be secure, Page avowed, until "Prussian militarism be utterly cut out, as surgeons cut out a cancer. And the Allies will do it—must do it, to live. It would dash our Monroe Doctrine. It wd even invade the U.S. in time." He conceded that a German defeat might entail "many objectionable things," especially the aggrandizement of Russia and Japan and further expansion of British colonialism. "But these are all lesser or less immediate evils."[10]

Those remarks disclosed a significant departure. By the end of the first month of the war, Page ventured beyond other Americans who were forming pro-Allied convictions by perceiving an American stake in defeating Germany. A month later the ambassador went further still. "I have my moods," he wrote to Wilson on 6 October, "when I wonder if we oughtn't to step in and end it [the war] on a definite programme of the reduction of armaments and the restriction of military authority and to make the acceptance of our programs a condition of our refraining from action. . . . There's no important influence we can have on the terms of peace by any mere offers of mediation." If the Allies won by themselves, there would be "no limitation of armament —except for Germany! And the U.S. will have no voice in the terms of settlements—and England will keep building her mammoth navy and Russia will keep her innumerable army." On the other hand, cobelligerency with the Allies could be conditioned on their agreement to postwar international reforms. "Perhaps we could drive a bargain in that way and really reduce the armaments of the world—and end the war almost at once." These ideas were, Page added, "speculations." He was "not commending—only trying to think the thing out."[11]

Page had certainly lost none of his capacity for spinning grand schemes. The proposal showed not only how early he contemplated American entry into the war on the Allied side but also what considerations were uppermost in his mind. The ambassador later struck a number of critics as a classic case of a diplomat who identified too closely with his hosts. Wilson and House came to believe not long afterward that the wartime atmosphere in London unbalanced Page and got him out of touch with American sentiment. In part, they were correct. Ever impressionable, Page admired the British people's spirit of sacrifice and common effort in going to war. "You needn't talk of decadence," he told Arthur in September 1914. "All their great qualities are in them here and now." Perhaps betraying a twinge of envy, he added, "The heroism of this people here is ours by inheritance—a very precious heritage, and we have room & sunlight for its better nurture." Page still thrilled to visions of Anglo-Saxon racial destiny, and, as he had done nearly twenty years before, he warmed to the notion that a war might provide an ennobling experience for his own people.[12]

Yet calculation played a larger part than sentiment in Page's pro-Allied views. His design for American world leadership in partnership with Britain impelled him to seek the best possible wartime relations with his hosts. "If England wins, as of course, she will," he warned House in September 1914, "it'll be a bigger and stronger England, with no strong enemy in the world, with her Empire knit closer than ever— . . . under obligation and *in alliance with Russia—and Japan*! England will not need our friendship as much as she now needs it; and there may come Governments here that will show they do not." The implied conclusion was that American power and self-interest might require grasping at opportunities to help the Allies win the war. Once more, Page's political thinking showed a striking resemblance to that of his fellow American imperialist Theodore Roosevelt. In August and September 1914 the ex-president's views followed a similar arc from initial detachment toward the war, through outrage over Belgium, to a mixture of strategic reckoning and hankering to get into the fight. As before, the congruence between Page's attitudes and Roosevelt's stemmed from neither influence nor admiration but from their unrecognized ideological kinship.[13]

By early October 1914 the ambassador had shaped the viewpoint that he was to hold throughout his tenure in London, and that viewpoint spelled trouble for himself and his country. Page saw no reason to change his ways as ambassador. He not only continued to think that the foreign secretary spoke to him with complete candor, but he also reciprocated with avowals of sympathy toward the Allies that bordered on indiscretion. For example, Grey noted that in a conversation on 29 August, "the ambassador said that [German] militarism must be broken—it would be hardly worth living if that were the rule." Page likewise assumed that he enjoyed the same special access as before to the president and his confidant, and he stepped up the flow of letters to Wilson and House. His correspondence with both men peaked in volume during the first year and a half of the war. But now, instead of delivering pleasantly abstract discourses on world leadership and Anglo-American unity, the ambassador was preaching a concrete diplomatic course that could lead to intervention in the bloodiest war in history. Page was right when he told Wilson that nothing remained the same as before the war. In October 1914 he discovered how different things were for his own views and behavior.[14]

Two areas in which the ambassador anticipated wartime gains for the United States—shipping and overseas trade—furnished the first diplomatic controversies with Britain. Both concerns stemmed from British determination to use naval power against the economies of the Central Powers. The most important aspect of this warfare was interdicting seaborne supplies to Germany through blockade, but two circumstances complicated British policies. One difficulty was the large trade that normally went to Germany through neighboring neutral nations, principally the Netherlands. Curtailing that trade raised delicate problems in international law and the treatment of neutrals. The second complication was the position of the United States as the largest and most powerful neutral nation and the major supplier of food, munitions, and later credit for the Allied war effort. Restrictions on American trade with the Central Powers had to be handled cautiously. Alienating the United States was, as Grey later observed, "one mistake that, if it had been made, would have been fatal to the cause of the Allies." At the beginning of the war, the foreign secretary stood firmly in command, and the British moved gingerly.[15]

The shipping issue arose first. The war's outbreak left a large number of German and Austrian vessels stranded in United States ports. To facilitate their purchase by Americans, the Wilson administration introduced legislation, including a controversial bill to establish a government-owned shipping corporation. Although the Allied governments bristled at the move as a possible violation of neutrality, only resistance on Capitol Hill over domestic issues and the adjournment of Congress prevented passage of the ship-purchase legislation, thus averting a diplomatic dispute. Undissuaded, Wilson announced that he intended to pursue his plans when Congress reconvened the following December. Trouble loomed ahead.

Before that dispute resurfaced, however, British restrictions on trade with the Central Powers caused a collision. At the beginning of hostilities, Page presented a circular request from Secretary Bryan that all the belligerents accept the provisions for maritime restrictions contained in the Declaration of London of 1909. That declaration was the product of an international conference dominated by trading nations likely to be neutral; it had gained approval from neither the British nor any of the other current belligerents. To Bryan's request, the British replied equably that they were willing to abide by the declaration "subject to certain modifications and additions," which dealt with neutral ports and definitions of contraband and effectively nullified the purported acceptance. In fact, the British had already arrogated to themselves sweeping discretion to intercept goods suspected of a Central Powers destination in an Order in Council. Meanwhile, Germany and Austria gladly acceded to Bryan's request. By the end of August 1914, it appeared that the British were throwing down the gauntlet for a diplomatic duel over the Allied blockade.[16]

A month later Page became embroiled in his government's response to the challenge. On 27 September the counselor of the State Department, Robert Lansing, who was substituting for the campaigning Secretary Bryan, presented the president a lengthy, truculently phrased draft of a protest note. Thanks to the intercession of House, who happened to be visiting at the White

House and who shared pro-Allied views, Wilson shelved the note in favor of a shorter, informal, but still strongly worded protest. When Page conveyed that protest to Grey on 29 September, he found the foreign secretary conciliatory. "He expresses the most earnest wish to avoid every action that will give offense to our Government or cause public criticism in the United States," reported the ambassador. Instead of a duel, the opening round of dealings over the blockade seemed to portend accommodation.[17]

These hopeful beginnings soured when the British drafted a new Order in Council on 9 October, enlarging their contraband lists and asserting further control over cargoes bound for neutral ports. Page reported that Grey insisted that the order "will not be issued till it has been discussed and he hopes approved" by the Americans. Lansing and Wilson found the new Order in Council unsatisfactory, and the counselor cabled on 13 October instructing Page to talk tough to the British.

This development rattled the ambassador. On 15 October he sent a long cable marked "CONFIDENTIAL FOR THE PRESIDENT" and transmitted at eleven o'clock at night. "In the controversy about shipping I cannot help fearing that we are getting into deep water needlessly," Page warned. No one in Washington grasped the nature of World War I. "It is a world-clash of systems of government, a struggle to the extermination of English civilization or of Prussian military autocracy." What did "a few shippers' theoretical rights" matter compared with those stakes? "Look a little further ahead," Page urged Wilson. "If Germany win it will make no matter what position Britain took on the Declaration of London. We shall see the Monroe Doctrine shot through. We shall have to have a great army and a great navy. If England win and we have an ugly academic dispute because of this controversy we shall be in a bad position for helping compose the quarrel or for any other service." The blockade controversy was unnecessarily jeopardizing "our friendly relations with Great Britain in the sorest time of need in her history. I know that this is the correct larger perspective."[18]

Page's telegraphic peroration elicited no immediate reply. Instead, the ambassador received a pair of cables from Lansing the following afternoon. The first one instructed him to protest formally Britain's refusal to adopt the Declaration of London without modification. The second cable, marked "To be decoded by Ambassador," suggested that Page "might in the strictest confidence intimate to Sir Edward Grey the Department's plan as follows stating very explicitly that it is your personal suggestion and not one for which your Government is responsible." He was to suggest that the British proclaim a new Order in Council accepting the Declaration of London. Then they should issue another order claiming, on the basis of fictitious secret evidence, that a neutral port or country had become an enemy supply base and was therefore not covered by the declaration. The cable reiterated that these suggestions "must be done in an entirely personal way and in the distinct understanding that this Government is in no way responsible for what you may say." The president's answer to Page's telegram arrived at noon the next day, 17 October; it was also marked "TO BE DECIPHERED ONLY BY AMBASSADOR." Wilson reproved him, "Beg that you will not regard the position of this Government as merely academic. Contact with opinion on this side the water would materially alter your views." The president admonished the ambassador "to use your utmost persuasive efforts to effect an understanding by the method which we have gone out of our way to suggest which will put the whole case in an unimpeachable form."[19]

That afternoon Page numbly proceeded to the Foreign Office to present the protest and the proposal to circumvent the Declaration of London. "I followed your instructions literally," he informed Lansing. Grey rejected the entire American position. Even a show of accepting the declaration was impossible, the foreign secretary once more explained, because the document contained too many unexamined implications and, more important, because Parliament had twice previously refused to ratify it. The simplest solution to the difficulty, he continued, lay in Britain's issuing the new Order in Council, to which the United States need make no response. Afterward the two countries could treat seizures of cargoes as individual cases. As for the plan to circumvent the declaration, Grey asked, "Do you mean that we should accept it and then issue a proclamation to get around it?" The query contained, Page observed, "some approach to irritation." The interview humiliated the ambassador. "I presented and 'pushed' every insistence," he maintained to Wilson, "—otherwise I should not have been excusable." Actually, Page did not offer the Declaration of London escape-hatch scheme as his own suggestion, as he had been instructed to do. He simply refrained from saying whose idea it was. "I must be spared from saying anything is my *personal suggestion and not one for which my Gov't is responsible*' when this is not true. . . . My relations with Sir Edw. have not been built up on this basis and could not survive this method of dealing—long."[20]

The following five or six days were harrowing for Page. For the first time since coming to London, his health suffered. He had trouble sleeping and his ulcer evidently flared up. Brooding at his desk and by his fireside, he afterward told the president, "I turned the matter over in my mind backward and forward 100 times a day, it seemed to me." He drafted long letters to Wilson and made notes to himself. He discussed the dispute with Laughlin and Chandler Anderson, a State Department legal adviser on loan to the embassy, who prepared a lengthy memorandum on the questions of international law. Each reexamination emphasized, he cabled Lansing on 20 October, "certain large facts to remember." Britain was determined to cut off the Central Powers from all potentially useful war materials. Law and precedent favored the British. Grey was eager to accommodate legitimate American commerce, adjudicate disputed cases as they arose, and compensate for economic losses. "Under these circumstances," Page wrote in one draft letter, "I can't see why we should quarrel." Blaming Lansing's background as a lawyer for the difficulties, Page reminded Wilson on 21 October, "I once heard you say that it took you twenty years to recover from your legal training—from the habit of mind that is bent on making out a case rather than on seeing the large facts of a situation in their proper proportion."[21]

The ambassador resolved to take drastic steps. On 20 October, he cabled his son Arthur, directing him to deliver an urgent message to House: "God delivers or can you deliver us from library lawyers. They often lose chestnuts while they argue about burns. See our friend and come here immediately if case not already settled. Of utmost importance." Two days later, on 22 October, Page sent House a letter threatening, "If Lansing again brings up the Declaration of London—after 4 flat and reasonable rejections—I shall resign." Relief was already on the way. The dispute ended abruptly on 21 October, before Page made his threat to resign and evidently without reference to his arguments. Lansing informally told the British ambassador in Washington, Spring Rice, that the United States was dropping its insistence upon the Declaration of London. Page received notification of the shift early on 23 October, and he rushed to inform the Foreign Office. The relieved ambassador filed the papers relating to the controversy away in a dispatch box. "The very sight of that locked box brings a shuddering memory," he wrote the president on 28 October, "of the worst nightmare I ever had. All for what, I don't even yet know."[22]

Page had reason to feel puzzled. An air of unreality still surrounds the controversy, inasmuch as Wilson and Lansing were merely fencing with the British and were prepared from the start to relent. The ambassador's remaining in the dark about their intentions evidently reflected habitual State Department inefficiency, as well as the president's frequently haphazard way of dealing with subordinates. The dressing down that Wilson gave Page showed how the two men's temperamental differences could cause friction under stress. In public and private during 1914 and 1915 Wilson stressed the need for national self-control toward the war. He seems to have been projecting onto the United States the same discipline that he was struggling to maintain against grief over his wife's death, which also occurred in August 1914. Page's display of emotion, therefore, angered Wilson. Explaining his attitude toward the ambassador, the president observed to House, "I fear that there is a slight danger in the intense feeling he has for the English case."[23]

Page's behavior was not completely beyond criticism either. His deepest distress sprang not from policy disagreement nor from what he was ordered to do but from what he was supposed to pretend was his own idea. In his letter to House, the sentence preceding the threat to resign read: "And he [Lansing] instructed me to propose this plan *as my own, saying distinctly that it was not proposed by my Government!*" Further on, Page declared, "Now the relations that I have established with Sir Edw. Grey have been built up on frankness, fairness, friendship, and certainly on truth-telling. I can't have relations of any other sort, nor can England & the U.S. have relations of any other sort." That was more of Page's diplomatic naiveté. One can sympathize with his refusal to tell a lie and share his distaste for the subterfuge about the Declaration of London as a shoddy scheme. But his reactions were not warranted or correct for a diplomat. Moreover, Page exaggerated the burden placed on him personally by the scheme involving the declaration. Lansing also divulged it to Spring Rice, for him to communicate to Grey. Likewise, the foreign secretary came no closer than before to reciprocating the ambassador's candor. Page told Grey that he disagreed with his own government on the blockade, but Grey revealed nothing to him about the divisions within the Foreign Office and among the Allies on the subject. The strains of war were creating a situation to which the ambassador's amateur approach to diplomacy was ill-suited, even dangerous.[24]

The controversy left lasting marks on Page's relations with nearly all the principal figures in his government. The ambassador and the president each expressed regret about having appeared to disagree, and each assured the other of undiminished regard. Yet neither man repented his stand. "The insistence on the Declaration of London came near to upsetting the whole kettle of fish," Page asserted to Wilson. " . . . I fancy we can manage a little more perspective than should be obtainable from any point of view on your side of the water," Wilson told Page. To Colonel House the president confided on 23 October, "I am a little disturbed by the messages Walter Page is sending recently. It is very necessary that he should see the difficult matters between us and the British Government in the light in which they are seen on this side of the water, and I am sorry that he should think the argument of them the work of mere 'library lawyers.' We are very much helped by his advice, but I hope that he will not get into an unsympathetic attitude." Those remarks denoted the beginning of a change in the relationship between Wilson and Page. The controversy had cracked their mutually held illusions of intimacy and agreement.[25]

The ambassador's standing with House also suffered from the dispute. When the colonel received Page's telegram on 21 October, he passed the message at once on to the president, adding, "I hardly know to what he refers, but perhaps you do." Privately, House's initial reaction was to agree with Page. "The State Department is not what it should be," he wrote in his diary. " . . . I am sorry to say, too, as I have said before, that the President does not seem to have a proper sense of proportion as between domestic and foreign affairs. I suppose it is the Washington atmosphere that has gripped him as it does everyone else who works there, and the work of the day largely obscures the tremendous world issues that are now before us." But when the president replied with the remarks about Page's not getting "into an unsympathetic attitude," House hastened to disassociate himself from the ambassador. "After I had sent that cablegram of Page's I regretted it," he responded to Wilson on 24 October, "for the reason that he seemed unduly disturbed." The little Texan was not about to let anyone come between him and the seat of power.[26]

Little that happened after the abandonment of the protests involving the Declaration of London served to restore Page's position. The British issued their new Order in Council on 29 October 1914, tightening the blockade. As the restrictions started to pinch certain American exports, particularly cotton and copper, representatives for those interests put pressure on the Wilson administration. Annoyance also rose among shippers and other businessmen because of delays and damage caused by the British blockade. Although Page dutifully passed along such complaints to the Foreign Office, his performance did not satisfy the State Department. Some of Page's comments about the war likewise displeased Bryan and Lansing. Early in December 1914 Wilson asked House, the colonel recorded in his diary, "to caution Walter Page about being too pro-British. Page is writing letters to the State Department which excite attention, and both Mr. Bryan and Mr. Lansing have spoken to him [Wilson] about it." House complied, writing his friend, "The President wished me to ask you please to be careful not to express any un-neutral feeling either by word of mouth, or by letter, and not even to the State Department. He said that both Mr. Bryan and Mr. Lansing had remarked upon your leaning in that direction, and he thought it would materially lessen your influence." Page brushed aside the warning, asking whether an ambassador ought "to keep another government friendly and in good humor. . . . Or is his business to snap and snarl and play 'smart' and keep 'em irritated—damn 'em—and get and give nothing?"[27]

Even a mild remonstrance to the British could put him in a bad light. On 26 December 1914 Bryan dispatched the first formal American diplomatic note to Britain about the blockade, raising only minor points of contention. "It is an admirable paper," Page cabled back, "it is a pleasure to present it." Another State Department leak marred the diplomatic exchange, however, and the British press greeted the action, Page reported to Bryan, with "a strong under current of comment . . . that the Note is proof of German propaganda in the United States." Many spokesmen in London, he added, scorned the United States for "protesting about trade and failing to protest about Belgium." Though simply reporting British reactions, Page emphasized the harshest of adverse comments, thereby echoing charges simultaneously leveled against the Wilson administration by Roosevelt and other pro-Allied stalwarts at home. The ambassador did not agree with those charges. "The old women of both sexes—here as well as in the U.S.," he told Chandler Anderson in February 1915, "—are making much fuss, to the confusion of straight thinking, about the failure of the President to 'protest' against the rape of Belgium." Still, relaying such comments from Britain hardly improved Page's standing in Washington.[28]

No dispute followed presentation of the note. Grey's reply in February 1915, with a defense of the blockade on legal and moral grounds, apparently satisfied Wilson and Bryan, since no further exchanges ensued. In the meantime, the shipping controversy erupted again with an incident that appeared to threaten a nasty clash. At the end of December 1914, the transfer of the German freighter *Dacia* to American registry for trade with Germany through the Netherlands angered the British, who threatened to seize the ship. Wilson and Bryan, in turn, refused to budge from their earlier approval of such ship transfers, and a diplomatic clash seemed in the making.

The incident worried Page because of the gravity with which the British regarded the *Dacia*. An inquiry at the Foreign Office on 18 January, Page cabled Bryan, "brought from Sir Edward Grey the most ominous conversation I have had with him." His description of the British state of mind made an impression on the president and secretary of state. On 23 January Page received a long cable from Bryan, marked "To be Deciphered by Ambassador Himself." The message, which Wilson had edited, maintained that the British misunderstood and exaggerated the importance of the *Dacia* case and that the United States government did not intend to provoke a controversy over the ship's seizure. That cable not only furnished all the reassurance that Page required, but conveying it soon became unnecessary because the British received other indications that the Americans did not plan to raise a major controversy and, ironically, because the French finally intercepted the *Dacia*.[29]

As the shipping controversy cleared up, a more complicated and much more dangerous situation was taking shape. On 4 February 1915 the German government proclaimed its intention to employ the new weapon, the submarine, to sink belligerent and neutral shipping engaged in trade with the enemies of the Central Powers. The submarine threat involved America's relations with Britain as well as Germany. The Germans justified submarine warfare in part as a retaliation against the Allied blockade, particularly on foodstuffs. The British likewise seized upon the submarine proclamation as an excuse for further tightening restrictions. These developments promised to plunge Page into fresh contentions over the blockade, with far bigger issues at stake.

One ray of hope did relieve gloomy prospects at the beginning of February 1915. The first American feelers toward mediation of the war involved the ambassador. In January 1915 Field Marshal Sir John French, the commander of the British Expeditionary Force on the western front, secretly told Page that he and other military leaders regarded the war as a deadlock and that they might welcome peace initiatives from the United States. At the same time, House cabled that he was sailing for Europe on 30 January on the British liner *Lusitania*, to visit the belligerent capitals. "The President and I find that we are going around in a circle in dealing with the representatives in Washington," House explained to Page in a letter, "and he thinks it advisable and necessary to reach the principals direct." The colonel's mission heartened the ambassador. "I guess he wished to look the ground over to see if he can find any peace-doves' nests," Page wrote to his wife, who was visiting in the United States. "Well I hope he'll succeed. I can't see any way out by keeping on this fighting." He also recognized that House's visit could help restore his touch with American opinion, which "is somehow remote to me." Page told Alice that he had "cabled House to come here and stay with me. I'm eager to get into his mind & to see precisely how they look at it." As before, the Tar Heel was looking to his Texan friend to set matters right.[30]

Colonel House and his wife arrived in London on the afternoon of Saturday, 6 February 1915. Ambassador Page met them at the railroad station with his car and chauffeur and helped them get settled at their hotel. Then the two men spent the rest of the day at the ambassador's residence discussing plans for the colonel's stay. To Page everything must have seemed intimate and productive. He had arranged for them to have lunch with Grey the following Wednesday, 10 February. "I did not tell him," House recorded in his diary, "the British ambassador has already arranged for me to meet Sir Edward tomorrow." The following morning at eleven o'clock, the colonel called at Grey's house on Eccleston Square for a two-hour conversation about possible peace terms. Except for Grey's brother, who joined them afterward for lunch, no one else was present. House told Page about the meeting that evening at dinner, but it was only the first in a series of secret contacts at the foreign secretary's home that took place without the ambassador's knowledge or involvement. As House described one meeting with Grey in his diary, "We sat by the fire in his library facing one another, discussing every phase of the situation with a single mind and purpose." The other encounters Page never learned about at all. "As far as he knows, I have only seen Sir Edward twice with him," House told Wilson. "He has not the faintest conception of the people I have met and what I have done, or the active cooperation of Sir Edward. I have enlightened him a little only for it seems best not to endanger our very warm and cordial relations by telling him of my activities without his participation."[31]

House's mission to Europe in 1915 hardly provided the significant diplomatic activity or frank discussion of policy that Page craved. Instead, the colonel's visit formed another episode in the gradual deterioration of the ambassador's position. The president's emissary remained in London for a month before he crossed over to the Continent to confer first in Paris, then in Berlin, and finally in Paris again. Late in April House returned to London, where he stayed until his departure for the United States at the beginning of June. The four months of House's mission coincided with the most important turning point in America's relations with the warring powers. Those months also began to confirm Page's estrangement from significant decisions and his disagreement about fundamental issues. House and Wilson evidently planned from the outset for the colonel to play a lone hand in dealing with the European leaders. House's prewar mission had convinced him that working through official channels was too confining. Not even his chosen ambassadorial instrument in London suited him. Directly after arriving there in February 1915, House regretted having to send cables to the president through the embassy, despite having arranged a private code with Wilson. "I could send them through the British Foreign Office," he explained to the president in a letter, "but I do not like to do this as it might indicate to them that Yucca [Page] was not in our full confidence, which might impair his usefulness."[32]

During House's first sojourn in London, Page seems to have remained unaware of how much the colonel shut him out. As before, he made contacts for his friend with various governmental and private figures. He took some part in the diplomatic business of the mission. At their meeting with Grey on 10 February, Page surprised House by favoring American participation in making peace. A week later, the ambassador and the colonel conferred with the prime minister as well as the foreign secretary. "During the luncheon," House wrote in his diary, "Page and Grey did most of the talking, Asquith and I listening. After lunch I did nearly all the talking with the others asking questions." As in the past, Page had long talks with House, in which he unburdened himself about the inadequacies and transgressions of the State Department. Toward the purpose of the colonel's visit, however, Page showed mixed reactions. Even before House's arrival, he had second thoughts about the United States trying to mediate the war. "Peace?" he wrote to Alice. "My Lord! I don't see how or when. And I have a feeling *that's* yet a dangerous subject." When House showed him Wilson's confidential letter of instruction, the colonel noted in his diary that the ambassador called it "a great document, one of the best the President had ever written and he said, 'he has given you a noble mission.'" But in a draft letter to Wilson, which he did not send, Page dwelled on the vagueness of House's proposals, and in his own diary he wrote on 11 March, "*E. M. House* went to Paris this morning, having no p[eace] message from this Kingdom whatever. This kind of talk here now was spoken of by the Prime Minister the other day 'as the twittering of a sparrow in a tumult that shakes the world.'" Those were Page's first aspersions on House.[33]

More serious friction between the two men originated with the colonel. On 20 February 1915 Secretary Bryan dispatched a note asking Britain and Germany to abandon their respective practices of food blockade and submarine warfare. Wilson cabled House the same day, urging forceful presentation of the note in London. "Please say to Page that he cannot emphasize too much in presenting the note to Grey the favorable opinion which would be created in this country if the British Government could see its way clear to adopt the suggestions made there." How the ambassador followed those instructions was disputed. Page reported to Bryan that he "urged" the proposal on Grey, who was "non-committal" but appeared favorable "at least in principle." But House claimed that Page balked at making a vigorous argument for the plan. "He put it very mildly to the British Government," the colonel wrote in his diary on 20 February, "although his instructions were to make it very strong." Two days later the two men reviewed the situation, and House recorded that "Page was inclined not to make a personal appeal to Grey in behalf of acceptance of the President's proposal concerning a compromise with Germany on the question of the embargo." When the colonel reminded him of Wilson's own urging, the ambassador consented to meet with Grey again, "though one could see that he had no stomach for it. He did not consider the suggestion a wise one, nor did he consider its acceptance favorable to the British Government." Doubting the sincerity of Page's presentation, House pressed the proposal on Grey at two of their private meetings. The colonel got the same amicably noncommittal response as the ambassador did from the foreign secretary.[34]

The greatest significance of those disagreements lay in their effect on the relationship between Page and House. Since the suggestion regarding the food blockade apparently had scant chance of acceptance, the ambassador's reluctance to keep urging it was hard to fault. But some of his motives were questionable. Page's doubt about whether acceding to the plan would be "favorable to the British Government" betrayed his pro-Allied views. Those views did not bother House. "I argued to the contrary," he observed in his diary, "and tried to convince him that the good opinion gained from the neutrals would be compensation enough for any concessions this [British] Government might make, and that the concessions were not really more than those made by Germany." The two men differed over means and strategies for achieving their common end of assuring the right kind of Allied victory. Page disturbed House for other reasons. The colonel again distrusted the ambassador's tendency toward indiscretion. Assessing Page's position in a letter to Wilson, House observed,

"He is so open, frank, and honest that he believes everybody is as much so as himself. He is inclined therefore to put too much trust in the people with whom he is thrown." The times seemed to require greater wariness and guile, gifts that House abundantly possessed.[35]

The colonel's reservations about the ambassador's effectiveness surfaced again in March 1915, in connection with the British moves to tighten the blockade further in retaliation against the German submarine decree. Page responded to these moves in his expected manner. To Grey he expressed the conviction that they "would not give rise to any trouble with the United States Government," while he cabled the State Department on 3 March advising that "we content ourselves for the present with a friendly inquiry how the proposed reprisal will be carried out." Page's reactions to the tightened blockade affronted House. When the ambassador showed him a draft of his cable to the State Department, the colonel remarked in his diary that "he had a lot of things in it which I advised eliminating. It was the strongest sort of pro-British argument, and I knew it would weaken his influence both with the State Department and with the President. He reluctantly cut it down to a short statement, merely making the request as I have outlined before."[36]

Despite these frictions between them, the two men came nowhere near any kind of break. For his part, House still felt affection for Page. "We talked of home, of the President, of McAdoo and conditions, and we had a genuinely good time," he wrote in his diary after an evening at the ambassador's house. "I like Page, he is direct and without guile." Nor did the colonel try to undercut the ambassador in the president's eyes. Although he criticized Page's lack of guile in a letter to Wilson early in March, House hastened to add, "They have the highest regard for him here in official circles and Sir Edward has spoken of his liking for him time and again. . . . I think this liking for Page here is of great value to our two countries at this present moment." So long as Page did not overstep himself too much, House seemed glad to tolerate him.[37]

Little that happened while House was away in Paris and

Berlin changed relations between him and Page. A long, complicated note authored by Lansing about the tightened blockade went to Page for presentation on 30 March. But the ambassador assured the foreign secretary, noted Grey, "that we would not be pressed for time. His own personal opinion was that one of the great objects of the American Note was to keep the record about international law straight." Meanwhile, tensions between the United States and Germany were growing because of submarine attacks on merchant shipping. In March, after the sinking of an American vessel, Page noted in his diary, "We'll see what we shall see."[38]

House and his wife arrived back in London on the evening of 28 April and stayed at the Pages' residence for several days before they moved into a rented house near Green Park. The colonel again met secretly with the foreign secretary, twice this time, immediately after his arrival. When Grey came to Page's house for tea on 30 April, House commented in his diary, "I took the precaution to remain downstairs in order to meet him when he first came in and to walk up to the drawing room with him. In this way there was no embarrassment nor any pretense of not having met before." The colonel did not tell the ambassador about their two previous conferences, and he and Grey barely mentioned the subject of those meetings in Page's presence. The ambassador recorded in his diary that on 30 April they had "little talk of the main subject, which is not yet ripe by a great deal." Actually, House and Grey were discussing a mediation initiative on the basis of "freedom of the seas." That was the colonel's formula for limiting naval warfare against neutral commerce, to which the Germans seemed attracted. Grey likewise showed some interest in the idea, provided international security guarantees were also part of a peace settlement. Discussions of freedom of the seas with British leaders formed House's principal business in London until he left for America on 4 June. Page evidently neither knew about nor participated in those talks.[39]

Bonds of friendship persisted between the two southerners. As on the colonel's earlier visits, the ambassador made contacts, provided entertainment, and advised on practical matters. But strain also grew. During the spring of 1915 Page's viewpoint toward the war hardened. After the meeting with the colonel and the foreign secretary on 30 April, the ambassador commented in his diary, "The ingenious loop-hole discovered by House is— mere moonshine, viz, the freedom of the seas in war. That is a one-sided proposition unless they couple with it freedom of the land in war also, wh. is nonsense." Four days later, he commented, "It's certain House can do nothing. Prudent as he is, one doubts whether his journeying and talks and presence in Europe really helps [*sic*] peace forward."[40]

Page now recognized, too, that House was undercutting him in London. Upon his return, the colonel solidified contacts through Sir Horace Plunkett, the English agrarian reformer to whom Page had introduced him, with Arthur James Balfour, the conservative leader who became first lord of the Admiralty in the government shakeup of May 1915. House arranged another private code with Plunkett so that he could maintain communication with Balfour after his return to America. Codes seem to have been a fetish with House. He established still another one with the Foreign Office just before his departure, expressly for the purpose of circumventing Page. On 3 June House spoke with Lord Crewe, who was substituting for Grey at the Foreign Office, "of my relations with Page and of how careful we must be not to offend his sensibilities. I suggested a private code between Grey and myself, by which we could talk unofficially, so that neither Embassy should be cognizant of it." The colonel likewise penetrated the embassy staff, enlisting Clifford Carver, the ambassador's secretary, as his agent. Carver, who had gotten his post the preceding November, believed that Page felt "petty jealousy" toward the colonel's contacts and activities. When Carver spent several days making arrangements for House's departure, the secretary noted in his own diary, "I am sure that the Ambassador feels that there is far too much ado about nothing."[41]

Most of Page's displeasure with House sprang from diplomatic issues. In the minds of Wilson and his advisers, the submarine dispute with Germany was becoming inescapably linked with responses to the British blockade. As tensions increased over submarine warfare during April 1915, the president grew uneasy about British dilatoriness in answering American representations. On 5 May he cabled House, asking him to convey a private message to Grey. "A very serious change is coming over public sentiment in this country because of England's delays and arbitrary interferences with our neutral cargoes," warned the president. Before the British could respond to that message, the submarine dispute exploded into a full-fledged crisis between the United States and Germany, raising for the first time the danger that America might be drawn into World War I.[42]

American leaders had been worried since February because they feared that their citizens might be killed by submarine attack and thereby cause an outraged public to demand war. Page thought that those kinds of events might occur. "Peace? Lord knows when," he told his son Arthur on 2 May. "The blowing-up of a liner with American passengers may be the prelude. I almost expect such a thing. . . . If a British liner full of Americans be blown up, what will Uncle Sam do? What's going to happen?" The ambassador was not alone in such speculations. Late in the morning of 7 May 1915, House and Grey went for a drive to Kew Gardens. "We spoke of the probability of an ocean liner being sunk," the colonel recorded in his diary, "and I told him if this were done, a flame of indignation would sweep across America, which would probably carry us into the war." Calling at Buckingham Palace after the drive, House found himself discussing the same subject "strangely enough" with the king. "Suppose they should sink the Lusitania with American passengers on board?" asked George V.[43]

Within two or three hours of the king's utterance, a German submarine did sink the *Lusitania*, the liner on which House had sailed to Europe and the largest passenger ship afloat. One thousand one hundred ninety-eight men, women, and children died, including 128 United States citizens. Rumors were afloat in London throughout the afternoon of 7 May about a submarine attack on the *Lusitania*, but news of the extent of the disaster did not reach the capital until evening. The Pages were entertaining the Houses and other guests for dinner at their residence on

Grosvenor Square when reports started to arrive. "The whole topic of conversation was the Lusitania," noted House. "Clifford Carver was at the telephone all evening bringing us despatches which grew worse as the evening passed." House remarked that he was "deeply concerned about the consequences of this last inhuman act." Page reacted more hotly. "Ambassador violent for war," his daughter wrote in her journal. Page may have openly advocated war to his dinner guests, or he may have exploded only privately to his family. Either way, he had cast his lot.[44]

The ambassador lost no time conveying interventionist sentiments to Washington. The next day he cabled, "The freely expressed unofficial view is that the United States must declare war or forfeit European respect. So far as I know this opinion is universal." Virtually "unanimous opinion" held that American belligerency would "bring peace quickly" and confer great influence in the peace settlement. Failure to fight would insure that "the United States will have no voice or influence in settling the war nor in what follows for a long time to come." Those views may indeed have held sway in Britain, but the ambassador had scarcely had time to assess public opinion since receiving the news about the *Lusitania* the night before. Rather, Page was reading his own beliefs into the situation. His cable annoyed Secretary Bryan, who was desperately seeking to avoid war. As soon as the communication arrived, Bryan remonstrated against the ambassador to Wilson. The president replied, "After all, this does not express Page's own opinion, but what he takes to be public opinion at the moment in Great Britain." Wilson was wrong. The *Lusitania* outrage had converted Page, along with other leading pro-Allied Americans, into an advocate of intervention.[45]

The sinking of the *Lusitania* brought out the worst in Page as an ambassador. His earlier pro-Allied advocacy shrank into insignificance compared with what followed. For nearly two years, until the United States finally did enter the war in April 1917, Page kept up a cannonade of cables and letters to the president, the secretary of state, Colonel House, and assorted friends and relatives. Nearly all his communications cajoled, reiterated, nagged away at a single point: the United States must take up arms for the sake of its own self-respect and the decent opinion of Britain. Early in June 1915, for example, he wrote his son Arthur, "We're in danger of being feminized and fad-ridden — ... pensions, Christian Science; peace-cranks; ... petty coats where breeches ought to be & breeches where petty coats ought to be; ... white livers and soft heads and milk-and-water;—I don't want war: nobody knows its horrors or its degradation or its cost. But to get rid of hyphenated degenerates perhaps it's worth while, and to free us from 'isms and soft folk & pious liars." Someone who did not know where those remarks came from could easily have mistaken them for the attacks on Wilson that were emanating publicly and privately from Theodore Roosevelt. Neither those views nor Page's tireless reiteration of them was going to strengthen his standing with Wilson in months to come.[46]

Colonel House reacted to the sinking of the *Lusitania* in almost exactly the same way. When Page showed him the cable of 8 May, the Texan raised no objections and apparently suggested some additions. The next day, the colonel likewise cabled Wilson to advocate a tough protest to Germany. "If war follows, it will not be a new war," House declared, "but an endeavor to end more speedily an old one." Echoing Page's contention, he asserted, "Our action in this crisis will determine the part we will play when peace is made, and how far we may influence a settlement for the lasting good of humanity. We are being adjudged by mankind." For his part, House displayed no more diplomatic finesse than Page did in responding to the sinking of the *Lusitania*. Plunkett recorded in his diary that the colonel avowed himself in favor of American intervention several times, at least once in Balfour's presence. On the day before House left, Plunkett asked him again "in all the circumstances whether he did not think it better for the U.S. to come in. He said (after a pause of thought), 'Yes, I do. We cannot take any risk of England's being beaten.'" Although no record indicates House's making as flat a statement to Grey, it seems safe to assume that the colonel at least left a similar impression during those long, private talks with the foreign secretary. Suppleness was not synonymous with discretion. The small, stealthy Texan could sometimes be as indiscreet as the big, blunt North Carolinian in talking with the British.[47]

Page's satisfaction in the colonel's newly belligerent views carried an overtone of contempt. On 4 June 1915 the ambassador wrote in his diary, "House has gone home while the going on an American ship is safe—running away from German submarines as the conclusion of his errand to get a peace-proposal from Germany to the Allies; he has gone red-hot for war between the U.S. and Germany. He's in a different mood from his coming!" Such a comment did not augur well for their friendship. But the pair parted at the beginning of June 1915 on good terms, and shortly afterward the colonel gave additional evidence of his wish to maintain their friendly relations. While House was at sea, Secretary Bryan resigned amid a flurry of public statements about his disagreements with the president over the *Lusitania* crisis. In seeking to replace the Commoner, Wilson sent Secretary of the Treasury McAdoo to New York to consult with House on 14 June, two days after the colonel landed. "I suggested your name," House wrote Page three days later, "and McAdoo said that the President thought it would not do to take an Ambassador from a belligerent country and make him Secretary of State. I disagree with this conclusion and I shall again urge the desirability of naming you." The colonel said that Page would make an excellent secretary of state because the president needed "someone who has his entire confidence and who would cordially co-operate in the work I am doing."[48]

Whether the colonel really promoted the ambassador as a successor to Bryan is questionable. Two letters to Page contain the only references to his possible appointment. House failed to mention him in his diary record of the 14 June conference with McAdoo. As it happened, no one but Lansing received serious consideration, and the counselor was named acting secretary of state on 23 June 1915. The appointment pleased Page, who was glad to see Bryan out and professed not to want the job himself.

"Rob't Lansing appointed Sec. State," the ambassador wrote in his diary, "—very good; no jarring of the machinery while we cross this bridge."[49]

Seven months elapsed between House's departure from Britain in June 1915 and his return on a second wartime mission at the beginning of January 1916. Those months marked a disheartening stretch of time for Page, a period of virtually unrelieved depression, disillusionment, and impotence. Part of the ambassador's gloom reflected the atmosphere in which he lived. "The general strain—military, political, financial—gets greater," he wrote his daughter Katharine in December 1915. "The streets are darker than ever. The number of wounded increases rapidly. More houses are turned into hospitals. The Manchesters', next door, is a hospital now. And everybody fears worse days are to come." The spirit of those remarks applied equally to the ambassador himself.[50]

Much of Page's discontent had a specific root in policy. After May 1915 he chafed at the failure of the United States to come into the war on the Allied side. The way that the sinking of the *Lusitania* galvanized him into an unflinching interventionist suggested that the disaster provided a welcome excuse for advocating American entry into the war. Page did not for a moment share what Wilson called the American people's "double-wish" to avenge the *Lusitania* outrage and yet avoid involvement in the frightful conflict. The ambassador made his choice without hesitation, second thought, or regrets. That reaction was completely in character for him. In switching his greatest cause from sectional reconciliation at home to partnership with Britain abroad, Page retained for himself the same role of secular preacher, with ambassadorial letters replacing magazines as his pulpit. His notions of salvation, too, continued to stress activity. For Page the submarine supplied an essential feature, hitherto missing, to the war. At last he could demand that the United States take vigorous action. His discontent seethed, as his government seemed to sit supine.

From Page's standpoint the situation did not start out badly.

He felt fairly confident at the beginning of June 1915 that his country would soon be at war. But his hopes dissipated as the Wilson administration settled into a long diplomatic siege over the submarine. As early as 8 June, the ambassador wrote House, "I must warn you that the President is being laughed at by our best friends for his slowness in action." Six weeks later, on 21 July, he reiterated to the colonel that the British were beginning to think "that the American Government is pusillanimous." Page himself regretted Wilson's patience with the Germans because, "looking at the thing in a long-range way, we're bound to get into the war. . . . And by dallying with them we do not change the ultimate result, but we take away from ourselves the spunk and credit of getting in instead of being kicked and cursed in." As usual, the ambassador addressed the president with greater restraint, but at the end of September Page stated to Wilson, "In the meantime our prestige (if that be the right word), in British judgment, is gone."[51]

A pair of related circumstances heightened the ambassador's distress. One was that House seemed to misunderstand his arguments. The colonel's warlike sentiments cooled rapidly after his return to the United States, especially when he caught the drift of the president's thinking. In July and August, House wrote several times to warn Page about the strength of antiinterventionist sentiment. "I doubt whether anything we could do short of intervention would satisfy the Allies," the colonel also asserted. Page replied to those warnings at the beginning of September with an eight-page handwritten letter that opened, "You write to me about pleasing the Allies, the big Ally in particular. That doesn't particularly appeal to me. We don't owe them anything." Page insisted, "My point is not sentimental. It is (1) We must maintain our own self-respect and safety. If we submit to too many insults, *that* will in time bring Germany against us and (perhaps even earlier) Japan and ultimately England, too. . . . (2) About nagging and forever presenting technical and legal points as lawyers do to confuse juries—the point is the point of efficiency. If we do that, we can't carry our main points."[52]

The gibe about lawyerish tactics referred to the second distressing circumstance for Page. He believed that Lansing's ardor for scoring legal points was again stirring up unnecessary blockade squabbles. In July 1915 Lansing again instructed Page to make strong protests to Grey concerning the legality of both general Allied restrictions and particular actions. Those instructions, together with other grumblings from the State Department about the British, predictably disturbed the ambassador. On 4 August he admonished House that "the lawyer-way in wh. the Dp't goes on in its dealings with Great Britain is losing us the only great international friendship that we have any chance of keeping or that is worth having." Repeating Wilson's quip about having needed twenty years to unlearn the legal habit of mind, Page snapped, "Well, his Administration is suffering from it to a degree that is pathetic & that will leave bad results for 100 years."[53]

Unfortunately the ambassador's overreactions further weakened his influence. In July, Page cautioned House against pressing blockade disputes with Britain while the United States teetered on the brink of war with Germany. The result could be that *we shall be at war with one side and not at peace with the other.* The advice was unnecessary, since House, Lansing, and Wilson each recognized the folly of getting into trouble with both sets of belligerents at the same time. Throughout the summer of 1915, the United States showed great restraint in dealing with the Allies, making no more formal note of protest about the blockade until the end of October, when the submarine crisis had temporarily subsided. Such forbearance in Washington made Page's admonitions and alarms go over even worse than earlier. Unfortunately, too, a fumbling effort by Colonel House to set his friend straight highlighted the ambassador's weaknesses at an inopportune moment.[54]

At the middle of July, House told Arthur Page that he thought his father "should have some sort of rest which he cannot get on the other side." When Ambassador Page got the message at the end of July, he cabled Lansing, "I can arrange for a visit almost immediately." Lansing, who knew nothing about House's plan, telegraphed the president, who was vacationing in

New Hampshire, for instructions. "I do not understand this at all," Wilson wrote back. "No one was authorized by me to convey any such intimation to Page, and, as a matter of judgment, I think it would be very unwise for him to come to America at this time." When Lansing accordingly cabled the president's view to Page on 3 August, that should have ended the matter. But Colonel House thought that he had some explaining to do. Again hastening to protect himself by shifting blame to the ambassador House commented, "Page is in a blue funk. . . . To read Page's letters one would think the Germans were just outside London and moving rapidly westward upon New York." House maintained that "it would be well to send for Page and let him have thirty or forty days in this country. The war has gotten on his nerves and he has no idea what the sentiment of the people in this country is in regard to it." House had meant well in hatching the plan, but he had ended up by disparaging Page.[55]

The incident coincided with the beginning of a sharp decline in Page's standing with Wilson. Up to that point and for a short while afterward, the president did not worry unduly about the ambassador. "With regard to Walter Page," he replied to House on 21 August, "I have this feeling: he is undoubtedly too much affected by the English view of things and needs a bath in American opinion; but is it wise to send for him just now and is it not, after all, rather useful to have him give us the English view so straight?" Despite his flare-up over the Declaration of London the preceding October, the president had continued to praise the ambassador to mutual friends. The president's failure to answer the ambassador's letters bothered Page, but Wilson finally wrote on 10 September, "I do not often acknowledge your interesting letters, but that is not because they are not of vital interest to me but only because I have nothing to write in return which compares in interest with what you write to me." Page's letters were "of real service to me," and Wilson hoped "that you will not leave out a single line or item which is interesting your own thought." That communication relieved the ambassador, Irwin Laughlin recalled, by showing that he continued to enjoy the president's confidence.[56]

Page took heart too readily. Wilson's letter had an undertone of impatience, and the president closed by wishing for a chance "to see you and have a long talk with you, and I think it would refresh you to get into the freer and cooler atmosphere of this country of course, where the majority are not half so much off their poise as a small minority seem to be, but we must postpone that pleasure for a little while." The hint of reproof was hard to miss. It was not long after this that Wilson stopped reading those letters to him on which Page lavished so much care. House remembered later that the president accumulated the ambassador's correspondence, planning for the colonel to go through it on his periodic visits to the White House. "Here's another from Page," Wilson would remark as he handed over a bulky packet of the handwritten correspondence. Wilson's continuing to read Page's letters as long as he did was a tribute to the ambassador's special relationship and gifts as a correspondent. Acting upon his belief in self-control, the president had stopped reading war news in the press as early as December 1914. "And so I manage most of the time to hold excitement at arm's length," he had then explained to a friend, "and escape their contagion." During the fall of 1915, Wilson added Page's letters to his list of contagious influences to avoid. The ambassador hardly knew it, but the cornerstone of his position was crumbling.[57]

Wilson would almost certainly have grown alienated from Page sooner or later, even without the misunderstanding about the ambassador's return. But House's characterization seemed to strike a responsive note at a time when the president was changing his mind. The colonel needed few hints to sense the shift in Wilson's attitude. House, too, was beginning to tire of the lengthy disquisitions that he received every few weeks from London. Page reached a peak of epistolary zeal during the fall of 1915, culminating with a twenty-five-page handwritten letter to the colonel at the middle of November. When Wilson met House in New York later in the month, the Texan recorded in his diary that they quickly agreed that Page had become "utterly hopeless." Neither of them thought of replacing the ambassador. Wilson and House simply decided to ignore him, especially because they were planning for the colonel to go on another mission to Europe in December. By the end of 1915, Page's standing with Wilson, and by extension with House, had skidded from the prewar pinnacle of intimacy and importance, through a long period of strain but still respect, to annoyance and disregard. The fall had been hard and it was not over yet.[58]

Deterioration in the relationships with Wilson and House occurred on Page's side as well. The earlier friction over the Declaration of London had not stopped the ambassador from lauding the president to friends. He evidently criticized Wilson just once during the first year of the war, on the familiar ground of inaccessibility. All the shortcomings of his country's policies Page blamed on either Bryan's incompetence and cowardice or Lansing's lawyerly limitations. But as the submarine crisis wore on through the summer of 1915 without American intervention, the first signs of disillusionment with Wilson appeared. "I cannot express my admiration of the President's management, so far at least, of his colossal task of leading us right," Page wrote around the end of August in a draft of a letter to House. That sentence may have been just a slip of the pen, but Page did not send that letter. His admiration for Wilson waned slowly, and he persisted in wanting to believe in his old acquaintance. In December 1915 he wrote about the president in his diary, "I think there is no expectation in any quarter here that he will ever do more than write notes. And yet, I believe that he will now." The statement sounded suspiciously like whistling in the dark. Throughout the fall of 1915 Page found Wilson's injunction to write openly hard to follow. Sitting by his fireside late at night, the ambassador composed even more extensive notes and drafts than before, weighing how much and in what forms to press his recurrent criticism of America's failure to enter the war.[59]

By contrast, Page had little hesitation about thinking the worst of House. In part he seems to have transferred to the colonel the same scorn that he had earlier felt for Bryan and continued to feel for Lansing. House's apparent deconversion from interventionism and his insinuations about the effects of the British atmosphere on Page likewise rankled. Page's long letters to House in September and November 1915 betrayed traces of irritation. Those were the first letters to the colonel for which Page set down preliminary notes and drafts, many of which he scrapped. Resorting to such deliberation with House showed that frankness and informality were going out of his friendship with the Texan. Page also knew that the colonel persisted in trespassing on his diplomatic territory. Clifford Carver's activities for House during the summer of 1915 were an open secret, and Page was glad to see the young man reassigned in the fall.

Word of the colonel's next mission brought no joy, either. Newspaper stories of his coming prompted Page to draft a letter to Wilson arguing, "House's visits, as your Envoy, have been a mistake." Not only had the colonel's missions created misleading impressions among the British, but they had also undermined the ambassador's position. "Everybody asked where in I had fallen short." Laughlin later recalled that only his own strenuous objections prevented that letter from being sent. On 23 December when the ambassador received a cable from the State Department instructing him to tell the British that House was not coming on a peace mission, he wrote in the margin, "Why lie to *me* about it?" A few days later, rumors circulated that Page might resign. He grumbled in his diary that the rumors had gotten started "partly because of House's pussy-cat way of slipping about & of purring at the wrong times and in the wrong tones." Such resentments did not presage a happy encounter when the colonel came back to London.[60]

Whatever influence Page was losing with his own government, he did enjoy affection and trust among his hosts. House accurately reported the British attitude toward the ambassador to Wilson. Grey told the colonel at the beginning of June 1915, "If you wish to communicate with me through Mr. Page there could be no more agreeable channel: I have a genuine liking & regard for him." The foreign secretary found dealing with the ambassador equally agreeable in blockade disputes later in 1915. The most serious concern involved a British decision in August to interdict all shipments of cotton destined for the Central Powers. Because of the centrality of cotton to the South's economy and because of the political dependence of the Wilson administration on the South, the move required delicacy and understanding. The essential element in the successful resolution of the problem was a scheme by which the British purchased the entire American cotton export crop. Page's contribution to steering relations around a potentially dangerous confrontation lay in his repeatedly warning Grey that the cotton question contained political dynamite. His expressions of sympathy for the Allies lent credence to his warnings, which, together with other information from Washington, helped shape Grey's resolve to couple the contraband announcement with a purchase plan. In this instance Page's ambassadorial approach did come in handy for both countries.[61]

His helpfulness also smoothed the handling of the myriad complaints involving American ships and cargoes detained by the British. Page, who had urged case-by-case responses to the blockade, suffered a certain poetic justice as shipping complaints brought steady increases in the embassy's routine business, outstripping additions to staff. Both the volume and the triviality of many of the complaints added to the ambassador's larger depression. Page's determination not to blow up those complaints avoided unpleasantness with the British, but Lansing's suspicions that the ambassador was not pressing hard enough hurt him further with the State Department. At the beginning of November, Frank Polk, Lansing's successor as counselor, told House that he considered Page "so pro-British that his judgment is of no value." The British, by contrast, began entrusting the ambassador with some special confidences. In September Page acted as the intermediary in releasing documents the British had captured from F. J. Archibald, a German agent. The documents implicated the Austrian ambassador and the German military and naval attachés in Washington in sabotage and espionage activities in the United States. Their publication raised a scandal that resulted in the expulsion of the three diplomats. The trust the British accorded Page would later lead them to pass on other secret information and to employ him as the principal intermediary in the most spectacular intelligence coup of World War I.[62]

But being agreeable and helpful to the British did not mean

that the ambassador was as effective as he could have been in dealing with them. Several years after his death, Page began to be viewed by both Wilson's defenders and critics as a diplomatic failure. The most common posthumous charges against him echoed House's and Wilson's contemporary criticisms—that excessive sympathy for the British and the wartime atmosphere in London got the better of his judgment of American interests. Page himself rebutted such charges in his letters to Colonel House in the fall of 1915, when he argued at length that strategy, not sympathy, shaped his views. In the twenty-five-page November letter, for example, Page condemned the program of the newly founded League to Enforce Peace, which Wilson later endorsed. "We had as well get down to facts," he asserted, "—the big facts in the world, the actual world not a dream world. The biggest fact in the real world—as regards peace—is the British navy. The next biggest fact is our navy. If they perfectly understand one another, there'll be no more great wars so long as this understanding continues." That argument against the league resembled Roosevelt's pronouncements on the organization. Like the ex-president, the ambassador was championing American intervention on the Allied side mainly through calculations of national interest and conceptions of international politics.[63]

A graver criticism of Page's diplomatic performance is that he did not adequately pursue his own objectives of promoting Allied victory and American intervention. By mid-1915 some perceptive figures in London could recognize that their side might not be able to win without assistance from the United States. An exchange crisis during the summer and the flotation of a $500-million Anglo-French loan in the fall exposed Allied financial dependence on America. At the same time, such military disappointments as continuing deadlock on the western front, the failure of the Dardanelles operation against Turkey, and the deterioration of Russia as a military factor cast growing doubt on the ability of the Allies to defeat the Central Powers. In view of all those conditions, British policy makers would have acted prudently if they had sought to avoid friction with the United States and to make themselves look attractive as possible partners in war. Germany's submarine warfare created an excellent chance for those objectives to be realized, provided Allied actions did not alienate the United States. Yet most British leaders seemed bent on a course that threatened to spoil relations with America, and Ambassador Page did almost nothing to deter them.

In May and June 1915 British policy toward the United States stood at a critical juncture. Asquith's new coalition government pondered Wilson's renewed request through House to abandon the food blockade in light of the submarine crisis. Grey and those closest to him in the Foreign Office favored risking relaxation of the blockade in exchange for American good will and the chance to put the Germans on the spot. The War Office and the Admiralty, with backing from France, wanted a still more stringent blockade and condemned any gestures toward loosening restrictions. The advocates of the tougher line prevailed easily. Not only did they have the argument of military necessity apparently on their side, but they also enjoyed the support of Lloyd George and the Conservative leaders, whom Asquith feared most politically. Meanwhile, failing eyesight required Grey to vacate his post for nearly two months after the middle of May. In his absence, arguments for relaxing the blockade received neither enthusiastic nor unanimous support from the Foreign Office. Refusal to relax the blockade in June 1915 effectively closed for Britain the option of pursuing an overriding policy of pleasing the United States. Thereafter, the proponents of such a policy steadily lost influence to hard-liners. British favor in American eyes came to depend more and more upon the Germans' looking worse than they did.

Page evidently knew nothing about the blockade debates of June 1915. His ignorance was not entirely his fault, since House barely informed him about the requests to the British. Yet if the ambassador had known what was going on, he might not have aided the advocates of a pro-American policy. Page had long since made up his mind that the burden of keeping relations harmonious fell on the United States. He never seems to have questioned either the necessity or the desirability of the blockade. Nor did he apprehend much about Grey's diplomatic thinking other than his manifest friendship for the United States. Just as he had remarked little on prewar divisions within Britain, Page showed scant appreciation for differences of opinion about the war because they did not suit his argument. Finally, he preferred the hard-liners in the British government, even at the expense of his friend Grey. "As the war goes on," Page wrote to Arthur at the end of August, "I become more and more doubtful about the ability and decisiveness of the British Gov't, especially the part of it that hangs on from the old Liberal Gov't. The popular idea, which is perhaps correct, is that Lloyd George is the only man of that group who is equal to the present job." Such views did not dispose the ambassador to help strengthen the hand of the foreign secretary or anyone else who wanted to put good relations with the United States uppermost in British policy.[64]

Page's sorest limitation as a diplomat was lack of perception and flexibility. With respect to Grey, he apparently never perceived the ambivalences and doubts that plagued the foreign secretary. On the American posture toward the war, he showed little appreciation of the need to placate domestic interests. Page recognized as well as anyone else the yoking of submarine and blockade issues in the minds of his countrymen, and he warned the British several times that any accommodation by Germany would immediately shift pressure to them. But the ambassador did not grasp that a forceful defense of his nation's trading and shipping interests might actually help prepare the British for facing such full-fledged protests. Although Grey liked the convenience of dealing with an ambassador like Page, the foreign secretary's own position needed more than sympathy—it would have been strengthened by a more vigorous presentation of the American side. One man who did mix those elements, together with recognizing and playing upon some of Grey's inner conflicts, was House. The colonel stood out, despite his flaws, as the most resourceful American representative to deal with the British during World War I. House presented a striking contrast to Page. Perhaps the ambassador could have acted more effectively if the colonel and the president had not bypassed him so often, but that seems doubtful. The intrigues and complexities of wartime dealings with the British, particularly with the enigmatic Grey, called for the subtlety and love of manipulation, if not the deviousness, of Colonel House. Even by his own pro-Allied, interventionist lights, Page was out of his element.

A few distractions eased the ambassador's gloom during the latter part of 1915. He still enjoyed occasional moments of recreation. In the summer Page managed to get in periodic rounds of his bad golf game again. He and Alice took a couple of short trips out of London, in May with the Houses to Bath and in August by themselves to the Cotswolds. The Pages' most significant and most pleasant distraction was the marriage of their daughter Katharine to Charles Loring, a Boston architect. At the insistence of the king and queen, the wedding ceremony took place on 4 August 1915 in the Chapel Royal of St. James's Palace. Even though wartime custom restricted its size, the wedding became a major social occasion. Guests included such prominent American residents in Britain as Henry James and the painter John Singer Sargent, together with the prime minister and the foreign secretary. "Sir E. Grey was most serious & devout," reported Frank Page, who was best man, "but Asquith did nothing but take in every thing & everyone in the place every time anyone prayed."[65]

Page needed distraction during the second half of 1915. He faced the overriding, depressing facts of the war, submarine blockade, shipping cases, and America's failure to intervene. He also passed another milestone of advancing age, turning sixty on 15 August 1915. Fortunately, Page's health seemed to be holding up well. It may have been coincidence, but his big burst of letter writing to House came soon after his birthday, along with fresh stabs at diary keeping. If Page was seeing solace in literary activity, he had reason. At the end of October, a long-awaited blockade protest arrived—a typical Lansing production, fifty-five pages that alternated between copious legal citations and truculently worded accusations that the British were using the blockade as a cloak for advancing their own economic interests. The note understandably dismayed the ambassador, who had received no advance indication of its length, tone, and contents.

Page grew even more troubled when the submarine crisis erupted again in November and still failed to incite his country to action.

The end of 1915 found him at a new low. For the first time, his pessimism was coloring his attitude toward Wilson. "The truth, as it seems to me here and now," he noted in his diary at the middle of December, "is that after his brave notes to Germany about the *Lusitania*, the President lost a chance for leadership." If public outrage now forced Wilson to take the country to war, he would be acting "somewhat too late to get credit for courage." Page viewed the president's predicament slightly more charitably in a Christmas letter to his sons. "I don't know what the President cd have done differently," he wrote, "—unless, before he sent the *Lusitania* notes he had called Congress together and submitted his notes to Congress." But, as matters stood, Wilson could no longer take forceful action because the American people would not run the risk of war, "—or the Administration thinks they will not. . . ." Page closed sourly, "Mere notes break nobody's skin." The last part of 1915 had gone badly for the ambassador and the policies that he desperately wanted his country to follow. In view of Page's doubts about Wilson and mutterings about House, who was on his way to London, the beginning of 1916 promised to be no better.[66]

CHAPTER 10

The Trials of Diplomacy

The onset of the year 1916 found Walter Hines Page in a desperate mood. On 3 January he cabled Lansing: "We have now come to the parting of the ways. If English respect be worth preserving at all, it can be preserved only by immediate action." Nothing less than "immediate severing of relations with both Germany and Austria" could retrieve even a shred of regard in British eyes. Writing Wilson on 5 January, the same day that House landed in Britain, Page described Allied feelings "of disappointment verging on contempt" for America. All classes were united in believing that the United States would never fight. "A common nickname for Americans in the financial and newspaper districts of London is," he noted, "'too prouds.'" That observation, made to the man who had coined the luckless phrase "too proud to fight," hinted at how badly Page wanted to provoke his government to act.[1]

House's arrival brought no reassurance. The colonel saw the foreign secretary alone hours after reaching London, and he held extensive discussions with him and other British leaders during the next two weeks, mostly without the ambassador's knowledge. House explained to Wilson on 13 January that he had to "move with some circumspection" on diplomatic matters "that properly belong to Page's duties, but I take some chances trusting that I do not offend. Page has been exceedingly cordial and pleasant and has done what he could. He does not know, of course, the purpose of my visit or what I am discussing with Grey and Balfour." Whatever Page knew or suspected, he used House as the outlet for his pent-up wrath toward their government. On his second day in London, the colonel wrote in his diary that the ambassador was "full of the growing unpopularity of the President" and that he "questioned whether the President would ever take decisive action concerning the Lusitania and other matters." Page kept on, according to House, "harping upon the same subjects" and remained "as pessimistic as ever. It has become a punishment for me to be with him because he is so critical of the President, Lansing and our people generally." House departed on 20 January, to visit Paris and Berlin, not to return to London until the second week in February.[2]

The colonel's departure did not relieve the ambassador's desperation. Mounting pressures in Britain and from the other Allies for further tightening of the blockade worried Page. On 22 January he sent Lansing a long cable in which he maintained that the United States's response to the forthcoming blockade measures would determine both the outcome of the war and the shape of future world peace. Three days later, Grey summoned Page to the Foreign Office to discuss an informal proposal that had come from Lansing. The latter had suggested a "*modus vivendi*," whereby the Germans would moderate submarine attacks in exchange for the Allies' disarming merchant vessels. "I was obliged to tell him that I knew nothing about such proposals," the ambassador reported back to Washington. Page added that he had not seen Grey "so grave and disappointed" since the dark days of August 1914. In his own opinion, the *modus vivendi* threatened to alienate the Allies completely. "For me, these are the most anxious days we've had," Page told his daughter Katharine shortly afterward. The ambassador read the situation correctly. Wilson's handling of the submarine issue, House's mediation efforts, and Lansing's blockade policies steadily deepened Page's desperation. He faced a time of unceasing trial in which virtually all his remaining influence would wither away.[3]

Colonel House's return to London in February 1916 precipitated a confrontation. Calling at House's hotel half an hour after his arrival on Wednesday, 9 February, Page launched into a tirade against administration policies, particularly the *modus vivendi*, and the next day he resumed, House recorded, "his denunciation of the President and Lansing, and of the Administration in general." Page joked that the best thing to do with the State Department might be to fire everybody, tear the building down, and start over with a whole new staff housed in a tent on the grounds of the Washington Monument. "I did not argue with him," noted House. "One might as well argue with a petulant woman." Finally, on 14 February, the ambassador bared the depth of his disaffection. The big North Carolinian paced back and forth in the little Texan's hotel suite, damning Wilson as a coward and comparing him to Jefferson, who had submitted to unremitting abuse from foreign powers without going to war. House set down in his diary that Page "said that the President was simply not a man of action; that he was like Jefferson whom [*sic*] he said ran away from Richmond when he was Governor of Virginia because of his fear of the British. It was as much as I could do to contain myself. I sat still and quiet looking into the fire until he had relieved his mind."[4]

In part, as the colonel thought, the ambassador was just letting off steam. Despite the violence of his denunciations, Page had not lost all faith in Wilson. Yet his utterances did express more than a passing mood. His accusations revealed how much the two men's temperamental differences were driving them apart. At one point House recorded in his diary that Page blamed the lack of American belligerency on Wilson's "preaching the duty of personal neutrality," behind which lay both "a lack of leadership" and "a mortal dread of war and therefore a mortal dread of Germany." At bottom, then, the trouble sprang from Wilson's repression of straightforward, manly feeling. Those charges sounded once more like the fulminations of Roosevelt. The day before, Page had written in his own diary, "There is a feeling here (no doubt premature, at least) that as Roosevelt by his Bull Moose defection elected Wilson, Wilson by his war-timidity may now elect Roosevelt." Curiously, even closer to the ex-president's thinking was the ambassador's scornful comparison of Wilson to Jefferson. Page had become an unwitting Rooseveltian in the Wilsonian camp.[5]

The collision occasioned by House's return to London focused on the colonel's mediation plan. At his meeting with the ambassador on 9 February, the president's confidant also disclosed the aim of his mission to Europe. "I have told Page for the first time something of what we have in mind," House reported to Wilson, "and later I shall see that he is brought into the conferences when they broaden sufficiently. I think this is essential because too many now know it and if he should hear of it from anyone excepting me, his sensibilities would be hurt to such an extent that he might resign." The colonel's newfound solicitude for the ambassador's position stemmed less from friendship than from prudence. House was about to present a plan by which the United States would offer mediation to the belligerents and go to war on the Allied side if the Central Powers rejected the offer. On 13 February he and the foreign secretary drew up what came to be called the House-Grey Memorandum, under which Britain pledged to cooperate with a mediation initiative and the United States promised to intervene if that initiative failed. With such a diplomatic coup in the offing, the Texas colonel wanted to prevent the ambassador from making trouble.[6]

House's overture failed to win Page over. Although the ambassador at first raised no objections, on 11 February, when the colonel came to tea at the ambassador's house, his host took him aside, as House recorded in his diary, "to say that he thought it best for him not to take part in any peace talks that I might have with the Cabinet." The colonel did not try to dissuade him, "because it suited my purpose to have him remain out of the conference, since in his frame of mind he is a hindrance rather than a help." Page wrote in his own diary, "I told House that I couldn't go with him into any such conference, & I wouldn't." He dismissed the plan as "purely academic nonsensical stuff," which contained "the fatal moral weakness" of promising that "we shd plunge into the war, not on the merits of the case, but by a carefully sprung trick! . . . Of course such a morally weak, indirect scheme is doomed to failure—is wrong, in fact." The ambassador likewise warned the colonel that the British would spurn the project. House, he noted, "didn't seem surprised" at his refusal to take part in the negotiations.[7]

House's scheme ignited Page's long-simmering sense of estrangement. The ambassador began to contemplate resigning in protest. On 13 February he noted in his diary, "My mood is—not to mention House in any letter or dispatch to Washton [*sic*], lest I be misunderstood. I must stick by the job now lest the public conclude that House's coming caused my withdrawal as personal pique. But if House proposes to come again, I think I shall simply say—'Well, I go at once, then.'" Again, on 24 February, the day that House sailed for home, Page wrote in his diary, "He cannot come again or—I go." Nor did the ambassador confine his disparagements to the privacy of his diary. His daughter later recalled that he told Balfour that he had refused to have anything to do with the House-Grey Memorandum. When Hugh Wallace, a wealthy American friend of both House and Page, visited London shortly after the colonel's departure, the ambassador reiterated his determination to resign if the Texan returned. As soon as Wallace got back to the United States at the beginning of May 1916, he repeated the story to House, thereby making the alienation mutual.[8]

Page attempted to counteract House's activities with a move of his own. On 13 February the ambassador also noted in his diary, "House is doing a lot of harm here wh. I must somehow turn to good—e.g. make it accentuate the crisis as soon as he is gone." The preceding day he had outlined his thoughts in a memorandum entitled "A Programme," in which he called for an immediate break with Germany and economic reprisals. "This wd lead to actual war. We cd use our navy & begin to prepare an army and—save our souls." Deciding not to wait for House's departure, Page dispatched a cable on 15 February, in which he exhorted Wilson at once to sever relations and institute an embargo against the Central Powers. Those steps alone, avowed Page, would end the war with a speedy Allied victory. "This action moreover will settle the whole question of securing permanent peace." Cooperation between "the great English speaking peoples without any formal alliance will control the conditions of permanent peace." Only these strong, bold acts would suffice. "Longer delay or any other plan will bring us only a thankless, opulent and dangerous isolation." The southerner had taken his stand.[9]

Page showed the cable to House on 15 February, either before or after its transmission. " 'Do you agree with me?' " the ambassador recorded in his diary. " 'No.' 'Wherein do you differ?' 'Oh, I can't tell you now: it'll take a long time.' " Page called House's refusal to talk "mere spinelessness," scoffed at his "vain & silly talk about 'intervention,' " and reaffirmed, "The only effective thing to do is to create a situation—or to recognize a situation and fall in with it." The colonel recorded the conversation differently in his diary, noting that he called the cable "a fine literary effort. . . . It was a stirring message and I told him so. He asked what I thought the President would do. I thought it would have no effect as to the real purpose he desired, but it would probably make the President careful not to do some of the things against Great Britain which he was contemplating." Both men's descriptions of the encounter highlighted the basic divergence between them. The ambassador contrasted his own bluntness with the colonel's subterfuge. House stressed his instinct for power and influence as opposed to Page's quixotic gesturing and love of luminous phrases. The Texan and the Tar Heel were like the fox and the bear. One was prowling for promising openings to approach his objective. The other was squandering his last strength in futile, headlong rampage.[10]

Page assessed the situation in London correctly when he told House that the British were interested only in military victory. In March and May 1916, the leaders of Asquith's coalition government twice declined to act upon the House-Grey Memorandum. Each time they spurned mediation because they hoped to defeat the Central Powers in the field. House would have done better not to dismiss Page's warning so casually. The negotiations surrounding the House-Grey Memorandum formed a sorry chapter in both British and American diplomacy. As Arthur Link has shown, House's reports to Wilson misrepresented British receptivity to his proposals. The colonel also painted different pictures for the president and for the British about whether the main purpose of his scheme was to secure mediation or to create a pretext for the United States to enter the war. The British leaders reciprocated both by appearing more sympathetic than they really were and, some of them, by eavesdropping on House's communications. The later famous cable-tapping and cipher-cracking operation, "Room 40" of the Admiralty, headed by Captain William Reginald Hall, the director of naval intelligence, began listening in on the American embassy's wires at least as early as May 1915. Because of the extreme secrecy surrounding Hall's activities, it is not certain to whom the captain showed the interceptions of House's messages, but it is clear that Hall passed some interceptions along to strategically placed confidants in the government, in hopes of undercutting Grey's apparent encouragement of mediation. For once, Colonel House had met his match in deviousness.[11]

The ambassador remained happily unaware of the different forms of British dalliance with the president's confidant. Instead, his own stand heartened him to fresh activity. Maintaining outward cordiality toward House, Page lunched with him on 23 February, the day before the colonel's departure. "Page is in great good humor," House noted in his diary, "because he believes the United States will be at war within a month." The ambassador also resorted to new heights of indiscretion. Two days later, he showed a copy of his cable to Wilson to Sir Horace Plunkett. "I got permission to show it to Arthur Balfour only," Plunkett noted in his diary, "and I promised not to keep any copy of it. B. said he had never seen any such communication from an ambassador to his master." Page probably showed the cable to Grey as well, since the foreign secretary commented the same day that "Mr. Page, Colonel House and others had often told me that they thought a rupture with Germany inevitable." Page also transmitted his views back to the United States. During March and early April, he wrote long letters telling his brother Henry and son-in-law Charles Loring that their country must get into the war at once. Most important, the ambassador appears to have dropped hints about resigning. The financier J. P. Morgan, who was in London in February 1916, told Page that he hoped the envoy was not contemplating resignation. Upon returning to

America in March, House wrote, "I think all should stand by the ship until calmer weather whether we like it or not. I know this is your view too for I have heard you express it."[12]

But things seemed to look up for Page during most of March and April 1916. Wilson and Lansing bowed to the combined importunings of House, Page, and the British and withdrew the *modus vivendi*. Their change of face sparked a revolt on Capitol Hill by antiinterventionist Bryanite Democrats, whom Wilson routed with a bold assertion of party leadership and presidential prerogative in foreign affairs. Best of all from the ambassador's standpoint, the submarine controversy dramatically worsened. The English Channel steamer *Sussex* was torpedoed on 24 March, and four American passengers were injured. Wilson threatened to sever relations with Germany, and United States entry into the war appeared imminent. On the last day of March, Page told Benjamin Strong, the governor of the New York Federal Reserve Bank, that if the United States did not become a full-fledged partner of the Allies, "Then we sh'd be only half-in, so far as our safety is concerned." Writing to his son-in-law four days later, the ambassador urged establishment of a big army. He dismissed allegations about militarism as "lying nonsense" peddled by "Chautauqua-millenium, halo-crowned, angel-winged idiots. . . . I want a real army—to clean this crowd up. I'd hang old William J. for treason and hang his followers to the nearest lampposts and put up big electric signs at night—'Now we propose to become men!'" With his fighting blood up, the Tar Heel sounded more Rooseveltian than ever.[13]

Page's springtime hopes for American intervention suffered a severe letdown. Wilson's threat to break relations caused Germany to accede to his demands for modification and limitation of submarine warfare. The ambassador professed delight at the outcome. "The more I have thought of your last Note to Germany," he wrote to the president on 12 May, "the more admirable its content and especially its strategy appear. They are bagged." Page expected that the Germans would soon renege on their pledges. "If they begin submarine deviltry again," he told his daughter Katharine the next day, "then we can't parley: we've got to break. They will begin again—after they see they can't now make peace." Page accurately forecast what happened at the beginning of 1917, when the Germans resumed and intensified submarine attacks and the United States did go to war. But those events lay in the future. In the meantime, relations between Britain and the United States turned swiftly and unremittingly sour.[14]

Page, among others, had repeatedly warned the British that if the Germans ever relented over the submarine the Americans would unleash accumulated grievances against the Allied blockade. Those predictions came true after May 1916, and additional complications made matters even worse. One complication was the decline of Grey's power. Failing eyesight and ambivalence about war policies weakened the foreign secretary and his pro-American viewpoint within the successive Asquith governments. The rejection of the House-Grey Memorandum confirmed the ascendancy of the war hawks, who scorned concern about the United States. That rejection further worsened relations by disenchanting Wilson about British motives in fighting the war. The pro-American position also lost ground within the Foreign Office in connection with the declining influence of the British ambassador in Washington, Sir Cecil Spring Rice. Lansing, House, and Wilson all grew weary of Spring Rice's testy assertions of his country's positions. Contrarily, a group of hard-liners in the Foreign Office ridiculed the ambassador's repeated warnings of the danger of offending the United States. Finally, the Easter Rebellion in Ireland in April 1916, followed by brutal attempts at suppression, disillusioned large numbers of Americans with the British.

The downturn in relations opened for Page with familiar blockade issues. The British did not reply to Lansing's long note of the previous October until 24 April, when they merely rehashed well-worn defenses. In May Lansing shifted his protests to a particularly touchy new practice—British interdiction of mail to European neutral destinations. Even Page could not avoid annoyance with his hosts. "I begin to understand their stupidity and their arrogance," he wrote to House on 23 May. "If your enemies are such fools in psychological tactics and Heaven is with you, why take the trouble to be alert? and why be modest?" A week later he added to the colonel, "I have moods in which I lose my patience with them and I have put on two muzzles and a tight corset to hold myself in."[15]

Still, exasperation did not alter the ambassador's views or conduct. During the spring and summer of 1916, Page maintained the flow of letters to Wilson and House, constantly counseling patience and understanding toward the British. "Picture to yourself the state of mind in Washington during the three days' battle of Gettysburg," Page told House in July, as the battle of the Somme was exacting its enormous toll of British lives. A comparable state of mind held sway in London: "Nobody has any time or mind for anything but to help the battle along—that's the whole truth." Page likewise persisted in relaying his interventionist views homeward. At the end of May, he sent his partners at Doubleday, Page a twenty-three-page handwritten letter in which he spelled out his ideas about immediate entry into the war, full-fledged partnership with the Allies, and large-scale armament. "All the foregoing I have fired at the Great White Chief for a year by telegram and by mail," he concluded, "and I have never fired it anywhere else but now. *Be very quiet*, then." Page hardly kept quiet himself, since he repeated most of those arguments a month later in a long letter to Edwin Alderman.[16]

The British gave the ambassador almost no help in shoring up crumbling relations. In addition to the long-standing blockade controversies and the mails dispute, fresh incidents further inflamed ill feeling. One was a shipping case that seemed a throwback to the previous century. In April the British had stopped an American steamer, the *China*, in the Far East and removed fifty suspected German nationals. Thanks mainly to Page's vigorous representations, the British released the captives, after several delays. Worse resentment arose in July when the British government published a "Black List," barring eighty-seven American businesses accused of trafficking with the Central Powers from all dealings with British subjects and firms. At the same time, the Irish troubles spawned a special martyr in Sir Roger Casement, the former British colonial official who had been captured just after coming ashore from a German submarine during the Easter Rebellion. Despite widely held doubts about Casement's sanity and the fairness of his trial and a United States Senate resolution urging clemency, the British refused to commute his death sentence.

These incidents pained the ambassador. He informed Wilson on 21 July that Grey "becomes more and more rigid" and that shipping and mails disputes had come to be chiefly the responsibility of Lord Robert Cecil, the minister of blockade and second in command at the Foreign Office. Page liked the tall, homely, intellectual Cecil but admitted that he was less sympathetic to the United States than Grey used to be. "He smooths many little paths. The broad highways are sometimes too much for him." Page told both Grey and Cecil that the Black List was a blunder. Yet the ambassador remained most distressed over his country's attitudes. Page continued to insist that the stakes of Anglo-American unity outweighed minor, ephemeral disputes over such matters as trade, mail, or even Ireland. He condemned the 1916 rebellion as a stab in the back of Britain's war effort, and he lost any sympathy for Casement when Captain Hall confidentially arranged for him to get a copy of the prisoner's diaries, which contained evidence of homosexuality. Passing the Casement diaries on to the ambassador showed once more how the British appreciated and were willing to use him.[17]

Probably nothing bothered Page more during 1916 than knowing that his views of the war differed from those of so many of his countrymen. "I can't understand the violence of feeling in the minds of Americans of many sorts—of hostility to England," he wrote in his diary in January. The ambassador importuned journalist friends and former members of his staff to send reports about politics and reactions to war issues in the United States. Also, since the middle of 1915 his son Arthur had been writing weekly letters surveying the American scene. The disagreements over the war supplied a personal wrench for Page early in 1916. Prominent among the antiinterventionist congressional insurgents against Wilson was his brother Robert, who announced in March that he refused to run for reelection rather than condone warlike administration policies. The two brothers had apparently been aware of their divergence for some time. Walter Page told their brother Henry that he considered Robert's action "a great mistake. . . . But I have felt for several years that he had too kindly a feeling for, and lived too close to, certain yellow dogs in Washington—the most ignorant men of any race or nation or time in the history of the entire human race." Even brotherly affection did not soften his hostility toward those who wanted to keep America out of war.[18]

Other matters added to the strain on Page during the spring and summer of 1916. The embassy's work load continued to outstrip its manpower, notwithstanding additional staff. New personnel, in turn, further overcrowded the quarters in Grosvenor Gardens. Some relief came with the appointment in May of Hugh Gibson, a bouncy, efficient younger career officer, as chief of staff. Gibson's reorganizations helped apportion duties more equitably, although the basic problems of insufficient staff and inadequate facilities went unmet. Overwork was also beginning to sap morale, particularly because staff officers had no time for even brief holidays. Worse, the embassy shared the ambassador's reputation for pro-British sentiment. Several career officers believed that the State Department was discriminating against them in promotions and assignments.

Page occasionally got some respite from his worries, including a few golf games in the spring and a few days at Bournemouth at the end of May. Although his health remained good, the weather offered scant consolation, as the never overly warm English summer failed to appear. Page wrote to Wilson in July by a blazing fire, and he reported to the president that he purposely lingered before the fireplace in the foreign secretary's office to draw Grey into general conversations about "any sort of thing that is big and interesting." Unhappily, their liking for each other and common interest in such topics as the future solidarity of the English-speaking peoples and Wordsworth's poetry did not long dispel their gloom about their countries' relations.[19]

Page would have felt even gloomier if he had known how low his own stock was sinking in Washington. The changed diplomatic climate exposed his weakness and isolation. Lansing continued to suspect him of lukewarmness in arguing blockade cases. In June a memorandum from him to Counselor Polk noted that "Mr. Page has not perceived that any general principles are involved in Trade matters." Polk had little use for the ambassador, either. Discussing mediation ideas with House in May, he remarked, according to the colonel's diary, that he "thought it a pity that we did not have someone as ambassador in London who could help in the general plan we have in mind." Polk also informed House that Chandler Anderson, the department's legal officer, was urging the ambassador's removal. On 17 May Anderson told Lansing "that we were making a mistake in keeping Page in London; that he has no influence; that he knows no one other than Grey, and that we could accomplish nothing through him."[20]

The most damaging effect of Page's moves in February 1916 involved his relationship with the president. In May 1916 the confrontation the ambassador had fomented three months earlier backfired on him. Wilson had not reacted to Page's cable of 16 February, except to seek Lansing's assurance that it did not reflect House's opinion, too. Dismissing the call for war as a typical expression of the ambassador's viewpoint, the president evidently gave him little further thought until May. Then Wilson became totally disillusioned with Page, through House's intervention. On 4 May Hugh Wallace told House about Page's threat to resign if the colonel came on another mission. House exploded. "Page is the only one of our ambassadors who is under real obligations to me," he wrote in his diary. Inasmuch as he had engineered the North Carolinian's appointment and defended him "where I conscientiously could," the Texan thought at the least "he would quietly get out upon some pretext other than the real one." House decided to cover himself with Wilson. "I think I shall take it up with the President and let him decide what is best in the circumstances."[21]

On 10 May, after learning more about Page's attitude from Wallace and after discussing the ambassador with Polk, House wrote to Wilson. The colonel explained that he had detected "signs of discontent in Page" as early as a year before, but he brushed aside as unimportant "the annoyance I was subjected to" on both his missions. "But what does count is that we have in Page a cog that refuses to work smoothly in the machinery you have set in motion to bring about peace and a reconstruction of international law." The ambassador's dissent encompassed "your foreign policy and the administration of the State Department," and Page threatened to resign in protest over any further missions by House. The colonel professed to be sorry to bother the president with the matter, but he commented in closing that no other ambassadors in European capitals had taken offense at his activities. "I therefore believe this feeling is confined to London alone —where, indeed, I least expected it."[22]

House's argument hit the mark with Wilson. The president replied on 17 May that he found the letter "painful reading. . . . It lowers my opinion of the man immensely. I thought he was more capable of gratitude (I mean gratitude to you, of which he must know he owes a great deal) than that." Wilson added that "Lansing is so dissatisfied with Page's whole conduct of our dealings with the Foreign Office in London that he wants to bring him back for a vacation to get some American atmosphere in him again. What do you think?" "I do not think we need worry about Page," House responded. "If he comes home at once I believe we can straighten him out." The colonel added, however, "He [Page] may wish to remain after he comes home, for private reasons, and if he does, I would not dissuade him." The president made no further comment about the ambassador except to tell House in July, "I wish that I could bring Page back, as Secretary of Agriculture, for example, in place of Houston when Houston is promoted to some one or other of the many posts in which he is needed." Ironically, Wilson was contemplating moving Page to the job that the editor had first wanted—as a demotion. Clearly, the North Carolinian's influence in critical foreign relations was gone.[23]

The expedient of bringing Page home finally bore fruit when, after two months of pushing by Counselor Polk, Lansing cabled on 21 July to request Page's return for consultations. Not suspecting the reason for his recall, the ambassador leaped at the request. "Such a visit will be of infinite help to me," he wrote the president. During the week before he sailed on 3 August, Page had private talks with Bryce, Grey, and Asquith about the issues and general state of relations between their countries. He wanted to strengthen his hand for achieving the great results from the visit. "Three and a half years is a long time," he also told Wilson, "especially when two have been war years." Page was about to learn how long those years had been and how many changes they had brought.[24]

The ambassador's journey back to the United States went badly from the moment his ship landed in New York on the evening of Friday, 11 August 1916. In place of the chilly English weather, the Pages found the eastern United States sweltering under a heat wave. Third Assistant Secretary of State William Phillips came into the dockside quarantine area to confer with the ambassador before he met waiting family members and newspaper reporters. Probably under Phillips's prompting, Page declined to comment on relations with Britain, although he did quip, "You might as well ask me about the length of the millennium as to give an opinion on the length of the war." The discomforts of their arrival turned trivial in the face of a family tragedy that awaited the Pages. Their twenty-four-year-old daughter-in-law, Frank's wife, Katherine Sefton Page, had fallen dangerously ill with poliomyelitis. The ambassador and his wife rushed to Garden City, where the young couple lived, but Katherine died the following afternoon. Instead of going to Washington at once, as he had planned, the ambassador accompanied the rest of the family to Auburn, New York, for the funeral. "15 Aug," he noted in his address book. "Buried Katherine at Auburn—Poor Frank." The melancholy day was also Page's sixty-first birthday.[25]

Immediately after the funeral the ambassador left for Washington. Arriving in the capital late on Wednesday, 16 August, he began a frustrating two-week sojourn. Although the president invited him to lunch at the White House the day after his arrival, the meeting featured only small talk. "Not a word about England," Page noted in his diary. "Not a word about foreign policy or foreign relations." Wilson explained that a threatened nation-wide railroad strike was occupying all his attention. Page asked if he could "have a talk with him when his mind shd be free." The president replied by dropping a hint that the ambassador did not pick up. Did Page not want, Wilson asked, to go off and take a rest before conferring? "I preferred to do my minor errands with the Dp't," the ambassador responded. "But I shd hold myself at his convenience and his command." Running the errands and awaiting the president's command proved disheartening experiences.[26]

The State Department fulfilled Page's worst forebodings on all levels. The ambassador had not met Secretary Lansing before, and his initial impression was not encouraging. As Page waited in the anteroom for their first meeting, Lansing came out to answer reporters' questions with no more than an almost curt "Yes" or "No." Page wrote in his diary that the secretary seemed like "an amateur oracle," thoroughly lacking "the slightest touch of wholesome human nature." Inside his office, Lansing received Page courteously but "talked vague nothings." When the ambassador expressed pleasure at being home again, the secretary observed that he ought "to get a different atmosphere: we all need a change of atmosphere." Page wondered whether "this remark implied a criticism of me," but he concluded after further talk "that he did not mean it as a serious criticism but only as a sort of obvious remark." Page was wrong. Lansing, like Wilson, was hinting that the ambassador needed to get back in tune with American opinion. In both cases, however, Page had some reason for failing to catch their drift. The president did not see him again for nearly two weeks, while Lansing persistently avoided discussing substantive issues. During their first interview, which lasted an hour, only two of the secretary's remarks impressed the ambassador as "at all definite"; the rest consisted of "pleasant nothings. . . ."[27]

That initial conversation offered a foretaste of Page's other contacts with Lansing. By the ambassador's count, they met five more times over the next two weeks, at the State Department and at small social occasions. "All the rest of his talk was about 'cases,' " Page complained in his diary. One evening, "almost in despair," he recounted, "I rammed down him a sort of general statement about the situation as I saw it; at least I made a start. But soon he stopped me and ran off at a tangent on some historical statement I had made, showing his mind was not at all on the real subject, the large subject." Such behavior confirmed what Page had thought all along about Lansing. "A mere routine-clerk, law-book-precedent man," he fumed in a memorandum just after leaving Washington: "No grasp, no imagination, no constructive tendency or ability—measuring Armageddon, if he tries to measure it at all—with a 6-inch rule. . . . O God! What a crime and what a shame to have this manikin in that place now!" Lansing did not care for Page either. He later wrote in his memoirs that personal contact with the ambassador solidified his "conviction that it was useless to present protests and complaints through him." Lansing decided, therefore, to transfer shipping cases to the consul general in London, Robert Skinner, "who could be counted upon to do his duty, however unpleasant that duty might be, and to do it with tact and discretion."[28]

In one way, the antipathy between the ambassador and the secretary was ironic. No one else in the administration, not even House, came as close as Lansing to sharing Page's view of the war. Shortly after the ambassador's visit, the secretary set out his views in a memorandum in which he lamented the president's inability to perceive and "adopt the true policy, which is, 'Join the Allies as soon as possible and crush the German Autocrats.' " But it probably would not have helped if Page had recognized their common viewpoint. He and Lansing were antithetical in nearly every respect. Besides coming from dissimilar backgrounds, the two men did not look or act at all alike. The southern journalist's big frame, rumpled clothes, bald head, and scraggly moustache contrasted strikingly with the Yankee corporation lawyer's compact figure, dapper dress, silver hair, and immaculately trimmed moustache. The discrepancy between Page's outspoken informality and Lansing's closemouthed correctness betokened conflicting approaches toward their common goal of intervention on the Allied side. Lansing later claimed that his practice of arguing specific points of international law in long, detailed notes to Britain reflected a settled strategy of steering clear of larger controversies. The secretary also said that he feared that the ambassador's passionately pro-British posture might provoke the president in the opposite direction, making relations even worse. Lansing combined House's deviousness with Wilson's aloofness. Knowing him better would probably have made Page hate him more.[29]

The ambassador found dealing with others in the State Department and elsewhere in Washington equally unsatisfactory. His daughter-in-law's death from polio prevented Page from seeing Counselor Polk during his stay in Washington in August. Because "infantile paralysis" was considered primarily a child's disease, Polk left for his vacation without meeting with Page, for fear of transmitting infection to his young children. Spring Rice, the British ambassador, avoided Page in August for the same reason. The vacation season also meant that he could not discuss embassy administrative problems with William Phillips but had to deal instead with Assistant Secretary John E. Osborne, a dull-witted former political crony of Bryan's. Lansing sent Page to Capitol Hill to talk with senators and congressmen who had constituents with blockade grievances. Moreover, at a lunch at the Shoreham Hotel with several cabinet members, including Lansing and Daniels, Page heard only jokes, comments on the food, and "all sorts of silly commonplaces. Not a word was said to indicate that any man of thought sat at the table, hardly a word wh showed that anybody there knew that a war was going on."[30]

Page was like a front-line soldier home on furlough who found himself unable to relate to normal peacetime activities. Most officials were caught up, the ambassador recognized, in such domestic matters as the threatened railroad strike, the rush of legislation at the close of Congress, and the already-opened presidential campaign. But the president's and the secretary of state's shunning of Page reflected other considerations. His failure to take their hints showed that there was no gentle way to apprise him of their displeasure, and neither man liked personal conflict.

Something deep in Wilson's character, as Ray Stannard Baker first pointed out, made him shrink from face-to-face disagreement and controversy. That reluctance to engage in direct, inescapably emotional clashes may have been another manifestation of Wilson's need for self-control. Lansing's behavior sprang from the stiffness and pomposity that Page observed. The secretary never enjoyed relationships of equality, and he stood in an awkward position with the ambassador, who was not really his subordinate but, rather, the president's appointee and representative. Instead of locking horns with Page, Wilson and Lansing each tried to ignore him and his views in the vague hope that the American atmosphere would somehow inspire changes.[31]

Their treatment could scarcely have failed to register. "It wd be hard to forget these 2 weeks in Washton [sic] and their grave depressions," Page noted in his diary just after he left. "They called me home and then—skedaddled!" he wrote to House on 26 August. The same day he wrote to Alice, "I have found no man so far, except Houston, who has the slightest comprehension of our situation—not the slightest." Page had several long, satisfying talks with Houston, who criticized Wilson's solitary habits in running the government and his lack of social grace. The ambassador and his congressman brother apparently did not see each other. "I'm tired and hot," he also informed Alice on 26 August. Although he admitted that he had "little hope of any large good coming of my visit," he maintained that he was "not unhappy and hopeless in the long run." One reason for optimism remained. Page added to his wife, "Of course I have not yet talked with the President."[32]

The coveted chance came on Tuesday, 29 August, or so Page thought. He and William G. Sharp, the ambassador to France, who was also back on leave, received invitations to lunch at the White House with the president, his wife, and three of Wilson's spinster cousins, Helen Woodrow Bones and Lucy and Mary Smith. To Page's consternation, the conversation around the table proceeded in a light vein. There was no mention of international matters except for a brief monologue by Sharp, an Ohio manufacturer and big Democratic campaign contributor, who repeatedly affirmed, "Not one jot or tittle of criticism of the U.S. in France!" Two of Wilson's cousins remembered afterward that the president had asked them beforehand to avoid any discussion of foreign policy in front of Page. After lunch the party drove to the Capitol, where the president addressed a joint session of Congress on the impending railroad strike. Following the address, Page rode with the women, but not Wilson, back to the White House, where he learned that the president had already returned. "Does he expect me to go in and say goodbye?" the ambassador asked a doorman. The answer was, "No." Recognition finally dawned. "Thus he had no idea of talking w. me now, if ever," Page wrote in his diary the next day. "Not at lunch nor after did he suggest a conversation about American-English affairs or say anything about my seeing him again." Though the weather was hot, the ambassador was out in the cold.[33]

Page left Washington the following day in a rage. He must have brooded about his experiences all during the seven-hour train ride to New York and probably the night before as well. When he reached New York he discharged his fury, characteristically, by writing. On the stationery of a Manhattan hotel Page set down the first two pages of a fragmentary account of his stay in the capital, entitled "About Washton," in which he not only recounted his infuriating encounters with the president, secretary of state, and other officials but also laid blame for the situation squarely on Wilson. Firsthand observation of his old acquaintance confirmed Page's earlier suspicions. Wilson's insistence upon "personal neutrality" had stifled healthy popular reactions to the war, thereby leaving the masses "at their intellectual and moral ease—softened, isolated, lulled. That wasn't leadership in a democracy. Right here is the Prest's [sic] vast failure." Page harped on the president's lack of "social sense" and associating with "family connexions only" because those traits bore out his long-standing fear about Wilson's solitary habits depriving him of contact with vigorous people and fresh ideas. Page was determined to administer a dose of both. The afternoon after the White House lunch he wrote Alice, "I am simply waiting for the President. I can wait as long as he can."[34]

Page spent the next two and a half weeks at his son Arthur's on Long Island. He caught up with book and magazine publishing by going over to the Doubleday, Page offices in Garden City and by taking a short trip to Boston, where he talked with Mifflin and the current *Atlantic* editor, Ellery Sedgwick. But his chief concern lay with cornering the president. Burton Hendrick, *World's Work*'s managing editor, remembered Page vowing that he "was going to see Wilson if he had to sit on the curbstone until morning." Page also tried to get in touch with House. The trip to Boston seems to have been a ruse to smoke out the elusive colonel, who spent his summers nearby on the North Shore. Although House kept putting off another confrontation with Page, he played no overt part in the official cold shoulder. When he heard about the ambassador's reception, he wrote in his diary, "I think the President is wrong in not seeing Page for he should get his point of view, contrary to his own though it may be." Soon afterward, when James W. Gerard, the ambassador to Germany, returned to Washington, the colonel noted in his diary that he was taking steps to insure that Gerard did not "have any such experiences as Walter Page had." House finally consented to meet his former cohort in New York around the middle of September.[35]

Page did not wait idly. Besides his other activities, he occupied himself, as usual, with writing. Relations with Britain had taken a fresh turn for the worse when Congress, with Wilson's backing, enacted retaliatory legislation. The new laws empowered the president to shut off exports and deny port facilities to any nation that unlawfully discriminated against American businesses or interfered with trade with other countries—unmistakable slaps at the Black List and blockade. Page responded to this development by writing notes to himself, sometimes in Greek script, about "Relations, U.S. and G.B. and suggestions for improvement," and "Ask P. to give me a week's notice of any retaliatory proclamation he may have in his mind to make," and "Give final scotch to peace ideas." Other memoranda dwelled on the lack of vision in Washington. Page also started a letter to Laughlin in which he showed that renewed personal contact with Wilson had further exposed their temperamental gulf. "He is surrounded by the feminine Boneses and Smiths," wrote the ambassador. "The men about him (and he sees them only 'on business') are nearly all very, very small fry, or worse, the narrowest twopenny lot I've ever run across. He has no real companions. Nobody talks to him freely and frankly."[36]

Writing offered solace from frustration, and the descriptions of the stay in Washington also demonstrated that Page remained alive to the literary potential in his experiences. Later, probably on shipboard going back to Britain, he sketched an outline of the trip and noted, "Make the narrative of my visit home." Yet his main purpose in putting pen to paper was to affect events. On 14 September Page produced a fourteen-page handwritten essay entitled "Notes towards an Explanation of the British Feeling towards the United States." The "Notes," which he intended for Wilson, rehashed his familiar points about the quarrelsome impression left by blockade protests, the misunderstandings fostered by House's missions, and suspicions of pro-German influences. One remedy might be, he suggested, to send a high State Department official, preferably Frank Polk, to Britain to discuss differences. Above all, Page once more implored the president not to allow "trivial trade disputes" to overshadow "the great vision of the triumph of international good will and of democracy." The southerner was still trying to sway his old acquaintance with epistolary eloquence. Unfortunately, he had said nearly all those things many times before, and the two men's mutually held illusions of intimacy had long since evaporated.[37]

Prospects appeared to improve when a summons arrived for a meeting in Washington on Sunday, 17 September. Before the ambassador could reach the capital, however, he learned that the president had gone to Columbia, South Carolina, because of the death of his sister. Page partially retrieved the journey by getting together with Spring Rice and Sir Richard Crawford, the British embassy's financial expert. The two Englishmen warned him of the gravity of the retaliatory measures, and he told them about how much damage the Black List had done. After making a flying visit to North Carolina, Page stopped in Washington again for a meeting at last with Counselor Polk, who proved to be the first person in the department willing to speak frankly with him. "He and I spent many hours together," Polk informed House, "and I think before he left Washington, he modified his views." Whether the ambassador changed his views or not, the counselor's hard-hitting rebuttals of his arguments did impress upon him the depth of disaffection with Britain. But Page still wanted to see Wilson. On 21 September he sent the president accounts of his conversations with Grey and Bryce. He said that he also had "a most important and confidential message for you from the British Government which they prefer should be orally delivered." That message evidently induced Wilson to relent. A telegram went to Page inviting him to come to Shadow Lawn, the New Jersey seaside estate where Wilson was spending the duration of the campaign, to stay overnight on Friday, 22 September.[38]

Page arrived at Shadow Lawn late in the evening because a wreck on the line had delayed his train. He did not confer with the president until the next day, Saturday, 23 September. The two men spent the entire morning together, in what Wilson described to Lansing as "a talk of the most explicit kind." Page's opportunity for an extended, frank discussion had finally come, but he hardly got what he craved. The only account of the encounter is several pages of notes that Page scrawled in pencil in his address book, and the account has the curious feature of telling only what Wilson said. Page left no record of his side of the conversation. The ambassador referred to the meeting just once afterward, when he recalled in his diary the following March what the president had said about the causes of the war. It seems odd that Page's literary instinct should have failed him on this of all occasions. He knew that he had come to one of the most dramatic moments of his life. He sat facing his acquaintance of three decades, the strong-jawed fellow southerner whose magnificent career he had witnessed and helped further. They were debating issues that could decide the course of world history. If any experience ever promised to repay Page's belief that great events produced great literature, this was it. Yet he let it slip by.[39]

Page's reticence in describing the encounter probably stemmed from a mixture of fidelity, dismay, and chagrin. He may have recorded only Wilson's side of the discussion because Wilson did most of the talking. The notes depicted the president delivering a stern lecture on the ways in which the Allies had sacrificed American sympathy through their arrogance and high-handedness. Wilson's technique for fending off potentially unpleasant encounters was to seize the conversational initiative, deliver an overwhelming argument, and permit the other person to say little, if anything. Wilson told Lansing the following week, "I covered the whole subject matter in a way which I am sure left nothing to be desired in the way of explicitness or firmness of tone." The president likewise shocked the ambassador by stating that the war sprang from "many causes—some of long origin. He spoke of England's having the earth, of Germany's wanting it." This was the point to which Page later returned in his diary, where he recalled that Wilson viewed the war as "a quarrel to settle economic rivalries between Germany & England. He said to me last Sep. that there were many causes by [which] Germany went to war. He showed a great deal of toleration of Germany; and he was, during the whole morning I talked with him, complaining of England." When Page passed along his urgent "private message" that the British would reject any American collusion in a German request for an armistice, Wilson replied, "If an armistice, no, that's a military matter & none of my business. If it be a proposal looking towards peace,—yes, I shall be glad." The ambassador may have fallen silent out of numbness at the realization of how far he and the president had drifted apart.[40]

Page did elicit a promise from Wilson not to invoke the retaliatory legislation until after the election. "But he hinted that if there were continued provocation afterwards (in case he were elected) he would. One of the worst provocations was the long English delay in answering our Notes. Was this delay due to fear or shame?" In the face of Wilson's ire, Page may have decided that he could present his case more effectively through his essay, which he handed over during the interview. Not saying much would also have reflected Page's preference for avoiding personal clashes and his ability to submit to criticism. The encounter with

Wilson may have left Page doubly chagrined. At the time, he received tough criticism from the man whom he had once hero-worshiped. Later, he could recall his own timidity in not standing up to what he regarded as perniciously false arguments. By either light, his part in the encounter would not be something that he would care to write about. The scribbled notes in the address book may have embodied not Page's literary yearnings but his irrepressible journalistic yen for getting a story.[41]

When the president and the ambassador finished their conference, they went to lunch. Colonel House was waiting for them and the three men sat down at the table together. "The conversation was general and unimportant during the meal," the colonel wrote in his diary, "and Page left . . . shortly afterward." A little more transpired. House, whom Page was seeing for the first time on the trip, arranged to meet him two days later in New York. Also, according to one story, Page placed his hand on Wilson's shoulder as he said good-bye, and the president's eyes filled with tears. The story sounds apocryphal because neither man was given to demonstrations of sentiment. But the occasion probably did have a valedictory undertone. It was exactly thirty-four years and one day since the two southerners had first met and talked. Neither of them could help realizing that they had broken irrevocably, in spite of so much that they had formerly had in common. No matter what the future brought, they would almost certainly have no further momentous, face-to-face encounters like the one that had just ended. In fact, Page and Wilson would never see each other again, although they could not know that then. Yet they must have realized, even without gestures or tears, that their once illustrious relationship was over.[42]

The encounter made an impact. For the ambassador, the president's remarks deepened his appreciation of the bitterness toward the British and the tensions in Anglo-American relations. Wilson gauged accurately when he assured Lansing that Page "will be able to convey to the powers that be in London a very clear impression of the lamentable and dangerous mistakes they are making." Page also came away from the interview with sympathy for Wilson. "I think he is the loneliest man I have ever known," he reportedly told his son Frank. The ambassador contributed a small amount of money to the president's reelection campaign despite reservations about the Democrats' domestic policies. For a while he also moderated his private criticisms of Wilson's leadership. For the president, the interview seems to have implanted fresh doubts about the ambassador's loyalty, since ideas of replacing him would soon arise again.[43]

Most important, however, Page's visit to Shadow Lawn did gain a hearing for his views. Wilson and House spent the following morning, 24 September, as the colonel recorded, "going over foreign affairs, principally our differences with Great Britain. Page had left a mass of memoranda which the President read aloud." The ambassador's arguments apparently swayed House a bit. Although the colonel suggested that the root of Britain's irritation could be traced to the recent American decision to build a larger navy, he was shaken when the president replied, "Let us build a bigger navy than her's [sic] and do what we please." House tried to remind Wilson that naval rivalry with the Germans had pushed the British into the war. "I thought their alliance with France, Russia, Italy and Japan would make them a formidable antagonist, provided the Allies won," he added. "We came to no conclusion for lunch was served and the conversation was discontinued." House was not having an altogether easy time with Wilson, either.[44]

Page stayed in the United States another week after the meeting at Shadow Lawn, sailing for Britain the following Saturday, 30 September. He crammed a number of activities into that final week, including a long talk with House, which did nothing to alter Page's position but did deepen his appreciation of the perilous condition of relations with Britain, and a final unsatisfactory interview with Lansing. A few pleasanter matters also occupied Page during his last week in America. The night before his departure, a group of old friends from publishing circles and the Southern Education Board put on a testimonial dinner at the University Club, at which they presented Page with the fund they had subscribed for his portrait. Even there, the ambassador's main concern intruded. "I informally outlined the necessity of

WALTER HINES PAGE,
*United States ambassador to the Court of St. James's, 1917,
portrait by P. A. Laszlo*

*(by permission of the Division of Archives and History,
Raleigh, North Carolina)*

TO THE GLORY OF GOD
AND IN MEMORY OF
WALTER HINES PAGE
1855-1918
AMBASSADOR
OF THE UNITED STATES
OF AMERICA TO THE
COURT OF ST. JAMES'S
1913-1918
The friend of Britain in her
sorest need.

TABLET COMMEMORATING WALTER HINES PAGE,
in Westminster Abbey

(by permission of Dean and Chapter of Westminster)

sympathetic understanding between G.B. & the U.S.," he wrote in his diary. " . . . Buttrick & Rose informed me that they had never been so stirred in their lives."[45]

The return voyage to Britain was probably the best part of the trip for Page, although it too had bad moments. On the morning of 30 September, House came down to the dock to see the Pages off. The ambassador begged the colonel in parting to use his influence against any invocation of the retaliatory measures. House also recorded in his diary that Page "asked me why I had not written him more frequently, and I replied it was because he had not written me." The other great relationship between southerners had likewise disintegrated beyond repair. Accompanied by Arthur, the Pages spent nine days in a stormy Atlantic crossing. The ambassador kept to his stateroom, attacking what Alice called "an enormous amount of work." His labors most likely included writing some of the descriptions of the visit and the memoranda that went into his diary. When their ship entered the harbor of Liverpool on the night of 8 October, the total blackout of the city disconcerted Arthur Page. On the train to London the next morning, the Pages grew infuriated when they read a newspaper story of a campaign speech in which Wilson had publicly aired his belief that the causes of the war were "obscure." But the arrival at Euston Station cheered them up again, since most of the embassy staff were waiting on the platform to welcome them back. The ambassador's return to London on 9 October was the truest homecoming that he experienced in 1916.[46]

The joy of getting back faded overnight. The day after his arrival in London, 10 October 1916, Ambassador Page went to see the foreign secretary, who had been elevated during the summer to the peerage as Viscount Grey of Fallodon. Their interview must have made Page feel as if he had never left, since they immediately found themselves at loggerheads over the Black List. Lord Grey also opened his first official discussion with the ambassador about German submarines by protesting American recent actions in allowing the new long-range undersea warship, the *U-53*, to put into port at Newport, Rhode Island. That discussion introduced the subjects and the tenor of the relations that the ambassador had to conduct over the next four months. Abolition of the Black List became Page's foremost cause. When he paid a courtesy call at Buckingham Palace soon after his return, King George mentioned that the foreign secretary "has told me of the earnest remarks you made to him on this subject." The ambassador responded, "I wonder, Sir, if Lord Grey repeated to your Majesty all that I told him." Laughing, the king replied, "Quite enough, I assure you, to make your meaning clear." Despite Page's repeated requests, nothing came of his suggestion to send Polk over to discuss the Black List, but the ambassador's efforts apparently moved the British to reconsider the matter in January 1917, just before the renewed submarine crisis rendered the subject moot.[47]

Page must also have wondered many times whether he had been right to come back from the United States. Ever since House's visit to London the previous February he had been talking about either resignation or retirement at the end of Wilson's first term, on 4 March 1917. During the spring of 1916 the apparently excellent prospects of American entry into the war had ruled out any dramatic departure, but Page had nevertheless resolved to retire. "Three of my four years are gone," he had told his business partners in May, "and the fourth will quickly pass." Imminent retirement had evidently enabled him to put up with his myriad frustrations during the summer and fall of 1916. "We wish to come home March 4 at midnight and go about our proper business," Page had written Alice from Washington even before the fiasco of lunch at the White House. "There's nothing here that I wd for the world be mixed up with." After the president had snubbed him in Washington and revealed the irreconcilability of their views at Shadow Lawn, the ambassador could easily have decided to resign at once, as House had half expected him to do. But he had once more swallowed pride, accepted disappointment, and returned to his post.[48]

Page explained why he went back in the memorandum that he wrote, most likely on shipboard, about Wilson's leadership.

"Why do I support the P. since I hold this opinion of his forn [*sic*] policy?" he asked. "Because I have confidence in Mr. W., his aims & character, because I agree with his general political philosophy, because I hold it the better course to remain loyal to him & to do all I can to change his view, because, having won the confidence of the English, I may use whatever influence I have to keep the international situation tolerable, & because I have no good reasons for confidence in the wisdom of the opposite party —especially as regards domestic policy." He could serve his country best, he concluded, "by making the most of a difficult task." That statement disclosed elements of dutifulness and practicality in Page's conception of his ambassadorship. His meeting with the president had also, temporarily, rekindled his personal admiration.[49]

The memorandum likewise pointed toward broader aspects of Page's thinking. As his frequent allusions to "loyalty" and "dignity" suggested, a resignation in protest had never been a real possibility after the initial threats during House's mission. For such a resignation to have had an impact, Page would have had to speak out. To leave that way would have been, as House had shrewdly though unnecessarily reminded him in March 1916, to imitate Bryan's reviled example. Wilson thought Page capable of doing such a thing. "He expressed the opinion that Page would come home disgruntled and show his true state of mind through the pages of the *World's Work*," House recorded in his diary in January 1917. "I did not believe he would do this as there would be no excuse for such action." The colonel knew his man.[50]

Retirement was another matter, and it did not preclude lingering hopes of having some influence. Immediately after Wilson won his narrow reelection victory on 7 November, Page wrote him another long, carefully drafted letter in which he not only announced his desire to step down but also again urged American intervention on the Allied side. Appealing to the "Liberal idea," the ambassador argued that "only autocracies wage aggressive wars" and that the spread of democracy would eliminate militarism and conquest. By intervening now, Wilson could serve that end quickly and easily. "The United States would stand, as no other nation has ever stood in the world—predominant and unselfish—on the highest ideals ever reached in human government. It is a vision as splendid as the Holy Grail [*sic*]." That appeal to Wilson's idealism and vanity would hardly have swayed the president, even if he had read it. As House discovered shortly afterward, the letter remained unread among others from the ambassador. Not surprisingly perhaps, Page's impassioned appeal for intervention undermined his request to retire, since both the colonel and Mrs. Wilson, who also read the letter, believed that the ambassador really wanted to be asked to stay on.[51]

House and Mrs. Wilson were partially correct. The ambassador, and his wife even more so, sincerely wished to flee the strain and depression of wartime London. "The gloom deepens steadily," Page wrote his daughter Katharine on New Year's Day 1917. Yet the ambassador told his son Frank at the middle of December that if Wilson asked him to remain for a while longer, "I couldn't decently refuse such a request." Two weeks later Page reminded Wilson of his wish to retire, adding that he would be happy to stay a few months more "in wh time the war may end—a circumstance that might make my successor's induction somewhat easier." To Lansing in January 1917 he indicated his willingness to serve until the end of the war. When Lansing cabled on 5 February asking him not to leave for the time being, Page at once replied that he would stay for the duration of the war. In his diary he explained these offers to remain at his post as manifestations of "my loyalty to the President and to this job and my fundamental objection to being regarded as a 'quitter.' "[52]

Desire as well as duty moved Page. For one thing, the ambassador was unsure about what he would do back home. "I don't especially care for Garden City," he had confided to Arthur the previous March. " . . . I guess I'll have to do an old man's work at the Press for some years." Where his heart lay he had made plain in May 1916. "I begin today a fuller and more formal diary than I have hitherto kept," he had written then. "For whenever the war may end, the larger forces wh. will end it are now clearly seen, and the great dramatic events wh. will lead up to the end are probably already beginning to happen." Like Page's earlier diary-keeping resolutions, that one went astray, except during the visit home. With the new peace moves in December, however, the ambassador made his most assiduous effort yet at recording his experiences. Moreover, rumors were rife in January 1917 about still more peace overtures and renewed submarine warfare. The war appeared at last to be approaching a climax, and the ever-aspiring literary southerner did not want to give up his ringside seat.[53]

It was one thing for Page to want to stay on and something else for Wilson to keep him, especially now that House was conniving against him. After May 1916 the Texan treated his onetime friend with a contradictory mixture of sympathy and spite. Sometimes the colonel stuck up for the ambassador, such as when he noted in his diary in May that Chandler Anderson's charges against Page were "prejudiced" and "not true." House regarded Page as "clean, able and honest, and he may be right in his views, but they are not the President's view—hence the trouble." The fox, it seemed, felt a sneaking admiration for the bear's straightforwardness. Yet the colonel sought to undermine the ambassador. Also in May he suggested to Wilson that Cleveland Dodge might be a good replacement for Page. Besides friendship with Wilson and House, Dodge's only qualification for the post was wealth, but that did not bother the colonel. "He is loyal and has good sense," House told Wilson, "and that is all you want in an Ambassador." During the summer of 1916 House took to ridiculing Page behind his back with Clifford Carver. The pair dubbed the ambassador "P. O. P."—"Poor Old Page." When Page came back in August, House joked to Carver, "I am surprised to see you running away so soon after P. O. P. arrives." The colonel knew a lot about being a small man.[54]

Although dislike of the official cold shoulder toward Page on his visit home and meeting with the Tar Heel briefly revived the Texan's sympathy, he soon struck an even harder blow at the ambassador. At the middle of November 1916, in their first meeting after the election, House gave Wilson "some idea of

Page's feeling toward him." He characterized the ambassador's opinions as respect for the president's ability coupled with the belief that "he would not fight under any circumstances. In this he classed him with Jefferson. The President naturally was not pleased with Page's view of him, although he did not resent it." Wilson raised different possibilities for handling Page, including the ambassador's recall. "He declared that no man must stand in his way."[55]

For once, in undermining Page House nearly outfoxed himself. On 27 November he and Wilson again considered the ambassador in relation to the major mediation overture that they were planning. The president insisted that the colonel be present in London when the peace initiative took place. House demurred, arguing that his appearance might prompt Page's resignation. Wilson replied that he "felt quite content to have him resign in any way he would." House rejoined that Page's resignation in protest could hurt the mediation effort, "but I did not convince the President that it was a serious obstacle." The colonel did not want to remove himself from the scene, and he was using the ambassador's sensibilities as an excuse. Finally, on 1 December, probably at House's urging, Lansing dissuaded Wilson from sending the colonel.[56]

The question of Page's future came up once more when House was in Washington on 14 December and he discussed the ambassador's postelection offer to retire with the president and Mrs. Wilson. The colonel now suggested Thomas Jones, an old Princeton friend of Wilson's, and Hugh Wallace as possible replacements for Page. House again nearly overplayed his hand. Neither Jones nor Wallace had much to recommend him for the post except, like Cleveland Dodge, friendship with Wilson, wealth, and big campaign contributions. Wilson reminded House that Jones's appointment to the Federal Reserve Board had earlier been rejected by the Senate; Wallace struck him as an intellectual lightweight. Some years later House recalled, "I almost lost the confidence of Woodrow Wilson in pushing Wallace's claim for recognition upon him."[57]

Another influence also imperiled the colonel's intrigues. Edith

Bolling Wilson, the president's second wife, never liked the little Texan. On 3 January 1917, when House was once more visiting the White House, Mrs. Wilson suggested to the colonel in front of her husband that he go to London as Page's replacement. House had to talk fast to squelch the idea. He argued that becoming ambassador "would confine my activities to Great Britain" and thereby limit his usefulness in dealing with all the belligerents. The next day Wilson mentioned Dodge as a possibility for the London embassy. He subsequently told House several times during January, "that he intended to accept his [Page's] resignation."[58]

The ambassador had an inkling that he might be on the way out. "Of course I know that there are influences about the President (and perhaps even the President himself) that does [sic] not want a man here who tells him the whole truth," he wrote his son Frank in December. Page received no response from Wilson to either his original suggestion about retirement or a reminder to the president at the end of December. Finally, he wrote in desperation to Lansing at the middle of January, "It is now imperative that I know your mind and his." When Lansing raised the question, Wilson responded on 31 January, "It is a shame for me to have treated Page this way. The truth is, I have not known what course to pursue, whether it was best to retain him until the end of the war or let him retire now. What is your advice?" Lansing evidently recommended keeping Page, at least for a while, since he cabled the ambassador on 5 February that the president wanted him to stay on "at the present time."[59]

That did not close the question, however. The next day, 6 February, Wilson wrote to offer Dodge the ambassadorship, not immediately but at some future date. Dodge declined two days later, pleading ill health and lack of qualification, and offered to send more money to Page. House continued suggesting names until the end of March 1917, when Wilson stopped him by saying that " 'in a misguided moment,' he had told Page he could continue and he supposed 'we would be compelled to have a British American representing the United States at the Court of St. James'. One reason he gave for having told Page was that he could not find a suitable man to take his place."[60]

The whole consideration of replacing Page had an air of unreality. Wilson's dissatisfaction with him was understandable and justified. But he scarcely exerted himself to remove Page and usually only under House's prodding. He finally wound up allowing a man whom he mistrusted to remain as the nation's most important diplomatic representative because replacing him seemed inconvenient. It is hard to escape the conclusion that Wilson did not greatly care whether Page stayed or went. Nor, after a certain point, did House. The collapse of Page's influence, together with Spring Rice's parallel though somewhat different decline, had obviously created a dangerous situation in Anglo-American relations. Yet the lack of effective ambassadors enhanced the importance of House, who continued to develop special channels of communication with London. In December 1916 a junior British army officer on secret service assignment in America, Captain Sir William Wiseman, was assigned to act as a contact with House and to relay messages between the colonel and the foreign secretary. A fast friendship soon formed between House and Wiseman, with the familiar overtones of boyish conspiracy in managing great events. Their connection became the truly effective diplomatic link between Britain and the United States for the duration of the war. With matters thus composed, House became less interested in getting rid of Page, although he did deliver one last blow in February or March 1917, when he convinced Dodge to stop subsidizing the ambassador. The Texan knowingly hit the Tar Heel in his most sensitive spot—his pocketbook.

The prolonged uncertainty about whether he would remain as ambassador only deepened Page's gloom during the closing months of 1916. The Allied position grew shakier as the stalemate persisted on the western front, Russia neared collapse, and Italy showed signs of weakness. For Britain, the worst signs were mounting ship losses to the submarines, coupled with the growing likelihood that Germany would shortly launch an all-out undersea campaign, and the chilling discovery that British financial resources in the United States, upon which the whole Allied war effort depended, were nearing exhaustion. Those developments contributed to the mood of doubt and reappraisal in which Asquith's ministry fell at the beginning of December 1916. As before, Page noted almost none of the signs of Allied faltering or British internal division. Rather, he cheered Asquith's fall and the emergence of Lloyd George as prime minister of the new hardline War Cabinet, even though he regretted Grey's departure as foreign secretary. "To me, the new Government seems to promise well—very well," Page exulted to Wilson. "There's a snap about it that the old Government lacked."[61]

That gleam of hope swiftly paled, however, in the face of what the ambassador regarded as the most disheartening turn of all. At the middle of December 1916, Wilson fulfilled Page's worst fears that the United States might collaborate with Germany in an attempt to force unacceptable peace terms on the Allies. First, the United States relayed a German overture toward peace discussions, and Page had to perform the unpleasant task of presenting the German note to the British. Because Balfour, who had succeeded Grey as foreign secretary, was sick during much of December, Page dealt with Lord Robert Cecil, who had remained as second in command at the Foreign Office. The two tall, thin, homely men got the negotiations off to a decent start. The ambassador showed Cecil a rough draft of the German note the night before he formally presented the document on 18 December. They discussed the situation the following day. According to Cecil's record, Page called the German note "an offer to buy a pig in a poke," but he warned strongly against any impulses to brush the overture aside derisively. He also assured Cecil that any American peace note that might be forthcoming could not "be much more than a pious aspiration for peace; since that was the only thing that was equally applicable to the Germans and to us."[62]

Page must have felt humiliated the next afternoon, 20 December. His country's peace note, which he presented, not only called for the belligerents to state their peace terms, but it also observed that the aims of the warring nations "seem the same on both sides." That phrase in particular drew jeers from the British press and pro-Allied Americans when the note was published on 21 December. When Page presented the note, according to Cecil, he explained that he had not expected such a development. The ambassador added that President Wilson held mediation "very much at heart; that he was an idealist by temperament; and that this move of his, whether wise or not, was certainly dictated by the purest sentiment of humanity." Reporting to Lansing, Page feared that the note "will for a long time cause deep, even if silent resentment." On the morning of 26 December, the ambassador had to face vocal resentment from Cecil, who "talked at length personally," Page reported, expressing sorrow and anger at the American attitude. Page responded by telling him, Cecil recorded, that on his visit home he had been shocked to discover that Americans "did not seem to appreciate what the German really was, or that Prussian militarism was, as he put it, 'an organised crime.' Somehow or other, though facts crossed the Atlantic the spirit of the war did not." But, the ambassador reiterated sadly, most of his countrymen, even "men of the highest education and knowledge, had never really understood what was happening." The indiscretion and distaste of Page's remarks ironically helped convey the spirit behind the peace note.[63]

Despite his unhappiness with the mediation effort, Page behaved far more loyally than either of the two men closest to Wilson. Lansing made two attempts to subvert the move. On 20 and 21 December he assured the British and French ambassadors that Wilson was actually maneuvering to enter the war on the Allied side. Also on 21 December he told newspaper reporters, "Neither the President nor myself regard [*sic*] this note as a peace note. . . . We are drawing nearer the verge of war ourselves." Wilson ordered Lansing to issue an immediate retraction, and a flurry of clarifying statements poured out of the State Department and the White House, in an effort to repair the damage caused by Lansing's remarks. House moved more stealthily. On 20 and 22 December he talked privately with Sir Horace Plunkett, who was in New York. As Plunkett related to Balfour, House assured him that the peace note was a ploy aimed at "restraining the German submarine policy; and that if this restraint were removed England would not be able to hold out long enough for American assistance to become effective. House is very definite that this is the most serious consideration which makes the President hesitate to take up a strong attitude toward Germany." The colonel also had Plunkett use his new communication link through Sir William Wiseman to cable Cecil on 22 December, conveying House's assurance "that the attitude of the Administration towards Britain has not changed from that which he explained to Balfour in February." It was ironic that at the end of December 1916 Wilson was contemplating getting rid of the one honest man among his top diplomatic agents.[64]

The different impact upon the British of Lansing's, House's, and Page's representations contained poetic justice. Neither Lansing's public and private statements nor House's communications through Plunkett attracted a great deal of attention in London. Their efforts to mislead the British about the intentions behind the peace note stood little chance of success, anyway, since the prime minister and the foreign secretary were receiving interceptions of the cable traffic between Washington and Berlin. Page's remarks, by contrast, got an important hearing. The War Cabinet convened at Number 10 Downing Street to consider a reply to the American note on the morning of 26 December, immediately after the ambassador's conversation with Cecil. Substituting for Balfour at the meeting, Cecil recounted that Page "had urged the desirability of complete frankness" toward the United States, and he repeated the ambassador's observations on Americans' "very limited appreciation of what was involved in the war." The minutes noted, "The War Cabinet concurred in the view that frankness was desirable." At a conference with French representatives that afternoon, Cecil used Page's observations again to squelch a vague French draft reply. Cecil argued that their draft did not satisfy the need for openness and "might be read as missing a great opportunity" to present the Allied case to the American public. It would be an exaggeration to claim that Page's representations played a critical part in shaping the ultimately polite Allied reply to Wilson's peace note. But his truthful remarks, unlike Lansing's and House's misrepresentations, did help at a critical juncture.[65]

Page got a glimpse of how much he had helped Anglo-

American amity when he obtained an interview with Lloyd George on the morning of 29 December. The meeting furnished the ambassador with his first exposure to the dynamic little Welshman in his new capacity as prime minister and virtual wartime dictator of Great Britain. As Page described the encounter to Wilson, "I asked Lloyd George openly what the Allies would reply to your note." The prime minister "replied in as frank a way and a most emphatic one." He regarded "your peace inquiry as premature." But Lloyd George also avowed, "We are friends. We are kinsmen. We have common ideals and a common destiny." Reiterating that the Allies considered Wilson's note "premature," Lloyd George nevertheless disclosed that "both the British and French Governments had received it and would reply in good will recognizing and appreciating your high motive. Agreement had been reached between his Government and the French Government as to the reply to it which they have sent to the Governments of Italy and Russia. They had set down their terms of peace as specifically as possible. These were concrete enough to be clearly understood."

The only specific terms that Lloyd George revealed to Page concerned Poland and Christians in the Ottoman Empire. Yet he did state, "The Allies' reply must be published and not used for secret negotiations." Lloyd George then reached what he considered the most important part of his conversation. "He said that you are the one man in the world to end this slaughter when the appointed time for it to end came." Page asked how Wilson would know when that time arrived. "That is what I am coming to," Lloyd George answered. "I am now talking to you quite privately. I wish to establish a relation of confidential privacy with you as the representative of the President so that we may talk so to speak, in an extra-ambassadorial way." If such a connection were established, Lloyd George promised, "I shall promptly inform you when conditions seem to me to call for the President's good offices. It is not yet come. More peace agitation now would be unfortunate and almost or quite unfriendly." In all, the conversation seemed extremely gratifying in both revelations and prospects.

Unfortunately, further disappointment followed for Page. He cabled an account of the meeting at midnight on 29 December, "FOR THE PRESIDENT WITH THE GREATEST URGENCY AND IN THE GREATEST CONFIDENCE." Page closed, "Would you acknowledge this telegram by wire and any comment that you care to make I should be glad to have." No word came from Wilson. On 10 January 1917 the Allies replied to Wilson's peace note with a joint statement of relatively moderate and fairly specific peace terms. Their reply contrasted favorably with an earlier curt German refusal to state any terms. The Allied note relieved Page's gloom a little. On 10 January he informed the foreign secretary, Balfour recorded, "that the rumors, which attributed to President Wilson the immediate intention of issuing a further Note on the subject of Peace, had no foundation."[66]

Six days after, the ambassador endured yet another humiliation. He received the text of a speech in which Wilson intended to urge a compromise settlement, or in his words, "peace without victory." Page was aghast. The speech showed, he wrote in his diary, that Wilson "thinks he can play peace-maker." Fearing the offense that the phrase "peace without victory" might cause, the ambassador cabled on 20 January to implore the president to substitute "peace without conquest" or some other words. "The sentiments you express are the noblest utterance since the war began," he declared, "and with an explanatory modification of this passage the speech guarantees to greatly further the cause you plead, enhance your influence, and fix you at the front of the movement for securing permanent peace." When Lansing passed along Page's suggestion, Wilson snapped, "I'll consider it." The president delivered his address to the Senate on 22 January with "peace without victory" intact. Page evidently indulged in a bit of mendacious flattery in his telegram. He later annotated his diary with the comment that the speech "—a remote, academic deliverance, while G't Britain & France were fighting for their very lives—made a profoundly dejected feeling; & it made my place & my work more uncomfortable than ever."[67]

As before, other matters added to Page's discomfort. The work load for himself and his staff kept growing, and the mediation move increased their burdens. House's trespassing in his sphere continued to vex Page, too. The colonel sent Clifford Carver on a mission to Europe in October 1916, over the ambassador's protests, and in January 1917 House started using the journalist Norman Hapgood to gather information in London, likewise to Page's consternation. One of his few diversions came when he sat for his portrait with the renowned society painter Philip Laszlo during January and February. Revealingly perhaps, Page held a book and wore an academic gown while posing for the portrait. Except for those diversions, he wrote Katharine, between "war-strain" and the "general unpopularity of our Gov't, we live very quietly now." Page's health bothered him occasionally, and the weather again seemed to match his gloom. "It's an awful winter here," he wrote Frank in December, "—much the worst we've had. It's cold—really damp-cold; & the fogs are the old-time sort, dense, dirty, impenetrable. We have nights when nobody can go out. We keep lights burning all day." The ambassador had many reasons for thinking that the first few months after his return to Britain were his darkest hour.[68]

From Page's standpoint, however, a dawning quickly followed. On 9 January 1917, the kaiser signed a decree ordering an unrestricted submarine campaign to begin on 1 February, an action that the Germans knew would almost surely bring the United States into the war. No warning was to be given until the day before the campaign opened, 31 January 1917. The German ambassador in Washington was, however, apprised of the decision on 17 January, when he received the soon-to-be-famous "Zimmermann telegram," which offered Mexico restoration of Texas, New Mexico, and Arizona in return for cobelligerency against the United States. The Zimmermann telegram opened, "It is our purpose on the 1st February to commence unrestricted U-Boat war." One man in Britain knew the contents of the Zimmermann telegram within hours of its transmission. That was Captain Hall, the director of naval intelligence and head of Room 40, who decided to keep the telegram absolutely secret until after 1 February, locking it in his desk and not informing any of his superiors. Yet despite Hall's suppression of that vital piece of intelligence, Balfour and others in the Foreign Office may have had advance knowledge of the submarine campaign, and they may have passed the information on to the American ambassador several days before the event.

Almost five years later, Eugene Shoecraft, who had been Page's personal secretary, recalled that the ambassador asked to be driven to the Foreign Office at four o'clock on the afternoon of Friday, 26 January 1917. "Mr. Balfour had sent an urgent request to come," Shoecraft related. The ambassador stayed for over an hour. As he watched Page come down the steps of the Foreign Office, Shoecraft remembered thinking, "I knew by the curious smile that Mr. Page had rec'd some startling news. To tease me, he made me guess all the way back to the chancery." When they got there, Page called in Edward Bell, who served as the embassy's liaison with the British intelligence agencies, and told the two of them about his conversation with the foreign secretary. Shoecraft mistakenly believed that Balfour had given Page the Zimmermann telegram that afternoon, but Balfour could have told him about the resumption of submarine warfare. The ambassador wrote nothing in his diary on 31 January or 1 or 2 February about the German move or his own reactions—an uncharacteristic omission that might suggest that he was not taken by surprise. The foreign secretary might also have constrained him to secrecy. No record exists of any communication from the London embassy to the State Department about the renewal of hostilities until after the United States broke relations with Germany on 3 February. Whenever he got the news, Page was delighted to see the Germans unleash their submarines. At last, it seemed, his country would have to enter the war.[69]

The American ambassador in London first learned of the severance of diplomatic relations not from the State Department but from Captain Hall. For two days after the resumption of submarine warfare, the embassy received no word from Washington about any response. The silence was unsettling. When Page saw Balfour on 2 February, the two had what the foreign secretary described as "a long and friendly talk," but the ambassador declined to speculate on what Wilson would do. Alice Page burst out to Arthur the same day, "How one wishes there could be no question and no hesitation about what the answer would be—a righteous flaming sword." On 3 February British newspapers carried unofficial reports of a break with Germany, but still no confirmation came from the State Department. Everyone at the embassy was certain, Shoecraft recalled, that notification would arrive that night. The Pages, together with Laughlin and his wife, Bell, and Shoecraft, decided to wait in the ambassador's office at Grosvenor Gardens. "About 9 o'clock the front door bell rang," Shoecraft related. "I hurried downstairs and found Admiral [sic] Hall coming up." Hall exclaimed, "Thank God!" Then he read the message that he had just gotten from the British naval attaché in Washington, "Bernstorff has just been given his passports. I shall probably get drunk tonight." Although Shoecraft and Bell invited Hall downstairs for "generous whiskies and soda," the ambassador did not join them. The next morning he sent the president a short cable praising his "prompt action." "Mrs. Page thinks this telegram too impersonal," he added. "So it may be, but I am afraid to let myself go."[70]

For Page, those two days between the renewal of submarine warfare and the diplomatic break established a pattern that lasted until the United States went to war at the beginning of April 1917. During the next two months he continued to have moods of alternating elation and doubt. He likewise remained on intimate terms with certain British figures, particularly Hall. The ambassador greeted the break with Germany by savoring a personal pleasure. On 4 February he wrote to inform the Foreign Office that his embassy would no longer be overseeing German interests in London, and he closed the letter with a partial flourish underlining the signature, "Walter Hines Page." Not having to handle German interests temporarily lightened the embassy's work load. Page enjoyed extended, intimate talks with Balfour and Lloyd George on 5 February, during which neither British leader attempted to hide his relish at the prospect of American belligerency. In all his contacts since the break, Page told Lansing, he found the British government "even more communicative than before," while public opinion "continues to become more cordial."[71]

The ambassador's initial joy gave way to agony as Wilson made no moves closer to war during the next two weeks. "I am now willing to record my conviction that we shall not get into the war at all," he wrote in his diary on 19 February. If submarine atrocities worsened, Wilson would merely arm merchant vessels "or take some other precautionary measure stopping short of war: *he can't lead into action.*" Yet even on his most depressed days in February 1917 Page was kept busy with important new tasks. First came secret conversations about a separate peace between the Allies and Austria-Hungary. Following a directive from Wilson on 9 February, Page met four times with Lloyd George over the next two weeks. Those contacts with the wily Welshman, who wriggled away from any commitment, cooled Page's admiration for him, but they also instilled the thrill of participating in and recording great events. In one of several long diary entries about those talks Page wrote, "As I walked away from Downing St., This reflection occurred to me: I sat down & talked to this Dictator of the B. Empire as calmly & as easily as if I had gone to see a man on some trifling errand. . . . I fancy all great transactions and conferences are done so. The momentousness of such occasions comes afterwards—is a sort of afterthought."[72]

A much more immediately momentous occurrence grew out of the talks about a separate peace with Austria. In a letter on 22 February Page related to Wilson that, after his third inconclusive meeting with Lloyd George three days before, he had decided that he needed to know whether the British had any tricks up their sleeves. Taking Laughlin and Bell into his confidence, Page asked them to sound out their contacts elsewhere in the government. Bell went to the Admiralty to see Captain Hall. "What rows are brewing?" Bell inquired. "Sit down, and I'll tell you one," Hall answered, "—one that your ambassador ought to know." The director of naval intelligence then told the American that his sources in Washington had learned that a peace move involving Austria was afoot. That much the ambassador wrote to the president on 22 February. But that was not everything that Hall told Bell on 19 February and it was not all that Page knew about his subordinate's visit to the Admiralty. When Bell called there, Hall also told him for the first time about the Zimmermann telegram. Hall asked Bell to let his chief know about the telegram, but he warned that he did not yet have the Foreign Office's consent to turn over the document. This was the opening of the most dramatic episode of Page's ambassadorship, probably of his whole life. [73]

William Reginald Hall fitted none of the usual images of a master spy. Far from being a faceless or secretive director of naval intelligence, he had become well known in London since assuming the post at the beginning of the war. Among his early acquaintances had been the American ambassador, whom he had known for the past two years, and "Ned" Bell, with whom he had established a working relationship since passing along the Archibald papers in August 1915. Hall practiced calculated indiscretion with both his own and foreign governments. He frequently withheld important pieces from his superiors, as with the Zimmermann telegram, and leaked interceptions in various quarters, as with House's messages. Although he apparently never informed anyone in the American embassy of his tap on their cables, he did make Bell and other members of the pro-Allied staff regular recipients of information, stories, and gossip gathered elsewhere. When the ambassador's son visited London in October 1916, for example, the captain showed him and Hugh Gibson a subsequently notorious photograph of the German ambassador in Washington with two women that, Arthur Page commented, "would damage his career in any Puritanical country." Gibson observed, "Too bad his disclosures will not bear writing."[74]

Hall's biggest coup occurred sometime during 1916, when Room 40 succeeded in breaking the German diplomatic ciphers. With the Zimmermann telegram, however, that feat proved a mixed blessing. Hall believed that if he let anyone else know about the telegram, at least before 1 February, the Germans might catch some hint of the interception and change their ciphers, and, like Page and others, he originally hoped that the submarine attacks would bring the United States into the war at once, so that he would not have to divulge the telegram. After 3 February, however, the captain took steps to release his bomb-shell. On 5 February he told the Foreign Office for the first time about the telegram. At the same time, Hall began operations to obtain a deciphered copy in Mexico, to use as a cover for Room 40's interception. By 19 February the cover operation was completed, and the captain let Bell in on the secret and told him to alert the ambassador. The following day, Wednesday, 20 February, Hall obtained Balfour's permission to inform the Americans and to make whatever arrangements with them he thought appropriate for turning over the Zimmermann telegram.

The captain must have gone straight from the Foreign Office to the embassy in Grosvenor Gardens. As Hall later recounted, he called first on Laughlin, who now held the title of counselor of the embassy. Hall sat down in a chair next to the counselor's desk. "I've got something for you," he said, smiling, and handed Laughlin some sheets of paper. "Read that! It might interest you." As the counselor looked over the papers, an expression of astonishment spread over his face. Laughlin started patting the top of his bald head, a nervous habit of his whenever he was excited. "This is wonderful!" he exclaimed. "Where did you get it?" The captain merely grinned. Then Laughlin asked, "May I show it to the Ambassador at once?" Hall nodded and Laughlin took him into Page's office. The ambassador was working away at his littered desk, as usual, oblivious to his surroundings. "May I bring Admiral [*sic*] Hall in?" Laughlin asked. "He has brought some papers that you might like to read." Page reached out for them in a leisurely way and started to look them over. As he became aware of the contents, he grasped the pages more tightly, then held them with both hands. Presently, he adjusted his glasses and bent down over the desk. He read the papers through several times. At length, wordlessly, Page banged his big fist down on the desk. "This document must be cabled immediately to Washington," he declared. "See that it is sent at once."[75]

That last remark sounds apocryphal. The ambassador could recognize that communicating the Zimmermann telegram to his government was going to be a delicate task. Not only did he have to insure that the secrecy of the source was not breached, but he also had to forestall the doubts that were sure to arise about the telegram's authenticity. Along with Laughlin and Bell, Page conferred with Hall during the next three days about proper methods of conveying the message. In those discussions the captain told many fascinating tales. He related how the Germans had sent the Zimmermann telegram over several different cable routes and how Room 40 had broken the cipher, including the sizable coincidences originating in Persia that had brought a code book into their hands. "What a story is here!" Page wrote in his diary on 24 February. During the following year, the ambassador became even better acquainted with Hall, who never ceased to amaze him. "If there be any life left in me after this war," Page wrote Wilson in March 1918, "and if Hall's abnormal activity and ingenuity have not caused him to be translated, I wish to spend a week with him at some quiet place, and then spend a year in writing out what he will have told me. That's the shortest cut to immortality for him and for me that has yet occurred to me." Sticking at his post was rewarding the ambassador with undreamed-of experiences to be fashioned into literature—provided only time remained to give him the chance.[76]

The immediate problem remained how to communicate the Zimmermann telegram to the United States. Hall and Page finally agreed that the best procedure would be for the foreign secretary to present the telegram to the ambassador. The formal exchange took place in Balfour's office on the afternoon of Friday, 23 February. The excitement of the episode infected even the sixty-eight-year-old Balfour, who usually treated all human affairs with passionless detachment. "As dramatic a moment as I remember in all my life," he later remarked about handing the Zimmermann telegram to Page. The ambassador instructed Bell and Shoecraft to encipher the English and German texts of the telegram. The work took the whole night. At eight o'clock the next morning, 24 February, the ambassador cabled the State Department, "In about three hours I shall send a telegram of great importance to the President and Secretary of State." Page sent the telegram at one o'clock in the afternoon. In his covering message, he told Lansing that the British "earnestly request that you will keep the source of your information and the British Government's method of intercepting it profoundly secret," and added, "but they put no prohibition on the publication of Zimmermann's telegram itself."[77]

The ambassador's concerns did not cease with the dispatch of the telegram. "This wd precipitate a war between almost any 2 nations," he wrote in his diary just after sending the message. "Heaven only knows what effect it will have in Washton [*sic*]!" Fortunately, no one in the administration doubted the telegram's authenticity, although Page did arrange for its verification a week later. The State Department cabled the cipher copy that had gone to Mexico over regular American telegraph lines from the German embassy in Washington. Bell went to the Admiralty where, under Hall's watchful eye, he deciphered that version, using Room 40's German code book. Without waiting for the verification, Wilson ordered Lansing to release the Zimmermann telegram to Congress and the press on 28 February. The next day, the ambassador sent the foreign secretary a handwritten note informing him that the secretary of state conveyed "thanks to Mr. Balfour for this information of such inestimable value" and that the president wished "to express his very great appreciation of so marked an act of friendliness on the part of His Majesty's Government."[78]

The Zimmermann telegram's reception in Washington pleased Page but did not quell his misgivings. "Nobody knows what our Gov't will do," he noted in his diary on 26 February. Wilson's request to Congress to arm merchant ships brought a flicker of hope. "Apparently there is only one step more possible," Page recorded on 27 February. "Or can there be any intermediate step?" After a German submarine sank the British liner *Laconia*, killing two American women passengers, he drafted a letter to Wilson, which he marked "Not sent!!" in which he said that the British viewed the incident as a repetition of the *Lusitania*, proving once more "that our Government is determined at all hazards to avoid war." News of publication of the Zimmermann telegram convinced him on 2 March that "if the Pres't were really to lead all the people wd follow. Whether he will even now lead—remains to be seen." The ambassador did not like what he soon saw. After a filibuster by antiinterventionist senators stymied the armed-ships bill and Zimmermann astonishingly admitted the authenticity of the telegram to Mexico, Page grew enraged at the president's apparent indecision. In his diary he pasted newspaper clippings of Wilson's second inaugural address on 4 March 1917. Next to the clippings he penned such comments as "No, no," "That's a pity!" and "Good God!" To his son Arthur he lamented, "I've just read the P's Inaugural—Words again. . . . Same old thing. Unless public opinion bodily pushes him over, we'll never get into the war."[79]

The friendly attention Page was now getting from the British leaders somewhat eased his pain over Washington's inaction. He confessed to Arthur on 4 March that he enjoyed being "very much 'in'" with such men as Lloyd George, Balfour, and Conservative party leader Andrew Bonar Law. "They dine with us and give us their confidence." For a change, he did not exaggerate his hosts' intimacy. At the beginning of March 1917, the British apprised Page of their most pressing reason for wanting the United States in the war. On 7 March he conferred for over an hour at the Foreign Office with Balfour and Bonar Law, who was now chancellor of the exchequer. They informed Page of the Allies' impending financial collapse. The ambassador noted in his diary that Balfour believed "that the problem of exchange is the great problem—not the submarine." Yet when he cabled the secretary of state on 5 March, the ambassador dissembled by asserting that a "condition most alarming to the American financial and industrial outlook" had arisen because the submarines prevented the Allies from shipping gold to pay for their war orders. Page did not inform Lansing that the British were actually running out of all collateral. He urged a quick, massive credit, not to save the Allies, but to stave off economic collapse in America.[80]

Discussions of possible belligerent cooperation helped pass what seemed an interminable wait for the United States to come into the war. The ambassador directed his staff early in March to feel out different parts of the British government about the most desirable forms of assistance. Besides money, Page found that merchant shipping and naval coordination against submarines topped everyone's list, together with the immediate dispatch of a token force of American troops as a symbolic gesture. Page likewise continued to take some consolation from his vantage point for writing about momentous events. "The climax of things seems near," he recorded on 25 February. "I, therefore, will at least for a time, keep a diary in some detail." The weather bolstered the ambassador's spirits a little, too. On 16 March Page wrote to Katharine that they were having the first half day of sunshine in months. On the main question, however, he conceded, "It's a mere waiting time." Also at mid-March, Wilson's call for Congress to assemble a month hence instilled momentary hopes, but those quickly gave way to doubts about whether, as Page complained in his diary, "If we 'get into the war,' we'll get in with only 1 foot." The waiting even seemed to affect the ambassador's health. "It is making daddy ill," Mrs. Page told Katharine on 21 March. "I have never seen him so depressed."[81]

As always, action offered an antidote to depression. The president's hesitation did not prevent exploratory moves toward belligerent cooperation from starting in Washington as well as in London. Naval coordination looked critical to leaders in both capitals. The ambassador held several discussions on the subject with Balfour and Admiral Sir John Jellicoe, the British fleet commander. The highest priority, Page reported, was "that our Government send here immediately an admiral of our navy who will bring our navy's plans and inquiries." He added that Balfour "expressed his enthusiastic hope that such a plan would be immediately carried out." The suggestion helped produce results. Frank Polk took the matter up at once with Secretary of the Navy Daniels, who had just received authorization from President Wilson to establish secret naval contacts with the British. On 27 March Daniels ordered Rear Admiral William S. Sims to sail for Britain as soon as possible, aboard a merchant steamer, in civilian clothes and under an assumed name. Sims carried a letter of introduction to Page from his old antagonist. The admiral came, Daniels stated, "on the mission outlined in your recent letter to the Secretary of State. You will find him one of the world's ablest naval officers and a gentleman you will be glad to know well."[82]

Page also tried to keep his spirits up with writing. On 25 March he sent Arthur a letter in which he expounded at length the benefits of entering the war. Belligerency would "unhorse our cranks and soft-brains . . . revive our real manhood—put the mollycoddles in disgrace as idiots & dandies are. . . . Break up our feminized education—make a boy a vigorous animal & make our education rest on a wholesome physical basis." Behind those assertions lay a profound distaste for the president and his whole approach to world politics. In the letter to Arthur, Page again dismissed Wilson's advocacy of a postwar league of nations as a way "to waste time." A week later, in a long letter that he may not have sent, he ridiculed "Leagues to Enforce Peace" to David Houston. "These things are mere intellectual (or idiotic) diversions of minds out of contact with realities." In his diary the same day, Page hoped that the people and Congress, which was on the eve of convening, would force the country into war, in spite of "the President's Neutrality-in-Thought and Peace-Itch." Wilson was "*not* a leader, but rather a stubborn phrasemaker." In the throes of belligerence, Page's expressions once more acquired an uncannily Rooseveltian ring, and this tone lasted to the end. Congress assembled on 2 April 1917. Everyone waited to hear what Wilson would say when he went to Capitol Hill that night. "Here we are in London," Page wrote in his diary, "fearing the President's timidity—I hope without warrant. And the suspense is pretty wearing."[83]

The suspense ended the next day. During the early hours of 3 April, the embassy received a cable from the State Department reporting that the president had asked Congress to declare that a state of war existed between the United States and Germany. The morning newspapers carried the text of Wilson's address. In an entry in his diary that he entitled "*The Day*," the ambassador recorded that his whole staff "has never been so delighted." Page called them together for a short speech. "Now we have greater need than ever," he exhorted, "every man to do constructive work—think of plans to serve. We are in this excellent strategical position in the capital of the greatest belligerent—a position [for] which I thank my stars, the President and all the powers that be going for us. We can each strive to justify our existence." In the afternoon Page went to the Foreign Office. Balfour shook his hand with unwonted warmth and said, "It's a great day for the world." The ambassador spent several hours discussing various forms of cooperation with Balfour and Cecil.[84]

Page had to wait another four days, while Congress deliberated, before his country officially became a belligerent. The war resolution passed overwhelmingly in the Senate on 4 April, by a margin of 82 to 6, and two days later in the House, 363 to 50. Page may have taken some satisfaction that only one of the dissenters in the Senate and eleven in the House were southern Democrats—a rump of Bryanite recusants. Robert Page was no longer in Congress, but two of his remaining North Carolina colleagues in the House opposed the war resolution. Official word of belligerency reached the London embassy in the evening of 6 April 1917. The following morning, the ambassador sent the Foreign Office formal notification "that a state of war exists between the United States and the Imperial German Government." This time a full flourish underlined the signature, "Walter Hines Page." The rush of new tasks kept him from pausing much to relish his altered condition until the end of the month, when he wrote to Arthur, "I cannot conceal nor can I repress my gratification that we are in the war at last." He felt personal vindication for "my letters & my telegrams" in which he had pounded away at Wilson "for nearly two years" with every conceivable argument for going to war. "I *have* accomplished something," Page insisted, perhaps partly to reassure himself. "I swear I have." Such thoughts may have made him feel better, but he came nearer the mark when he also told Arthur, "I have such a sense of relief that I almost feel my job is now done." During the following year, Page would discover how much of his job lay behind him.[85]

CHAPTER 11

Allied Standardbearer

During the summer of 1917 a woman friend wrote to salute Page as "an Allied Ambassador (how delicious that sounds!)." Strictly speaking, the entrance of the United States into World War I did not make Page an Allied ambassador. Because Wilson refused to heed his pleas, as well as House's and Lansing's, to contract formal ties with the Allies, the United States retained the ambiguous status of an "Associated Power." But cobelligerency gave Page new heart. The first few months of Anglo-American comradeship in arms formed a springtime of hope after a two-year winter of discontent. "We can now begin a distinctly New Era in the world's history and its management, if we rise to the occasion," he rejoiced to Frank Polk at the beginning of May 1917. America could "play a bigger part than we have yet dreamed of if we prove big enough to lead the British and the French. . . . See how a declaration of war has cleared the atmosphere!" For Page, 1917 was 1898 all over again, only better. Fighting in Europe alongside the Allies appeared to promise even more than empire toward fulfilling American destiny. "Delicious" aptly described much of the way that he felt after 6 April 1917.[1]

The spring and early summer of 1917 marked the emotional high point of Page's ambassadorship. During those months he tasted again many of the pleasures of his prewar year in London, while at the same time he quickened with a new sense of importance brought by intervention. America's entry into the war allowed Page to deal more easily, in private and in public, with the British than he had done for nearly three years. Shortly after the declaration of war, the ambassador had an audience at Buckingham Palace. The king laughed, slapped the table, and called out as Page bowed to leave, "Ah—ah—we knew where *you* stood all the time." On 12 April Page delivered his first major speech since the outbreak of the war. Speaking to the Pilgrims, the same group that had heard his first public address in Britain almost four years before, the ambassador refused "to talk too sentimentally," but he swore that the two great English-speaking nations had formed an "indissoluble companionship" that was "the moral union for a new era in international relations." On 20 April a service at St. Paul's Cathedral, which Page helped to plan, commemorated American entry into the war. The royal family attended, together with the archbishop of Canterbury and nearly every member of the cabinet. One observer remembered that the ambassador marched down the aisle "so full of enthusiasm and satisfaction that he looked almost 6″ taller!"[2]

More than ceremonies and speech making fed Page's excitement. Two days after the president's war address, the foreign secretary again alluded to the Allies' desperate financial and shipping situation. Because of submarine sinkings and the dependence of the western powers upon overseas supplies of food, fuel, and munitions, Balfour explained to Page, "tonnage is as much a military as an economic necessity." Further, "our power to finance, not merely ourselves, but all our Allies, has inevitable limitations." Those statements, Page soon discovered, downplayed the Allied predicament. He learned both from British sources and through Admiral Sims that the submarines were much closer to cutting the Allies' overseas lifeline than anyone dared admit publicly. Equally bad, Britain's ability to finance purchases in America virtually collapsed in June 1917, so that only immediate, massive loans from the United States could keep the Allied war effort going. By the end of June 1917, the ambassador recognized, as he told the president, that American intervention had prevented a "premature peace" because of finances. "And now we are all in bad straits because of this submarine destruction of shipping. And time is of the essence in the matter."[3]

Coordination with the British effort occupied Page even

before the United States formally took up arms. As soon as the news of Wilson's call for intervention reached London on 3 April, the Imperial War Cabinet proposed that a special mission headed by "someone of the highest status" should go as soon as possible to Washington to inform the Americans about Allied needs. The following morning, Balfour broached the idea to Page, who responded warmly, especially when he learned that the foreign secretary himself would head the mission. The ambassador cabled the proposal to the State Department early on 5 April, with the admonition, "An intimation from the President that it will be agreeable would be welcomed." For the next four days, Page heard nothing, even though the War Cabinet officially approved the mission and Balfour began making preparations to leave. After two further cables raised no response, the ambassador urged the foreign secretary to go anyway. "Nothing is more certain," Page assured him, "than the complete and enthusiastic satisfaction and gratification that your going will give. The President will feel honoured & be deeply touched by your visit.—I am hoping hourly to send you word that I have heard this from Washington." Finally, on the morning of 9 April, Page received authorization from Lansing to assent to Balfour's mission. "Not a word at all came from the President or for the President," the ambassador grumbled to himself, and the secretary of state's reply hardly amounted to a warm invitation. Cooperation in arms did not seem to be getting off to a promising start.[4]

Not all his dealings with British leaders were reassuring, either. Page remained in close contact with Balfour and Lloyd George, both of whom excited his admiration. He told Wilson in May that although he had "almost outgrown my living hero-worship," first Grey and now Balfour, they "by birth and cultivation have at least sometimes seemed of heroic size to me." Lloyd George inspired him on different grounds. The prime minister had, Page added, "greater moral force" than Grey or Balfour, along with what they lacked, "—a touch of genius,—whatever that is—not the kind that takes infinite pains but the kind that acts as an electric light flashed in the dark." But Lloyd George's genius often spelled trouble.[5]

The foreign secretary's trip to the United States presented an occasion for one of the prime minister's typical entanglements for the ambassador. After talking with House in New York and seeing for himself in Washington, Balfour grasped the deterioration of British representation in the United States. On 6 May he cabled back to London to urge Grey's appointment as "Special Envoy" to replace Spring Rice. Despite reluctance on the part of Lloyd George, who disliked Grey, the War Cabinet approved the request on 11 May. When the prime minister conferred with the former foreign secretary five days later, however, he described the ambassadorship in such a way that Grey declared himself unsuitable for the post. The same day, 16 May, Lloyd George informed the War Cabinet that Grey "was not the right man for Washington at this juncture." Britain required a strong figure there, the minutes recorded the prime minister declaring, "to direct the people of the United States into doing things instead of talking about them. . . . He himself believed that Lord Northcliffe would be a good selection." Other members of the War Cabinet immediately objected. The flamboyant Alfred Charles William Harmsworth, Viscount Northcliffe, was well known on both sides of the Atlantic; with his brother, Lord Rothermere, he owned the largest chain of newspapers in Britain. Besides lacking diplomatic experience, however, his renowned arrogance and short temper hardly fitted him for an ambassadorship. The War Cabinet meeting adjourned without reaching any decision.[6]

According to two observers close to the scene, Lloyd George had ulterior motives in pushing Northcliffe. Colonel Sir Maurice Hankey, the War Cabinet's secretary, noted in his diary that the prime minister's argument for a forceful representative in America "of course, is really a dodge to get rid of Northcliffe, of whom he is afraid." C. P. Scott, the editor of *The Manchester Guardian* and Lloyd George's close friend, wrote in his diary that the prime minister urged Northcliffe's appointment "quite frankly on the ground—which obviously was the determining motive—that it was essential to get rid of him." Lloyd George apparently feared political attack from the Harmsworth press. Faced with strenuous dissents cabled by the foreign secretary, the prime minister pressed for Northcliffe to be sent as an addition to, rather than as a replacement for, Spring Rice. On 31 May the War Cabinet finally detailed Cecil to sound out Page, who jumped at the idea. Cecil reported that the American ambassador believed that Northcliffe "would be particularly suitable to discharge the duties indicated." Page's declaration "enthusiastically in favour of the suggestion," the War Cabinet minutes recorded, sealed the press lord's appointment. Subsequently, Northcliffe's presence in America further damaged the British position, as he and Spring Rice conducted a semipublic feud over prerogatives and jurisdiction during the summer and fall of 1917. A third emissary, the Earl of Reading, had to be appointed in August with powers to overrule them both in financial matters. At a time when the fate of the Allies hinged upon aid from the United States, the "Welsh Merlin," as Lloyd George was nicknamed, chose to perform political tricks with representation there. He sought to use the American ambassador as his dupe.[7]

Page had reasons of his own for falling in with the scheme. He respected Northcliffe, whom he had known for several years, and he shared Lloyd George's professed convictions about the need for force and vigor. More important, in keeping with his own background as an editor and publicist, Page recognized that diplomacy had acquired an important public dimension. He believed that one of the keys to winning the war lay in molding and guiding public opinion. Admiration for his hosts' wartime fortitude did not erase the ambassador's criticisms of British society. The day after he talked with Cecil about Northcliffe, Page wrote to Wallace Buttrick, "They have neither popular education nor democracy in this Kingdom, and this war has proved to them for the first time the absolute necessity of having both." By the same token, mutual ignorance and misunderstanding between the British and American peoples had to be overcome. Page was writing to Buttrick to extend an invitation from the British government to come and speak about the United States. "If I were free from the trammels of official life," the ambassador avowed, "I'd travel around the world to do a great good work and to have an experience whereby a man may grow." Page hoped that Northcliffe would similarly enlighten American opinion. The two men must have discussed propaganda possibilities before Northcliffe's departure. In July the press lord reported to the ambassador, "I do wish you would beg our people to realize that this nation is the decider of the war and we should pay more attention than we do." Northcliffe seemed to be playing the kind of role that Page wanted in the United States.[8]

The ambassador's concern about public opinion affected one of his two most critical dealings with the British. Since February 1917 the War Cabinet had deliberately minimized the extent of submarine sinkings, which by April were claiming a staggering 865,000 tons of merchant shipping a month. When Admiral Sims reached London on 10 April, his British opposite numbers learned to their horror that he and everyone in the United States had assumed that the submarine problem was well in hand. Sims warned that in order to get needed naval cooperation from America, leaders in Washington would have to be disabused of the optimism that the British themselves had instilled. The situation bore out the ambassador's fears about the lack of publicity. "This submarine business is most threatening," he informed Polk in May. "This fool Government doesn't tell the facts to the public; and presently (it may be) the public will turn out the Government." At the same time, he confided to Doubleday that although Britain stood in imminent peril of being starved out, "These silly English do not publish these harrowing facts, & nobody knows them but a very few people." After both his own admonitions and Balfour's pleas from Washington failed to prod the War Cabinet into publicizing submarine losses, Page concluded that their failure to own up to the disaster epitomized the worst shortcoming of British officialdom. "This stolidity is the same quality that led to the tragedies of Gallipoli and Mesopotamia," he told Wilson in July. "The British will not confess that any danger awaits them."[9]

Despite those frustrations, facing the submarine challenge comprised one of Page's happiest tasks. True to Daniels's prediction, the ambassador formed a fast friendship with Sims. In May, he told the president that the lean, trim-bearded admiral "strikes me (and the English so regard him) as a man of admirable judgment—unexcitable and indefatigable." Immediately upon his arrival in London, Sims met the submarine threat by siding with a group of younger British naval officers who were pushing use of the convoy system for merchant vessels. The convoy proved to be the long-sought defense against the submarine, and its adoption during the summer of 1917 brought a sharp reduction in the rate of sinkings. But that solved only part of the problem. The Allies still required additional naval craft for antisubmarine patrols and convoy escorts and replacement of already-lost merchant tonnage. Vessels for antisubmarine duty off the British and French coasts presented the most pressing need. At Sims's behest Page barraged the White House and State Department with communications in June and July urging the transfer of all available craft to European waters. The ambassador likewise lent his voice to appeals for a shift in American naval building from capital ships to lighter, antisubmarine vessels and for release of newly constructed freighters to Allied supply duty. Although Page's efforts probably did not make the decisive difference, his work did help to defeat the submarine.[10]

Page's other critical dealing with the British involved money. The British reached the end of their financial rope in the United States in late June 1917, when their American agents, J. P. Morgan and Company, demanded repayment of a $400-million overdraft. The disbursements that Britain had received from the United States Treasury since April did not begin to cover that amount, much less pay for steadily mounting new war orders. On 28 June Page cabled Lansing, "It was disclosed that financial disaster to all the European Allies is imminent unless the United States Government advances to the British enough money to pay for British purchases in the United States." Page affirmed that he was "convinced that these men are not overstating their case. Unless we come to their rescue we are all in danger of disaster." That cable, together with messages sent to House through Wiseman, led to a series of talks from which measures eventually emerged to alleviate the Allies' financial plight.[11]

For all their flaws, the British continued to inspire the ambassador, especially because the war appeared to be democratizing them. "This experience is making England over again," Page told Doubleday in May 1917. "There never was a more interesting thing to watch & to be part of." The ambassador likewise enjoyed his renewed standing as a public figure. Ceremonial occasions proliferated from the moment that the United States entered the war. During the first two months of belligerency, for example, in addition to addressing the Pilgrims and arranging the service at St. Paul's, Page spoke twice to the American Luncheon Club, went to Cambridge to receive an honorary degree, accepted a Shakespeare folio at the University of London, and entertained all ranks of visiting fellow countrymen. Although Page complained of fatigue, he admitted to Arthur that he and Alice enjoyed their activities. "Your mother is kept busy in 'opening' and 'patroning' things," he explained. "But she thrives on it. I cd be orator all day and every day & every night if it were physically possible. We ought to organize this eagerness while it lasts."[12]

Page himself strove to organize wartime eagerness through propaganda and public speaking. The invitation to Buttrick in June was one of several the ambassador arranged for the British to extend. During the summer of 1917, he worked closely with John Buchan, the novelist and publisher, who served as the British government's chief propagandist. Buchan followed the ambassador's suggestions both in inviting Americans to Britain and in coaching them about what to say after they arrived. Page proposed a number of other projects, too. In April he forwarded to House a suggestion by Frederick William Wile, an American newspaperman, to set up a propaganda agency in Britain. "The thing that counts here—as in the United States," asserted Page, "—is public opinion throughout the country and—the press." The ambassador must have broached the idea to Balfour before the foreign secretary's departure for America. When Balfour met with House in New York, the colonel noted in his diary that they discussed "Page's suggestion as to American propaganda in England. My personal impression was that it would be better not to do so, but leave our interests in the hands of the British themselves, provided they would undertake to set the public right."

Page did not let official coolness at home dampen his ardor for propaganda. After Buttrick arrived in London in August, the ambassador started hatching plans with his old friend for a large-scale private venture to foster Anglo-American understanding.[13]

Page likewise promoted solidarity through his own speeches. In frequent public appearances, the ambassador dwelled on the "new era" in international relations based upon Anglo-American unity. His most important utterance came on 4 August, in an address at Plymouth entitled "The Union of Two Great Peoples." The speech marked a personal comeback for Page, since almost exactly four years before he had delivered his first address as ambassador outside London at Plymouth, that ringing and controversial avowal of Anglo-Saxon racial destiny. In August 1917 Page reaffirmed that Britain and the United States possessed the same "racial and national characteristics," and he insisted that in the American Revolution his nation "fell apart from the Old Land *only* in political allegiance." Now, World War I had "swept away incidental differences between us as a harrow smooths a field." The great task remained to implant future unity "on the broad base of friendly and informed public opinion in both countries." Page advocated extensive cultural exchanges and massive educational campaigns, and he dismissed the criticism "that these things cost money. They are less costly than ignorance of one another." The Tar Heel was applying his fundamental theme from southern reform to the world scene. On the nurturing of understanding between the English-speaking peoples, he concluded by declaring, "There is no other task in the world so important for the security of civilization."[14]

The trip to Plymouth capped an exhilarating five months for Page. His speech commemorated the third anniversary of the outbreak of the war. It was part of a festive occasion that also featured parades, a triumphal ride for him through cheering crowds, and a round of parties. After his return to London, the ambassador got away for ten days' vacation at a large country house, where he occupied himself as usual by writing notes and long letters. Even at the height of his activities during the spring and summer of 1917, Page's mind turned to the potential for writing about his dealings with the British leaders. "All this ought to make good 'copy' sometime," he told Doubleday in May. "The trouble is it ought not to be published till most of these men are dead, and many of 'em will outlive me. But, when I get a little time to think it all out, I'll see if some plan can't be made to use some of it." Page also responded enthusiastically to Doubleday's ideas for starting a new magazine and publishing a series of books to boost Anglo-American cooperation and international concord. "The thing to do is some big thing worthily," he asserted, "—as big as the world and its needs." The ambassador's holiday in August 1917 took him away from London when the first American troops passed through on their way to France. Despite the embassy's insistence on no fanfare, the four thousand men in khaki presented a stirring sight as they marched down Whitehall on 15 August. It was the ambassador's sixty-second birthday.[15]

The excitement of the first months of belligerency never totally eclipsed Page's misgivings about whether his main work was over. Outwardly, his misgivings appeared ridiculous. Belligerency brought an even bigger work load, attested by the swollen size of the embassy. The chancery and the military, naval, and financial missions spread out to occupy all the adjoining buildings on the block in Grosvenor Gardens. Within a year the staff had grown to 137 members, not counting the other missions, and in January 1918 the embassy sent nearly double the number of cables it had the year before. Yet neither work nor symbols of importance allayed Page's doubts, particularly as the summer of 1917 passed. In September he confessed to Arthur, "My job is really done here. When I pulled thro' the neutrality period & won the confidence of this Gov't & people so that they understood &—saw us come in, *that* was really the end of my job."[16]

Page did well not to quench his skepticism completely. Silence from Washington continued on many matters, and although it was nothing new, it gave the ambassador reason to sense that he was not at the center of things. Not only did his own government largely continue to ignore him, but the British began increasingly to bypass him. Reports of Page's fall from Wilson's graces had been reaching the Foreign Office at least since the beginning of 1917. In January Balfour had noted on one such report, "The President is unjust to Page. Can we do anything to help the latter?" When the foreign secretary was in the United States in May, Cecil cabled to remind him to express "to the President & the U.S. Govt our very high appreciation of all that Mr. Page has done for the relations between our two countries both before & since America entered the war." But appreciation did not mean that the British leaders intended to rely upon an ineffective instrument of communication in vital matters. Starting with the foreign secretary's invitation in April, the British used the channel to House through Wiseman as a supplement to Page. Possible peace overtures went to the colonel alone, and neither the British nor the American ambassadors was informed. In late September Balfour's secretary, Sir Eric Drummond, observed, "Col. House is one of our best & strongest friends & it seems to me that we are coming to rely on him more & more in emergencies." Page would have been downcast if he had known how small a part he was really playing in the great events of the war.[17]

As earlier, Page's not being replaced owed less to affection in London than to lack of will in Washington. In September 1917, for example, Wilson and House discussed ways to fire Lansing. The colonel suggested giving the secretary an ambassadorship; Wilson objected that no embassies were open. "I replied," House recorded in his diary, "'you could make a vacancy at London. That between hurting the sensibilities of Page and Lansing there was less reason for sparing Page.'" House believed that if Lansing were promised a place at the peace conference he would go to London. Wilson disliked the scheme because he thought Lansing unfit "for a peace commissioner; that he would give out statements at that congress, just as he does in Washington, thereby nullifying his, the President's work." Wilson agreed simply to offer Lansing Page's ambassadorship, House noted, but evidently he never did. The underlying reason for letting Page stay still seemed to be Wilson's failure to become greatly aroused about the reliability of his subordinates.[18]

Nor was the ambassador's conduct toward his superior completely aboveboard. Although Page kept up his flow of letters to Wilson after the United States went to war, the correspondence contained more of the insincere flattery that had first appeared in January and February 1917. Actually Page neither forgave nor trusted his old acquaintance. In July 1917 he told Arthur, "We waited to come in far too long—far past the time when victory cd have been quickly and cheaply won." In March 1918 he stated to his son, "The Great White Chief is at bottom a pacifist, has always been so & is now." Relations with House likewise remained a trial. Page kept up his correspondence with House through the summer of 1917, and in August he offered his and his staff's services to assist the colonel in his new official assignment of planning for the postwar peace conference. That gesture led to another humiliation for the ambassador, for House not only failed to respond to Page's offer, but he also turned the member of Page's staff who was studying peace possibilities, William Henry Buckler, into his own agent. At the end of August, Page discovered that Buckler was reporting to the colonel without his knowledge, and he forbade Buckler further correspondence with House. Buckler asked the colonel not to have the ambassador officially overruled because "this would mortify Mr. Page, & might cause his staff to regard you as a 'hidden Hand,' and me as a sort of outside conspirator."[19]

Page soon suffered mortification at House's hands, anyway. In November 1917 the colonel crossed the Atlantic with an entourage of experts, nicknamed the "House Party," to confer with the British and French governments and attend the Inter-Allied Conference in Paris. Page received word of the mission only after arrangements with the British had already been made. He stood with Balfour on the platform at Paddington Station to greet the delegation when they arrived at midnight on 8 November, and he escorted House and the ranking military members to lunch at Buckingham Palace on 16 November. Otherwise, except for giving two or three informal dinners and handling routine chores, the ambassador took no part in the activities of the "House Party." Page was present at none of the colonel's meetings with Lloyd George and the War Cabinet. His former work of advising and making arrangements for House fell to Wiseman, who was also staying at Chesterfield House, the residence provided for the colonel, his wife, and son-in-law. The ambassador preserved dignity throughout the visit. "Page has done everything that could be desired, so far," House noted in his diary, "and has shown a disposition to play the part one might properly expect." On his side, the colonel no longer showed any malice toward the ambassador. "I shall do everything possible not to offend his dignity," he also recorded, "and I trust we may get away without any hurt feelings."[20]

The next four months, December 1917 through March 1918, comprised a low period for Page. The principal source of depression remained the course of the war. It had been clear since midsummer 1917 that Page's hopes that American intervention would bring a speedy victory were vain. Calamities mounted during the summer and fall—unbroken deadlock on the western front, near collapse in Italy, Russian disintegration, and finally the Bolshevik takeover in the November revolution. Pessimism grew in official circles in Britain, while a number of figures outside the government began advocating a compromise settlement. "This is the weariest Christmas in British annals—certainly since the Napoleonic wars," Page reported to Wilson at the end of 1917. From his standpoint, prospects did not brighten during the opening months of 1918. The Bolshevik capitulation to the Germans at Brest-Litovsk disturbed Page, as did talk among British conservatives about peace with Germany at the expense of Russia. Wilson's Fourteen Points rekindled his doubts about the president's "pacifism." By the end of February 1918 Page had sunk into a temporarily defeatist mood. It was the only crack in his optimism during the entire war.[21]

Personal disappointments likewise buffeted the ambassador. The "House Party" experience understandably fueled doubts about his usefulness. "Events will now go on till peace come without much real work for an ambassador to do," Page noted in his diary the day after the colonel's departure. A month later, his two largest propaganda and cultural exchange projects went awry. One was a plan that he had earlier worked out with Buttrick to invite a delegation of distinguished Americans to visit Britain early in 1918. The other, longer-range project developed late in November from a meeting with Lord Reading and Thomas Lamont, a partner in the Morgan firm. Page, Reading, and Lamont proposed to raise five hundred thousand dollars to finance an organization over ten years to promote Anglo-American understanding. It was to be called "The Kinsmen" and patterned after the General Education Board. Both projects foundered on Wilson's objection. When Taft, whom Buttrick had asked to head the delegation to Britain, called at the White House in December 1917, the president squelched the plan. Taft later recalled that Wilson had scoffed, "Page is really an Englishman, and I have to discount what ever he says about the situation in Great Britain." Also, according to a thirdhand account of the interview in House's diary, Wilson "said he did not desire any closer relations with England than we have now." In January 1918 Buttrick informed Page that the visit would be abandoned. In view of the president's attitude, he and Lamont had also "agreed that the big scheme will have to be laid aside for a while." Page replied at the beginning of February, "The misfortune . . . is a far greater misfortune than has come to me for a very long time indeed."[22]

Other blows soon fell from House. The colonel bore the ambassador no ill will, and, aside from the suggestion about moving Lansing to London, he showed no interest in replacing Page. Yet he did intend to sideline the ambassador, as he had done in London in November. After Lord Reading went to Washington as Spring Rice's successor in February 1918, the colonel devised another set of codes for the new British ambassador to use in telephoning and writing through Wiseman. The code included no cover name for Page. Later in the month, House requested Ray Stannard Baker to undertake a mission to Britain. As House noted in his diary, he asked Baker "to gather information regarding liberal thought there. We find it impossible to get this from Page." Baker later remembered asking House how much he should tell Page about the reason for his visit. "I was told to use my own judgment." Again, during the summer of 1918, the colonel discussed fresh trouble in Mexico entirely with Wiseman and Reading, as he wrote in his diary, "without the London Embassy having known that it was even brewing." House noted that he had not informed Page for fear "that he would take offence because the matter had not been referred to him for action in the first place, which was not possible in the circumstances."[23]

Yet the ambassador did not feel as downcast as he had before American intervention. Page never regretted that his country had come into the war. In December 1917 he told Arthur, "The greatest thing we'll get out of it will be our emancipation from Pacifism and all forms of softness & from the debilitation of surplus wealth." When his son Frank joined the army in March 1918, Page rejoiced that "you'll come out of this experience with great development of judgment, of sturdiness, of balance and calm, which will serve you well all your life." The ambassador found staying at his post easy to justify. "Now, if I quit before the end," he confided to Arthur in March, "the next man will get much of the credit for my work and will be, in the popular mind, *the* war ambassador." Page's public image mattered to him, as he continued making speeches in late 1917 and early 1918. On 6 April 1918 he and Balfour jointly addressed a banquet given at Mansion House by the lord mayor of London to mark the anniversary of American entry into the war. Baker, who was present, noted that Page spoke well. The ambassador pledged that British and American victory was going to be "won by the stout heart of every man and woman of the conquering races." Baker also noted, "Mr. Page was greatly cheered. . . . People *like* him."[24]

Even the increased work load had compensations. Cobelligerency brought a number of American officials to London, including senators and representatives in November and December 1917 and Secretary of War Newton D. Baker in March 1918. Their visits lessened the ambassador's sense of isolation and provided him with opportunities to promote cooperation with Britain. Contacts with the British continued to offer satisfaction.

Page maintained friendly personal relations with Lloyd George and Balfour, and he sometimes dealt with important diplomatic matters, such as another Austrian peace feeler in February 1918. Hall continued to pass along sensitive intelligence data, including Room 40's interceptions of earlier communications between Berlin and the German embassy in Washington and the Austrian emperor's letter to the Spanish king in the 1918 peace overture. The expanding embassy size and burgeoning routine work bothered Page, but the presence of other American missions in London actually lightened the embassy's duties. "My own personal work is less than it has been for a very long time," Page observed to Arthur in May 1918, "great as the volume of routine work continues to be."[25]

Writing plans still cheered the ambassador, too. Sometime during the year following American intervention, Page jotted down a note in Greek script on "Possible Minor Tasks After the War." Among them were "Lectures to College & the Like" and "Novels?" At another time he commented to himself: "Fuller account must be written of (1) Russian Revolution (2) Our Entry into War." Early in 1918 Page once more started keeping a notebook, in addition to his always fitful diary, in which he set down ideas for essays, lectures, and books. The book projects included "(1) My Engl. Life—In Diary form—or in chapters by subjects? (2) My Own Life (for my children) including sketches of the Old Man, of A. F. P. [his father], K. F. P. [his mother], &c. &c.—(3) The King—A Novel—." Hall's disclosures prompted Page to remark to Wilson in March about how much he wanted to tell his story. The trouble was, he added, so much of Hall's material was locked up in a safe marked " 'not to be opened till 20 years after this date.' I've made up my mind to live twenty years more. I shall be present at the opening of that safe!" Ray Stannard Baker recorded in his journal that Page showed him a chapter of the personal autobiography in May 1918. "I hope he will go on!" Baker noted. "If only he would write indiscreetly! Could set down the things he really sees and feels. But," Baker reflected, "no ambassador can ever do that!"[26]

Page's happiest revelation of literary yearnings in 1918 involved his eldest son Ralph, who had recently given up peach farming in North Carolina to take up writing and was publishing a book entitled *Dramatic Moments in American Diplomacy* with Doubleday, Page. "What you write about Ralph and his writing gives me pleasure beyond anything that has recently happened," Page responded to Arthur in January. In March he wrote Ralph a long letter of advice and admonition. "Style is good breeding— and art—in writing," he avowed. " . . . You'll get a good style if you practice it. It is in your blood & temperament and way of saying things." When *Dramatic Moments in American Diplomacy* appeared in April 1918, one of the most favorable reviews came from Theodore Roosevelt. In *The Outlook*, the ex-president not only commended Ralph Page's "truthful and interesting" book, but he also lauded his father, "who for the last five years in England has shown himself not only a most loyal and able representative of America, but a staunch champion of the rights of civilized mankind." In March Roosevelt wrote the ambassador to tell him that he had "represented America in London during these trying years as no other ambassador in London has ever represented us, with the exception of Charles Francis Adams, during the Civil War." Those words may have given balm to the disappointments Page had suffered at the hands of Wilson and House.[27]

The ambassador's health continued to form another source of consolation after American entry into the war. Throughout this period Page generally enjoyed better health than he had previously, despite strain, overwork, London fogs, and the British climate. But the onset of 1918 brought an unwelcome change. Persistent exhaustion and weight loss forced Page, at his wife's insistence, to take off the first two weeks in March for a holiday in Cornwall. "The rest down here is doing him a world of good," Mrs. Page wrote Arthur, "but it is also boring him." The Pages both believed that the vacation restored him to full vigor. To be on the safe side, the ambassador had an examination at the beginning of April by Sir William Osler, the most renowned physician in Britain. "He finds things sound for a man nearly 63

& gives me at least 15 y'rs—78," Page exulted in his diary. "Let's call it 80 in round numbers!"[28]

That clean bill of health provided false reassurance. At the middle of April, Page suffered what Alice called "three little break downs," and by the beginning of May the ambassador could not meet some of his commitments. During the second week in May, Page came down, Alice related, "with an attack of acute indigestion that lasted nearly four hours and then the Dr. said to him it is no use, you must take a complete rest." Page arranged for a two-month leave of absence, and he and Alice left London on 18 May for a coast estate in Kent. For a while the seaside sojourn seemed to help, but late in June Page started having difficulty breathing and could not lie down without choking. "I have said he was tired and worn out and needs rest," Alice wrote to Frank. "But sometimes I am afraid it is more than that."[29]

The respiratory condition persisted, making Page's doctor suspect heart complications, but the ambassador insisted upon going back to work when his leave expired on 18 July. During the next week, he met with Balfour at the Foreign Office, dispatched a long cable to the State Department about threatened strikes in the British munitions industry, and gave a luncheon, which Lloyd George attended, for the visiting assistant secretary of the navy, Franklin D. Roosevelt. At the same time, the ambassador was relaying the doleful news back to North Carolina that his brother Chris's nineteen-year-old son, Allison, was missing in action and presumed killed with the United States Marines at Belleau Wood.

But Page was never able to resume his full duties. Alice reported to Katharine that he was "weak, no strength at all. He doesn't walk at all, and at times his breathing is bad." Because his doctors gave differing opinions, they urged him to leave his post again and undergo tests and additional convalescence at the famed sanatorium Duff House, at Banff in Scotland. Alice and the two sons, Arthur and Frank, who had come to London on military service, pleaded with the ambassador to relent in his determination to stay on until the end of the war. As Arthur later recalled, it finally took Sir William Osler's professional insistence to persuade Page to resign. On 1 August Page wrote to the president explaining that "a progressive digestive trouble which does not yield to the usual treatment" necessitated at least six months rest, under doctor's care. "I see nothing else to do, then, but to bow to the inevitable and to ask you to be kind enough to relieve me and to accept my resignation to take effect as soon as I can go to Washington and make a somewhat extended report."[30]

On 2 August Page left for the sanatorium in Scotland, where he received, as he told Alice, "the most thorough examination and tests that minds and experience of medical men can devise." The results appeared encouraging. Page reported to Alice that he had "no disease at all but a general weariness, to the point of breakdown, from overwork; and there is no reason why I shd not become myself again if I quit work for a time and live right, eat right, and let nothing worry me at all." Page's condition was actually far graver than his doctors realized. The diagnosis at Duff House revealed that he was suffering from hardening of the arteries, high blood pressure, and an early stage of emphysema. Given the state of medical knowledge at the time, there seemed every reason to assume that retirement and abstemious habits would allow Page, who turned sixty-three on 15 August, to live years longer. What the doctors did not know was that Page's combination of arterial hardening and elevated blood pressure formed the dire and then untreatable condition "hypertension," which was almost certain to cause heart attack, congestive heart failure, stroke, kidney failure, or some combination of those within weeks or a few months at the latest—any of which alone or together would probably bring death. Neither Page nor his physicians knew it, but he was dying.[31]

The ambassador and his doctors did feel sure about the cause of his illness. "It's the war, five London winters, the monotony of English food and the unceasing labor which is now the common lot," Page complained to Wilson in his letter of resignation. In an earlier draft of that letter he alluded to "the difficult work during our period of neutrality (wh., I suspect, is what ails me)." Attributing the breakdown of Page's health to the emo-

tional stress and overwork of his ambassadorship seemed warranted at the time, but that judgment now appears dubious in
light of subsequent medical research. Not only do the causes of
hypertension still remain obscure, but two other factors in Page's
life were much more likely contributors to his hypertension. One
was simply age, inasmuch as hardening of the arteries is part of
the aging process. The other contributor was Page's heavy smoking. He had been a constant smoker for over forty years, and as
late as the spring of 1918 he had been consuming at least fifty
big, strong cigars a week. In short, by the time he reached the age
of sixty-three Page had probably lived out his allotted span, no
matter what kind of work he was doing.[32]

As far as the ambassador knew in August 1918, his biggest
problems were winding up his affairs in Britain and getting
home. Page and his family had to suffer through another prolonged silence from Washington. After three weeks passed with
no reply, Arthur insisted that his father announce his resignation
anyway. But a cable arrived on 25 August, in which the president
declared that he had no "right to insist on such sacrifice as your
remaining in London. Your resignation is therefore accepted."
Wilson agreed to make the resignation effective as of the time
that Page reported to Washington, and he congratulated him on
"knowing that you have performed your difficult duties with
distinguished success." The delay in answering reflected some
dilatoriness on Wilson's part. He and House had first discussed
possible successors to Page on 16 August. By the time the ambassador got the president's cable, the colonel had recommended
John W. Davis, the solicitor general, for the post. On 31 August
the offer of the ambassadorship went to Davis, who was then
sailing for Europe on another mission and did not learn about
the proposal until he reached London on 5 September. After
balking for a few days at the expense of the post, Davis accepted
on 11 September. The way was clear for Page to come home.[33]

Obedient to doctors' orders, the ambassador got away with
as little ceremony and delay as possible. He remained in Scotland
until mid-September, while Alice and Arthur handled the details
of the departure. Back in London, he attended to only the most

necessary official matters. Ambassador and Mrs. Page journeyed to Windsor on 16 September for a brief formal leave-taking from the king and queen. As Alice reported to Katharine, their majesties were "very gracious" and gave them a pair of beautifully framed, signed photographs, which were "intended as a special mark of honour." She also noted that "your father got on very well except for the steps. I did not realize how they made him pant." Another disturbing sign also appeared. Since his return to London, Page had complained about his vision. An examination revealed retinal hemorrhages in both eyes—another unmistakable symptom of hypertensive degeneration. Time was running out for Page.[34]

The ambassador left London on 2 October 1918. Balfour and Cecil came to Waterloo Station to see him off. Laughlin and Shoecraft had to support Page on each arm as he hobbled the short distance from his automobile to a private railroad car provided by the British government. The sight was so sad that even the unemotional Balfour later admitted, "I almost wept when he left England." After Page boarded the British liner Olympic with Alice and Frank the following day, his condition took an alarming turn. The ship's doctor observed on first day at sea that Page grew drowsy, inattentive, and frequently delirious. Those symptoms suggested a possible stroke. When the Olympic docked in New York on 12 October, an ambulance was waiting to rush Page to St. Luke's Hospital. The doctors at St. Luke's found that he was suffering from heart congestion, kidney failure, further retinal hemorrhages, and consistently high blood pressure. His family feared for his life.[35]

Page's condition stabilized and then apparently improved during the next few weeks. By later October he had regained his full attentiveness, and early in November he began to walk around a little. "Your father is perfectly normal and his mind clear down to the last detail," Alice wrote Frank. "He is discouraged because he is so weak, and still more because he can't see to read." The armistice on 11 November naturally heartened him, and at the middle of the month Page sent congratulatory telegrams to Balfour and Bonar Law on the Conservatives' victory in coalition with Lloyd George in the British elections. Those messages disclosed Page's concern about his ambassadorship, which he had not yet formally relinquished. On 23 November, in his clearest sign of strength, he penned his first letter in three months, asking Wilson to release him from his promise to make a personal report. The familiar, neat handwriting began shakily but grew steadier as the letter went on. "I never wrote anything, Mr. President, with such regret," Page avowed. He felt particularly disappointed not to be present when Wilson visited Britain before the peace conference, but he would always have "profound appreciation of your giving me the most interesting and (I hope also by far) the most useful experience of my life." Wilson replied three days later with a brief letter of good wishes for Page's recovery. "I hope that the time is not far off," he closed, "when I can see you and catch up with things in a long talk." The exchange recaptured a hint of the two men's former friendship, thereby concluding Page's ambassadorship on a pleasing note.[36]

The note was partly false. Wilson and House sent Page get-well cards in October, but neither of them visited him at St. Luke's, even though the president was in New York several times while the ambassador was in the hospital and the colonel lived just across town. Behind Wilson's neglect lay unassuaged bitterness toward his old acquaintance. In September Wilson told House, as the colonel recorded in his diary, that to Page's request to resign "he has replied only by cable. He said he did not dare write expressing cordial regrets fearing lest it might place him in Page's unfriendly hands." House responded, "I did not think Page would write or say anything unfriendly while either of them was alive, but I did believe that, sooner or later, Page's criticism of him would be given to the world." Since Allied victory looked certain, House and Wilson thought that Page's views would carry little weight. That was House's last reference to Page in his diary during the ambassador's lifetime. The colonel evidently failed to see his one-time intimate because he no longer considered him worth taking time from his busy schedule. One other lingering sore spot involved money. Page's hospitalization in New York and transportation to North Carolina in December cost over six thousand dollars, and Alice worried constantly about meeting the expenses. In that way, too, his ambassadorship ended on a familiar note.[37]

Page's spirits were as good as could be expected when he surrendered his title at the end of November 1918. Five or six days after writing to Wilson, he penciled a draft of a letter declining an invitation to speak, in which he declared that complete accord between the English-speaking peoples was "the only basis for the continued progress of civilization." He affixed a bold signature to the draft and scribbled in the margin, "Cheddar cheese not be grape juice"—a final slap at Bryan. At the end of November, he suffered a relapse, but it did not last long. His vision meanwhile improved to the point at which he could resume some reading. Page's recovery satisfied his doctors at St. Luke's, who offered encouragement that he might eventually return to normal health.[38]

On 11 December Page left the hospital to travel to North Carolina in a private railroad car. As soon as he had agreed to resign, he had begun looking forward to going to Pinehurst. "I find myself thinking of the winter down South," he had written Alice in September, "—of Thanksgiving Day dinner for the older folks of our family, of a Xmas tree for the kids, of frolics of all sorts, of Rest, of some writing (perhaps not much), of going over my papers with Ralph—that's what he wants, you know, &c. &c &c—." The first part of that vision came true. As he was carried from the train at Aberdeen, Page reportedly remarked to Frank, who accompanied his father and mother on the trip, "Well, Frank, I did get here after all, didn't I?" For a few days he appeared to grow stronger, and he enjoyed reunions with his sisters and brothers, including Robert. But on Thursday, 19 December, he weakened, and the end came swiftly. Page died quietly, evidently of heart failure, on Saturday evening, 21 December 1918. Of his children, Arthur and Frank were away in the army, but Ralph and Katharine were with him when he died, as were Alice and his brothers and sisters. Death found Walter Page at home.[39]

His funeral and burial took place in Aberdeen the following

Tuesday, Christmas Eve. Messages of sympathy from Britain came from the king and queen and the foreign secretary. Cables of condolence also came from the president, who was in London, and the secretary of state, in Paris. The first secretary of the British embassy in Washington represented his government at the services. The State Department issued an official statement mourning the former ambassador's passing, and Assistant Secretary Phillips attended the funeral. Newspaper editorials around the United States saluted Page and his work, and other published tributes soon followed from his fellow magazine editors. After a simple funeral at the Page Memorial Church, named for his father and mother, his body was laid to rest in a tree-shaded plot atop a small knoll in the Old Bethesda Cemetery outside Aberdeen. The site overlooked the graves of his parents and his young nephew recently killed in the war. The native son had come back to an honored place among his own people.

Walter Hines Page was not forgotten. Ironically, his greatest fame and influence came after he died. His two older sons, Ralph and Arthur, set to work immediately after his death to preserve his memory and tell his story. Ralph spent much of 1919 and 1920 gathering and arranging his father's papers, and early in 1920 Arthur assigned the writing of Page's biography to Burton J. Hendrick, the managing editor of *World's Work*. Hendrick received his regular salary and dividends from the magazine, in addition to a promised five percent book royalty, while he worked exclusively on the biography for the next two years. Besides the papers that Ralph Page collected, Hendrick secured extensive material from others close to Page. Colonel House granted long interviews and supplied all of his and the ambassador's correspondence with each other. The now-invalid President Wilson refused to release Page's letters to him or grant permission to quote from his letters, but a number of British figures, particularly Grey and Hall, proved more forthcoming when Hendrick spent the winter months of 1920–21 in London. *World's Work* serialized parts of the biography starting in September 1921, and in September 1922, less than four years after Page's death, Doubleday, Page published *The Life and Letters of Walter Hines Page*.

The *Life and Letters* became a publishing sensation. Despite a two-volume edition with a ten-dollar price, the biography became the third biggest nonfiction best-seller for 1923. The two-volume set sold 62,000 copies during the first year after publication. In all editions, the two original volumes of the *Life and Letters* amassed sales of over 156,000 copies in the United States over six years. Nor was that all. After Wilson's death in 1924, his widow permitted publication of Page's letters to him, although she remained obdurate in her ban on any use of the late president's own letters. Between June and November 1925 *World's Work* ran a second set of installments by Hendrick based on Page's correspondence with Wilson. A third volume of the *Life and Letters* appeared in September 1925 and sold close to 60,000 copies in America before the end of the year. All three volumes likewise enjoyed large sales in Britain. Hendrick produced one further volume, based on Page's preambassadorial career, entitled *The Training of an American* and published in 1928. Evidently because of less timely subject matter, *The Training of an American* sold only about 5,600 copies. Still, the four biographical volumes posthumously gave Page the best-selling books that he had so coveted during his lifetime.[40]

The biography owed its spectacular success largely to three factors. One was Hendrick's talent. In a curmudgeonly reminiscence near the end of his life, Hendrick dismissed his effort as high-class hack work. That estimate contained some truth, inasmuch as he worked with Arthur Page, sometimes literally and always figuratively, looking over his shoulder. Hendrick's writing also had to gain clearance from Mrs. Page and Katharine, and the ambassadorial chapters additionally had to pass muster with Irwin Laughlin. For his part, Hendrick wrote in unfailingly laudatory, often saccharine tones. Yet he brought more to the biography than a facile pen. Hendrick did assiduous research, gathering voluminous papers from Page's family, friends, and associates, and collecting a great deal of collateral information and description from interviews. For the final volume, he garnered facts and insights about Page's childhood and formative experiences that would otherwise have been lost. In that last work Hendrick functioned more as a biographer fashioning a portrait of Page and less as a compiler of letters, as in the earlier volumes. He won the Pulitzer Prize for both the original two-volume *Life and Letters* and *The Training of an American*. Hendrick may have deprecated his contribution, but he wrought better than he knew.

Timing formed the second factor in the biography's success. Because Page was the first high-ranking member of the Wilson circle to die, his story became the earliest version of the administration's inner history, especially regarding World War I, to reach the public. Hendrick's dispatch in producing the *Life and Letters* helped insure the freshness of readers' memories. But the main credit for divining the potential appeal of Page's story belonged to his son Arthur. At least since 1916, Arthur Page had been approaching prominent Wilson administration figures about publishing memoirs with Doubleday, Page. The company eventually corralled most of the cabinet members, along with Admiral Sims, Henry Morgenthau, and Ray Stannard Baker, who became Wilson's authorized chronicler of the peace conference and his biographer after the ex-president's death. Yet none of those books achieved the popular and critical acclaim of the *Life and Letters*. It was also true that Doubleday, Page did not invest as much money and effort in the other Wilson-administration books; his father's biography was both a labor of love for Arthur Page and a triumph of public relations, the field in which he pursued a highly successful career after his break with the Doubledays in 1927. Yet timeliness alone did not completely account for the biography's success. In 1922 Doubleday, Page also published Baker's *Woodrow Wilson and the World Settlement*, which treated more recent and more immediately controversial events from the vantage point of exclusive access to the ex-president's papers. Hendrick's volumes still got better notices and outsold Baker's.

The strongest appeal of the *Life and Letters* lay with Page himself, who, far more than most biographical subjects, told his own story. Over nine-tenths of the text of the three volumes of the *Life and Letters* and about three-quarters of *The Training of an American* consisted of Page's own words, chiefly his letters.

Every reviewer, even those who disliked his views of the war, praised the letters' vividness and vigor. Letters had been Page's literary forte, and the biography furnished a perfect vehicle for releasing his best writings to the public while they were still timely. If Page had lived longer, discretion would almost certainly have curbed his pen, and his more formal writing had seldom matched his correspondence in force and interest. In a way, death had permitted Page to write the compelling books that he had yearned to produce throughout his life.

The success of the biography in turn brought honors that would have gratified Page beyond all expectations. Sales of the *Life and Letters* in Britain at the beginning of 1923 coincided with a diplomatic need to smooth postwar controversies. The two circumstances dovetailed to foster a drive to commemorate the ambassador's services with a memorial in Westminster Abbey. An impressive service took place there on 3 July 1923, at which Grey eulogized Page and unveiled a white marble tablet bearing his name, dates of service, and the inscription, "The Friend of Britain in Her Sorest Need." The only other Americans honored in Westminster Abbey were, and still are, Henry Wadsworth Longfellow and James Russell Lowell, whose busts stand in Poet's Corner. That association might have pleased Page almost as much as the diplomatic tribute.

Other monuments followed, including the naming of the new high school at Cary and the library at Randolph-Macon College after him. For some years, his grave under the oaks at Aberdeen became a pilgrimage spot for North Carolinians and visitors to nearby Pinehurst. The highest accolade besides the tablet in Westminster Abbey came in the spring of 1924, when the Johns Hopkins University announced the founding of the Walter Hines Page School of International Relations. The nature and location of the various memorials had a fitting, though ironic, symbolism. His grave, the school at his birthplace, and the library at his college all marked the measure of honor that fellow southerners were at last willing to accord him. The international relations school at the Johns Hopkins attested recognition by national leaders and the academic community. The tablet in

Westminster Abbey commemorated his brief but eventful passage across the world scene at a decisive moment in history. It is doubtful that any of the memorials would have come into being except for his ambassadorship, which was the least successful and unhappiest period of his life. Yet each of them represented one or more of the many fields in which he had moved and tried to bring reconciliation.

The erection of those monuments in the five and a half years after Page's death signaled an apotheosis of his reputation that would have more than requited his deepest lifetime desires. The renown started to slip soon afterward, first as the controversiality of his ambassadorship began to be revived and later as time passed and memories faded. Yet Page never quite became the character of his famous speech, "the forgotten man." He kept being rediscovered for his involvement in the sixty-three years of his lifetime. His life continued to draw significance from the representative quality that had led him to undertake such an astounding variety of enterprises and to seek to bridge some of the most important conflicts of the last century and a half of American history. Page remains one of the most illuminating figures of his time and of the consequences that have flowed from that time. Such significance would have gratified him. In *The Southerner* Page wrote, "It is just as well to pass deep shadows as fast as you can—not from fear, of course, but because we are children of light." Those were words by which he lived, for better and worse. His worst failings sprang from trying to pass by dark shadows in his native region, his nation, and his world. Yet more often he tried to dispel the shadows. Walter Hines Page sought to be and was a bringer of light.[41]

NOTES

BIBLIOGRAPHY

INDEX

———

NOTES

These notes refer only to direct quotations and certain other citations in the text. Locations of all manuscript collections cited and full citations to all works by Walter Hines Page are given in the selected bibliography. Those who wish to delve further into the sources for this book are urged to consult the copies of an earlier, somewhat longer, and more extensively annotated manuscript version deposited with the collection of biographical materials on Page in the Walter Hines Page Library, Randolph-Macon College.

ABBREVIATIONS IN NOTES

BJH	Burton J. Hendrick
BJH MSS	Burton J. Hendrick Papers
CAB	Cabinet Papers, Public Record Office, London, followed by series, volume, and (where available) document number—e.g., CAB 24/1/15.
CU	Columbia University Oral History Collection
EMH	Edward M. House
EMH MSS	Edward M. House Papers, Yale University Library
FO	Foreign Office Papers, Public Record Office, London, followed by series, volume, and (where available) document number—e.g., FO 371/1702/7914.
LC	Library of Congress
NA	National Archives
PUL	Princeton University Library
RCL	Rollins College Library
WHP	Walter Hines Page
WHP MSS	Walter Hines Page Papers, Houghton Library, Harvard University—with the following abbreviations for the principal divisions of the correspondence: AP — American Period EP — English Period
WW	Woodrow Wilson
WW MSS	Woodrow Wilson Papers, Library of Congress

CHAPTER I

1. WHP, *The Southerner*, pp. 3–4, 8–11, 13–15.

2. WHP to Catherine R. Page, Dec. 1876, WHP MSS, AP, file 813.

3. F. A. Olds interview, *Raleigh News and Observer*, 23 Dec. 1918, clipping, ibid., notes on early life; WHP to Catherine R. Page, 12 Apr. 1874, ibid., AP, file 813.

4. WHP, "The Old Place where little Grand Pa lived," ibid., speeches, box 5; U.S. Census, 1860, manuscript population and slave schedules, N.C., Wake County.

5. BJH interview with R. N. Page, 18–20 Mar. 1926, BJH MSS; Augustus White Long, *Son of Carolina: A Segment of the American Scene* (Durham, N.C.: Duke University Press, 1939), p. 150.

6. WHP speech, Oct. 1891, *Raleigh State Chronicle*, 20 Oct. 1891, clipping, WHP MSS, speeches, box 3; J. L. Prudhomme story, *Baltimore Evening Sun*, [1913], clipping, ibid., box 6.

7. WHP, *The Southerner*, p. 37; WHP to EMH, 24 Nov. 1916, EMH MSS.

8. Genealogical notes, WHP MSS, biographical material, box 1.

9. WHP, *The Southerner*, p. 46.

10. WHP to A. Frank Page, 12 May 1886, WHP MSS, AP, file 810.

11. BJH interview with R. Young, Mar. 1926, BJH MSS; Josephus Daniels, *Tar Heel Editor* (Chapel Hill, N.C.: University of North Carolina Press, 1939), p. 440.

12. WHP to Catherine R. Page, 2 Oct. 1872, WHP MSS, AP, file 813.

13. WHP to Catherine R. Page, 16 Oct. 1872, 15 May 1873, ibid.; Trinity College grade report, Dec. 1872, ibid., biographical material.

14. WHP to Catherine R. Page, 12 Feb., 15 May 1873, ibid., AP, file 813; *Randolph-Macon College Catalogue* (1874–75), pp. 29–30, copy in Randolph-Macon College Papers.

15. *Randolph-Macon College Catalogue* (1874–75), p. 28, copy in Randolph-Macon College Papers; A. G. Wardlaw reminiscence, Aug. 1924, BJH MSS.

16. Report card and distinction certificates, June 1874, WHP MSS, AP, file 922.

17. W. F. Tillett to WHP, 16 Aug. 1916, ibid., EP, file 1348; H. A. Tillett to WHP, 7 July 1913, ibid., file 1347.

18. J. B. Wardlaw to WHP, 6 Mar. 1876, ibid., AP, file 1090; WHP to Wardlaw, 2 June 1877, ibid.

19. WHP, obituary notice, *Literary World*, 24 Sept. 1881, clipping in ibid.

20. WHP to Catherine R. Page, 12 Apr. 1874, ibid., file 813; W. F. Tillett to BJH, 27 Nov. 1920, BJH MSS.

21. WHP to Catherine R. Page, 10 June 1874, WHP MSS, AP, file 813.

22. W. F. Tillett to BJH, 27 Nov. 1920, BJH MSS; WHP, annotated copy of *Randolph-Macon College Catalogue* (1872–73), WHP MSS, AP, file 922.

23. BJH interview with Cary Harris, 17 Mar. 1926, BJH MSS; BJH interview with Young, 12 Mar. 1926, ibid.

24. WHP to Catherine R. Page, 20 June 1875, WHP MSS, AP, file 813.

25. WHP, *The Southerner*, p. 327; "Study of an Old Southern Borough,"

pp. 650–51; WHP to James Lane Allen, 22 Sept. 1897, WHP MSS, AP, file 28; WHP, *The Rebuilding of Old Commonwealths*.

26. WHP to Catherine R. Page, 20 June 1875, WHP MSS, AP, file 813.

27. WHP to Catherine R. Page, 10, 31 Oct. 1875, ibid.

28. WHP to W. F. Tillett, ca. autumn 1876, quoted in C. O. Edwards to BJH, 4 July 1923, BJH MSS; Sarah J. Hanks to BJH, 3 Apr. [1922], ibid.

29. WHP to Sarah Jasper, 25 Aug. 1877, WHP MSS, AP, file 558.

30. WHP to Catherine R. Page, 31 Jan. 1876, ibid., file 813.

31. Basil L. Gildersleeve to WHP, 9 June, 1 Aug. 1876, ibid., file 419.

CHAPTER 2

1. WHP to Sarah Jasper, 30 Sept. 1876, quoted in BJH, *The Training of an American: The Earlier Life and Letters of Walter Hines Page* (Boston: Houghton Mifflin Company, 1928), p. 74; S. F. Clarke to BJH, 4 June 1923, BJH MSS; H. Sewall to BJH, 29 May 1923, ibid.

2. T. H. Huxley, *American Addresses* (New York: D. Appleton & Company, 1877), pp. 125, 126.

3. WHP to Jasper, 15 Oct., 30 Nov. 1876, quoted in BJH, *Training*, pp. 75, 76–77.

4. Basil L. Gildersleeve to Edwin Mims, 26 Nov. 1908, WHP MSS, AP, file 733.

5. E. G. Sihler, "Confessions and Convictions of a Classicist," *Johns Hopkins Alumni Magazine* 4 (1916): 277.

6. W. W. Jacques reminiscence, Aug. 1923, BJH MSS.

7. WHP to Catherine R. Page, 23 Feb. 1877, WHP MSS, AP, file 813; WHP to Jasper, 15 Oct. 1876, quoted in BJH, *Training*, pp. 75–76.

8. W. F. Tillett to BJH, 27 Nov. 1920, BJH MSS.

9. WHP to Jasper, 15 Oct. 1876, quoted in BJH, *Training*, p. 71.

10. WHP, undated MSS, WHP MSS, speeches, box 5; WHP to [Jasper?], 12 June 1877, ibid., notes on early life, box 3.

11. WHP to Catherine R. Page, 2 July 1877, ibid., AP, file 813.

12. WHP letter, 18 Sept. 1877, *Raleigh Observer*, 3 Oct. 1877.

13. WHP to Catherine R. Page, 29 Sept. 1877, WHP MSS, AP, file 813; WHP to [Jasper?], n.d., quoted in BJH, *Training*, pp. 105–6.

14. WHP to Gildersleeve, 6 May 1878, Gildersleeve Papers.

15. WHP to [Jasper?], 4 May 1878, WHP MSS, speeches, box 6.

16. WHP letter, 22 Nov. 1877, *Raleigh Observer*, 25 Nov. 1877.

17. WHP, "Henry Timrod," pp. 359–67.

18. Sidney Lanier to D. C. Gilman, 17 Dec. 1879, quoted in Hugh Hawkins, *Pioneer: A History of the Johns Hopkins University, 1874–1899* (Ithaca, N.Y.: Cornell University Press, 1960), p. 165; WHP to Gilman, 21 Nov. 1900, WHP MSS, AP, file 421.

19. E. A. Alderman, "A Great Ambassador: A Personal Impression," *Outlook* 135 (1923): 444; A. W. Long, "Walter Hines Page as an Editor in Raleigh," *The State* 1 (1937): 1.

20. WHP letter, 22 Nov. 1877, *Raleigh Observer*, 25 Nov. 1877; K. P. Battle to WHP, 25 Oct. 1878, WHP MSS, AP, file 84.

21. G. T. Winston to WHP, 18 July 1878, WHP MSS, AP, file 1142.

22. WHP, "Study of an Old Southern Borough," p. 651; WHP to Catherine R. Page, WHP MSS, AP, file 813; registration forms, 25 Jan. 1879, ibid., file 35.

23. *The Age* 1 (4 Jan. 1879): 1; editorial notice and advertisement, 5 Jan. 1879, WHP MSS, AP, file 652.

24. *The Age* 1 (15 Feb. 1879): 97–99, (17 May 1879): 278–79, (31 May 1879): 302–3, copy in WHP MSS, speeches, box 6.

25. WHP to A. Frank Page, 20 Apr. 1879, WHP MSS, AP, file 810.

26. BJH interview with Cary Harris, 17 Mar. 1926, BJH MSS; Bliss Perry, *And Gladly Teach* (Boston: Houghton Mifflin Company, 1935), p. 164.

27. WHP to Catherine R. Page, 22 Dec. 1878, 2 Mar. 1879, 11 July 1880, WHP MSS, AP, file 813.

28. BJH interview with Harris, 17 Mar. 1926, BJH MSS; clipping, WHP MSS, biographical material, box 1.

29. WHP letter, 17 Dec. 1878, *Raleigh Observer*, 31 Dec. 1878; essay fragments, WHP MSS, speeches, box 5.

30. WHP to Alice Wilson, 4 Jan. 1880, WHP MSS, AP, file 832.

31. WHP to E. E. Hale, 6 Jan. 1880, ibid., biographical materials, box 1.

CHAPTER 3

1. J. N. Burnes to WHP, 17 Jan. 1880, WHP MSS, AP, file 960.

2. *St. Joseph Gazette*, 15 July 1880.

3. Ibid., 30 Oct., 7 Nov. 1880.

4. WHP, "Study of an Old Southern Borough," pp. 648–58.

5. *St. Joseph Gazette*, 27 Nov. 1880; WHP to Catherine R. Page, [May 1881], WHP MSS, AP, file 813; WHP interview, *Charlotte Observer*, [1903], clipping, ibid., speeches, box 6.

6. WHP letter, 2 July 1881, *New York World*, 8 July 1881.

7. WHP letter, 9 Aug. 1881, *Boston Post*, 22 Aug. 1881.

8. WHP letters, 25 July, 10, 19 Aug. 1881, *New York World*, 29 July, 17, 23 Aug. 1881.

9. WHP letters, 12 July, 10, 27 Aug., 8 Sept. 1881, ibid., 18 July, 17 Aug., 5, 12 Sept. 1881.

10. WHP, "The Southern Educational Problem," pp. 309–20.

11. WHP letters, 25 July, 28 Sept. 1881, *Boston Post*, 2 Aug., 3 Oct. 1881; WHP to J. B. Wardlaw, [1881], WHP MSS, AP, file 1090.

12. WHP to A. Frank Page, 9 Oct. 1881, WHP MSS, AP, file 810.

13. WHP interview, *Charlotte Observer*, [1903], ibid., speeches, box 6.

14. *New York World*, 13 Feb. 1882.

15. E. I. Renick to WW, 15 Jan. 1882, in Arthur S. Link, ed., *The Papers of Woodrow Wilson* (Princeton, N.J., 1967), 2, p. 96.

16. WW to R. Bridges, 28 Oct. 1882, ibid., pp. 147–48; WW to R. H. Dabney, 11 Jan. 1883, ibid., pp. 285–86; *New York World*, 24 Sept. 1882.

17. BJH interview with J. Daniels, 21 Mar. 1926, BJH MSS.

18. *Boston Post*, 7 Mar. 1883.

19. J. Pulitzer quoted in W. A. Swanberg, *Pulitzer* (New York: Charles Scribner's Sons, 1967), p. 70; *Boston Post*, 18 May 1883.

20. A. W. Long, "Walter Hines Page as an Editor in Raleigh," *The State* 1 (1937): 16.

21. *Raleigh State Chronicle*, 15 Sept. 1883.

22. WHP to Catherine R. Page, 28 Dec. [1883], WHP MSS, AP, file 813.

23. H. Parker to BJH, 5 Aug. 1926, BJH MSS.

24. Advertising broadside, WHP MSS, AP, file 920.

25. *Raleigh State Chronicle*, 10 Nov. 1883.

26. Charles W. Dabney memoirs, Dabney Papers, box 15.

27. Watauga Club petition, 5 Feb. 1885, WHP MSS, AP, file 1101.

28. Report appended to petition, ibid.

29. WHP, "The Man behind the Plow," 27 May 1903, ibid., speeches, box 3.

30. *Raleigh State Chronicle*, 26 Jan. 1884.

31. Ibid., 1 Dec. 1883; WHP letter, 15 Feb. 1886, ibid., 18 Feb. 1886.

32. Ibid., 22 Sept., 24 Nov. 1883.

33. Ibid., 8 Dec. 1883, 14 June 1884.

34. Ibid., 14 June 1884; WHP to [H. W. Lilly], 24 Feb. 1885, WHP MSS, biographical materials, box 1.

35. WHP to [Gavin Hogg?], n.d., Hogg Papers; WHP to [Lilly], 24 Feb. 1885, WHP MSS, biographical materials, box 1.

36. *Raleigh State Chronicle*, 23 Feb. 1884.

37. Long, "Page as Editor in Raleigh," p. 16.

38. WHP to Alice W. Page, 6 Apr. 1885, WHP MSS, AP, file 832; WW to R. H. Dabney, 11 May 1883, in Link, *Papers of Woodrow Wilson*, 2, p. 320.

39. WHP letters, n.d., 2 Nov. 1885, 25 Jan. 1886, *Raleigh State Chronicle*, 30 Oct., 6 Nov. 1885, 28 Jan. 1886.

40. WHP letter, 1 Feb. 1886, ibid., 4 Feb. 1886.

41. *Atlanta Constitution*, 4 June 1885; WHP letters, 15 Feb., 8 Mar. 1886, *Raleigh State Chronicle*, 18 Feb., 11 Mar. 1886.

42. C. B. Aycock to WHP, 26 Feb. 1886, WHP MSS, AP, file 45.

43. WHP to A. Frank Page, 12 May 1885, ibid., file 810; WHP letter, 18 Feb. 1886, *Raleigh State Chronicle*, 25 Feb. 1886.

44. WHP letter, 1 Feb. 1886, *Raleigh State Chronicle*, 4 Feb. 1886.

CHAPTER 4

1. WHP letter, 17 May 1886, *Raleigh State Chronicle*, 20 May 1886; WHP to Alice W. Page, 4, 6 Apr. 1885, WHP MSS, AP, file 832; WHP to A. Frank Page, 12 May 1886, ibid., file 810.

2. WHP, "The 'New' Southern Problem," p. 712–13; WHP essay fragment, [1886], WHP MSS, speeches, box 5.

3. WHP letter, 19 May 1885, *Boston Post*, 22 May 1885; WHP letter, 13 July 1886, *Raleigh State Chronicle*, 15 July 1886.

4. *Raleigh State Chronicle*, 9 Feb. 1884.

5. WHP letters, 22 Dec. 1885, 5 Apr., 13 July, 27 Sept. 1886, *Raleigh State Chronicle*, 24 Dec. 1885, 8 Apr., 15 July, 30 Sept. 1886.

6. W. C. Dreher reminiscence, Apr. 1923, BJH MSS.

7. WHP interview, *Charlotte Observer*, [1903], clipping, WHP MSS, speeches, box 6; WHP to L. S. Metcalf, 23 Oct. [1887], ibid., AP, file 722.

8. Metcalf to L. F. Ward, 25 Sept., 16 Oct. [1886], Ward Papers.

9. Arthur E. Bostwick, *A Life with Men and Books* (New York: H. W. Wilson Company, 1939), p. 122.

10. I. L. Rice to WHP, 3 Aug. 1888, WHP MSS, AP, file 938; N. Bijur to WHP, 28 June 1889, ibid., file 99; WHP to Bijur, 1 Feb. 1891, ibid.

11. WHP to Bijur, 1 Feb. 1891, ibid.; Bostwick, *Life with Men and Books*, p. 122.

12. *Raleigh State Chronicle*, 15 Mar. 1884; Bostwick, *Life with Men and Books*, pp. 122–23.

13. WHP interview, *New York Herald*, 8 Oct. 1893, clipping, WHP MSS, speeches, box 6; WHP to Dreher, 3 Apr. 1893, ibid., AP, file 326; WHP to Charles F. Thwing, 4 Apr. 1894, ibid., file 1045.

14. WHP to Albert Shaw, 26 Mar. 1892, Shaw Papers; WHP to H. L. Higginson, 14 Sept. 1892, H. L. Higginson Papers, section 12, box 3.

15. *Forum* account book, Feb. 1893, WHP MSS, diaries 1; *Forum* 16 (Dec. 1893): cover.

16. WHP to Catherine R. Page, 19 Dec. 1893, WHP MSS, AP, file 813; WHP memorandum, 28 Feb. 1895, ibid., file 385; "THE FORUM: Business Statement by Walter H. Page, Editor," [Jan. 1894], H. B. Adams Papers.

17. Frank Luther Mott, *A History of American Magazines* (Cambridge, Mass.: Harvard University Press, 1957), 4:3–4, 8.

18. WHP to H. B. Adams, 27 Apr. 1894, H. B. Adams Papers.

19. Arthur Page reminiscence (CU), p. 6.

20. WHP memorandum, [May 1894], WHP MSS, AP, file 421.

21. WHP to Catherine R. Page, 19 Dec. 1893, ibid., file 813.

22. WHP to B. N. Duke, 15 Jan. 1892, Duke Papers.

23. WHP to G. W. Cable, 24 Apr. 1891, Cable Papers; WHP, "The Last Hold of the Southern Bully," pp. 303–14.

24. WHP to Shaw, 11 Aug. 1892, 11 Jan. 1893, Shaw Papers.

25. WHP, "Address at the Inauguration of President Winston," pp. 61–71.

26. [WHP], "Mr. Cleveland's—Failure?" pp. 129–38; [WHP], "Political Career and Character of David B. Hill," pp. 257–69.

27. WHP memorandum, [May 1894], WHP MSS, AP, file 421.

28. WHP to Andrew Carnegie, 12 Dec. 1893, ibid., file 204; WHP to H. B. Adams, 13 Feb. 1894, H. B. Adams Papers; WHP to Thwing, 13 Feb. 1894, WHP MSS, AP, file 1045.

29. WHP memorandum, [May 1894], WHP MSS, AP, file 421.

30. R. Frothingham to BJH, 29 Dec. 1924, BJH MSS.

31. WHP to Shaw, 3 July 1895, Shaw Papers; WHP to H. E. Scudder, 9 July 1895, WHP MSS, AP, file 973.

32. Entry, 2 Aug. 1895, Scudder Diary.

CHAPTER 5

1. *St. Joseph Gazette*, 27 Nov. 1880.

2. WHP to H. E. Scudder, 20 July 1895, WHP MSS, AP, file 973.

3. Entry, 17 June 1890, Scudder Diary; M. Jenkins to BJH, 23 Jan. 1925, BJH MSS; I. N. Hollis to BJH, 2 Feb. 1925, ibid.

4. Jenkins to BJH, 23 Jan. 1925, BJH MSS; Bliss Perry, *And Gladly Teach*, (Boston: Houghton Mifflin Company, 1935), pp. 177–78; Ellery Sedgwick, *The Happy Profession* (Boston: Little, Brown and Company, 1946), pp. 155, 178; G. H. Mifflin to WHP, 1 Nov. 1901, WHP MSS, AP, file 728.

5. Scudder, to H. O. Houghton, 3 Sept. 1894, Houghton Papers.

6. Entry, 5 July 1895, Scudder Diary. The crack about Scudder is quoted in Ellen B. Ballou, *The Building of the House: Houghton Mifflin's Formative Years* (Boston: Houghton Mifflin Company, 1970), p. 436.

7. Entries, 16, 25, 31 July 1895, Scudder Diary.

8. Entry, 14 Apr. 1896, ibid.

9. Mifflin to WHP, 31 Aug. 1895, WHP MSS, AP, file 728.

10. Entries, 15 Oct., 20 Nov. 1895, Scudder Diary; WHP to F. W. Atkinson, 28 Jan. 1896, WHP MSS, AP, file 28.

11. Entries, 21, 27, 29 Apr. 1896, Scudder Diary.

12. Entry, 7 May 1896, ibid.

13. Entry, 30 Mar. 1897, ibid.

14. Entry, 5 July 1898, ibid.

15. Entry, 18 Aug. 1896, ibid.

16. Ellery Sedgwick, "Walter Hines Page," *World's Work* 38 (1919): 375–76; WHP to John Jay Chapman, 26 Sept. 1896, WHP MSS, AP, file 28.

17. WHP to F. J. Turner, 29 May 1896, WHP MSS, AP, file 1057; WHP to Royal Cortissoz, 20 May 1896, Houghton Mifflin Co. Papers, letterbook 15.

18. WHP to W. A. White, 18 Dec. 1896, Houghton Mifflin Co. Papers, letterbook 16.

19. WHP to George Kennan, 1 Nov. 1898, ibid., letterbook 22.

20. WHP to Paul Shorey, 29 May 1896, WHP MSS, AP, file 28; WHP to J. B. Chamberlain, 30 Sept. 1896, ibid.

21. Profit and loss sheets and grand balance sheets, Houghton Mifflin Co. Papers (uncatalogued series); Mifflin to A. F. Houghton, 12 Mar. 1900, ibid., letterbook 21.

22. WHP to Robert Sharp, 13 Mar. 1897, WHP MSS, AP, file 983; WHP to John Burroughs, 8 Jan. 1898, ibid., file 28.

23. J. F. Rhodes to WHP, 2 Mar. 1907, ibid., file 935.

24. Profit and loss sheets, Houghton Mifflin Co. Papers (uncatalogued series).

25. WHP to Mary C. de Graffenreid, 12 Feb. 1896, WHP MSS, AP, file 28.

26. For the *David Harum* story, see Ballou, *The Building of the House*, p. 416.

27. WHP, "The Making of Literature," p. 468; WHP to Mifflin, 23 Feb. 1899, WHP MSS, AP, file 728.

28. WHP to Julia Magruder, 15 Sept. 1897, WHP MSS, AP, file 28; WHP, "The Making of Literature," pp. 461–71.

29. WHP to Brander Matthews, 7 Mar. 1897, Matthews Papers; WHP to Margaret Deland, 2 Dec. 1897, WHP MSS, AP, file 28; WHP to Anna M. Sholl, 4 Jan. 1899, Houghton Mifflin Co. Papers, letterbook 22; WHP, "Literature and Its Making," 18 June 1900, clipping, WHP MSS, speeches, box 3.

30. WHP to Rhodes, 22 June 1896, WHP MSS, AP, file 28.

31. WHP to W. L. Wilson, 10 Aug. 1896, Houghton Mifflin Co. Papers, letterbook 15; WHP to Chapman, 16 November 1896, Chapman Papers; WHP speech to Harvard Southern Club, 22 Feb. 1898, WHP MSS, speeches, box 3.

32. WHP, "The War with Spain and After," pp. 721–27.

33. WHP speech, 15 Dec. 1898, clipping, WHP MSS, speeches, box 3; WHP speech, Mar. 1899, clipping, ibid.; WHP, "The End of the War and After," pp. 430–32; WHP, "A Wholesome Stimulus to Higher Politics," pp. 289–92.

34. WHP to H. Scudder, 18 Mar. 1899, WHP MSS, AP, file 973; Scudder to WHP, 25 May 1898, ibid.

35. Theodore Roosevelt, *Autobiography* (New York: Macmillan Company, 1913), p. 217.

36. WHP to T. F. Bayard, 8 Oct. 1897, WHP MSS, AP, file 28; WHP to J. Bryce, 9 May 1898, ibid.

37. E. A. Alderman to WHP, 8 Aug. 1896, ibid., file 10; WHP to Alderman, 21 Aug. 1896, Alderman Papers.

38. WHP, "The Forgotten Man," pp. 1–47.

39. R. N. Page to WHP, 24 May [1897], WHP MSS, AP, file 827; C. D. McIver to WHP, 22 July 1897, ibid., file 677; *Raleigh News and Observer*, 20 May 1897.

40. Sedgwick, "Walter Hines Page," p. 376; WHP to W. P. Trent, 6 Oct. 1896, Houghton Mifflin Co. Papers, letterbook 16.

41. WHP, *The Southerner*, pp. 103–4.

42. WHP to C. B. Chesnutt, 14 Nov. 1898, WHP-Chesnutt Papers; WHP speech, 15 Dec. 1898, clipping, WHP MSS, speeches, box 3.

43. WHP to Alice W. Page, 15, 17 Feb., 2, 7 Mar. 1899, WHP MSS, AP, file 832; WHP to Mifflin, 23 Feb. 1899, ibid., file 728; WHP to Scudder, 28 Feb., 18 Mar. 1899, ibid., file 973.

44. WHP to Alice W. Page, [Mar. 1899], ibid., file 832; WHP speech, 5 Mar. 1899, clipping, ibid., speeches, box 3; WHP speech, 11 Apr. 1916, clipping, ibid., box 2.

45. WHP, *The Rebuilding of Old Commonwealths*, pp. 105–53.

46. Entry, 24 Apr. 1896, Scudder Diary; Jenkins to BJH, 23 Jan. 1925, BJH MSS.

47. WHP to Scudder, 13 Sept. 1897, 4 Nov. 1899, WHP MSS, AP, file 973.

48. WHP interview, *Charlotte Observer*, [1903], clipping, ibid., speeches, box 6; WHP to W. R. Thayer, 5 Dec. 1900, Thayer Papers, box 11.

49. WHP to Scudder, 2 Aug. 1899, WHP MSS, AP, file 973.

50. Sedgwick, *The Happy Profession*, p. 154; WHP to Chapman, 10 Mar. 1897, Chapman Papers.

51. E. H. Rowe to BJH, 2 July 1923, BJH MSS.

52. S. S. McClure to WHP, 19, 24 June 1899, WHP MSS, AP, file 666.

53. McClure to WHP, 7 July 1899, ibid.

54. Entry, 10 July 1899, Scudder Diary; WHP to Scudder, 2 Aug. 1899, WHP MSS, AP, file 973.

55. WHP to Thayer, 5 Dec. 1900, Thayer Papers, box 11; Perry, *And Gladly Teach*, p. 164.

56. WHP to Scudder, 4 Nov. 1899, WHP MSS, AP, file 973.

57. Entry, 14 Dec. 1899, Scudder Diary.

CHAPTER 6

1. On the firm's earnings see Doubleday, Page & Co. confidential statement [1911], H. L. Higginson Papers, series 12, box 12.

2. WHP, *A Publisher's Confession*, p. 91; O. Henry, quoted in H. Casey, "A New 'Page' in Diplomacy," clipping [1913], WHP MSS, speeches, box 6.

3. WHP to V. F. Boyle, 5 Feb. 1901, WHP MSS, AP, file 135; WHP, *A Publisher's Confession*, pp. 30–31.

4. WHP to T. Dreiser, 9 June 1900, Dreiser Papers.

5. T. H. McKee to R. N. Elias, [Mar.], 3 Apr. 1949, Elias Collection.

6. WHP to Dreiser, 23 July 1900, Dreiser Papers.

7. H. S. Houston radio broadcast, 15 Aug. 1930, reprint, WHP MSS, biographical material, box 1; R. C. Ogden to G. F. Peabody, 12 June 1905, Ogden Papers, box 15.

8. WHP, *A Publisher's Confession*, pp. 9–10, 17–18, 23, 25–28, 36, 61, 109, 127, 153, 169–70; reactions to book, WHP MSS, criticism file.

9. WHP, "An Organized Plan for Books for the Proper Study of English," [1899], WHP MSS, AP, file 638.

10. WHP to M. H. Liddell, 21 July 1903, ibid., file 638; Liddell to WHP, 22 July 1903, ibid.

11. WHP to C. Alphonso Smith, 18 Apr., 2 June 1908, 9 April 1911, ibid., file 996; Smith to BJH, 20 May 1924, BJH MSS.

12. WHP, "The Cultivated Man in an Industrial Era," pp. 4980–84.

13. Speech fragment, [1898], WHP MSS, speeches, box 3.

14. *World's Work* 2 (1902): 2695–96; WHP, "On a Tenth Birthday," pp. 13903–6.

15. WHP to J. C. Harris, 2 Aug. 1900, WHP MSS, AP, file 472.

16. WHP to J. Muir, 25 Nov. 1901, ibid., file 761; Henry Page to WHP, 8 Oct. 1901, ibid., file 818.

17. *World's Work* 1 (1900): 3–9, 18, 119.

18. WHP to Harris, 2 Aug. 1900, WHP MSS, AP, file 472.

19. *World's Work* 1 (1901): 247, 20 (1910): 12877; Thayer to WHP, 4 Dec. 1900, WHP MSS, AP, file 1039; WHP to W. B. Thayer, 5 Dec. 1900, Thayer Papers, box 11.

20. *World's Work* 1 (1900): 3.

21. WHP to R. S. Baker, 14 July 1908, WHP MSS, AP, file 57; WHP to E. Mims, 1 Nov. 1911, ibid., file 733; WHP to Francis J. Dyer, 11 July 1908, Dyer Papers.

22. WHP to B. I. Wheeler, 12 Sept. 1900, Wheeler Papers.

23. *World's Work* 12 (1906): 7477.

24. Houston to WHP, 20 Feb. 1903, WHP MSS, AP, file 526; WHP, "On a Tenth Birthday," p. 13914.

25. Arthur Page reminiscence (CU), p. 18.

26. WHP to H. Holt, 7 May 1912, Holt Papers (RCL).

27. WHP to H. Croly, 9 Feb. 1915, WHP MSS, EP, file 942.

28. WHP to J. S. Bassett, 1 Feb. 1904, Bassett Papers.

29. Alice W. Page to BJH, 15 July 1926, BJH MSS.

30. Arthur Page reminiscence (CU), pp. 13–14.

31. Ralph W. Page to WHP, 20 Oct. 1912, WHP MSS, AP, file 825.

32. WHP to W. H. Hoggson, 17 Aug. 1909, ibid., file 511; WHP memorandum, 29 Apr. 1910, ibid., biographical materials, box 1.

33. WHP to C. W. Dabney, 24 June 1910, Dabney Papers, folder 109; WHP to Bassett, 21 Jan. 1910, Bassett Papers.

34. WHP, "The Writer and the University," pp. 43–54. Cooper, Notes, Galley 197 (chapters 6 and 7

35. E. Glasgow to WHP, 4 Jan. 1902, WHP MSS, AP, file 423.

36. F. Strother reminiscence, 3 May 1926, BJH MSS.

37. Ferris Greenslet, *Under the Bridge* (Boston: Houghton Mifflin Company, 1943), p. 140; Christopher Morley, *"Effendi": Frank Nelson Doubleday, 1862–1934* (Garden City, N.Y.: privately published, 1934), pp. 1–2.

38. McKee to Elias, 3 Apr. 1949, Elias Collection.

39. Arthur Page reminiscence (CU), pp. 68–70, 72, 77; George H. Doran, *Chronicles of Barabbas, 1884–1934* (New York: Harcourt, Brace and Company, 1935), p. 223–24.

40. F. N. Doubleday to H. L. Higginson, 5 Dec. 1911, H. L. Higginson Papers, section 12, box 12.

41. WHP to Mary Johnston, [10 Mar. 1900?], Johnston Papers.

42. *Presbyterian Standard*, 2 Apr. 1902, clipping, WHP MSS, notes on early life, box 3.

43. WHP to Alice W. Page, 15, 17, 21 Mar. 1905, ibid., AP, file 832.

44. WHP, *The Southerner*, pp. 203–4, 314.

45. WHP to Alice W. Page, 21 Mar. 1905, WHP MSS, AP, file 832.

46. WHP to N. O. Nelson, 6 Dec. 1909, ibid., file 776; earnings statements, ibid., *Southerner* file.

47. WHP to Ogden, 26 June 1910, ibid., AP, file 804; promotional brochure, ibid., *Southerner* file.

48. J. G. de R. Hamilton review, *Raleigh News and Observer*, clipping, ibid.; WHP to Arthur Page, ibid., EP, file 989b.

49. Entry, 9 Jan. 1911, daybook 1911, ibid., diaries 1; entry, Notebook B [ca. Dec. 1912], ibid., speeches, box 4.

50. WHP speech, 8 Oct. 1912, ibid., box 6.

51. WHP to E. Alderman, 9 Dec. 1912, Alderman Papers.

CHAPTER 7

1. WHP to E. G. Murphy, 5 Apr. 1900, WHP MSS, AP, file 766.

2. WHP to G. F. Peabody, 17 Aug. 1904, Peabody Papers, box 57.

3. Peabody to R. C. Ogden, 4 June [1905], Ogden Papers, box 9.

4. WHP to J. H. Kirkland, 13 Aug. 1908, WHP MSS, AP, file 604.

5. Ogden to G. S. Dickerman, 18 June 1901, Southern Education Board Papers, box 15.

6. Murphy to C. D. McIver, 30 Mar., 4 Apr. 1903, McIver Papers, box 1.

7. Ogden to A. Carnegie, 10 July 1906, Ogden Papers, box 15; Louis R. Harlan, *Separate and Unequal: Public School Campaigns and Racism in the Southern Seaboard States, 1901–1915* (Chapel Hill, N.C.: University of North Carolina Press, 1958), esp. pp. 92–101.

8. WHP to Ogden, 17 Dec. 1903, WHP MSS, AP, file 804.

9. Murphy to WHP, 10 Dec. 1903, ibid., file 766.

10. Murphy to WHP, 16 Oct. 1909, ibid., *Southerner* file.

11. WHP to B. N. Duke, "Thanksgiving Day" 1903, B. N. Duke Papers.

12. WHP, "A Journey through the Southern States," pp. 9006–42.

13. WHP to C. T. Nesbitt, 15 May 1911, WHP MSS, AP, file 777; WHP to W. Rose, 24 Feb. 1910, ibid., file 954.

14. WHP to S. C. Mitchell, 2 Jan. 1908, Mitchell Papers, box 1.

15. *World's Work* 5 (1902): 2820.

16. WHP to O. G. Villard, 20 May 1913, Villard Papers, file 2936; WHP speech, 11 Apr. 1916, clipping, WHP MSS, speeches, box 2.

17. *World's Work* 1 (Nov. 1900): 19020; 3 (Nov. 1901): 1355.

18. Ibid. 1 (1901): 574–75.

19. Ibid. 5 (1902): 2705, 7 (1904): 4502.

20. Ibid. 9 (1905): 5776, 11 (1906): 7362–63, 14 (1907): 9384.

21. Ibid. 6 (1903): 3603, 16 (1908): 10172–73.

22. WHP speech, 11 Apr. 1916, clipping, WHP MSS, speeches, box 2.

23. *World's Work* 16 (1908): 10408–09; WHP to H. D. Wallace, 8 Nov. 1912, WHP MSS, AP, file 1083; WHP to Nesbitt, 19 Aug. 1912, ibid., file 777.

24. T. Roosevelt to WHP, 10 Aug. 1908, WHP MSS, file 952.

25. WHP to L. H. Bailey, 24 Apr. 1909, ibid., file 54.

26. BJH, *The Training of an American: The Earlier Life and Letters of Walter Hines Page* (Boston: Houghton Mifflin Company, 1928), pp. 370–71.

27. WHP, "The Hookworm and Civilization," pp. 504–18.

28. WHP to K. L. Butterfield, 25 Jan. 1909, WHP MSS, AP, file 186; WHP to Sir Horace Plunkett, 5 May 1909, Plunkett Papers.

29. *World's Work* 26 (1913): 17–18; WHP speech, 3 Dec. 1912, WHP MSS, speeches, box 3.

30. *World's Work* 8 (1904): 5332–33.

31. Ibid. 9 (1904): 5440, 14 (1907): 8816.

32. H. J. Ford, "An Explanation of Mr. Bryan," ibid. 16 (1908): 10215–23.

33. WHP to A. J. Montague, 21 Apr., 28 July 1908, Montague Papers, file 7/5.

34. WHP to W. H. Taft, 7 Nov. 1908, WHP MSS, AP, file 421.

35. WHP speech, 7 Dec. 1908, pamphlet, ibid., file 794; Taft speech (typewritten copy), ibid., file 1026.

36. WHP to Taft, 7 Nov. 1908, ibid.; *World's Work* 16 (1908): 10516–17.

37. *World's Work* 18 (1909): 11971–72; WHP to R. S. Baker, 12 July 1910, R. S. Baker Papers (LC), box 93.

38. *World's Work* 20 (1910): 13093.

39. W. L. McCorkle memorandum, [11 Feb. 1911], WHP MSS, AP, file 669; entry, 24 Feb. 1911, daybook 1911, ibid., diaries 1.

40. WHP memorandum, [ca. Mar. 1910], ibid., biographical material, box 1; WHP to WW, 8 Feb. 1911, ibid., AP, file 1136; *World's Work* 13 (1907): 8377, 21 (1910): 13588–707.

41. WW to WHP, 10 Feb. 1911, WHP MSS, WW letters; WHP to WW, 15 Feb. 1911, ibid., AP, file 1136; WHP to McCorkle, 13 Mar. 1911, ibid., file 669.

42. F. P. Stockbridge to WHP, 28 Apr. 1911, ibid., file 1015.

43. WHP to McCorkle, 17 June 1911, ibid., file 669; WW to WHP, 7 June 1911, ibid., WW letters.

44. WHP to McCorkle, 17 June 1911, ibid., AP, file 669; B. R. Newton to BJH, 14 Jan. 1925, BJH MSS.

45. W. G. Brown to EMH, 9 Dec. 1911, EMH MSS.

46. WHP to Wallace, 6 Aug. 1912, Wallace Papers; WHP to EMH, 6 Sept. 1912, EMH MSS.

47. F. P. Stockbridge, "How Woodrow Wilson Won His Nomination," *Current History* 20 (1924): 572; WHP to WW, 3 July 1912, WW MSS (PUL), "Correspondence B" file; *World's Work* 25 (1912): 138.

48. WHP to WW, 5 Nov. 1912, WHP MSS, AP, file 1136; WHP memorandum, 15 Nov. 1912, diary 1912, ibid., diaries 1.

49. WHP to WW, 27 Nov. 1912, ibid., AP, file 1136.

50. WHP to E. Alderman, 31 Dec. 1912, Alderman Papers; WW to Ellen Axson Wilson, 22 Aug. 1899, in Arthur S. Link, ed., *The Papers of Woodrow Wilson* (Princeton, N.J., 1971), 11, p. 237.

51. Entry, 15 Mar. 1913, EMH Diary.

52. Entry, 8 Jan. 1913, ibid.

53. Entries, 22, 23 Feb. 1913, ibid.

54. Entry, 24 Feb. 1913, ibid.

55. *World's Work* 25 (1913): 483; WHP to J. Y. Joyner, 25 Mar. 1913, Joyner Papers.

56. Entries, 26, 28 Mar. 1913, EMH Diary; WHP, "The Consecutive Story: The Ambassadorship," WHP MSS, diaries 2, box 1; WHP to WW, 1 Apr. 1913, ibid., AP, file 1136.

57. WHP, "Consecutive Story," ibid., diaries 2, box 1.

58. Entries, 14 Feb., 25 Mar. 1913, EMH Diary.

59. Entry, 30 Mar. 1913, ibid.

60. WHP, "Consecutive Story," WHP MSS, diaries 2, box 1.

61. WHP to Mary E. Page, 16 May 1913, ibid., EP, file 996.

CHAPTER 8

1. WHP to R. N. Page, 22 Dec. 1913, WHP MSS, EP, file 999; R. E. Blackwell to WHP, 2 June 1913, ibid., file 176; WHP, "Consecutive Story," ibid., diaries 2, box 1; WHP speech, 6 June 1913, ibid., speeches, box 1.

2. WHP, "Consecutive Story," ibid., diaries 2, box 1.

3. Entry, 29 June 1913, EMH Diary.

4. WHP to Alice W. Page, 7 June 1913, WHP MSS, EP, file 1002a; WHP to Arthur W. Page, 13 July 1913, ibid., file 989.

5. Entry, 19 June 1913, EMH Diary.

6. WHP to Mary E. Page, 16 Mar. 1914, WHP MSS, EP, file 996; WHP to WW, 18 Mar. 1914, ibid., file 1482.
Cooper, Notes, Galley 199, chapter 8

7. WHP to EMH, 8 Jan. 1914, EMH MSS; E. Bell to Arthur W. Page, 23 Apr. 1920, BJH MSS.

8. WHP to WW, 21 Dec. 1913, 25 Jan. 1914, WHP MSS, EP, file 1482; WHP to EMH, 23 Nov. 1913, EMH MSS.

9. WHP to EMH, 8 Jan., 27 Apr. 1914, EMH MSS.

10. WHP to Arthur W. Page, 27 Sept. 1913, WHP MSS, EP, file 989.

11. WHP to EMH, 25 Aug. 1913, EMH MSS.

12. WHP to EMH, 28 Aug. 1913, ibid.

13. WHP to EMH, 26 Oct. 1913, ibid.

14. WHP to EMH, 26 Oct. 1913, ibid.; Sir E. Grey to Sir W. Tyrrell, 17 Nov. 1913, FO 371/1678/52367.

15. WHP to EMH, 8 Jan., 2 Mar. 1914, EMH MSS; WHP speech, 11 Mar. 1914, WHP MSS, speeches, box 1; WW to WHP, 2 Apr. 1914, ibid., WW letters.

16. WHP to WW, 8, 12 June 1914, WHP MSS, EP, file 1482.

17. WHP to EMH, 13 Feb. 1914, EMH MSS; Viscount Grey of Fallodon, *Twenty-five Years, 1892–1916* (London: Hodder and Stoughton, 1925), 2, p. 100.

18. WHP, "Some Notes that I'll Work into a Letter to the President," [Mar. 1916], WHP MSS, EP, file 1482; WHP speech, 15 Aug. 1913, ibid., speeches, box 1; WHP to EMH, 28 Aug. 1913, EMH MSS.

19. WHP memorandum, Aug. 1913, WHP MSS, EP, file 187.

20. WHP to EMH, 23 Sept. 1913, EMH MSS; WHP to WW, 25 Oct. 1913, 31 Mar. 1914, WHP MSS, EP, file 1482; WHP to E. Alderman, Christmas 1913, Alderman Papers.

21. WW to WHP, 7 Mar. 1914, WHP MSS, WW letters.

22. Ray Stannard Baker, *American Chronicle* (New York: Charles Scribner's Sons, 1945), pp. 369, 379; Hamilton Fish Armstrong, *Peace and Counterpeace: From Wilson to Hitler* (New York: Harper and Row, 1971), pp. 445–46.

23. WHP to Grey, [June 1913], WHP MSS, EP, file 570; WHP to EMH, 8 July 1913, EMH MSS.

24. EMH to WHP, 4 Jan. 1914, WHP MSS, EP, file 683.

25. WHP to EMH, 2 Jan. 1914, EMH MSS; EMH to WW, 28 May 1914, ibid.; EMH to WHP, 28 May 1914, WHP MSS, EP, file 558; entry, 12 June 1914, EMH Diary.

26. Entries, 17 June, 4 July 1914, EMH Diary; EMH to WW, 17 June 1914, EMH MSS; WHP to WW, 5 July 1914 (two letters), WHP MSS, EP, file 1482.

27. EMH to WHP, 10 Sept. 1913, WHP MSS, EP, file 658; entry, 24 Dec. 1913, diary 1913, ibid., diaries 2, box 1; WHP to EMH, 27 Apr. 1914, EMH MSS.

28. Entries, 19, 30 June 1914, EMH Diary; WHP to WW, 5 July 1914, WHP MSS, EP, file 1482.

29. WHP to WW, 12 Sept. 1913, WHP MSS, EP, file 1482; WW to WHP, 6 Dec. 1913, ibid., WW letters; I. Laughlin to WHP, 6 May 1914, ibid., EP, file 755; entry, 4 Jan. 1914, diary 1914, ibid., diaries 2, box 1.

30. Entry, 20 Jan. 1914, ibid., diaries 2, box 1; WHP speech, 8 Dec. 1913, ibid., speeches, box 1.

31. Lord Cowdray, "Interview & Exchange of Views with the American Ambassador: *Strictly Private and Confidential Memo Re Mexico*," 9 Jan. 1914, S. Pearson & Sons, Ltd. Papers, box A 3.

32. Laughlin to Baker, 29 June 1935, Baker Papers (LC), box 41; WW to WHP, 24 Feb. 1914, WHP MSS, WW letters.

33. WHP to WW, 7 Apr., 5 June 1914, WHP MSS, EP, file 1482; WW to WHP, 19 June 1914, ibid., WW letters; WHP to EMH, 30 Jan. 1914, EMH MSS.

34. WW to C. H. Dodge, 12 July 1914, Baker Papers (LC), box 5; EMH to WHP, 3 Oct. 1914, WHP MSS, EP, file 658.

35. WHP, "Consecutive Story," WHP MSS, diaries 2, box 1; WHP to Arthur W. Page, 6–10 Nov. 1914, ibid., EP, file 989.

36. Grey, *Twenty-five Years*, 1, p. 269; WHP to R. N. Page, 22 July 1914, R. N. Page Papers; WHP to Arthur W. Page, 19 July 1914, WHP MSS, EP, file 989.

37. Alice W. Page to Arthur W. Page, 16 Aug. 1914, WHP MSS, notes on early life, box 5.

CHAPTER 9

1. WHP to WW, 29 July, 2, 9 Aug. 1914, WW MSS, series 2; entry, 4 Aug. 1914, diary 1914, WHP MSS, diaries 2, box 1.

2. WHP to WW, 9 Aug. 1914, WW MSS, series 2; WHP to Arthur W. Page, 9 Aug. 1914, WHP MSS, EP, file 989; BJH interview with I. Laughlin, ibid., file 755.

3. Emily Bax, "England Declares War," BJH MSS.

4. BJH interview with H. Hoover, WHP MSS, notes on early life, box 5.

5. WHP to Mary E. Page, Christmas 1915, ibid., EP, file 996; WHP to Arthur W. Page, [Sept. 1914], ibid., file 989; WHP to Alice W. Page, 7 Jan. 1915, ibid., file 1002b.

6. WHP to Arthur W. Page, 23 Aug. 1914, ibid., file 989; WHP to WW, 22 Sept., 29 Oct. 1914, WW MSS, series 2.

7. WHP to WW, 23 Aug. 1914, WW MSS, series 2; WHP to Arthur W. Page, 9 Aug. 1914, WHP MSS, EP, file 989.

8. WHP to WW, 29 July, 2, 9 Aug. 1914, WW MSS, series 2.

9. WHP to Arthur W. Page, [Sept.], 13 Oct. 1914, WHP MSS, EP, file 989; WHP to WW, 15 Oct. 1914, WW MSS, series 2.

10. Entry, 2 Aug. 1914, diary 1914, WHP MSS, diaries 2, box 1; Alice W. Page to Katharine Page, 19 Aug. 1914, ibid., EP, file 798; WHP to WW, 9 Aug., 6 Sept. 1914, WW MSS, series 2.

11. WHP to WW, 6 Oct. 1914, WW MSS, series 2.

12. WHP to Arthur W. Page, [Sept. 1914], WHP MSS, EP, file 989.

13. WHP to EMH, 22 Sept. 1914, EMH MSS.

14. Sir E. Grey to Sir C. Spring Rice, 29 Aug. 1914, FO 371/2223/45254.

15. Viscount Grey of Fallodon, *Twenty-five Years 1892–1916*, (London: Hodder and Stoughton, 1925), 2, p. 160.

16. Sir Eyre Crowe to WHP, 22 Aug. 1914, WHP MSS, EP, file 1202.

17. WHP to W. J. Bryan, 30 Sept. 1914, ibid.

18. WHP to Bryan, 9 Oct. 1914, ibid.; WHP to WW, 15 Oct. 1914, WW MSS, series 2.

19. R. Lansing to WHP, 16 Oct. 1914, WHP MSS, EP, file 1202; WW to WHP, 16 Oct. 1914, ibid.

20. WHP to Lansing, 19 Oct. 1914, ibid.; WHP to WW, 21 Oct. 1914, WW MSS, series 2.

21. WHP to Lansing, 20 Oct. 1914, WHP MSS, EP, file 1202; WHP draft letter, ibid., diaries 2, box 1; WHP to WW, 21, 28 Oct. 1914, WW MSS, series 2.

22. WHP to Arthur W. Page, 20 Oct. 1914, encl. WHP to EMH, 21 October, 1914, EMH MSS; WHP to EMH, 22 Oct. 1914, ibid.; WHP to WW, 28 Oct. 1914, WW MSS, series 2.

23. WW to EMH, 29 Oct. 1914, EMH MSS.

24. WW to EMH, 22 Oct. 1914, ibid.

25. WHP to WW, 28 Oct. 1914, WW MSS, series 2; WW to WHP, 28 Oct. 1914, WHP MSS, WW letters; WW to EMH, 23 Oct. 1914, EMH MSS.

26. EMH to WW, 21, 24 Oct. 1914, WW MSS, series 2; entry, 22 Oct. 1914, EMH Diary.

27. Entry, 3 Dec. 1914, EMH Diary; EMH to WHP, 4 Dec. 1914, WHP MSS, EP, file 658; WHP to EMH, 15 Dec. 1914, EMH MSS.

28. WHP to Bryan, 28 Dec. 1914, *Papers relating to the Foreign Relations of the United States: The Lansing Papers* (Washington: Government Printing Office, 1939), 1, p. 259; WHP to Bryan, 30 Dec. 1914, WHP MSS, EP, file 1202; WHP to C. P. Anderson, 4 Feb. 1915, Anderson Papers, box 26.

29. WHP to Bryan, 18 Jan. 1915, WHP MSS, EP, file 1202; Bryan to WHP, 23 Jan. 1915, ibid.

30. EMH to WHP, 18 Jan. 1915, ibid., file 658; WHP to Alice W. Page, 17, 24 Jan. 1915, ibid., file 1002a.

31. Entries, 6, 7, 13 Feb. 1915, EMH Diary; EMH to WW, 9 Mar. 1915, WW MSS, series 2.

32. EMH to WW, 9 Feb. 1915, WW MSS, series 2.

33. Entries, 14, 17 Feb. 1915, EMH Diary; WHP to Alice W. Page, 24 Feb. 1915, WHP MSS, EP, file 1002a.

34. WHP to Bryan, 23 Feb. 1915, WHP MSS, EP, file 1202; WW to EMH, 20 Feb. 1915, EMH MSS; entries, 20, 22 Feb. 1915, EMH Diary.

35. Entry, 22 Feb. 1915, EMH Diary; EMH to WW, 9 Mar. 1915, WW MSS, series 2.

36. Grey to Spring Rice, 1 Mar. 1915, FO 382/185/24928; WHP to Bryan, 3 Mar. 1915, WHP MSS, EP, file 1202; entry, 3 Mar. 1915, EMH Diary.

37. Entry, 5 Mar. 1915, EMH Diary; EMH to WW, 9 Mar. 1915, WW MSS, series 2.

38. Grey to Spring Rice, 13 Apr. 1915, FO 382/186/43896; entry, 12 Mar. 1915, diary 1915, WHP MSS, diaries 2, box 1.

39. Entry, 30 Apr. 1915, EMH Diary.

40. Entry, 3 June 1915, ibid.; entries, 30 Apr., 3 May 1915, diary 1915, WHP MSS, diaries 2, box 1.

41. Entry, 3 June 1915, EMH Diary; entries 3, 4 June 1915, diary, Carver Papers, box 1.

42. WW to EMH, 5 May 1915, EMH MSS.

43. WHP to Arthur W. Page, 2 May 1915, WHP MSS, EP, file 989; entry, 7 May 1915, EMH Diary.

44. Entry, 7 May 1915, EMH Diary; Katharine Page journal, WHP MSS, biographical materials, box 1.

45. WHP to Bryan, 8 May 1915, WHP MSS, EP, file 1202; WW to Bryan, 10 May 1915, Bryan MSS (NA).

46. WHP to Arthur W. Page, 6 June 1915, WHP MSS, EP, file 989.

47. EMH to WW, 9 May 1915, WW MSS, series 2; entry, 3 June 1915, Plunkett Diary.

48. Entry, 4 June 1915, diary 1915, WHP MSS, diaries 2, box 1; EMH to WHP, 17 June 1915, ibid., EP, file 658.

49. Entry, 23 June 1915, diary 1915, ibid., diaries 2, box 1.

50. WHP to Katharine Page Loring, 7 Dec. 1915, ibid., EP, file 797.

51. WHP to EMH, 8 June, 21 July 1915, EMH MSS; WHP to WW, 26 Sept. 1915, WW MSS, series 2.

52. EMH to WHP, 19 Aug. 1915, WHP MSS, EP, file 658; WHP to EMH, 2 Sept. 1915, EMH MSS.

53. WHP to EMH, 4 Aug. 1915, EMH MSS.

54. WHP to EMH, 21 July 1915, ibid.

55. EMH to Arthur W. Page, 15 July 1915, WHP MSS, EP, file 658; WHP to Lansing, 31 July 1915, ibid., file 1210; WW to Lansing, 2 Aug. 1915, Lansing Papers (PUL), box 3; EMH to WW, 4 Aug. 1915, WW MSS, series 2.

56. WW to EMH, 21 Aug. 1915, EMH MSS; WW to WHP, 10 Sept. 1915, WHP MSS, WW letters.

57. WW to WHP, 10 Sept. 1915, WHP MSS, WW letters; WW to EMH, 18 Oct. 1915, EMH MSS; H. F. Armstrong, *Peace and Counterpeace: From Wilson to Hitler* (New York: Harper and Row, 1971), pp. 445–46; WW to Nancy Toy, 12 Dec. 1914, Baker Papers (LC), box 16.

58. Entry, 28 Nov. 1915, EMH Diary.

59. WHP to EMH, [draft, ca. 1 Sept. 1915], WHP MSS, EP, file 658; entry, 17 Dec. 1915, diary 1915, ibid., diaries 2, box 1.

60. WHP to WW, draft, with BJH notation, ibid., EP, file 1482; Lansing to WHP, 23 Dec. 1915, with WHP notation, ibid.; entry, 28 Dec. 1915, diary 1915, ibid., diaries 2, box 1.

61. Grey to EMH, 3 June 1915, EMH MSS.

62. Entry, 1 Nov. 1915, EMH Diary.

63. WHP to EMH, 12 Nov. 1915, EMH MSS.

64. WHP to Arthur W. Page, 30 Aug. 1915, WHP MSS, EP, file 989 .

65. Frank Page to Arthur W. Page, 23 Aug. 1915, ibid., notes on early life, box 5.

66. Entry, 13 Dec. 1915, diary 1915, ibid., diaries 2, box 1; WHP to Arthur, Frank, and Ralph Page, Christmas 1915, ibid., EP, file 989.

CHAPTER 10

1. WHP to R. Lansing, 3 Jan. 1916, WHP MSS, EP, file 1213; WHP to WW, 5 Jan. 1916, ibid., file 1482.

2. EMH to WW, 13 Jan. 1916, WW MSS, series 2; entry, 6 Jan. 1916, EMH Diary.

3. WHP to Lansing, 28 Jan. 1916, WHP MSS, EP, file 1202; WHP to Katharine Page Loring, 18 Feb. 1916, ibid., file 797.

4. Entries, 10, 14 Feb. 1916, EMH Diary.

5. Entry, 12 Jan. 1916, ibid.; entry, 11 Jan. 1916, diary 1916, WHP MSS, diaries 2, box 2.

6. EMH to WW, 9 Feb. 1916, WW MSS, series 2.

7. Entry, 11 Feb. 1916, EMH Diary; entry, 11 Feb. 1916, diary 1916, WHP MSS, diaries 2, box 2.

8. Entries, 13, 24 Feb. 1916, diary 1916, WHP MSS, diaries 2, box 2.

9. Entries, 13, 14 Feb. 1916, ibid.; WHP to WW, 16 Feb. 1916, WW MSS, series 2.

10. Entry, 15 Feb. 1916, diary 1916, WHP MSS, diaries 2, box 2; entry, 15 Feb. 1916, EMH Diary.

11. Arthur S. Link, *Wilson* (Princeton, N.J.: Princeton University Press, 1964), 4, pp. 130–41.

12. Entry, 23 Feb. 1916, EMH Diary; entry, 25 Feb. 1916, Plunkett Diary; Grey memorandum, 25 Feb. 1916, FO 800/96; entry, 12 Feb. 1916, diary 1916, WHP MSS, diaries 2, box 2; EMH to WHP, 10 Mar. 1916, ibid., EP, file 658.

13. Entry, 31 Mar. 1916, diary 1916, WHP MSS, diaries 2, box 2; WHP to C. G. Loring, 3 Apr. 1916, ibid., EP, file 797.

14. WHP to WW, 12 May 1916, WW MSS, series 2; WHP to Katharine Page Loring, 13 May 1916, WHP MSS, EP, file 797.

15. WHP to EMH, 23, 30 May 1916, EMH MSS.

16. WW to EMH, 21 July 1916, ibid.; WHP to Doubleday, Page & Co., 29 May 1916, WHP MSS, EP, file 418.

17. WHP to WW, 21 July 1916, WW MSS, series 2.

18. Entry, 30 Jan. 1916, diary 1916, WHP MSS, diaries 2, box 2; WHP to Henry Page, [Mar. 1916], ibid., EP, file 994.

19. WHP to WW, 21 July 1916, WW MSS, series 2.

20. Memorandum, L. H. Woolsey, to J. H. Patchin, 29 June 1916, Polk Papers; entries, 15, 17 May 1916, EMH Diary.

21. Entry, 4 May 1916, EMH Diary.

22. EMH to WW, 10 May 1916, WW MSS, series 2.

23. WW to EMH, 17 May, 2 July 1916, EMH MSS; EMH to WW, 18 May 1916, WW MSS, series 2.

24. WHP to WW, 21 July 1916, WW MSS, series 2.

25. *New York Times*, 12 Aug. 1916; entry, 15 Aug. 1916, addressbook 1916, WHP MSS, diaries 2, box 2.

26. WHP memorandum, [Sept. 1916], diary 1916, ibid.; WHP, "About Washton [*sic*]," 30 Aug. 1916, ibid.

27. WHP, "Lansing," ibid.

28. WHP memorandum, [Sept. 1916], ibid.; WHP, "About Washton [*sic*]," ibid.; Robert M. Lansing, *War Memoirs* (Indianapolis: Bobbs-Merrill Company, 1935), p. 170.

29. Robert M. Lansing, "The President's Attitude toward Great Britain and Its Dangers," [Sept. 1916], Lansing Papers (LC), vol. 66.

30. WHP, [Sept. 1916], diary 1916, WHP MSS, diaries 2, box 2; fragmentary account, ibid.

31. Ray Stannard Baker, *Woodrow Wilson: Life and Letters* (Garden City, N.Y.: Doubleday, Doran and Company, 1937), pp. 322–23.

32. WHP, "About Washton [*sic*]," diary 1916, WHP MSS, diaries 2, box 2; WHP to Alice W. Page, 26 Aug. 1916, ibid., EP, file 1002a; WHP to EMH, 26 Aug. 1916, EMH MSS.

33. WHP, "About Washton [*sic*]," diary 1916, WHP MSS, diaries 2, box 2.

34. Ibid.; WHP to Alice W. Page, 29 Aug. 1916, ibid., EP, file 1002a.

35. BJH reminiscence (CU), p. 34; entries, 19 Sept., 10 Oct. 1916, EMH Diary.

36. WHP memorandum, "Addenda," diary 1916, WHP MSS, diaries 2, box 2; WHP to I. Laughlin, [Sept. 1916], ibid., EP, file 755.

37. WHP, memoranda and notes, diary 1916, ibid., diaries 2, box 2; WHP, "Notes towards an Understanding of the British Feelings towards the United States," 14 Sept. 1916, ibid.

38. F. Polk to EMH, 29 Sept. 1916, EMH MSS; WHP to WW, 21 Sept. 1916, WW MSS, series 2.

39. WW to Lansing, 29 Sept. 1916, *Papers relating to the Foreign Relations of the United States: The Lansing Papers* (Washington, D.C.: Government Printing Office, 1939), 1, p. 319.

40. WW to Lansing, 29 Sept. 1916, ibid.; entry, addressbook 1916, WHP MSS, diaries 2; entry, 1 Mar. 1917, ibid.

41. Entry, addressbook 1916, WHP MSS, diaries 2.

42. Entry, 23 Sept. 1916, EMH Diary; BJH, *The Life and Letters of Walter Hines Page* (Garden City, N.Y.: Doubleday, Page & Company, 1922), 2, p. 188.

43. BJH, *Life and Letters of WHP*, 2, p. 188.

44. Entry, 24 Sept. 1916, EMH Diary.

45. WHP memorandum, [Oct. 1916], diary 1916, WHP MSS, diaries 2, box 2.

46. Entry, 30 Sept. 1916, EMH Diary; Alice W. Page to EMH, 11 Oct. 1916, EMH MSS.

47. WHP to Lansing, [Oct. 1916], WHP MSS, EP, file 1213.

48. WHP to Doubleday, Page & Co., 29 May 1916, ibid., file 448; WHP to Alice W. Page, 26 Aug. 1916, ibid., file 1002a.

49. WHP memorandum, [Oct. 1916], ibid., diaries 2, box 2.

50. Entry, 12 Jan. 1917, EMH Diary.

51. WHP to WW, 29 Nov. 1916, WW MSS, series 2.

52. WHP to Katharine Page Loring, 1 Jan. 1917, WHP MSS, EP, file 797; WHP to Frank Page, 16 Dec. 1916, ibid., file 993; WHP to WW, 30 Dec. 1916, WW MSS, series 2.

53. WHP to Arthur W. Page, 26 Mar. 1916, WHP MSS, EP, file 989; entry, 10 May 1916, diary 1916, ibid., diaries 2, box 2.

54. Entry, 17 May 1916, EMH Diary; EMH to WW, 18 May 1916, WW MSS, series 2; EMH to C. Carver, 8 Aug. 1916, Carver Papers, box 13.

55. Entry, 14 Nov. 1916, EMH Diary.

56. Entry, 27 Nov. 1916, ibid.

57. Entry, 28 Mar. 1926, ibid.

58. Entries, 3, 12 Jan. 1917, ibid.

59. WHP to Frank Page, 16 Dec. 1916, WHP MSS, EP, file 993; WHP to Lansing, 19 Jan. 1917, ibid., file 753; WW to Lansing, 31 Jan. 1917, Lansing Papers (PUL), box 3; Lansing to WHP, 5 Feb. 1917, *Foreign Relations: Lansing Papers*, 1, p. 716.

60. Entry, 28 Mar. 1917, EMH Diary.

61. WHP to WW, 30 Dec. 1916, WW MSS, series 2.

62. R. Cecil to Sir C. Spring Rice, 19 Dec. 1916, FO 371/2805/269669.

63. Cecil to Spring Rice, 20 Dec. 1916, FO 371/2805/259670; Cecil to Spring Rice, 26 Dec. 1916, FO 371/2805/263429; WHP to Lansing, 22, 26 Dec. 1916, *Foreign Relations, 1916: Supplement, The World War* (Washington, D.C.: Government Printing Office, 1929), pp. 108–9, 115–16.

64. *New York Times*, 22 Dec. 1916; Sir H. Plunkett to A. J. Balfour, 22 Dec. 1916, also containing Plunkett to Cecil, 22 Dec. 1916, FO 800/209.

65. Minutes of War Cabinet meeting, 26 Dec. 1916, CAB 23/1/18; minutes of Anglo-French conference, 26 Dec. 1916, CAB 28/2/13.

66. WHP to WW, 29 Dec. 1916, State Department Papers, R. G. 84, E21, vol. 2; Balfour to Spring Rice, 10 Jan. 1917, FO 371/3075/9750.

67. WHP to Lansing (for Wilson), 20 Jan. 1917, *Foreign Relations: Lansing Papers*, 1, pp. 715–16; Lansing, *War Memoirs* (Indianapolis: Bobbs-Merrill Company, 1935), p. 195; entry, 16 Jan. 1917, diary 1917, WHP MSS, diaries 2, box 2.

68. WHP to Katharine Page Loring, 1 Jan. 1917, WHP MSS, EP, file 797; WHP to Frank Page, 16 Dec. 1916, ibid., file 993.

69. E. Shoecraft to BJH, 17 Dec. 1921, BJH MSS.

70. Balfour to Spring Rice, 2 Feb. 1917, FO 800/199; Alice W. Page to Arthur W. Page, 2 Feb. 1917, WHP MSS, notes on early life, box 5; Shoecraft to BJH, 17 Dec. 1921, BJH MSS; WHP to WW, 4 Feb. 1917, WW MSS, series 2.

71. WHP to Balfour, 4 Feb. 1917, FO 371/3108/27765; WHP to Lansing, 6 Feb. 1917, *Foreign Relations, 1917: Supplement 1, The World War* (Washington, D.C.: Government Printing Office, 1931), pp. 119–20.

72. Entry, 19 Feb. 1917, diary 1917, WHP MSS, diaries 2, box 2.

73. Sir William James, *The Eyes of the Navy: A Biographical Study of Admiral Sir William Reginald Hall* (London: Methuen, 1955), p. 142.

74. Entry, Oct. 1916, Arthur W. Page Diary, WHP MSS, diaries 2, box 2; H. Gibson to Mrs. F. A. Gibson, 8 Oct. 1916, Gibson Papers, box 8.

75. BJH MSS account, WHP MSS, notes on early life, box 4.

76. Entry, 24 Feb. 1917, diary 1917, ibid., diaries 2, box 2; WHP to WW, 17 Mar. 1918, WW MSS, series 2.

77. Balfour, quoted in Blanche E. C. Dugdale, *Arthur James Balfour* (London: Hutchinson & Company, 1936), 2, p. 191; WHP to Lansing, 24 Feb. 1917, State Department Papers, file 862, 20212/69; WHP to Lansing, 24 Feb. 1917, *Foreign Relations, 1917: Supplement 1*, pp. 147–48.

78. Entry, 24 Feb. 1917, diary 1917, WHP MSS, diaries 2, box 2; WHP to Balfour, 1 Mar. 1917, Balfour Papers, vol. 49742.

79. Entries, 26, 27 Feb. 1917, diary 1917, WHP MSS, diaries 2, box 2; draft letter to WW, ibid.; annotated clippings, ibid.; WHP to Arthur W. Page, 6 Mar. 1917, ibid., EP, file 989.

80. WHP to Arthur W. Page, 4 Mar. 1917, ibid.; entry, 2 Mar. 1917, diary 1917, ibid., diaries 2, box 2; WHP to Lansing, 5 Mar. 1917, *Foreign Relations, 1917: Supplement 1*, pp. 516–18.

81. WHP to WW, draft letter, [Mar. 1917], WHP MSS, EP, file 1482; entries, 25 Feb., 20 Mar. 1917, diary 1917, ibid., diaries 2, box 2; WHP to Katharine Page Loring, 16 Mar. 1917, ibid., EP, file 797; Alice W. Page to Katharine Page Loring, 21 Mar. 1917, ibid., file 798.

82. WHP to Lansing, 23 Mar. 1917, ibid., file 1215; Daniels to WHP, 27 Mar. 1917, ibid., file 2248.

83. WHP to Arthur W. Page, 25 Mar. 1917, ibid., file 989; WHP to D. Houston, 1 Apr. 1917, ibid., file 695; entries, 1, 2 Apr. 1917, diary 1917, ibid., diaries 2, box 2.

84. Entry, 3 Apr. 1917, ibid.

85. WHP to Balfour, 7 Apr. 1917, FO 371/3110/73441; WHP to Arthur W. Page, 28 Apr. 1917, WHP MSS, EP, file 989.

CHAPTER 11

1. Minnie Burnaby to WHP, 2 July [1917], WHP MSS, EP, file 219; WHP to F. Polk, 3 May 1917, ibid., file 1069.

2. Entry, "Spring 1917," diary 1917, ibid., diaries 2, box 2; speech, 12 Apr. 1917, ibid., speeches, box 2.

3. A. J. Balfour to WHP, 5 Apr. 1917, FO 371/3112/72286; WHP to WW, 29 June 1917, WW MSS, series 2.

4. Imperial War Cabinet minutes, 3 Apr. 1917, CAB 23/40/7; WHP to R. Lansing, 5 April 1917, WHP MSS, EP, file 1199; WHP to Balfour, 8 Apr. 1917, Balfour Papers, vol. 49742.

5. WHP to WW, 4 May 1917, WW MSS, series 2.

6. Secret War Cabinet minutes, 16 May 1917, CAB 23/13/140A.

7. Entry, 24 May 1917, diary, Hankey Papers, 1/3; entry, 27 June 1917, in Trevor Wilson, ed., *The Political Diaries of C. P. Scott* (London: Collins, 1970), p. 296; War Cabinet minutes, 31 May 1917, CAB 23/2/151.

8. WHP to W. Buttrick, 1 June 1917, WHP MSS, EP, file 252; Lord Northcliffe to WHP, 20 July 1917, ibid., file 958.

9. WHP to Polk, 3 May 1917, ibid., file 1069; WHP to F. N. Doubleday, 3 May 1917, ibid., file 145; WHP to WW, 6 July 1917, WW MSS, series 2.

10. WHP to WW, 4 May 1917, WW MSS, series 2.

11. WHP to Lansing, 28 June 1917, WHP MSS, EP, file 1216.

12. WHP to Doubleday, 3 May 1917, ibid., file 415; WHP to Arthur W. Page, 28 Apr., 15 June 1917, ibid., file 989.

13. WHP to EMH, [Apr. 1917], EMH MSS; entry, 13 May 1917, EMH Diary.

14. WHP, "The Union of Two Great Peoples," 14 Aug. 1917, WHP MSS, speeches, box 2.

15. WHP to Doubleday, 3 May 1917, ibid., EP, file 415.

16. WHP to Arthur W. Page, 26 Sept. 1917, ibid., file 989.

17. "Notes by Mr. Balfour and Sir E. Drummond on letter from Mr. F. Cunliffe-Owen of 12 January 1917," [ca. 23 Jan. 1917], FO 800/383; Sir E. Drummond memorandum, 23 Sept. 1917, FO 800/209.

18. Entry, 9 Sept. 1917, EMH Diary.

19. WHP to Arthur W. Page, 8 July 1917, 8 Mar. 1918, WHP MSS, EP, file 989; W. H. Buckler to EMH, 26 Oct. 1917, Buckler Papers, box 1.

20. Entry, 16 Nov. 1917, EMH Diary.

21. WHP to WW, 22 Dec. 1917, WW MSS, series 2.

22. Entry, 24 Nov. 1917, diary 1917, WHP MSS, diaries 2, box 2; Buttrick to WHP, 14 Jan. 1918, ibid., EP, file 252; BJH interview with W. H. Taft, ibid., notes on early life, box 5; entry, 3 Jan. 1918, EMH Diary.

23. Entries, 22 Feb., 24 Aug. 1918, EMH Diary; R. S. Baker reminiscence, Jan. 1925, BJH MSS.

24. WHP to Arthur W. Page, 23 Dec. 1917, 24 Mar. 1918, WHP MSS, EP, file 989; WHP to Frank Page, 12 Mar. 1918, ibid., file 993; speech, 6 Apr. 1918, ibid., speeches, box 2; entry, 6 Apr. 1918, journal, Baker Papers (LC), box 124.

25. WHP to Arthur W. Page, 20 May 1918, WHP MSS, EP, file 989.

26. Memoranda, [ca. 1917], ibid., file 1002d; notebook, 1918, ibid., speeches, box 4; WHP to WW, 17 Mar. 1918, WW MSS, series 2.

27. WHP to Arthur W. Page, 2 Jan. 1918, WHP MSS, EP, file 989; WHP to Ralph W. Page, 12 Mar. 1918, ibid., file 997; T. Roosevelt to WHP, 1 Mar. 1918, ibid., file 1148; Roosevelt, "Dramatic Moments in American Diplomacy," *Outlook* 69 (1918): 62.

28. Alice W. Page to Arthur W. Page, [Mar. 1918], WHP MSS, EP, file 989b; entry, 2 Apr. 1918, diary 1918, ibid., diaries 2, box 3.

29. Alice W. Page to Frank Page, 17 Apr., 20 May, 18 June 1918, ibid., EP, file 993.

30. Alice W. Page to Katharine Page Loring, 8 Aug. 1918, ibid., file 798; WHP to WW, 1 Aug. 1918, WW MSS, series 2.

31. WHP to Alice W. Page, 11 Aug. 1918, WHP MSS, EP, file 1002a.

32. WHP to WW, 1 Aug. 1918, WW MSS, series 2; WHP to WW, draft, WHP MSS, EP, file 1482.

33. WW to WHP, 24 Aug. 1918, WHP MSS, EP, file 1482.

34. Alice W. Page to Katharine Page Loring, 16–17 Sept. 1918, ibid., file 758.

35. Balfour, quoted in BJH, *The Life and Letters of Walter Hines Page* (Garden City, N.Y.: Doubleday, Page & Company, 1922), 2, p. 403.

36. Alice W. Page to Frank Page, 1918, WHP MSS, EP, file 993; WHP to WW, 23 Nov. 1918, WW MSS, series 2; WW to WHP, 26 Nov. 1918, WHP MSS, WW letters.

37. Entry, 24 Sept. 1918, EMH Diary.

38. WHP draft letter (with note, Katharine Page Loring to BJH, 25 June [1921]), WHP MSS, EP, file 310.

39. WHP to Alice W. Page, 2 Sept. 1918, ibid., file 1002a; remark to Frank Page, quoted in BJH, *Life and Letters of WHP*, 2, p. 406.

40. Doubleday, Page & Co. sales figures, [ca. 1928], BJH MSS; Houghton, Mifflin Co. to author, 21 Feb. 1975.

41. WHP, *The Southerner*, p. 29.

SELECTED BIBLIOGRAPHY

I. Manuscripts Consulted

A. Great Britain

Admiralty Papers, Public Record Office.

Earl of Balfour Papers, British Museum.

Viscount Bryce Papers, Bodleian Library, Oxford.

Cabinet Papers, Public Record Office.

Viscount Cecil of Chelwood Papers, British Museum.

Marquess of Crewe Papers, University Library, Cambridge.

Foreign Office Papers, Public Record Office.

Lord Hankey Diary and Papers, Churchill College, Cambridge.

Lord Hardinge of Penshurst Papers, University Library, Cambridge.

Earl Lloyd-George of Dwyfor Papers, Beaverbrook Library, London.

Andrew Bonar Law Papers, Beaverbrook Library, London.

Reginald McKenna Papers, Churchill College, Cambridge.

Earl of Oxford and Asquith Papers, Bodleian Library, Oxford.

Sir Ralph Paget Papers, British Museum.

S. Pearson and Son Company Papers, Science Museum, London.

Sir Horace Plunkett Diary and Papers, Plunkett Foundation, London.

Sir William Robertson Papers, Centre for Military Archives, King's College, University of London.

Sir William Robertson–Sir Archibald Murray Correspondence, British Museum.

C. P. Scott Papers, British Museum.

J. A. Spender Papers, British Museum.

Sir Cecil Spring Rice Papers, Churchill College, Cambridge.

J. St. Loe Strachey Papers, Beaverbrook Library, London.

Treasury Papers, Public Record Office.

War Office Papers, Public Record Office.

B. United States

Henry Carter Adams Papers, Michigan Historical Collections, University of Michigan.

Herbert Baxter Adams Papers, Johns Hopkins University Library.

Edwin A. Alderman Papers, Alderman Library, University of Virginia.

Thomas Bailey Aldrich Papers, Tulane University Library.
Ben Allen Papers, Hoover Presidential Library, West Branch, Iowa.
Chandler P. Anderson Papers, Library of Congress.
A. W. Anthony Collection, New York Public Library.
Autograph Collection, Iowa State Department of History and
    Archives.
Autograph File, Houghton Library, Harvard University.
Ray Stannard Baker Papers, Library of Congress.
————, Princeton University Library.
Frederic Bancroft Papers, Columbia University Library.
Clifton W. Barrett Collection, Alderman Library, University of
    Virginia.
John Spencer Bassett Papers, private possession.
Edward Bellamy Papers, Houghton Library, Harvard University.
R. R. Bowker Papers, New York Public Library.
William Garrot Brown Papers, Duke University Library.
William Jennings Bryan Papers, Library of Congress.
————, National Archives.
William H. Buckler Papers, Yale University Library.
Nicholas Murray Butler Papers, Columbia University Library.
George W. Cable Papers, Tulane University Library.
James Cannon, Jr. Papers, Duke University Library.
Clifford Carver Papers, Princeton University Library.
Century Collection, New York Public Library.
John Jay Chapman Papers, Houghton Library, Harvard University.
Ernest H. Cherrington Papers, Temperance Education Foundation,
    Westerville, Ohio.
John Clopton Papers, Duke University Library.
Charles W. Dabney Papers, Southern Historical Collection,
    University of North Carolina, Chapel Hill.
Josephus Daniels Papers, Library of Congress.
John W. Davis Papers, Yale University Library.
Lewis H. Dent Papers, Southern Historical Collection, University of
    North Carolina, Chapel Hill.
John M. Dickey Papers, Lilly Library, Indiana University.
Frank N. Doubleday Papers, Princeton University Library.
Theodore Dreiser Papers, University of Pennsylvania Library.
Benjamin N. Duke Papers, Duke University Library.
Francis J. Dyer Papers, Bancroft Library, University of California,
    Berkeley.
W. G. Eggleston Papers, Bancroft Library, University of California,
    Berkeley.
Robert H. Elias Collection of Theodore Dreiser Materials, private
    possession.

Charles W. Eliot Papers, Harvard University Archives.

Richard T. Ely Papers, State Historical Society of Wisconsin.

Edward Payson Evans Papers, Michigan Historical Collections, University of Michigan.

William P. Few Papers, Duke University Library.

Annie Adams Fields Papers, Houghton Library, Harvard University.

————, Henry E. Huntington Library and Art Collection, San Marino, California.

W. Cameron Forbes Papers, Houghton Library, Harvard University.

William Goodell Frost Papers, Berea College Library.

Hamlin Garland Papers, University of Southern California Library.

General Education Board Papers, Rockefeller Foundation Archives, New York.

Henry George Papers, New York Public Library.

Hugh Gibson Papers, Hoover Institution for the Study of War, Revolution and Peace.

Richard Watson Gilder Papers, New York Public Library.

Basil L. Gildersleeve Papers, Johns Hopkins University Library.

Daniel Coit Gilman Papers, Johns Hopkins University Library.

E. L. Godkin Papers, Houghton Library, Harvard University.

George Bird Grinnell Papers, Bancroft Library, University of California, Berkeley.

Paul H. Hanus Papers, Harvard University Archives.

William Rainey Harper Papers, University of Chicago Library.

Joel Chandler Harris Papers, Woodruff Library, Emory University.

Paul Hamilton Hayne Papers, Duke University Library.

Hemphill Family Papers, Duke University Library.

Burton J. Hendrick Memoir, Columbia University Oral History Collection.

Burton J. Hendrick Papers, private possession.

Henry Lee Higginson Papers, Baker Library, Harvard Business School.

Thomas Wentworth Higginson Papers, Houghton Library, Harvard University.

————, University of Southern California Library.

Walter B. Hill Papers, University of Georgia Library.

Gavin Hogg Papers, Duke University Library.

Hamilton Holt Papers, Rollins College Library, Winter Park, Florida.

————, University of Southern California Library.

Herbert Hoover Papers, Hoover Presidential Library, West Branch, Iowa.

Henry Oscar Houghton Papers, Houghton Library, Harvard University.

Houghton Mifflin Company Papers, Houghton Library, Harvard University.

Edward M. House Diary and Papers, Yale University Library.

David F. Houston Papers, Houghton Library, Harvard University.

Mark A. DeWolfe Howe Papers, Houghton Library, Harvard University.

William Dean Howells Papers, Houghton Library, Harvard University.

Johns Hopkins University Alumni Records Collection, Johns Hopkins University Library.

Hiram Johnson Papers, Bancroft Library, University of California, Berkeley.

Mary Johnston Papers, Alderman Library, University of Virginia.

J. Y. Joyner Papers, North Carolina State Department of Archives and History.

Keats Collection, Houghton Library, Harvard University.

Helen Keller Papers, American Foundation for the Blind, New York.

William Kent Papers, Yale University Library.

John C. Kilgo Papers, Duke University Library.

Grace King Papers, Southern Historical Collection, University of North Carolina, Chapel Hill.

Burton Kline Papers, Houghton Library, Harvard University.

Robert M. Lansing Papers, Library of Congress.

————, Princeton University Library.

Amy Lowell Papers, Houghton Library, Harvard University.

S. S. McClure Papers, Lilly Library, Indiana University.

Samuel McCoy Papers, Lilly Library, Indiana University.

Charles D. McIver Papers, University of North Carolina Library, Greensboro.

St. Clair McKelway Papers, New York Public Library.

William McKinley Papers, Library of Congress.

Dumas Malone Biographical Material on Edwin A. Alderman, Alderman Library, University of Virginia.

Josephine Peabody Marks Papers, Houghton Library, Harvard University.

Brander Matthews Papers, Columbia University Library.

Miscellaneous Collections, Henry E. Huntington Library and Art Collection, San Marino, California.

Miscellaneous Papers, New York Public Library.

Miscellaneous Papers, University of Delaware Library.

Samuel Chiles Mitchell Papers, Library of Congress.

Andrew Jackson Montague Papers, Virginia State Library.

Francis G. Newlands Papers, Yale University Library.

Robert C. Ogden Papers, Library of Congress.

Edward A. Oldham Papers, Duke University Library.

Fred A. Olds Papers, North Carolina State Department of Archives and History.

Arthur W. Page Memoir, Columbia University Oral History Collection.

Arthur W. Page Papers, State Historical Society of Wisconsin.

Robert N. Page Papers, Duke University Library.

Thomas Nelson Page Papers, Duke University Library.

————, Alderman Library, University of Virginia.

Walter Hines Page Papers, Duke University Library.

————, Houghton Library, Harvard University.

————, North Carolina State Department of Archives and History.

————, Biographical Materials Gathered by John Milton Cooper, Jr., Walter Hines Page Library, Randolph-Macon College.

Walter Hines Page–Charles W. Chesnutt Correspondence, Houghton Library, Harvard University.

Albert Bigelow Paine Papers, Henry E. Huntington Library and Art Collection, San Marino, California.

George Foster Peabody Papers, Library of Congress.

Bliss Perry Papers, Houghton Library, Harvard University.

James D. Phelan Papers, Bancroft Library, University of California, Berkeley.

William Phillips Diary, Houghton Library, Harvard University.

Clarence Poe Papers, North Carolina State Department of Archives and History.

Frank L. Polk Papers, Yale University Library.

William Sydney Porter Papers, Duke University Library.

Randolph-Macon College Papers, Walter Hines Page Library, Randolph-Macon College.

Paul S. Reinsch Papers, State Historical Society of Wisconsin.

James Whitcomb Riley Papers, Lilly Library, Indiana University.

Rockefeller Sanitary Commission Papers, Rockefeller Foundation Archives, New York.

Franklin D. Roosevelt Letter, Duke University Library.

Theodore Roosevelt Papers, Library of Congress.

Edward A. Ross Papers, State Historical Society of Wisconsin.

Lucy M. Salmon Papers, Vassar College Library.

Horace E. Scudder Diary, Houghton Library, Harvard University.

Albert Shaw Papers, New York Public Library.

Furnifold M. Simmons Papers, Duke University Library.

William S. Sims Papers, Library of Congress.

Upton Sinclair Papers, Lilly Library, Indiana University.

Southern Education Board Papers, Southern Historical Collection, University of North Carolina, Chapel Hill.

James Southgate Papers, Duke University Library.

State Department Papers, National Archives.

Edmund Clarence Stedman Papers, Columbia University Library.

Lincoln Steffens Papers, Columbia University Library.

George Stephens Papers, Southern Historical Collection, University of North Carolina, Chapel Hill.

William Howard Taft Papers, Library of Congress.

William Roscoe Thayer Papers, Houghton Library, Harvard University.

Daniel Augustus Tompkins Papers, Library of Congress.

Trinity College Papers, Duke University Library.

Frederick Jackson Turner Papers, Houghton Library, Harvard University.

————, Henry E. Huntington Library and Art Collection, San Marino, California.

Moses Coit Tyler Papers, Cornell University Collection of Regional History and Archives.

United States Census, Population and Slave Schedules (manuscript), North Carolina, 1850, National Archives.

————, 1860, National Archives.

Oswald Garrison Villard Papers, Houghton Library, Harvard University.

Frederic C. Walcott Papers, Yale University Library.

Henry D. Wallace Papers, University of Iowa Library.

Lester Frank Ward Papers, Hay Library, Brown University.

Charles Dudley Warner Papers, Trinity College Library, Hartford, Connecticut.

Booker T. Washington Papers, Library of Congress.

E. Y. Webb Papers, Southern Historical Collection, University of North Carolina, Chapel Hill.

Edgar H. Wells Papers, Houghton Library, Harvard University.

Benjamin Ide Wheeler Papers, Bancroft Library, University of California, Berkeley.

Andrew D. White Papers, Cornell University Collection of Regional History and Archives.

William G. Whitney Papers, Yale University Library.

Woodrow Wilson Papers, Library of Congress.

————, Princeton University Library.

II. *Interviews and Personal Communications*

Lady Elizabeth Mary Arthur, 14 Feb. 1972.
Richard H. Bassett, 16 Oct. 1969.
Jonathan Daniels, 28 Sept. 1970; 24 Nov. 1973.
Margaret Digby, 31 Mar. 1970.
John H. Finley, 2 Mar. 1969.
Sir Ralph Hawtrey, 14 June 1970.
Broadus Mitchell, 28 Aug. 1969.
Thaddeus S. Page, 29 June 1973.
Lady Percy of Newcastle, 22 April 1972.

III. *Works of Walter Hines Page* (*excluding newspaper letters and unsigned* World's Work *editorials*)

"Address at the Inauguration of President Winston." *North Carolina Magazine* 11 (1891): 61–71.
Nicholas Worth [pseud.]. "The Autobiography of a Southerner since the Civil War." *Atlantic* 98 (1906): 1–12, 157–76, 311–25, 474–88.
"Charles D. McIver." *South Atlantic Quarterly* 5 (1906): 389–92.
"A Closer Relation between Librarians and Publishers." *Library Journal* 27 (1902): 166–70.
"A Comprehensive View of Colleges." *World's Work* 12 (1906): 7789–94.
"The Country Man." *Proceedings of the Thirtieth Annual Session of the State Literary and Historical Association of North Carolina*. Raleigh, 1913. Pp. 30–42.
"The Cultivated Man in an Industrial Era." *World's Work* 8 (1904): 4980–84.
"Dedicatory Address." *The Formal Opening of the Trinity College Library, February 23, 1903*. Durham, 1903. Pp. 14–23.
"The End of the War, and After." *Atlantic* 82 (1898): 430–32.
"The Farmer's Credit." *Proceedings of the Fifteenth Conference for Education in the South, Nashville, Tennessee, April 3d, 4th, and 5th, 1912*. Washington, [1914]. Pp. 97–101.
"Gifford Pinchot, the Awakener of the Nation." *World's Work* 19 (1910): 12662–68.
"A Glance at the Ending Year." *World's Work* 11 (1905): 7003–8.
[Anon.]. "Henry Timrod." *South Atlantic* 1 (1878): 359–67.
"The Hookworm and Civilization." *World's Work* 24 (1912): 504–18.
"An Intimate View of Publishing." *World's Work* 4 (1902): 2561–65.

"A Journey through the Southern States." *World's Work* 14 (1907): 9003–42.

"The Last Hold of the Southern Bully." *Forum* 16 (1893): 303–14.

"McIver, a Leader of the People." *World's Work* 13 (1906): 8565–67.

"The Making of Literature." *State Normal Magazine* 3 (1899): 461–71.

"Independent" [pseud.]. "Mr. Cleveland's—Failure?" *Forum* 17 (1894): 129–38.

"Mr. Washington's Book." *Book Buyer* 20 (1900): 144–45.

"The Negro on the Negro." *Independent* 39 (1886): 7–8, 43–44, 107, 137–38, 202–3, 235.

"The 'New' Southern Problem: From a Southern Point of View." *Independent* 37 (1885): 712–13.

"On a Tenth Birthday." *World's Work* 21 (1911): 13903–17.

"The Pan-American Exposition." *World's Work* 2 (1901): 1015–48.

"The People as an Exhibit." *World's Work* 7 (1904): 5110–13.

"Independent" [pseud.]. "Political Career and Character of David B. Hill." *Forum* 18 (1894): 257–69.

[Anon.]. *A Publisher's Confession*. New York: Doubleday, Page & Company, 1905.

"The Rebuilding of Old Commonwealths." *Atlantic* 89 (1902): 651–61.

The Rebuilding of Old Commonwealths: Being Essays towards the Training of the Forgotten Man in the Southern States. New York: Doubleday, Page & Company, 1902. Reissued as *The School That Built a Town*. Introduction by Roy E. Larsen. New York: Harper & Brothers, 1952.

"The Southern Educational Conference." *Independent* 54 (1902): 1156–58.

"The Southern Educational Problem." *International Review* 11 (1881): 309–20.

Nicholas Worth [pseud.]. *The Southerner: A Novel*. New York: Doubleday, Page & Company, 1909.

"Study of an Old Southern Borough." *Atlantic* 48 (1881): 648–58.

"Teaching Morals by Photographs." *World's Work* 19 (1910): 12715–25.

"The Unfulfilled Ambition of the South." *Proceedings of the Eleventh Conference for Education in the South: The Seventh Session, Birmingham, Alabama, April 26th to April 28th, 1904*. New York, [1904]. Pp. 98–110.

"The War with Spain and After." *Atlantic* 81 (1898): 721–27.

"What the World's Work Is Trying to Do." *World's Work* 25 (1913): 265–68.

"A Wholesome Stimulus to Higher Politics." *Atlantic* 83 (1899):
289–92.
"The Writer and the University." *University Record* 12 (1907): 43–54.
Also in *Atlantic* 100 (1907): 685–95.

INDEX

THE AUTHOR

John Milton Cooper, Jr., a Princeton graduate with a Ph.D. from Columbia, is professor of history at the University of Wisconsin. He is author of *The Vanity of Power: American Isolationism and the First World War, 1914–1917* (1969) and editor of *Causes and Consequences of the First World War* (1972).

A NOTE ON THE BOOK

Text set in Photocomposition Sabon
Composition by The University of North Carolina Press

Printed on sixty-pound Olde Style by
S. D. Warren Company, Boston, Massachusetts

Binding cloth by
Holliston Mills, Inc., Norwood, Massachusetts

Printing and binding by
Kingsport Press, Kingsport, Tennessee

Designed by
Joyce Kachergis

Published by
The University of North Carolina Press